The
J. Paul Getty
Museum

HANDBOOK OF THE
Antiquities Collection

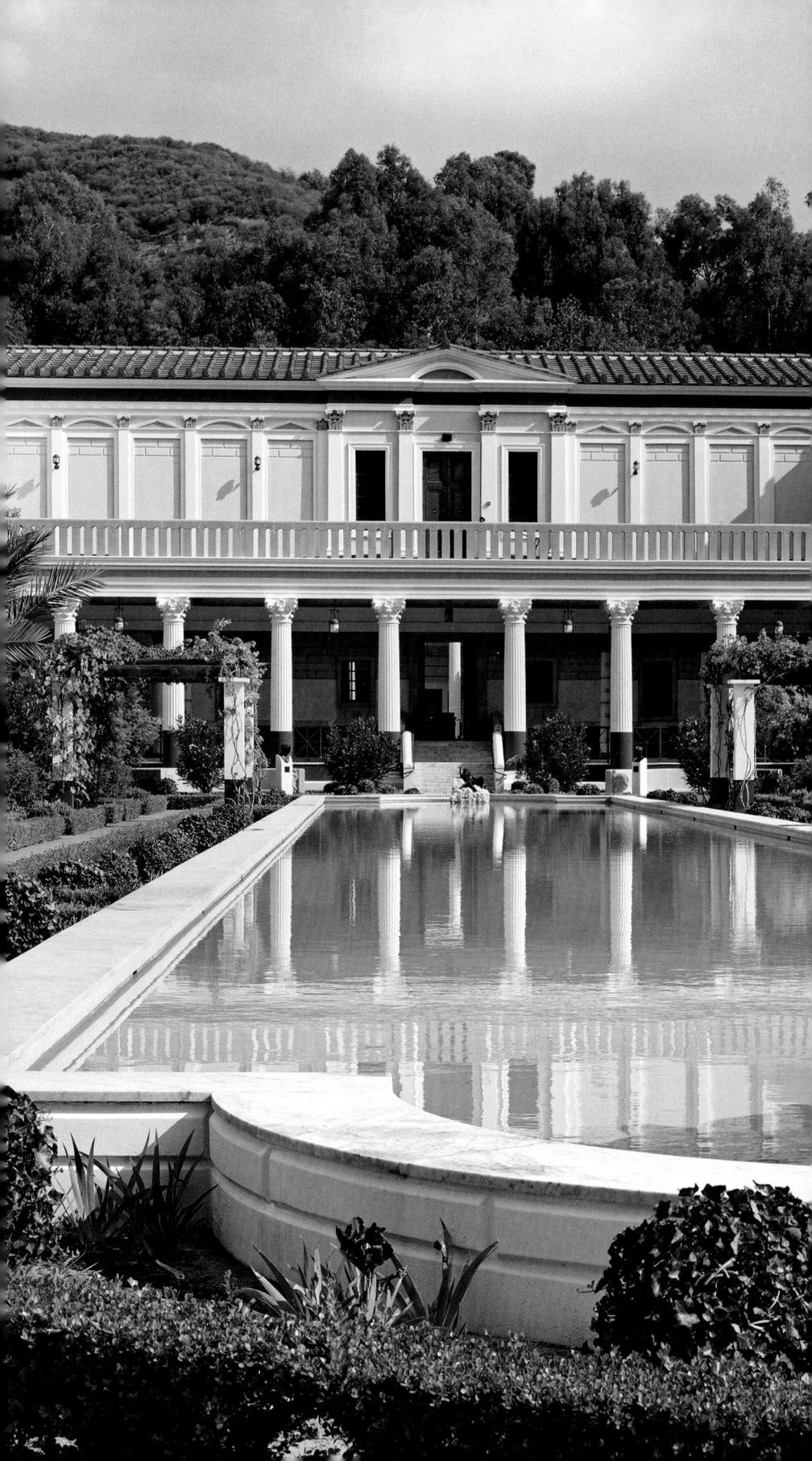

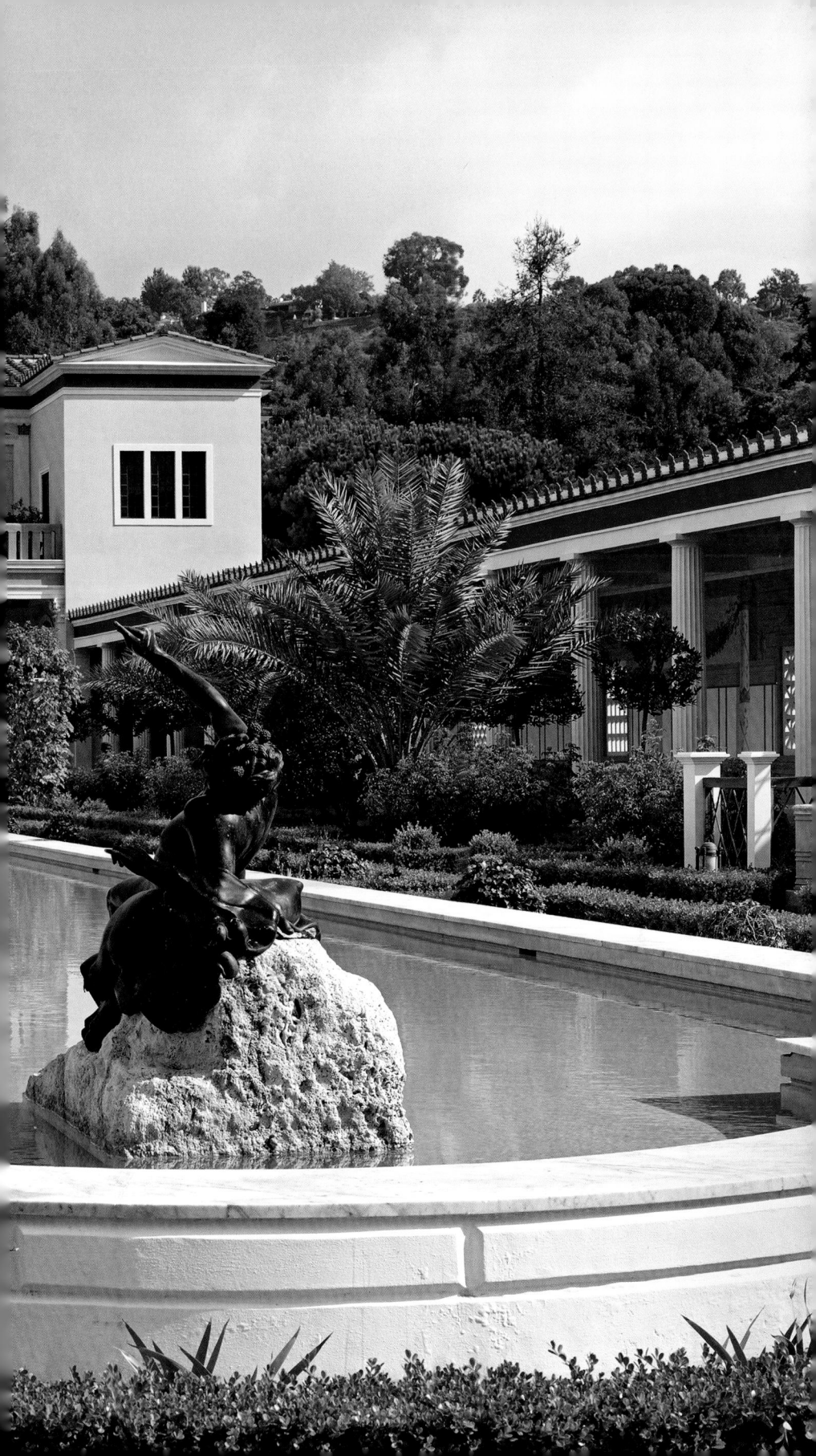

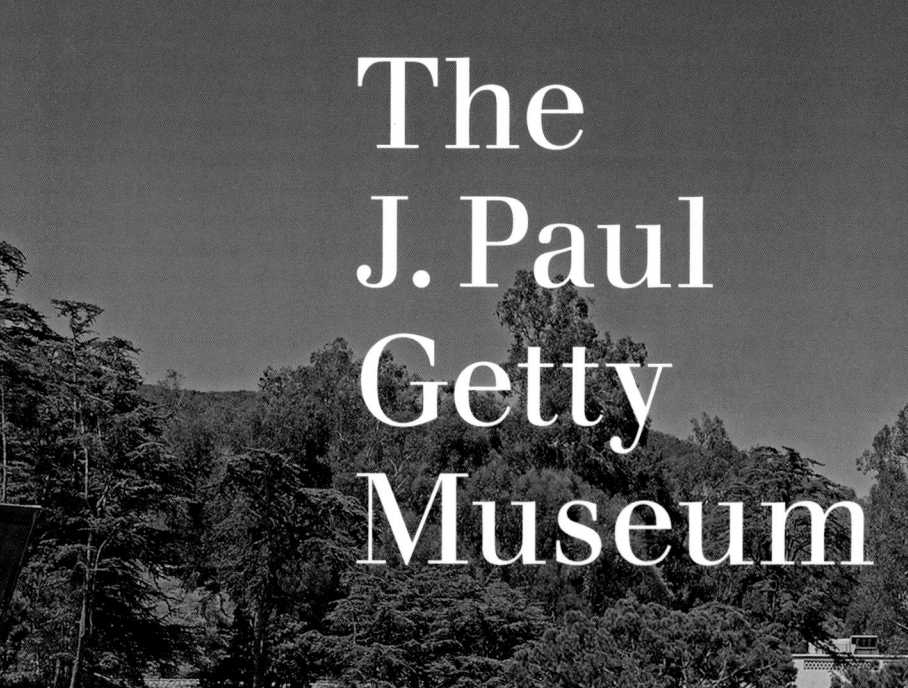

The
J. Paul
Getty
Museum

LOS ANGELES

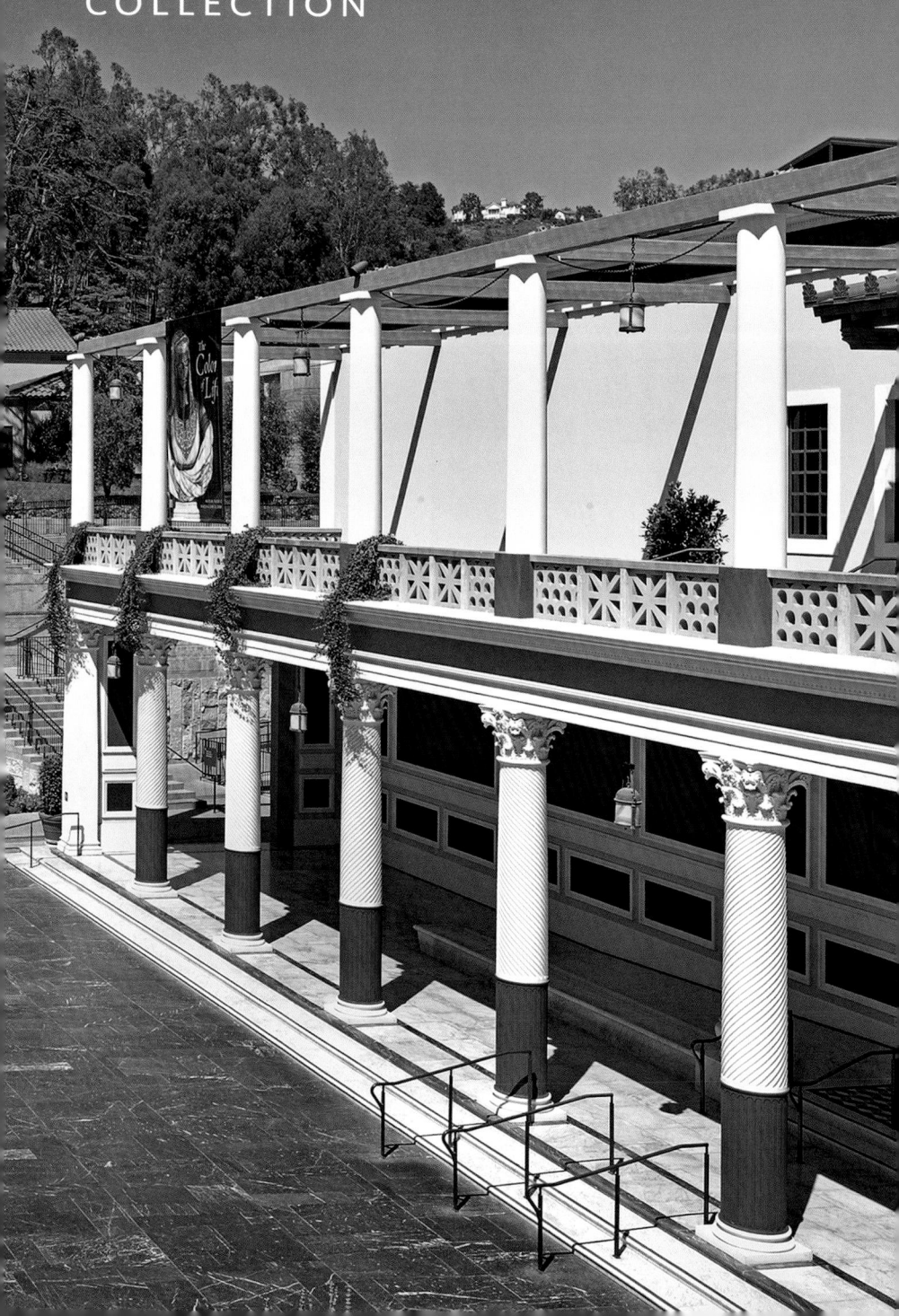

HANDBOOK

OF THE Antiquities

COLLECTION

© 2010 J. Paul Getty Trust
Second edition

Published by the J. Paul Getty Museum
Getty Publications
1200 Getty Center Drive, Suite 500
Los Angeles, CA 90049-1682
www.gettypublications.org

Gregory M. Britton, *Publisher*

Kenneth Lapatin and Karol Wight, *Editors*
Catherine Chambers, *Copy Editor*
Benedicte Gilman, *Editorial Coordinator*
Pamela Heath and Elizabeth Chapin Kahn,
Production Coordinators
Jeffrey Cohen, *Designer*
Tahnee Cracchiola, Lou Meluso, Ellen Rosenbery,
Jack Ross, and Bruce White, *Photographers*
David Fuller, *Cartographer*

Diane Franco, *Typesetter*
Color separations by Professional Graphics Inc.,
Rockford, Illinois
Printed in Singapore by Tien Wah Press (Pte) Limited

Front cover: Detail of statue of Venus; see pages 164–65.
Back cover: View across the Inner Peristyle of the
Getty Villa.
Pages ii–iii: The larger pool in the Outer Peristyle and the
façade of the Museum building of the Getty Villa.
Pages iv–v: The Barbara and Lawrence Fleischmann Theater
and the west façade of the Museum building of the
Getty Villa. The Ranch House is in the middle background.
Page viii: The Men's Gallery on the second floor of the
Getty Villa.
Page xxvi: Detail of jug; see page 3.
Page 14: Detail of mosaic glass bowl; see page 103.
Page 104: Detail of altar; see page 113.
Page 124: Detail of pithos; see page 134.
Page 144: Detail of fresco; see page 222.

Library of Congress Cataloging-in-Publication Data

J. Paul Getty Museum.
    The J. Paul Getty Museum handbook of the antiquities
collection.—2nd ed.
        p. cm.
    Includes index.
    ISBN 978-0-89236-998-0 (pbk.)
    1. Art, Classical—Catalogs. 2. Classical antiquities—
Catalogs. 3. Art—California—Malibu—Catalogs. 4. J. Paul
Getty Museum—Catalogs. I. Title. II. Title: Handbook
of the antiquities collection.
    N5603.M36J25 2010
    709.38'07479493—dc22

                                        2009033976

The Antiquities Collection

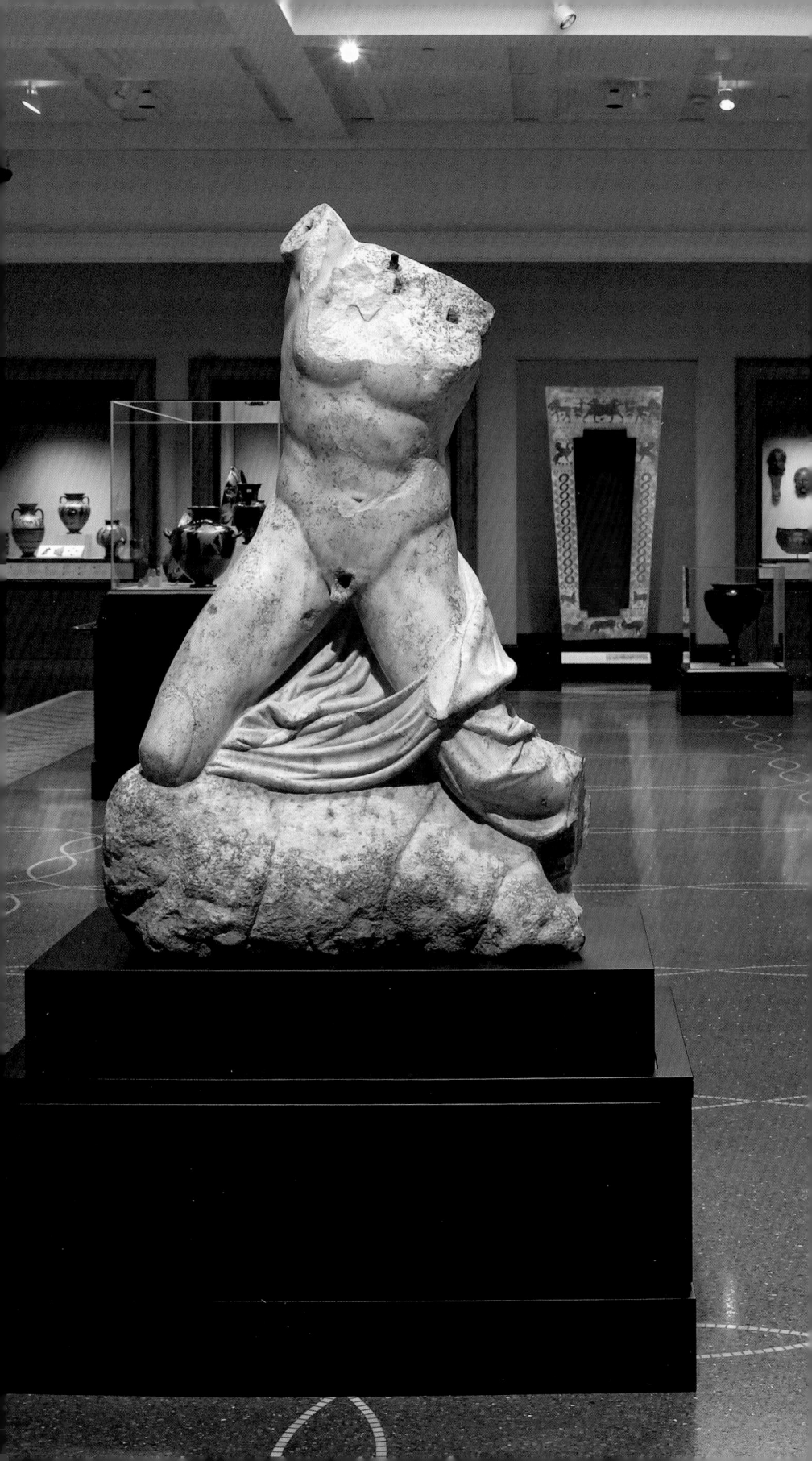

Foreword

PERHAPS NO COLLECTION in the Museum better exemplifies the passions, interests, and ambitions of its founder, J. Paul Getty, than that of Greek and Roman antiquities. Through his travels in the Mediterranean, his reading of specialized literature, his own fictional writing set in Greece and Italy, and, above all, his ardent collecting of antiquities, Mr. Getty exhibited a profound personal engagement with the ancient world that lasted from his first purchase in 1939 until his death in 1976. The reasons for his fervent interest were many and included his admiration for the great personalities of ancient history, his nearly equal emulation of or rivalry with other celebrated collectors of ancient art—from Emperor Hadrian to Cardinal Mazarin to Lord Lansdowne to William Randolph Hearst—and his perception of ancient art's ability to evoke the magnificence of the classical age. This latter concern, not only to evoke, but to replicate antique splendor, was the driving force behind his re-creation of the ancient Villa dei Papiri in Herculaneum as the setting for his collection in Malibu, California.

The Museum's collection of antiquities has grown significantly since Mr. Getty's death and his subsequent bequest to the institution, expanding into new areas—such as Greek vases, funeral objects, and Cycladic art—to the extent that it now rivals the much older collections of New York's Metropolitan Museum of Art and Boston's Museum of Fine Arts, both founded in 1870. The collection is particularly rich in luxury objects and art associated with classical theater, so it offers a profound commentary on the culture of ancient society.

For the enduring quality and significance of the Museum's Antiquities collection, as well as its expansion, a debt of gratitude is owed to Marion True, Curator of Antiquities from 1986 to 2005, and to Karol Wight, Senior Curator of Antiquities since 2007. Karol and her staff have labored tirelessly to make this collection accessible and meaningful to both scholars and the general public, through exhibitions, publications, symposia, seminars, and lectures. Our desire to stimulate the understanding, preservation, and enjoyment of the ancient world through our collection and related educational programs culminated in the 2006 opening of the remodeled Getty Villa, with its scholars program, conservation training program, and its performances of ancient Greek and Roman drama. As a nexus for the study of ancient art and culture, the Villa has truly embodied J. Paul Getty's aim to evoke the splendors of antiquity in all their complexity.

Michael Brand
Director, The J. Paul Getty Museum

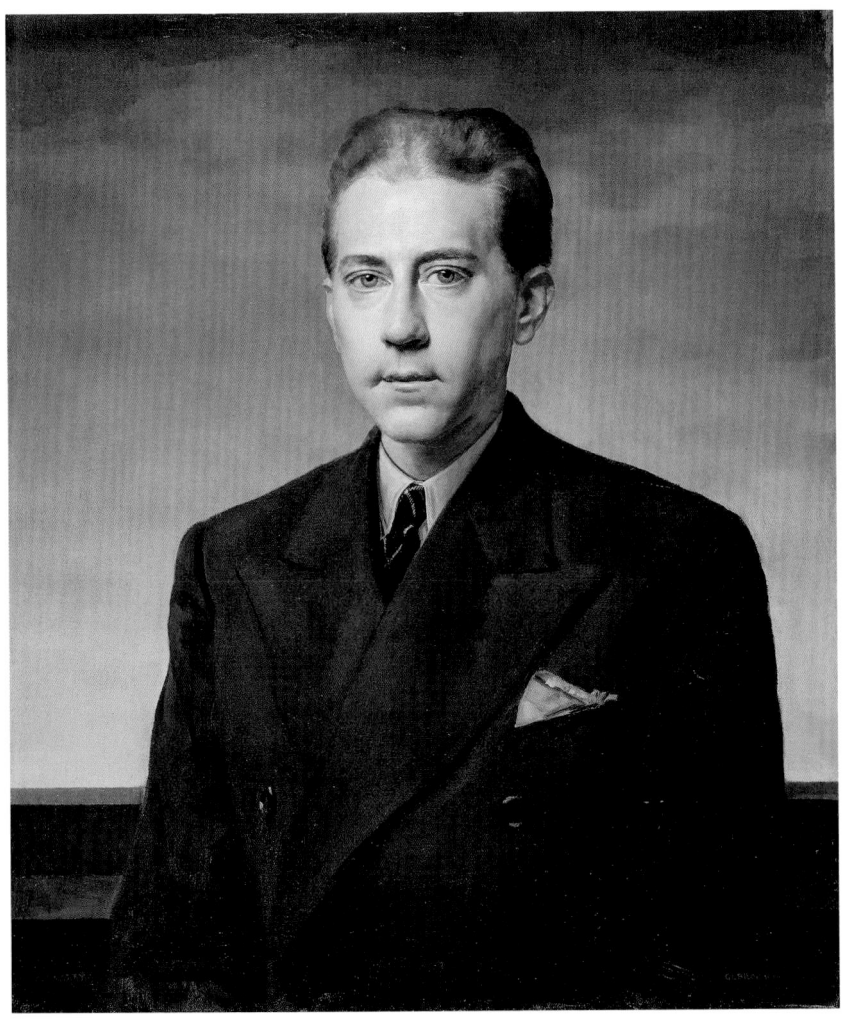

Gerald L. Brockhurst (English, 1890–1978), *Portrait of J. Paul Getty*, 1938. Oil on canvas, 67.PA.2.

A Brief History of the Collection

O N JANUARY 28, 2006, almost nine years after it closed for renovation and some thirty-two years after it had first presented its collections to the public, the Getty Villa reopened as a museum and educational center dedicated to the study of the arts and cultures of the ancient Mediterranean. The site's setting, collections, and programs are now woven together to create an integrated educational and cultural experience for our visitors. The architectural modifications and additions to the site were designed by the Boston firm of Machado and Silvetti Associates, in a manner sympathetic to the Roman design of the Villa building.

The J. Paul Getty Museum at the Getty Villa is the only art museum in the United States dedicated to the arts of ancient Greece, Etruria, and Rome. The new galleries contain more than twelve hundred objects from the Museum's Antiquities Collection, installed by themes such as Gods and Goddesses, Athletes and Competition, and Dionysos and the Theater. This new installation has allowed visitors to understand the ancient world in a more personal manner by using these broad themes to link the present with the past in order to understand how modern and ancient societies are both similar and different. In addition to the galleries for the permanent collection, the Getty Villa now contains galleries dedicated to changing exhibitions. To date, visitors have enjoyed exhibits focusing on such topics as Roman mosaics from Tunisia, masterpieces from the Hermitage Museum's collection of Greek art found on the northern shores of the Black Sea, the early history of the Society of Dilettanti, and new work by Jim Dine inspired by objects from the museum's collection. All this is a far cry from the Antiquities Collection's modest beginnings as a private assemblage of art formed by oil man J. Paul Getty.

Mr. Getty began acquiring ancient art in 1939 when he purchased at auction a small terracotta group depicting a female reclining on a couch attended by erotes (fig. 1). This composition was later discovered to be a nineteenth-century imitation of an ancient work, but it signaled a new direction for the 46-year-old collector's interests, which until then had been concentrated primarily on French decorative arts and Old Master paintings. The purchase of the terracotta was followed by the acquisition of marble portraits of Roman empresses, works that to this day remain cornerstones of the sculpture collection: a head of Agrippina (fig. 2) and the portrait bust of a woman (fig. 3; see also p. 162). Mr. Getty had an enduring fascination with ancient Roman culture and imperial personalities, and he continued to add portraits to his collection, as well as other important works of Roman sculpture, many from old and distinguished

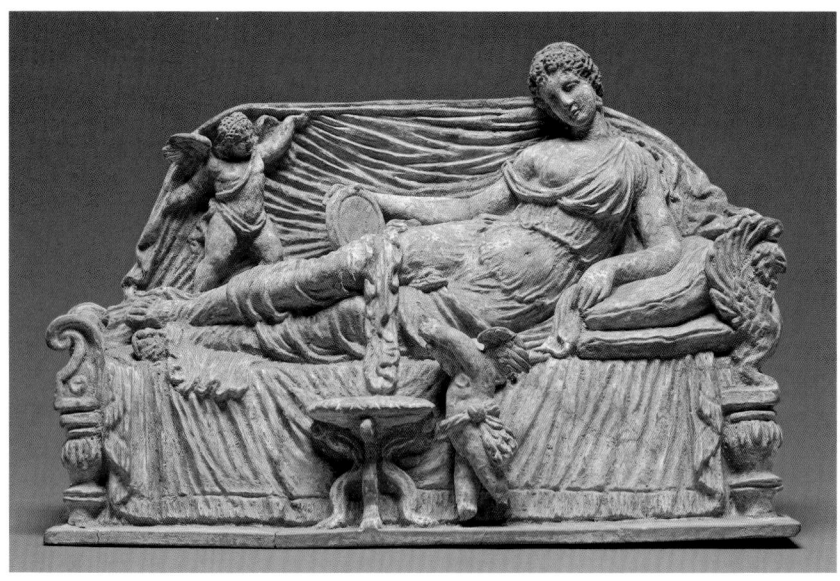

FIGURE 1

Female Reclining on a Couch with Erotes, 1850–1875, terracotta, H: 18.5 cm (7¼ in.); L: 27 cm (10⅝ in.), 78.AK.38.

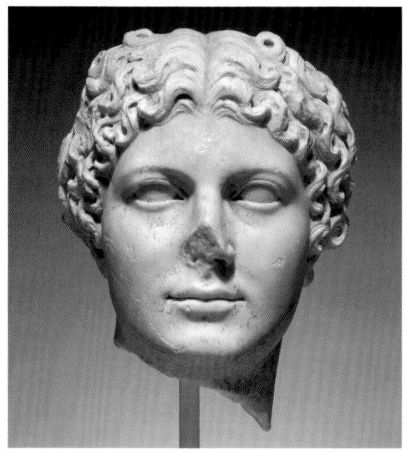

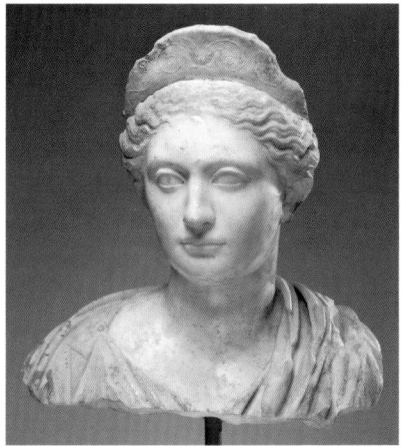

FIGURE 2

Portrait Head of Agrippina the Younger, Roman, circa A.D. 50, marble, H: 32 cm (12⅝ in.), 70.AA.101.

FIGURE 3

Portrait Bust of a Woman, Roman, circa A.D. 130, marble, H: 43 cm (16⅞ in.), 70.AA.100.

FIGURE 4

Statue of Hercules (The Lansdowne Herakles), Roman (found in Tivoli), circa A.D. 125, marble, H: 193.5 cm (76⅛ in.), 70.AA.109. The statue as first displayed in Malibu, outdoors in the courtyard of the Ranch House.

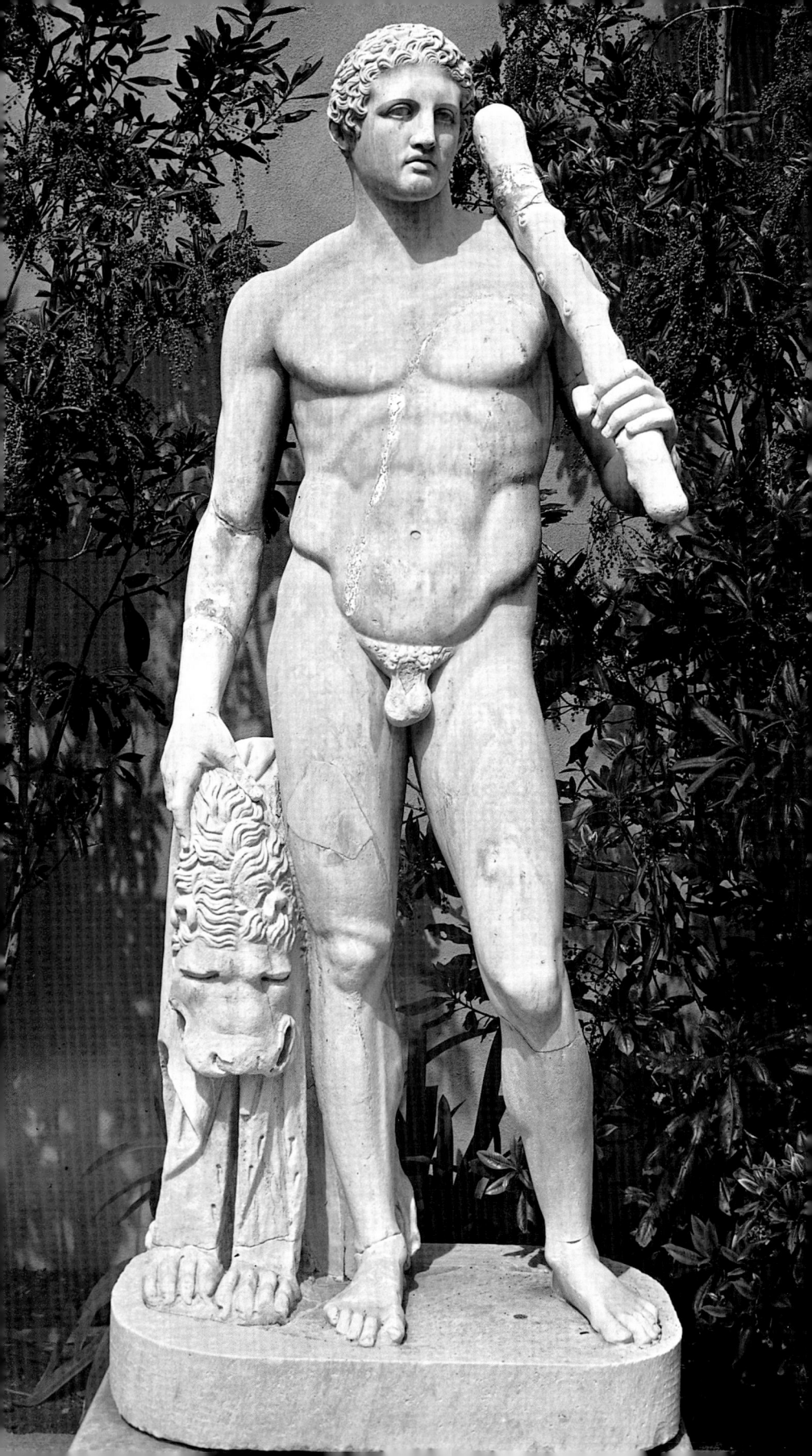

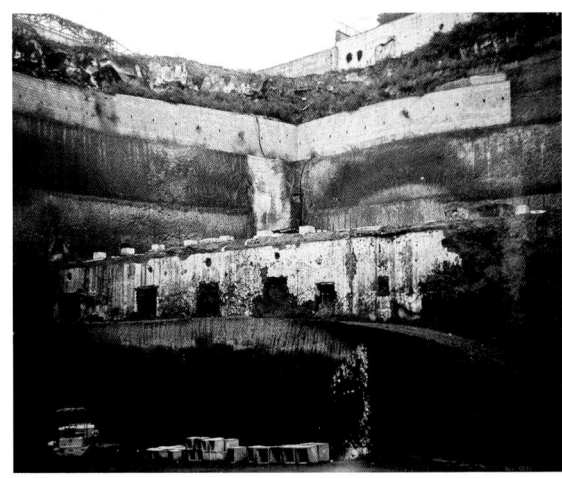

FIGURE 5

View of the Villa dei Papiri under excavation in Herculaneum (modern Ercolano, Italy), 1998.

collections. Over the next thirty years, he also added ancient bronzes, wall paintings, mosaics, and glass. The most important work acquired by Mr. Getty is a Roman statue of Hercules known as the Lansdowne Herakles (fig. 4), bought in 1951 from the collection of Lord Lansdowne in London (see also pp. 160–61). This piece had a well-documented modern history, having been discovered in 1790 near Hadrian's Villa in Tivoli, outside Rome. The statue became the inspiration for a novella by Mr. Getty, *A Journey from Corinth*, in which the statue of Hercules plays a key role as a coveted object that travels in antiquity from Corinth to the Bay of Naples. One of the settings for the story was the ancient Villa dei Papiri, a large residence on the outskirts of the town of Herculaneum. At the time Mr. Getty was writing, the villa was known only from the collection of ancient sculptures and wall paintings removed from the subterranean tunnels by the eighteenth-century excavators and from the ground plan made by their director, Karl Weber. Not until the late twentieth century was an attempt made to remove the more than sixty feet of volcanic debris that had buried the villa when Mount Vesuvius erupted in A.D. 79 (fig. 5). The famous carbonized papyrus book rolls (the vestiges of the ancient villa's Greek library) gave the building its modern name.

As the importance of his collection grew, Mr. Getty felt an increasing responsibility to make it accessible to the public. In December 1953 the J. Paul Getty Museum was officially incorporated, and in May 1954 it opened to the public in the Spanish-colonial Ranch House located on Mr. Getty's Malibu property (figs. 6, 7). (Today this building houses a library, conservation laboratories, and offices for curators and scholars.) Mr. Getty continued to add to his collections, many of which were placed on view in the Ranch House galleries. The expanding collection quickly outgrew the space available to display it. Toward the end of the 1960s Mr. Getty began to contemplate the idea of a new museum on the property. Although he seems to have flirted with the idea of a Neoclassical structure or an addition to the Ranch House in the same style, he decided, against the advice of his archi-

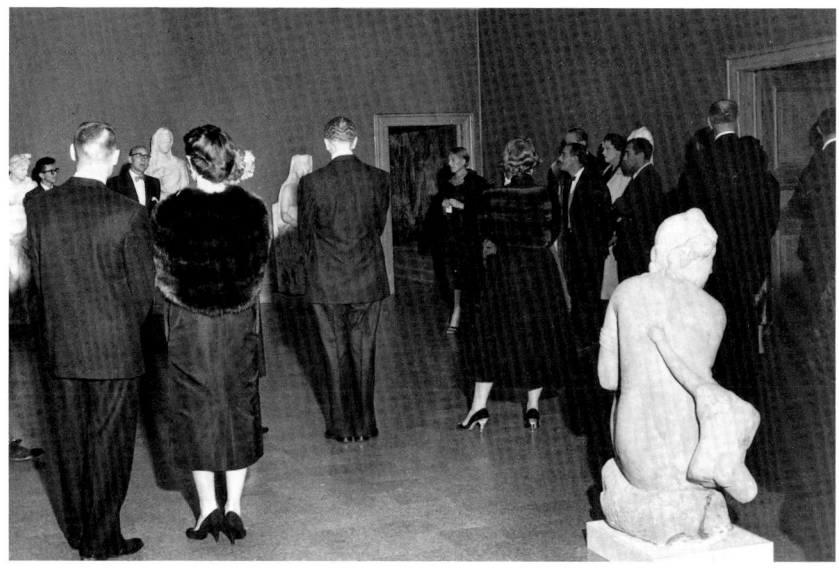

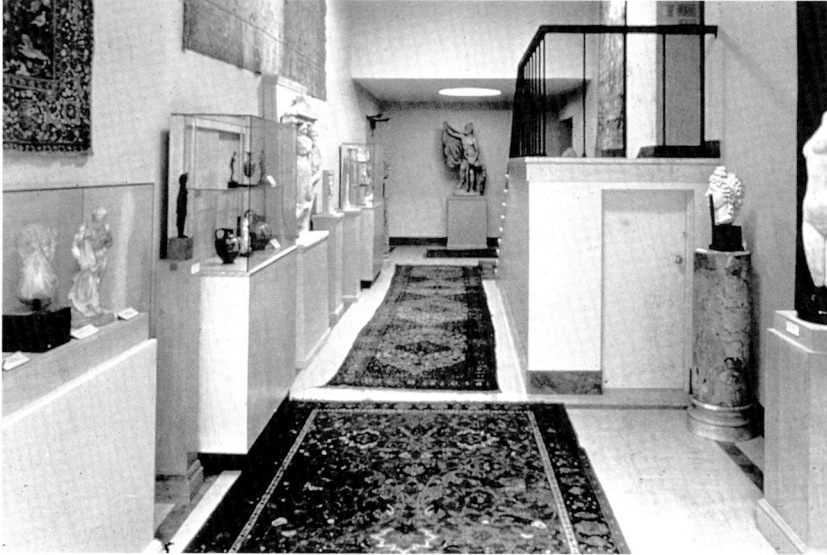

FIGURE 6

A reception at the opening of
the Ranch House Museum in
Malibu, 1954.

FIGURE 7

View of the new gallery for
antiquities in the Ranch
House in Malibu, shortly
after its opening in 1957.

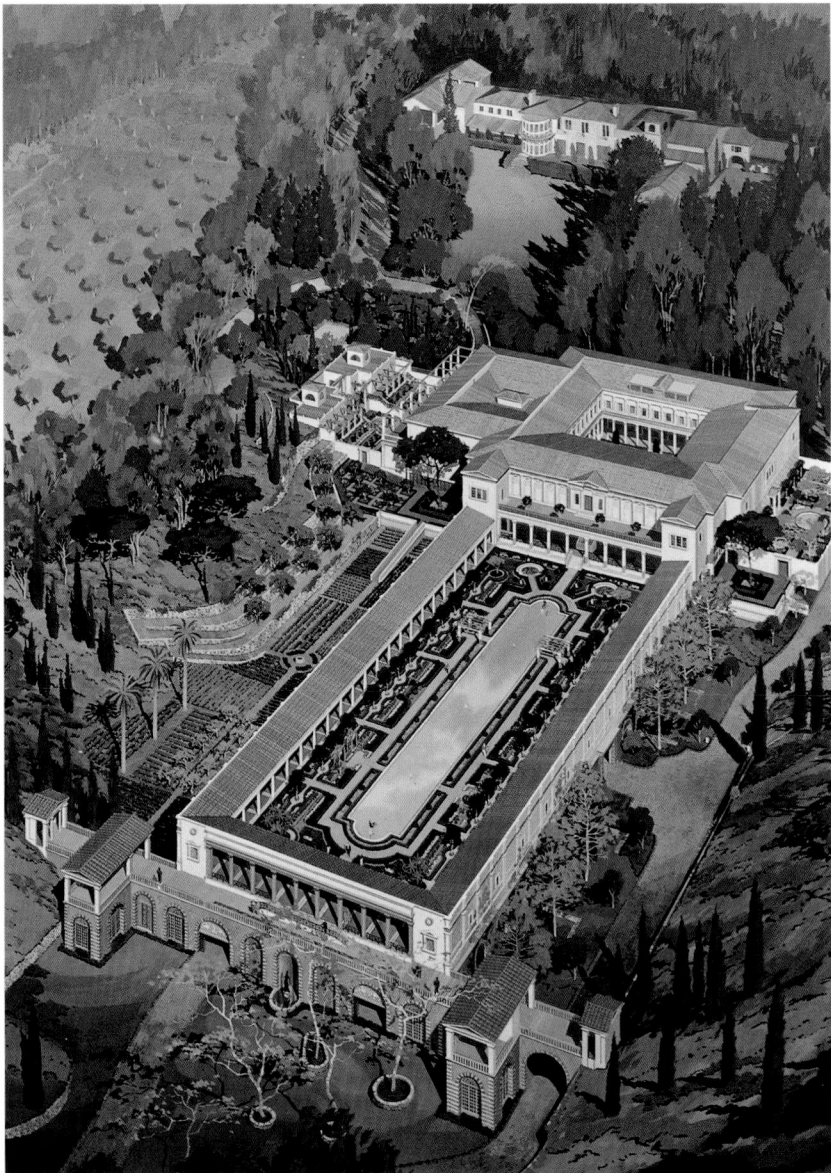

FIGURE 8

Watercolor rendering of the
proposed Getty Museum in
Malibu, 1972. Mr. Getty's Ranch
House (top) is behind the
Museum. Artist: Dave Wilkins.

tectural consultants, to build a replica of an ancient Roman villa, the opulent Villa dei Papiri that had provided the setting for *A Journey from Corinth*.

Working with the architectural historian Norman Neuerburg and the Los Angeles architectural firm of Langdon and Wilson, Mr. Getty set out to design and construct an opulent *villa marittima*, or seaside villa (fig. 8). As he himself wrote, "the principal reason [for building a new museum] concerns the collection of Greek and Roman art which the museum has managed to acquire…and what could be more logical than to display it in a classical building where it might originally have been seen?" Surely the Lansdowne Herakles, which in Mr. Getty's novella had been transported from Corinth to the Villa dei Papiri, was foremost in his mind among the antiquities that inspired this decision. Indeed, he had a special gallery created in the new museum specifically for its display.

The Getty Villa opened in January 1974 to great publicity and criticism. Derisively reviewed at the time as a rich man's folly that seemed to be an uncomfortable mixture of Hollywood and Herculaneum, the Villa proved to be enormously popular with the public. The lush gardens and seaside setting provided the perfect ambience for the enjoyment of the collections installed in the much-expanded galleries.

Mr. Getty made a number of significant purchases for the new museum. In this process he was aided by the expert advice of Bernard Ashmole, Lincoln Professor of Archaeology at the University of Oxford, and by Jiří Frel, the curator he hired in 1973 to oversee the Antiquities Collection. According to Frel, Mr. Getty's guiding principles for acquisition seem to have been aesthetic appeal and how well a piece would fit into the Museum's existing collection. To ensure that the Villa had adequate materials to display at its opening, he authorized the purchase of the entire contents of a Madison Avenue antiquities gallery in 1971. Other Greek funerary monuments, Roman sarcophagi, and a good representative selection of Greek and Roman portrait busts were gradually added to the displays, as well as jewelry, terracottas, and the first Greek and South Italian vases. Finally, Mr. Getty participated in the discussions concerning the acquisition of a life-size Greek bronze, the Statue of a Victorious Youth (see pp. 44–45). Unfortunately, he died before the purchase was completed.

Following Mr. Getty's death in 1976, the Antiquities Collection continued to expand as lacunae were filled and whole new dimensions were added to the inventory. The Museum slowly built a remarkable group of Romano-Egyptian mummy portraits (fig. 9), which would offer an excellent complement to the portraits in stone and bronze, as well as a number of more specialized collections, including carved ambers, Greek and Latin stone inscriptions, engraved gems and cameos (fig. 10), and silver and gold *lamellae*, or curse tablets.

Opportunities to acquire existing collections were especially welcomed by the young institution. Mr. Getty had little interest in ancient vases, and for a long time the collections reflected this lack of enthusiasm. In 1983, Walter and Molly Bareiss's Greek and South Italian vases came to the

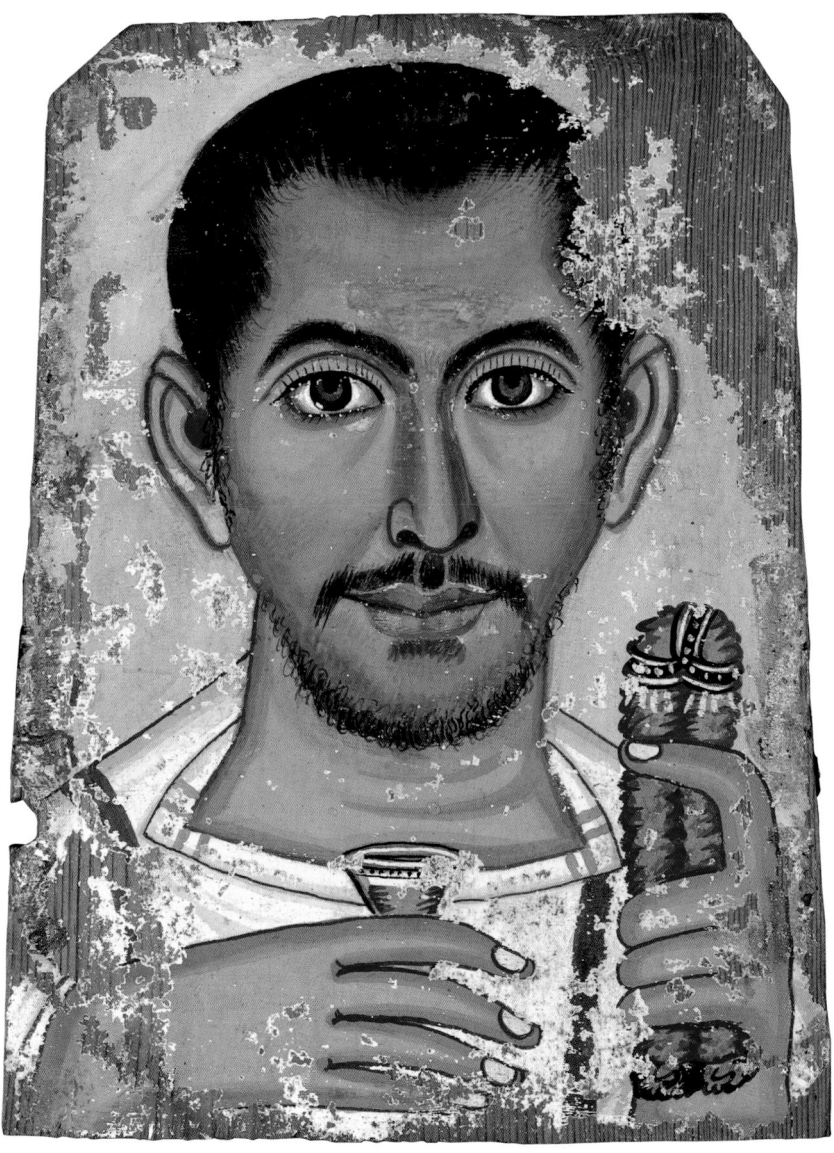

FIGURE 9

Mummy Portrait of a Bearded Man, Romano-Egyptian, from Egypt, A.D. 220–250, tempera on wood, H: 34 cm (13³⁄₈ in.), W: 25 cm (9⁷⁄₈ in.), 79.AP.142.

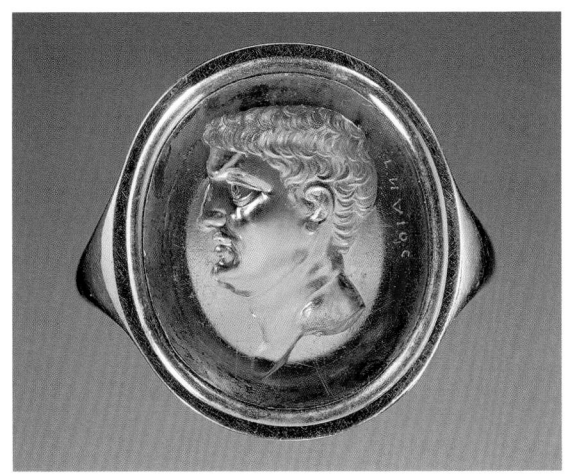

FIGURE 10

Intaglio of Marc Antony,
signed by Gnaios, Roman,
40–20 B.C., amethyst
and modern gold ring,
H: 1.7 cm (¾ in.), 2001.28.1.

Museum for a special exhibition. At the conclusion of the show, the owners were willing to part with their fine collection, built over thirty years, and by 1986 it had become the heart of the Museum's permanent collection. Another significant area of weakness among the Museum's holdings was in material from the Bronze Age, so when Paul and Marianne Steiner's group of large stone figures and related stone vessels became available in 1988, it was purchased for the Museum. The single most important acquisition opportunity for the Antiquities Collection came in 1996 with the addition of the collection of Lawrence and Barbara Fleischman. Following an exhibition of their collection held in Malibu and Cleveland, the Getty accessioned more than three hundred objects, including many important bronzes, as a combination gift and purchase from the Fleischmans. The most recent acquisition of a major collection occurred in 2003 with the purchase of a significant portion of the remarkable ancient glass collection of the late Erwin Oppenländer. Acquired by Mr. Oppenländer over a period of more than fifty years, the glass ranges in date from the second millennium B.C. to the tenth century A.D.

When a collection is actively formed within a matter of decades, it is inevitable that some mistakes are made. Two major acquisitions from 1979—a marble relief thought to be a Greek work of about 530 B.C. (fig. 11) and a marble head of Achilles once attributed to Skopas (fig. 12)—were both later determined to be modern forgeries. In 1985, the Museum acquired its most problematic object, the Getty Kouros (see p. 17), the authenticity of which is still debated. In spite of years of scientific research and scholarly inquiry, no decisive conclusions have been reached. Scholars and scientists are still firmly divided in their judgments, and the statue remains one of the enigmas of ancient art. As a healthy reminder of the limits of our knowledge about ancient art, the Getty Kouros has become an icon of the collection and is exhibited with other images of athletes, but with an extensive accompanying text that explores the issues surrounding its authenticity.

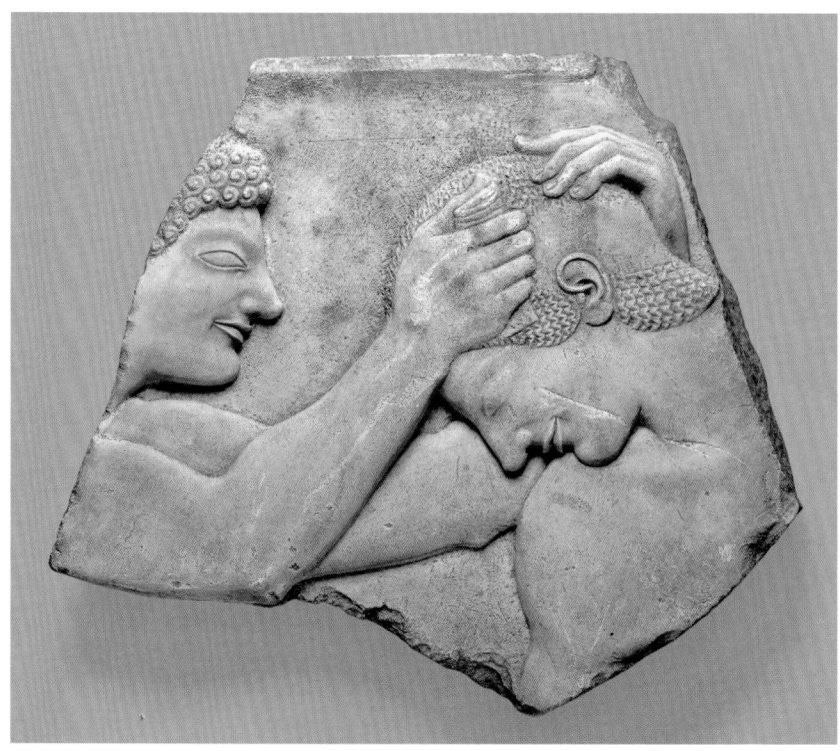

FIGURE 11

Fragment of a Grave Stele,
modern forgery based on a
Greek work of 520–510 B.C.,
marble, H: 50 cm (19⅝ in.);
W: 57.5 cm (22⅝ in.);
D: 9.2 cm (3⅝ in.), 79.AA.1.

FIGURE 12

Head of Achilles, modern
sculpture based on a
Greek work of 325–300 B.C.,
marble, H (approx.):
30.5 cm (12 in.), 79.AL.7.

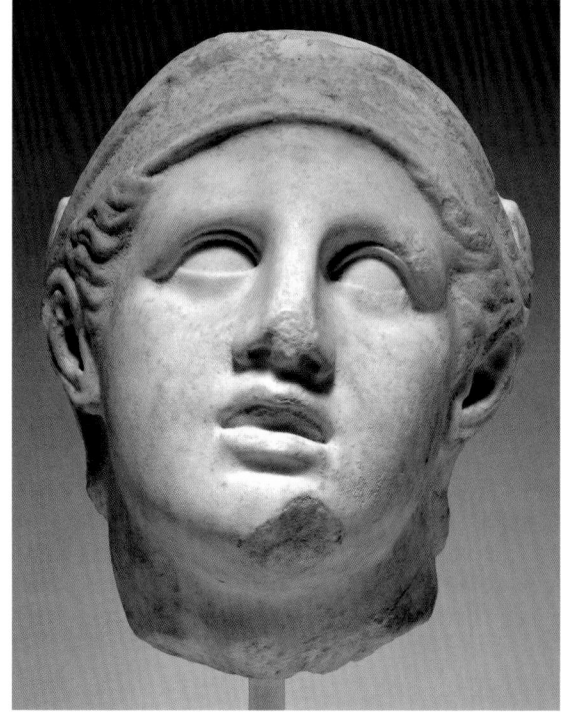

In 1997, just as the Getty Center opened to the public, the Villa in Malibu closed for renovations. As part of its architectural refurbishments, many much-needed public amenities have been added to the site. In the Villa itself, windows and skylights have been opened to provide abundant natural light appropriate for the display of ancient works of art, and colorful materials and rare stones reflect the influence of the sumptuous Roman seaside villa that served as the Museum's original model.

The closure of the museum did not prevent the continued growth of the collection. Mindful of the setting in which such objects would be displayed, the Museum acquired a solid gold beaker of the Roman period (see p. 206) —exactly the kind of luxurious vessel from which the original occupant of the Villa dei Papiri may have drunk—and a gilt silver statuette of a bull (see p. 207), excavated in Pompeii in the mid-eighteenth century, about the same time the Villa dei Papiri was being explored for the first time.

During the nine years that the Villa was undergoing renovation, a sea change was occurring in the art market for antiquities as the governments of countries around the Mediterranean began an intensive effort to try to regain what they considered their national patrimony. With the discovery of a large collection of photographs and other documents seized from the Swiss offices and warehouse of a major dealer in ancient art, legitimate claims were made to a number of collecting institutions in the United States and Europe for the return of objects to Italy and Greece. After lengthy negotiations with the Italian Ministry of Culture, the J. Paul Getty Trust reached an agreement for the return of thirty-nine objects from the Antiquities Collection. To date, thirty-eight of those pieces have been sent to Italy, while one, the Cult Statue of a Goddess, remains on view in the Getty Villa as an extended loan until the end of 2010. These returns have resulted in a wide program of cooperation with the Italian Ministry of Culture for the exchange of works of ancient art of the highest artistic quality, special exhibitions, and conservation projects. This collaboration will allow our visitors access to works not normally seen outside Italy, displayed in an environment perfectly suited to their history. In addition, four objects were sent to Greece in 2007, and plans for a similar agreement for cultural collaboration are being discussed.

Echoing the sentiments of the antiquities curators who have preceded me, it is my hope that the renewed Villa, filled with a superb collection of ancient art, will continue to delight the public just as its founder intended.

Karol Wight
Senior Curator of Antiquities, The J. Paul Getty Museum
August 2009

Notes to the Reader

Objects in this Handbook are grouped by culture; within culture, they are organized by medium; within medium, they are generally presented chronologically.

Unless otherwise noted, the largest measurement for a specific dimension is the one given. The following abbreviations are used:

H: Height
W: Width
D: Depth
DIAM: Diameter
L: Length
pl.: plural

To show the imagery on engraved gems more clearly, impressions are made. Black-and-white photographs of such impressions accompany the gem entries in this book.

Names of Greek Divinities with Their Roman and Etruscan Equivalents

GREEK	ROMAN	ETRUSCAN
Adonis	Adonis	Atunis
Aphrodite	Venus	Turan
Apollon	Phoebus Apollo	Apulu/Aplu
Ares	Mars	Laran/Maris
Artemis	Diana	Aritimi/Artumes/ Aretume/Artemes
Athena	Minerva	Men[e]rva
Demeter	Ceres	Vei
Dioskouroi *Kastor, Polydeukes*	Dioscouri *Castor, Pollux*	Tinas Clenar
Dionysos	Bacchus	Fufluns/Pacha
Eos	Aurora	Thesan
Ge/Gaia	Tellus	Cel
Hades	Pluto	Aita
Hephaistos	Vulcan	Sethlans
Hera	Juno	Uni
Herakles	Hercules	Hercle
Hermes	Mercury	Turms
Persephone	Proserpina	Phersipnai
Poseidon	Neptune	Nethuns
Zeus	Jupiter	Tin/Tinia/Tina

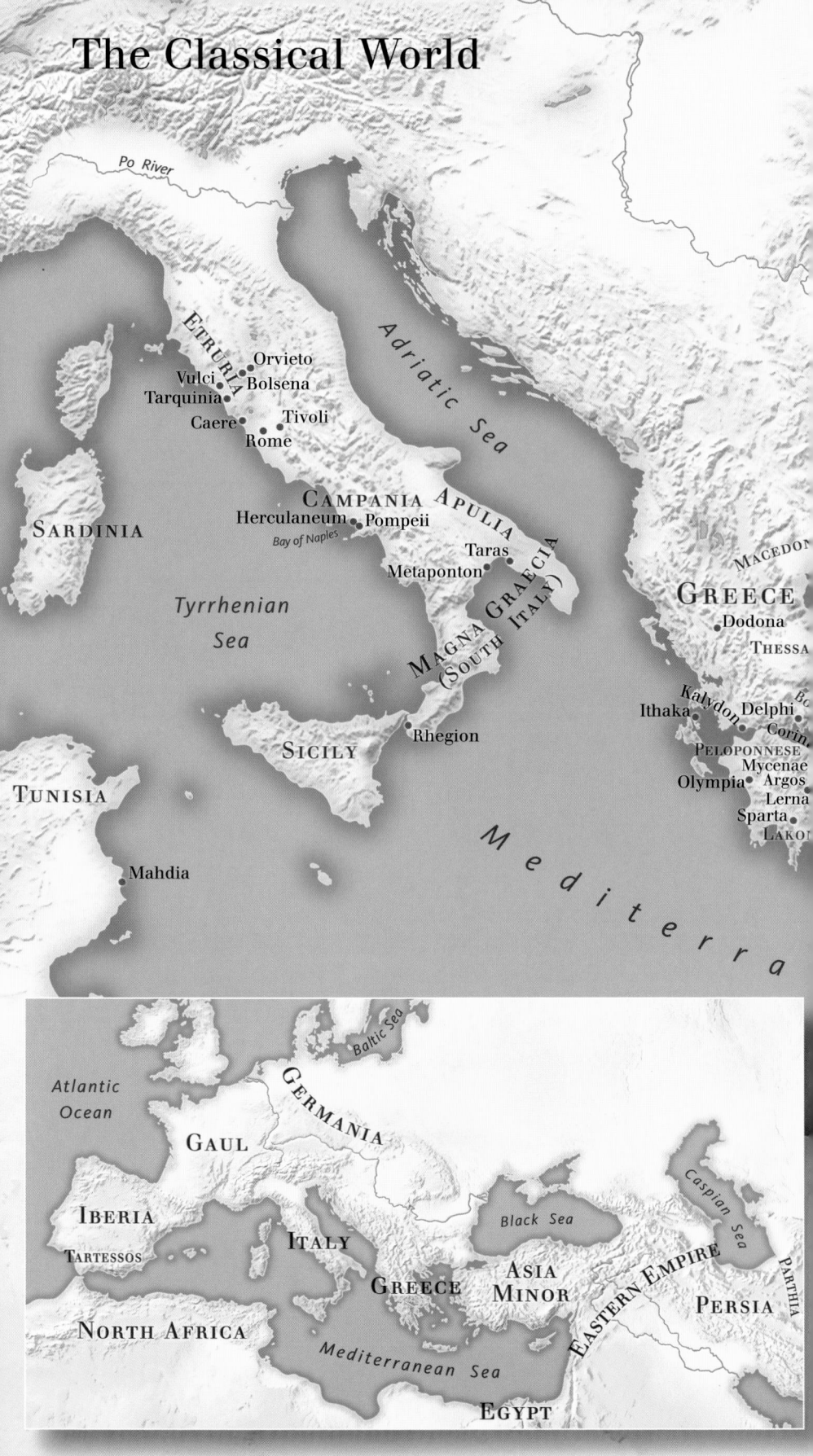

The Classical World

Po River

ETRURIA

Orvieto
Vulci
Bolsena
Tarquinia
Caere
Tivoli
Rome

Adriatic Sea

CAMPANIA APULIA
Herculaneum Pompeii
Bay of Naples
Taras
Metaponton

SARDINIA

Tyrrhenian Sea

MAGNA GRAECIA
(SOUTH ITALY)

MACEDON

GREECE
Dodona
THESSA

Kalydon Delphi
Ithaka Corin
PELOPONNESE
Mycenae
Olympia Argos
Lerna
Sparta
LAKON

SICILY
Rhegion

TUNISIA

Mediterra

Mahdia

Mediterra

Atlantic Ocean

Baltic Sea

GERMANIA

GAUL

IBERIA

ITALY

TARTESSOS

Black Sea

GREECE

ASIA MINOR

EASTERN EMPIRE

Caspian Sea

PARTHIA

PERSIA

NORTH AFRICA

Mediterranean Sea

EGYPT

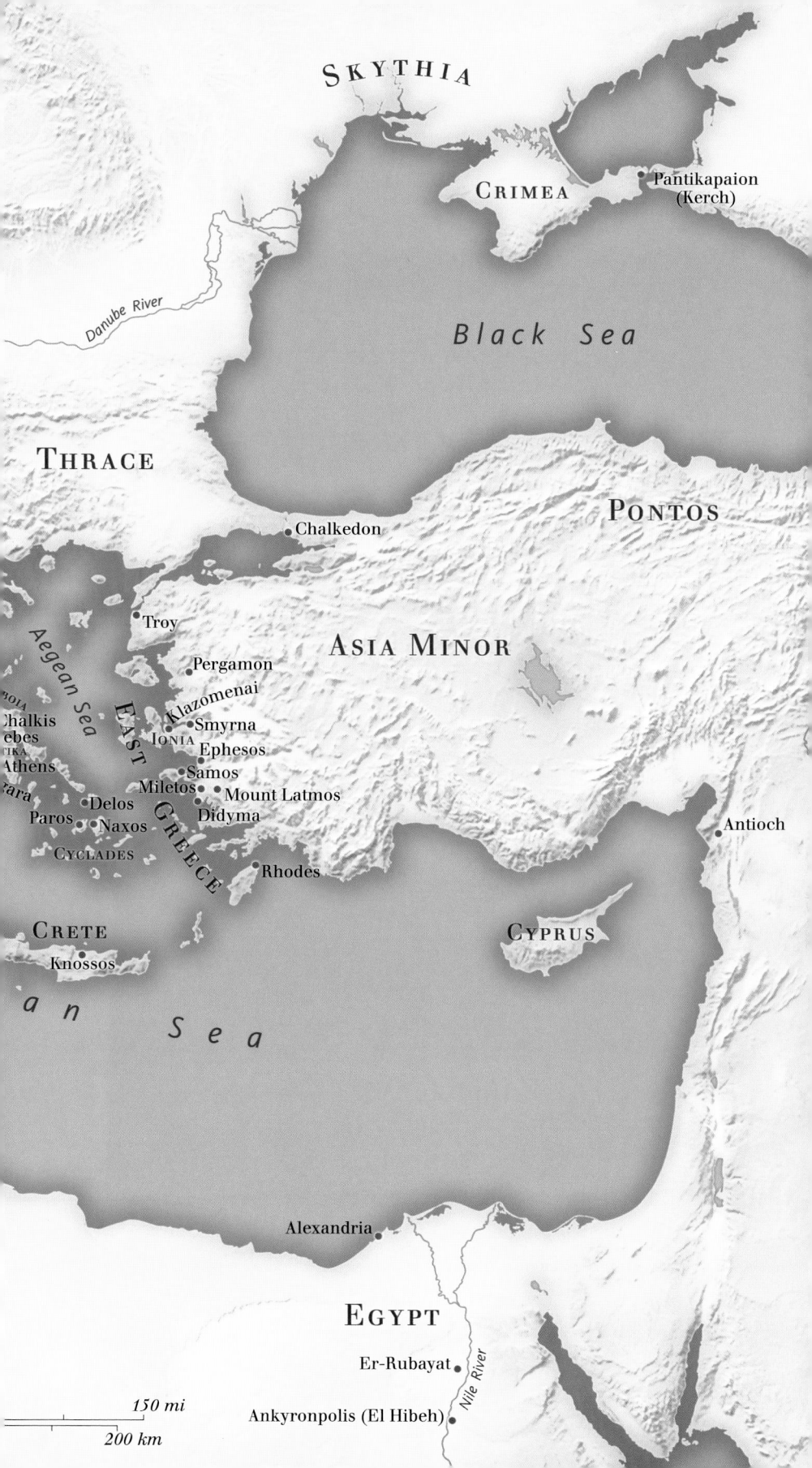

SKYTHIA

CRIMEA

Pantikapaion
(Kerch)

Black Sea

Danube River

THRACE

PONTOS

Chalkedon

Troy

ASIA MINOR

Aegean Sea

Pergamon

Klazomenai

Smyrna

IONIA

Ephesos

Samos

Miletos

Mount Latmos

Delos

Didyma

Paros

Naxos

CYCLADES

Rhodes

CRETE

CYPRUS

Knossos

Antioch

an

Sea

Chalkis

ebes

Athens

gara

Alexandria

EGYPT

Er-Rubayat

Ankyronpolis (El Hibeh)

Nile River

150 mi

200 km

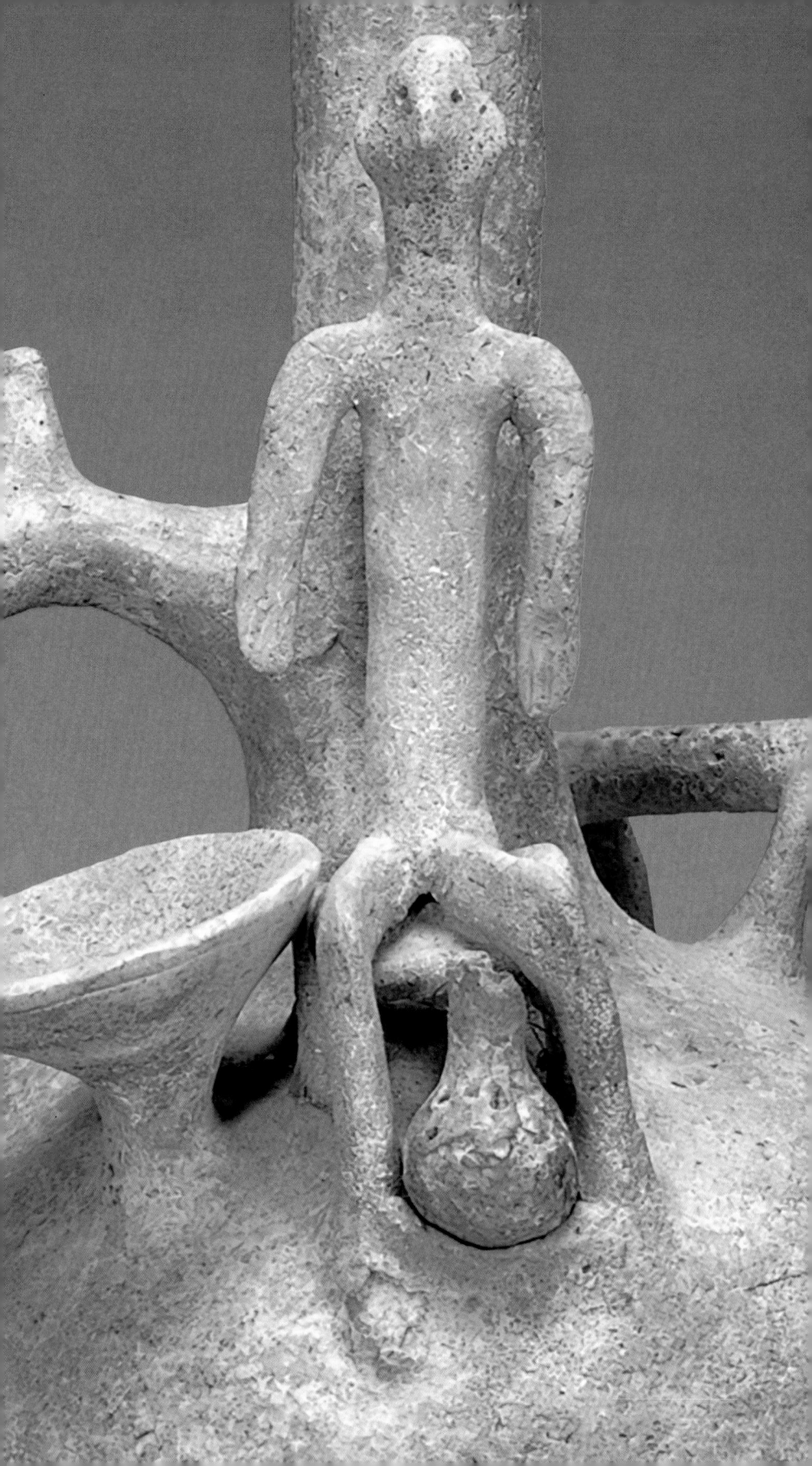

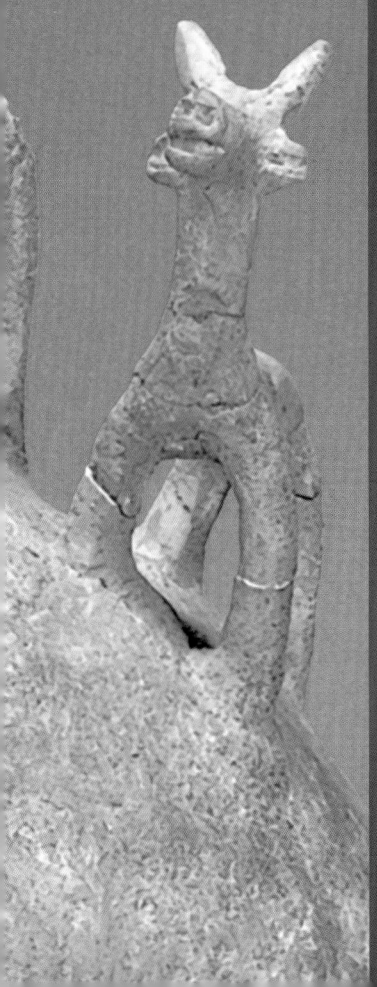

Preclassical
Cultures

Cypriot

**STATUETTE
OF A
FERTILITY
GODDESS**

Cypriot, 3000–2500 B.C.
Limestone
H: 39 cm (15⅜ in.)
W (arm to arm): 26.1 cm
(10¼ in.)
83.AA.38

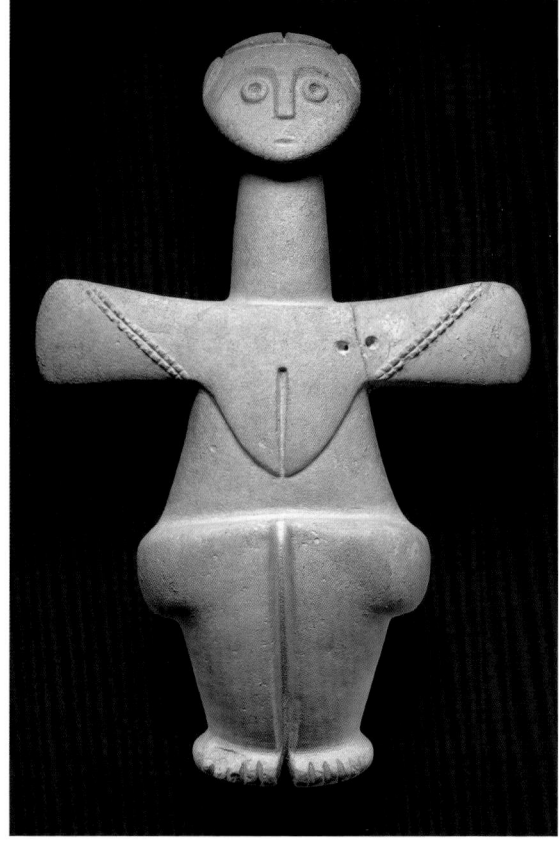

Carved from the local limestone of Cyprus, this female figure is one of the largest and most imposing sculptures from the Chalcolithic period (3000–2500 B.C.) in the eastern Mediterranean. Although the symbolic significance of the cruciform shape is lost to us, the various elements of the figure stress fertility. With head raised, arms extended, and legs drawn up, the statue appears to be in a semisquatting position, perhaps giving birth. The phallic character of the head and neck seems intentional, and the configuration of the breasts —the central focus—implies female genitalia. The V-shape of the breasts is further accentuated by the double bands on each arm, perhaps representing jewelry. Most contemporary Cypriot cruciform figures are considerably smaller than this large figure, suggesting that the Getty piece might have served as a cult image of a fertility or mother goddess. The attachment holes used to repair the left arm in antiquity attest to the importance of the object. The detailed rendering of the face, which includes nose, mouth, ears, hair, and an open-eyed expression, further highlights the figure's uniqueness.

The economy and boldness of design, coupled with an ampleness and clarity of individual forms, set this sculpture apart, imbuing it with a monumental presence unsurpassed in early Cypriot and Mediterranean sculpture.

BEAK-SPOUTED JUG WITH MODELED FIGURAL DECORATION

Cypriot, 2300–1650 B.C.
Terracotta
H: 44.2 cm (17³⁄₈ in.)
2001.79

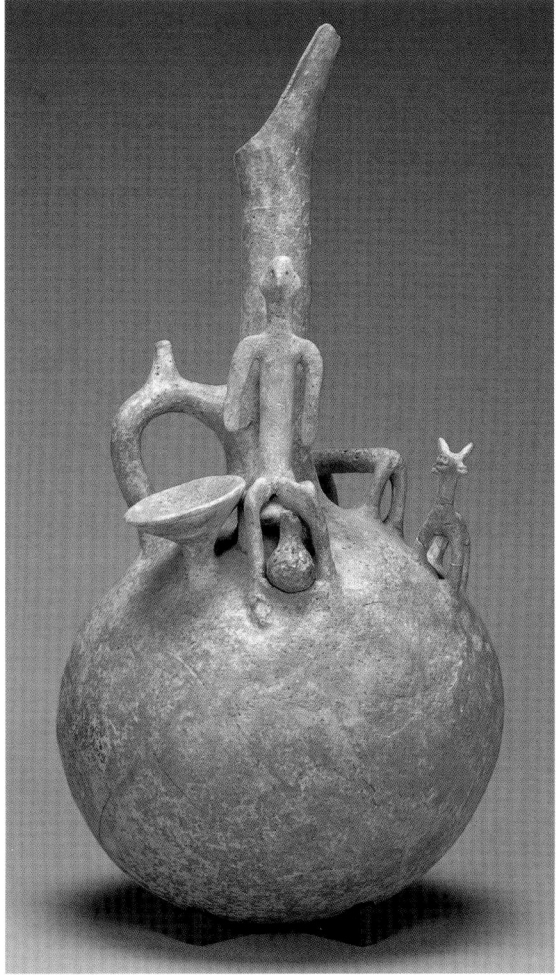

Globular jugs with cutaway or "beak" spouts first became common in Cyprus in the early Bronze Age (2700–1900 B.C.), perhaps as a result of interaction between the inhabitants of Cyprus and people from mainland Anatolia (Turkey), where such vessels were already traditional by that time. This jug is of a pottery type known as polished ware, perhaps of the red or the so-called drab variety. Although polished ware was common in early Cyprus, this jug is exceptional, as it is embellished with figures modeled in the round along the shoulder. The figures include two deer and a man seated on a stool. On the ground beside the man are a wide-brimmed bowl and

a jug, not unlike this one. The scene may portray preparations for milking the deer, or perhaps the moment before bloodletting or ritual sacrifice. In either case, the bowl and jug would be used to collect the liquid. The presence of the miniature jug within the scene suggests that the full-size jug could likewise have been used for milking or bloodletting activities.

Vases with modeled figural compositions are most often found in tombs, and this jug may similarly have been a burial object. The liquid it held may have been used in funerary rituals or may have been intended to sustain the deceased in the afterlife.

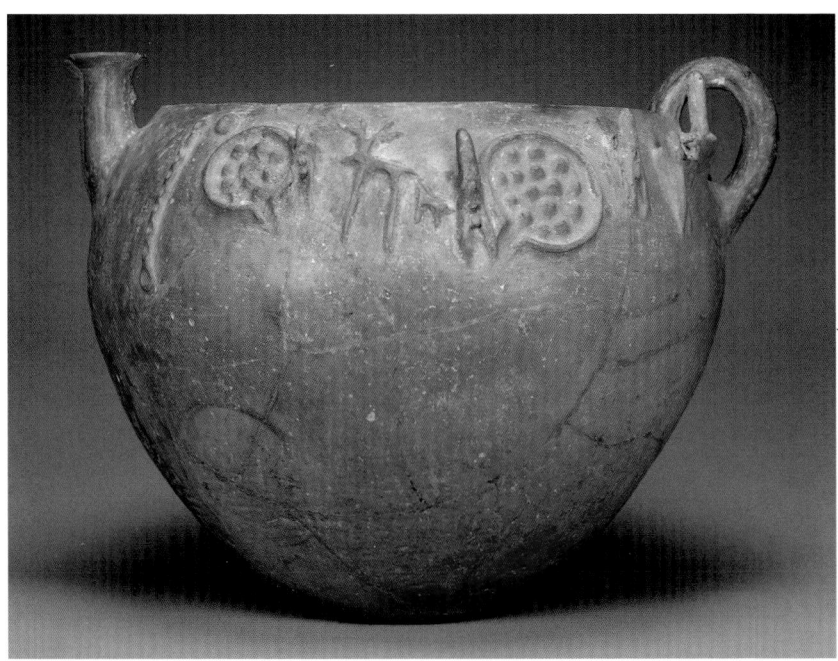

BOWL
WITH HIGH-RELIEF
DECORATION

Cypriot, 2000–1900 B.C.
Terracotta
H: 42.5 cm (16¾ in.)
DIAM (rim): 38.1 cm (15 in.)
2001.78

This bowl is of a ceramic type called red polished ware
that is characteristic of the early Bronze Age in Cyprus
(2700–1900 B.C.). The bowl features figural scenes
modeled in high relief around the vessel's shoulder.
On one side (pictured here), four schematically
rendered men are accompanied by a deer and another
animal, perhaps a fawn or dog. Interspersed between
the figures are several unidentifiable objects, including
two examples of a circular ridge enclosing a number
of small, conical lumps. These enclosures may represent troughs filled with piles of crude copper ore,
and the men are perhaps in the act of refining the ore,
an important industry in copper-rich Cyprus. The
distinctly male individuals seen here contrast with the
seemingly sexless figures on the other side of the
bowl, which, because of this disparity, are thought to
be female. The female figures are at work processing
small lumps of clay in what has been interpreted as
a scene of breadmaking. Indeed, the two sides of the
bowl may depict complementary views of men's
and women's daily tasks. Scenes of breadmaking also
appear on other Cypriot ceramic objects, often from
burial contexts. The small breadmakers were perhaps
intended to be of service in the afterlife, preparing
food to sustain the deceased. In the same way, the
men here could be in the act of supplying the deceased
with metal goods, such as the adzes, knives, pins,
and other implements that are commonly found in
Bronze Age Cypriot tombs.

Cycladic

Beaker

Cycladic, 3200–2800 B.C.
Marble
H: 15.5 cm (6⅛ in.)
DIAM: 12.4 cm (4⅞ in.)
90.AA.10

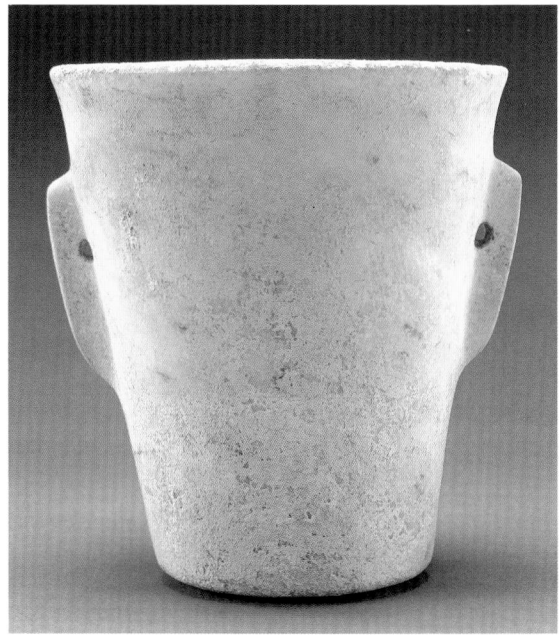

Sculpture in marble, particularly the figurative so-called idols, constitutes the most distinctive product of the culture that flourished in the archipelago at the center of the Aegean in the third millennium B.C. The production of stone vases was also an important and characteristic industry of the Cyclades, and it was only on those islands that white marble was used as a primary material for such vessels. The sculptors who carved the Cycladic figures probably also made the stone vases. The beaker, one of the four basic early Cycladic I shapes, is among the most appealing of the common early Cycladic marble vessels, and this particular example is typical of the shape. There are some sixty known examples of the type, which vary in height from a diminutive 7.8 cm to a large 33.9 cm, although most do not exceed 20 cm. The body is essentially a truncated cone and the plain rim is very slightly everted. A pair of vertical suspension lugs is set on opposite sides of the vessel. In rare cases, a female torso is represented on one side of a beaker. In the Cyclades, the beakers from known sources were evidently associated exclusively with graves. It is unclear precisely how they functioned as sepulchral vessels, and there is as yet no evidence that they played a role in rituals of a nonfunerary nature. Their shape, however, suggests that they served as containers for liquids rather than solids.

HEAD OF A
FIGURE
OF THE EARLY
SPEDOS TYPE

Cycladic, 2600–2500 B.C.
Marble with polychromy
H: 22.8 cm. (9 in.)
W: 8.9 cm. (3½ in.)
D: 6.4 cm. (2½ in.)
96.AA.27

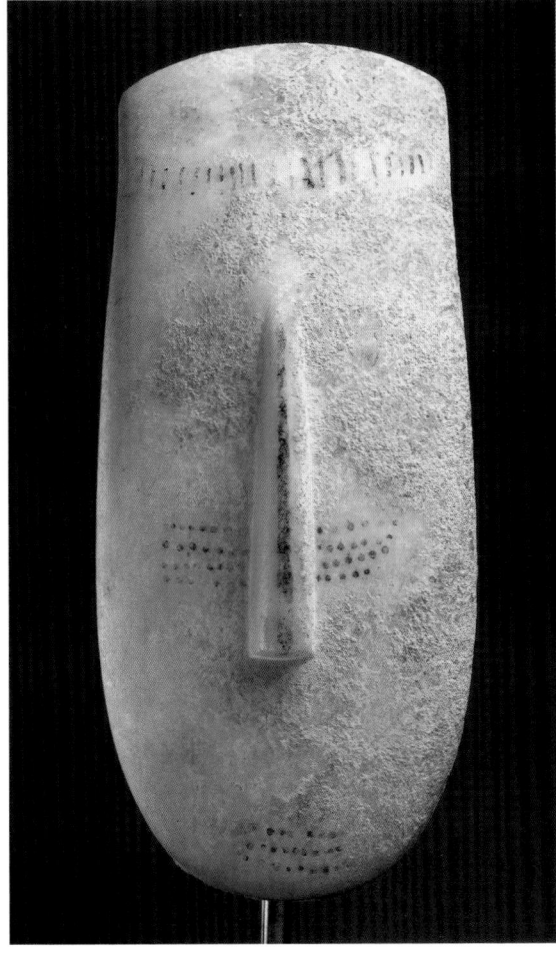

The appearance and elegance of the flattened and, above all, simplified rendering of the human form in Cycladic marble sculptures often strike viewers as quite modern. Although most figurines were less than 30 cm tall, this head, of early Spedos type (named after a cemetery on the island of Naxos), was broken from one of the few examples that was approximately life size. The head is also quite rare in that it preserves some of the paint that originally adorned these figures. Here short vertical lines on the forehead, a stripe on the nose, and bands of dots on the cheeks and chin—all added in a red pigment—may be cosmetic lines or tattooing. The faint bluish paint on the top and back of the head represented hair. Large almond-shaped eyes are preserved as "ghosts," areas that were once painted but are now lighter in color, as well as smoother and slightly raised in comparison to the adjacent marble surface. Although the findspot of the great majority of Cycladic figures is unknown, many of those with known contexts were found in graves. This has prompted scholars to suggest a ritual function connected with death and the afterlife. Not all early Cycladic graves contain such sculptures, however, and some have been found in settlement and sanctuary contexts, indicating a more complex and perhaps multifaceted usage.

FEMALE FIGURE OF THE LATE SPEDOS TYPE

Name-piece of
the Steiner Master
Cycladic, 2500–2400 B.C.
Marble
H: 59.9 cm (23⅝ in.)
W: 12.1 cm (4¾ in.)
88.AA.80

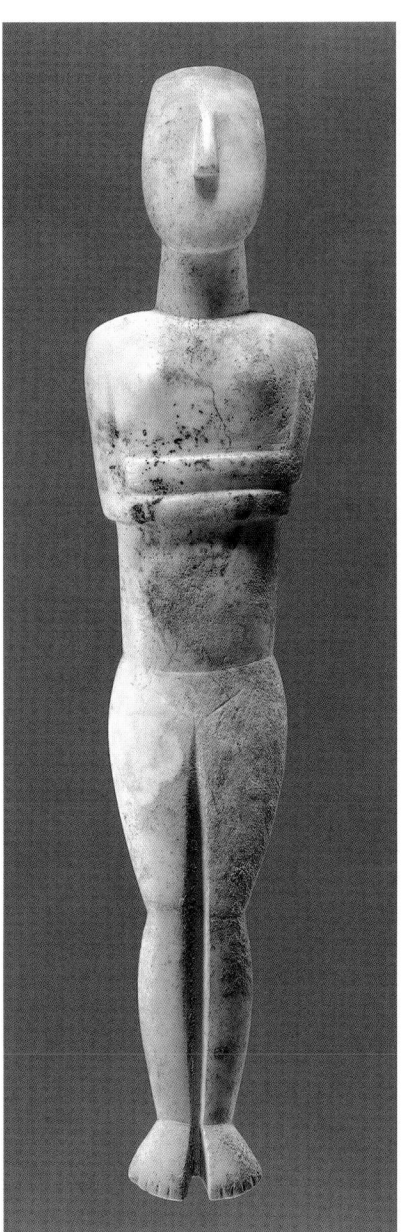

Cycladic figurines formed a special class of object that conformed to a strict traditional typology, within which the Spedos variety (named after a cemetery on the island of Naxos) is one of the most common and longest-lived examples of the canonical female figure with folded arms.

Incisions on this figure delineate the arms from the body, separate the thighs, define the abdomen and pubic triangle, and indicate fingers and toes. The breasts are lightly modeled. The nose is the only carved feature on the U-shaped head, though other details may originally have been enhanced with brightly colored pigments. Viewed from the side, the back is straight and continues the line of the neck, the head is slightly arched and the knees are gently flexed, so that the thighs and calves do not form a single straight line. The feet are bent forward in such a way that the figure cannot stand. Details of the human form are reduced to a minimum, and the figure is a flattened, schematic representation that approaches pure abstraction. Yet the figure is clearly a female, and male figures are rare in comparison to such canonical female idols. Ranging from delicate miniatures to robust works of impressive size, Cycladic idols often show a striking purity of form, beauty of material, and excellence in their workmanship.

STATUETTE OF A HARPIST

Cycladic, circa 2500 B.C.
Marble
H: 35.8 cm (14⅛ in.)
D: 28 cm (11 in.)
85.AA.103

As one of just ten known Cycladic harpists in the world, this figure is quite unusual, and unique in the Museum's collection. Sitting erect on a simple four-legged stool, the harpist lifts his head, perhaps in song. His left hand holds the frame of the harp; his right hand rests on its sound box. Originally, the sculpture's visual impact would have been quite different, because the figure's eyes and hair were once added in paint.

The instrument held by the musician, a frame harp, originated in the Near East and is the ancestor of the modern harp. At the top of the harp is an extension in the form of a swan's head, a common feature on ancient stringed instruments. The swan's elongated neck facilitated the projection of sound from the harp.

Because there are no known images of a harp-playing god at this early date, Cycladic statuettes of harpists may represent humans rather than deities. Musicians were important figures in such prelite-rate societies; they not only provided entertainment but also transmitted common history, mythology, and folklore through their stories and singing.

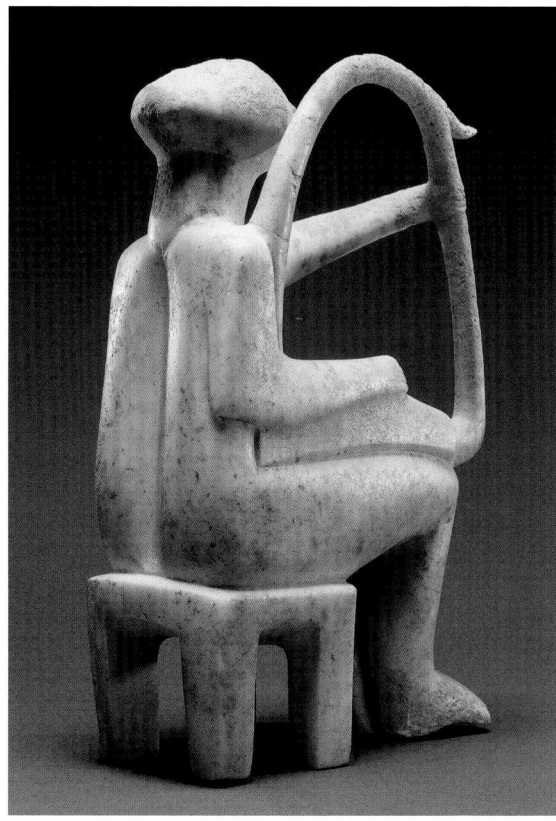

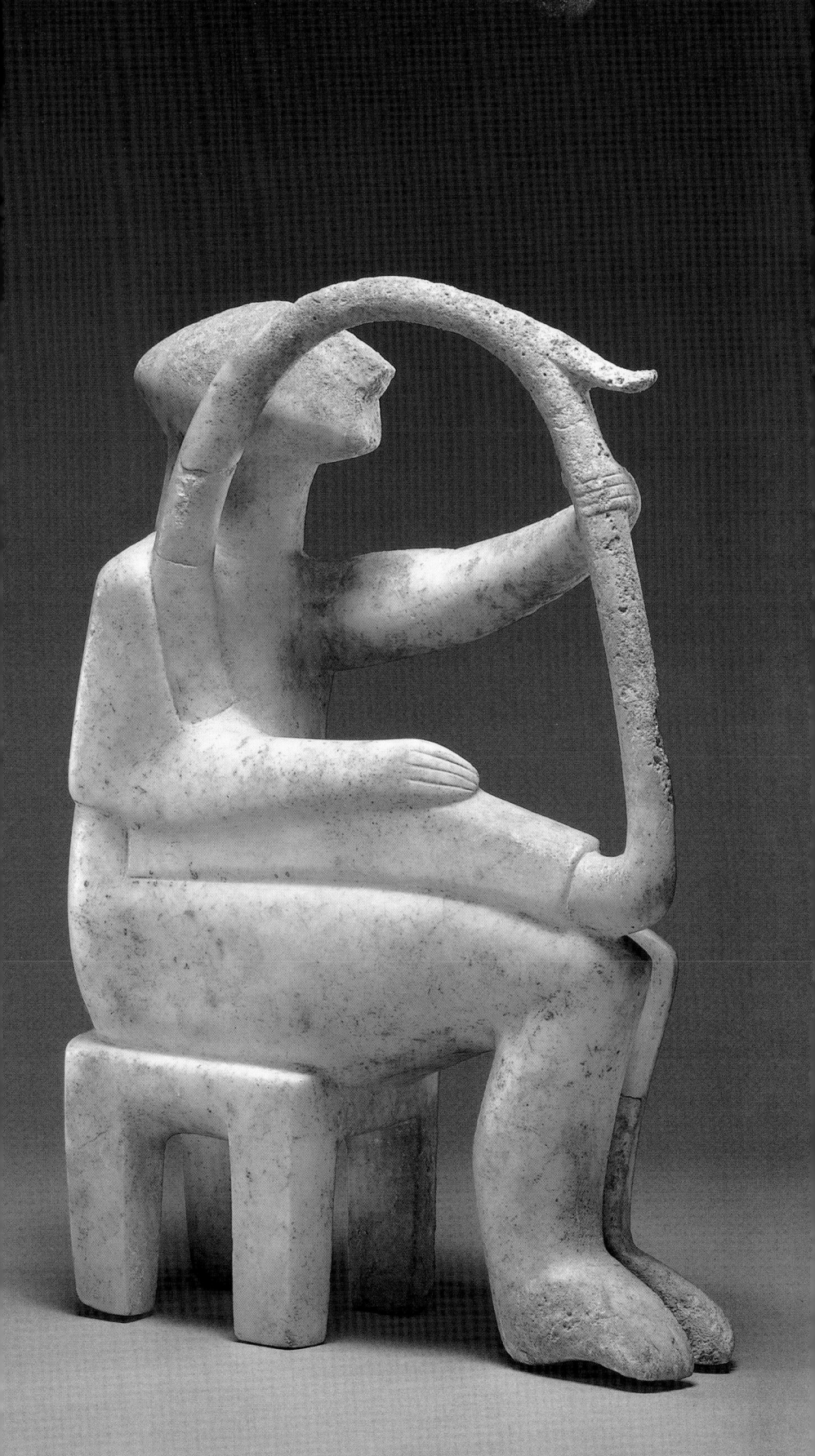

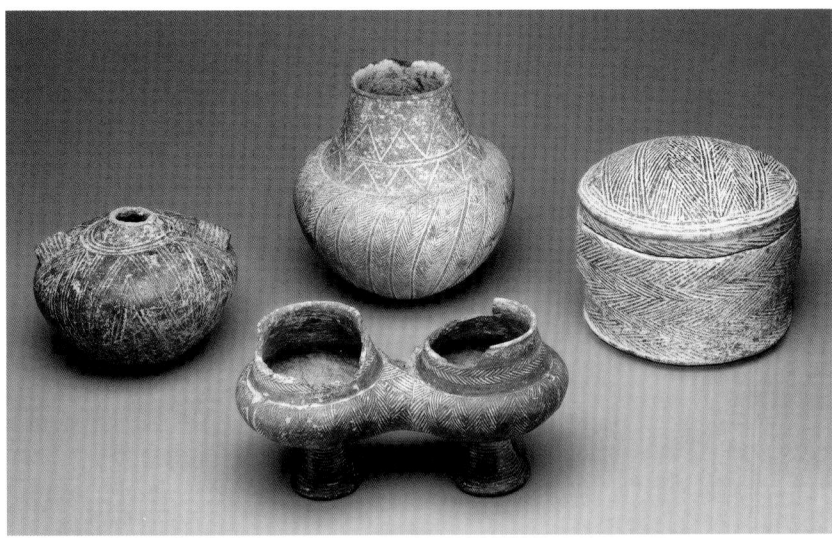

GROUP OF TERRACOTTA VASES

Cycladic, 3000–2700 B.C.
Terracotta
H: various, from 9.7 cm
(3⅞ in.) to 14.8 cm (5⅞ in.)
91.AE.28–.31

These four vases are typical of those produced during the early Cycladic period. They include a bottle, two collared jars (one of which is a double-pedestal vase, also known as a *kandila*), and a cylindrical pyxis with lid. Although surely used for a variety of functions in life, many of these vases accompanied the deceased in graves. Shaped by hand, the vessels were burnished smooth before firing, thereby creating a shiny, compacted, and less porous surface.

Cycladic potters of this period often decorated their pots with geometric designs incised into the surface of the vessel; these were usually filled with a white chalky substance that contrasted with the darker surface. The linear decoration may reflect the woven patterns of baskets, although no baskets from the time have survived.

The pottery and other material culture of the period in the Cyclades have been systematically organized into a series of cultures or groups, each named after a specific island or site. The shapes of the Museum's Cycladic terracotta vessels, coupled with the distinctive incised herringbone motifs found on the jar, the pyxis, and the twin *kandila*, are typical features of the earliest stage of the early Cycladic period, known as Grotta-Pelos culture (3000–2800 B.C.). However, the form of the bottle decorated with the opposed diagonal lines is more characteristic of the next stage, called the Kampos Group (2800–2600 B.C.).

Minoan

ENGRAVED SEAL DEPICTING A BULL LEAPER

Minoan, from Crete,
1450–1300 B.C.
Blue-gray hematite
DIAM: 1.9 cm (¾ in.)
2001.14.1

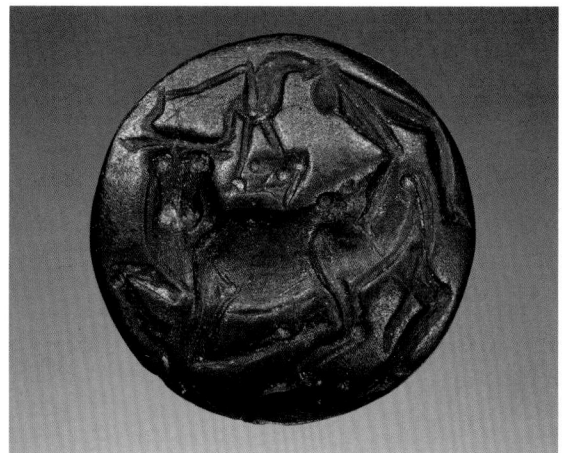

A male acrobat leaps over a bull, grasping one of its horns with his left hand. Such scenes of *taurokathapsia* (bull leaping) are typical of the art of late Bronze Age Crete (1600–1200 B.C.). They appear not only on engraved gems but also in frescoes and as statuettes. The ancient gem carver has organized the composition to fill the circular field of the lentil-shaped stone. While the bull's body is seen in profile, its head is depicted frontally. The male leaper, meanwhile, has flipped himself over the animal. Nude but for a loincloth and codpiece, he has the tall, thin proportions and muscular legs that are associated with male figures in Minoan art.

The practice of engraving semiprecious stones with geometric and figural motifs originated in Mesopotamia around 5000 B.C. The technique soon spread to Egypt and eventually the Aegean. Using a lathe with minute drills and wheels dipped in a slurry of oil and abrasive powder that actually cut the stone, Minoan craftsmen fashioned intaglios (from the Italian verb *intagliare*, "to cut into") that would produce relief images when pressed into soft clay or wax. Such impressions were employed as signatures on documents and to seal pots, chests, doors, and other containers to control, guarantee, or label their contents or to authorize a specific course of action. Although stones found locally, such as hematite, carnelian, steatite, agate, and jasper were commonly used, seals were also produced from exotic materials, such as amethyst, lapis lazuli, and hippopotamus ivory.

Mycenaean

SIDE-SPOUTED
SIEVE JUG

Attributed to Painter 20
Mycenaean, 1250–1225 B.C.
Terracotta
H: 16.6 cm (6½ in.)
DIAM (body): 13 cm (5⅛ in.)
85.AE.145

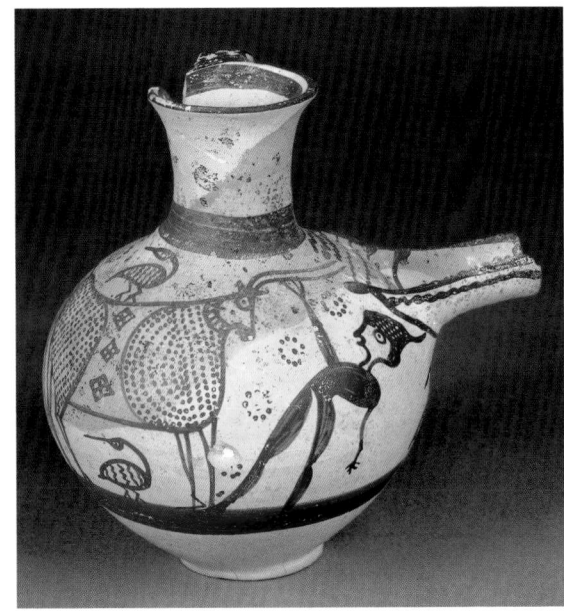

During the final stages of the Aegean Bronze Age, from about 1400 B.C. on, Mycenaean potters developed one of the earliest figurative styles in Greek painted pottery. The inspiration for this new style may have been fresco painting. Referred to as the Pictorial style, this type of pottery became progressively more popular in the fourteenth and thirteenth centuries B.C., but accounted for only a small percentage of Mycenaean pottery production. Although the majority of Pictorial-style vases have been found in Cyprus and the Near East, recent discoveries, along with scientific analysis, suggest that most were made in the Argolid, the broad plain that was home to Mycenae, Tiryns, and other important Mycenaean centers in the Peloponnese.

Wrapped around the body of this jug are many of the figurative elements that are found on other Pictorial-style vases: either a sphinx or a Centaur holding a pomegranate branch or a spray of opium poppies; a bull; four birds; and a man, who grasps one of the bull's horns. The connection between bull and man may allude to the ritual or athletic performance of bull leaping, which had its origins in Minoan Crete, but this is not a typical bull-leaping scene. Based on the way specific details are rendered and repeated and on the overall drawing style, a number of these vases have been attributed to individual vase-painters. Their names remain anonymous, but their styles have been differentiated and identified by numbers. Although the precise function of this jug is uncertain, the strainer holes suggest that it was designed for a liquid requiring filtering, perhaps beer.

Tartessian

FURNITURE SUPPORT REPRESENTING A WINGED FELINE

Tartessian, 700–575 B.C.
Bronze
H: 61 cm (24 in.)
D: 33 cm (13 in.)
79.AC.140

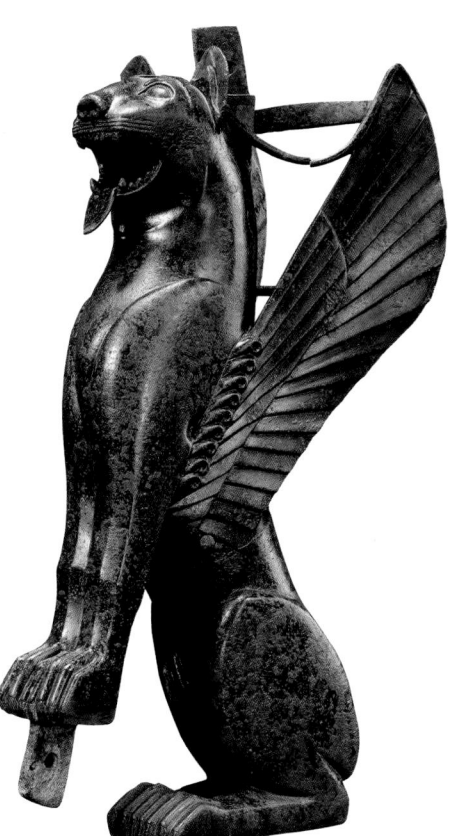

Stylistic details on the wings and head of this fierce, pantherlike creature and the general method of its manufacture suggest that it comes from the kingdom of Tartessos on the Atlantic coast outside the Strait of Gibraltar in modern Spain. Due to its rich mineral resources, Tartessos was an important port on Greek, Phoenician, and Etruscan trade routes in the western Mediterranean. The art of Tartessos combines native Iberian elements with influences brought by traders and colonists.

The form of the feline's brow is distinctively Tartessian, as is the triangle design in the creature's ears. Artists of the region were influenced by the animal-style tradition of the Phoenicians who first established colonies there. Felines, in particular, were popular in the art of many Mediterranean and Near Eastern cultures.

This beast was cast in two separate pieces, which are joined with rivets just below the wings. The thin bronze rods between the head and wings could be design features, but more likely they are part of the bronze mold's internal system of tubes, which facilitated the flow of the molten metal. The pierced projections behind the head and below the front paws of the winged creature indicate that it was attached to a larger structure, such as a wooden throne. It was not uncommon in antiquity for ceremonial chairs and thrones constructed of wood to be embellished with elements made of bronze and other metals.

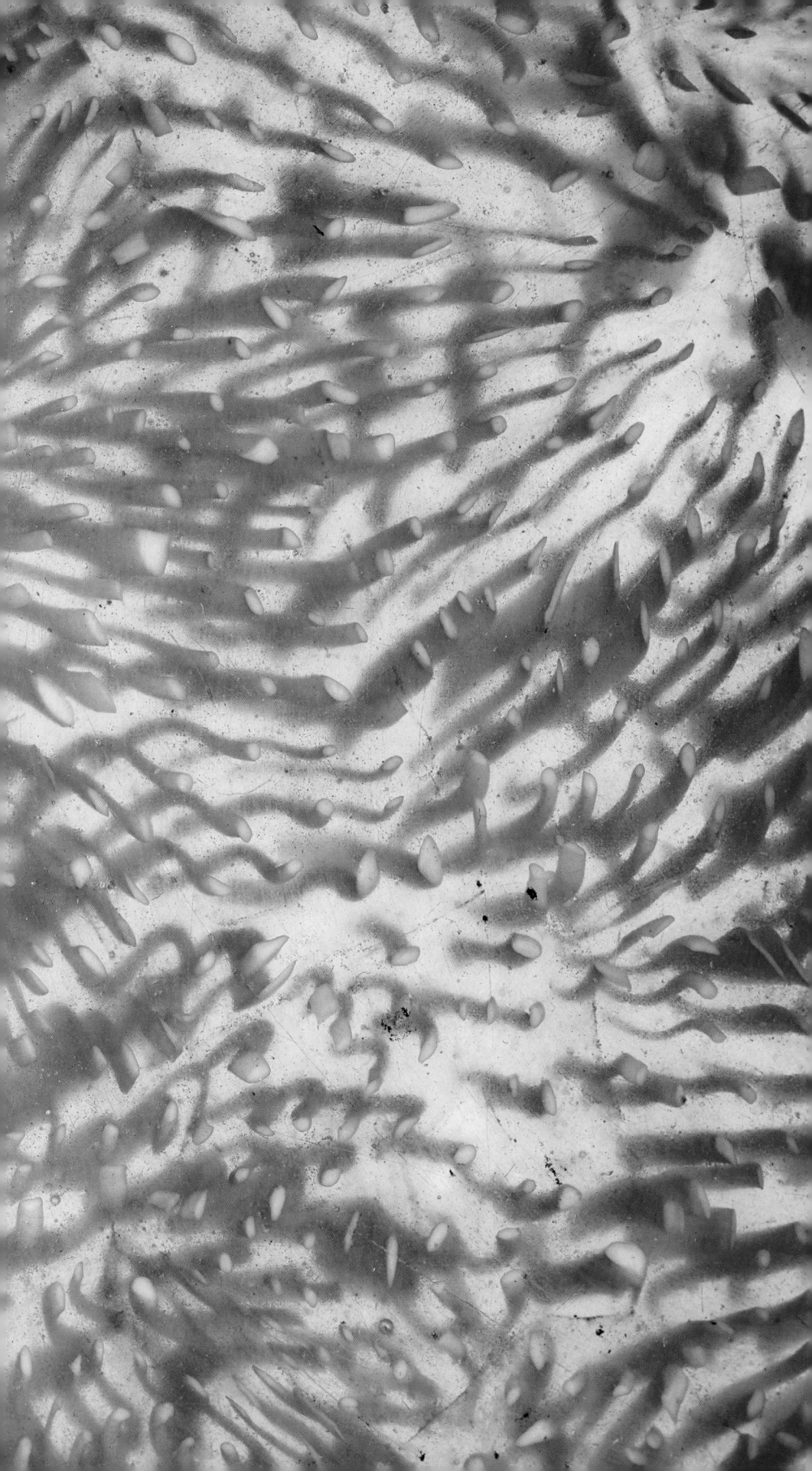

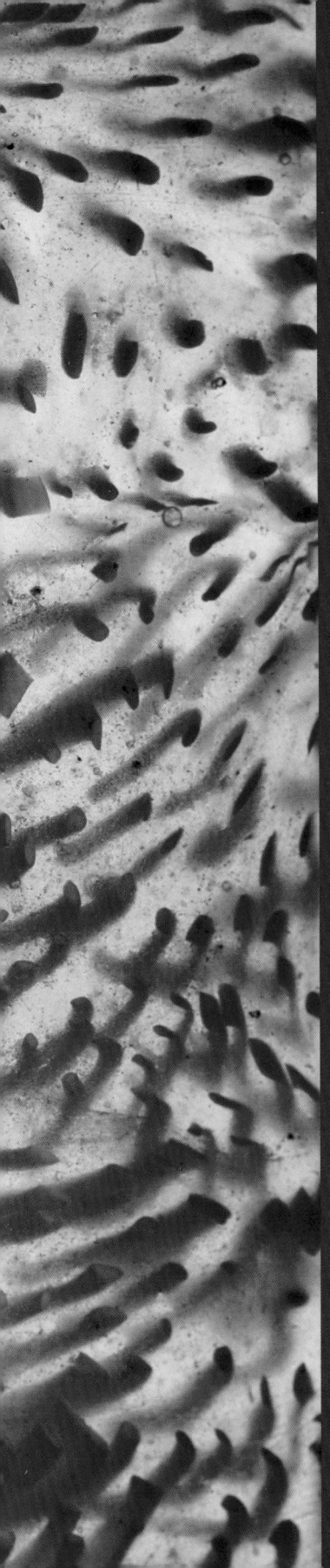

Greek and Eastern Mediterranean

STATUE OF A KOUROS

East Greek, from Didyma
550–525 B.C.
Marble
H: 51.5 cm (20¼ in.)
W: 28.9 cm (11⅜ in.)
D: 24.5 cm (9⅝ in.)
91.AA.7

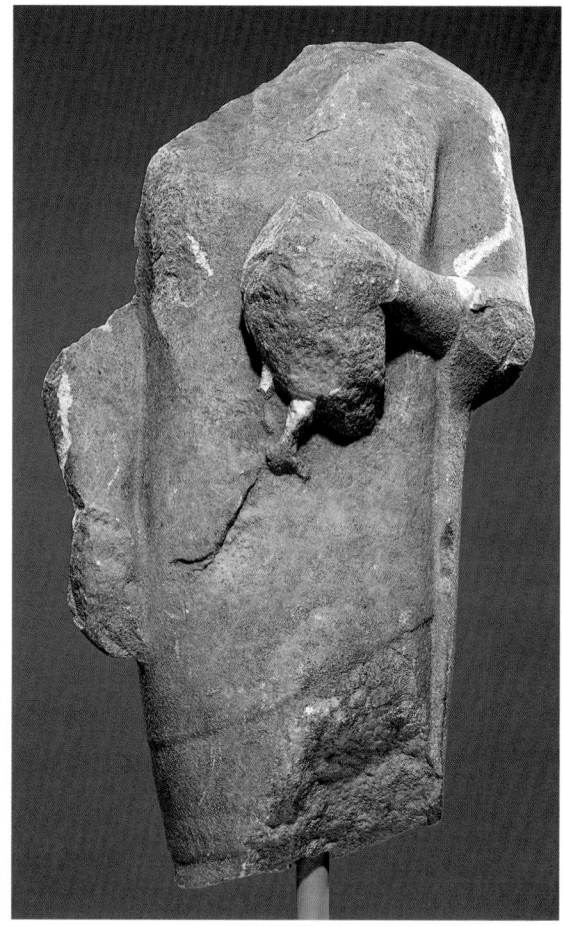

In the 500s B.C., the Greeks, in both Greece itself and its colonies, frequently dedicated statues of young men such as this as offerings to the gods in religious sanctuaries or erected them as funerary monuments. Most kouroi emphasized the figure's youthfulness, athletic build, and vitality. The word kouros (pl. kouroi) means "a youth" in Greek. Statues of kouroi embodied an ideal of physical and moral beauty valued in Greek society. Although usually portrayed nude, kouroi were also depicted clothed, particularly in Greek colonies located east of the Greek mainland in Ionia (the west coast of modern Turkey and the nearby islands), reflecting a regional preference. This half-life-size kouros wears a himation, or cloak, over a long tunic. A double incised line decorates the edge of the cloak. In his left hand, he holds to his chest a bird (whose head is missing) as an offering to the gods; his right hand is at his side. The figure stands frontally, with his left leg placed in front of the right. His shoulders are broad, his hips narrow; both buttocks are well defined. Kouroi often had long hair, and here the ends of long locks of hair are preserved on the upper back of the statue. The rounded muscular body of this kouros, his delicately sculpted fingers, and the smooth carving of his clinging garment suggest that the statue was sculpted in the East Greek city of Didyma.

STATUE OF
A KOUROS

Greek, circa 530 B.C.
or modern forgery
Marble
H: 206 cm (81¹/₈ in.)
W (at shoulders): 60.5 cm (23⁷/₈ in.)
D (at base): 57.5 cm (22⁵/₈ in.)
85.AA.40

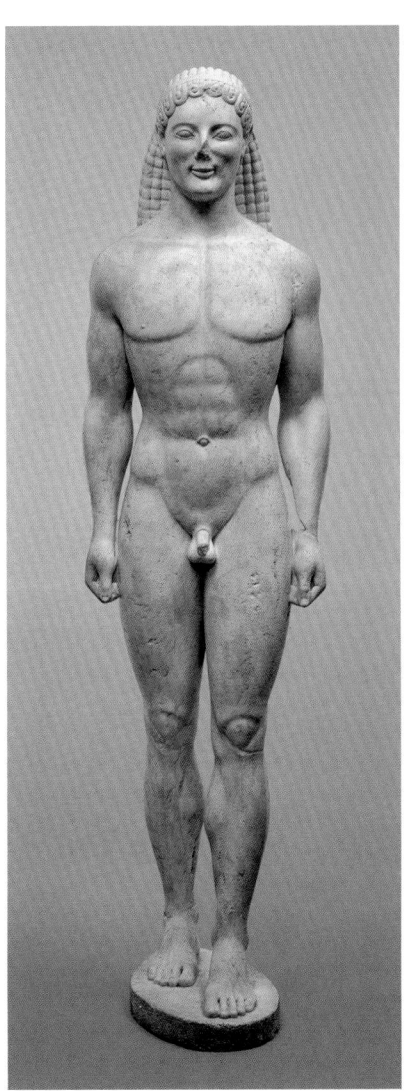

The earliest monumental sculpture in
Greece dates to around 650 B.C. and
appears to have taken its inspiration
from Egypt and the Near East. From
this time on there was an active artistic
output of life-size and over-life-size
statues throughout Greece. Most
consist of standing male and female
figures—kouroi and korai—and most
were carved from marble or limestone
that was often brightly painted. The
kouros, or standing male figure, was
an established type throughout the
sixth century B.C. Standing erect with
the left foot forward, the arms lowered
by the side of the body, and the eyes
looking straight ahead, these statues
were either dedicated in sanctuaries
or stood above tombs as grave monuments. Archaic Greek statues are
uniquely interesting because they
show the progression of Greek understanding about human anatomy.
Step by step, Greek sculptors learned
to represent in detail the complex
structure of the head, torso, arms,
legs, and feet.

Neither scientists nor art historians
have been able to resolve completely
the issue of the authenticity of the
Getty Kouros. Certain elements of the
statue, such as a mixture of earlier
and later stylistic traits and the use of
marble from the island of Thasos, have
led scholars to question its veracity.
Yet the apparent anomalies of the
Getty Kouros may indicate our limited
knowledge of Archaic Greek sculpture
rather than be evidence of a forger's
mistakes.

GRAVE STELE OF
THE HOPLITE POLLIS

Greek, from Megara, circa 480 B.C.
Marble
H: 153 cm (60¼ in.);
W: 45.1 cm (17¾ in.);
D: 15.9 cm (6¼ in.)
90.AA.129

"I speak, I, Pollis, the beloved son of
Asopichos, not having died a coward,
with the wounds of the tattooers, yes
myself," reads the inscription carved
on this sculpted stele, or commemorative stone slab, used here as a gravestone for the hoplite Pollis. Hoplites
were heavily armed foot soldiers.
Pollis here advances into battle,
helmeted with his shield raised and
his spear ready, but he is otherwise
ideally nude. A sword hangs at his
side, suspended from a strap that was
originally added in paint, as were
other details of the decoration.

Pollis probably was killed while
defending Greece from invading
Persians. The tattooers, the enemy
named in the inscription, were most
likely the Thracians, a fierce people
who occupied the area to the north of
Greece and who fought against the
Greeks under the Persian commander
Xerxes in 480 B.C.

In form the stele retains the tall
narrow shape popular in the Archaic
period, yet its decoration looks forward
to the early Classical period. Sculptors
of the period from about 480 to 450 B.C.
displayed a new interest in the representation of space, movement, and
human anatomy. Shown mostly in
profile view with accurate musculature
and a foreshortened shield, the figure
of Pollis conveys a sense of three-
dimensionality. Given the stele's very
shallow carving, this effect is all the
more remarkable.

The stele's inscription combines the
alphabets of both Athens and Corinth.
This kind of writing was typical of
Megara, the city-state located between
Athens and Corinth.

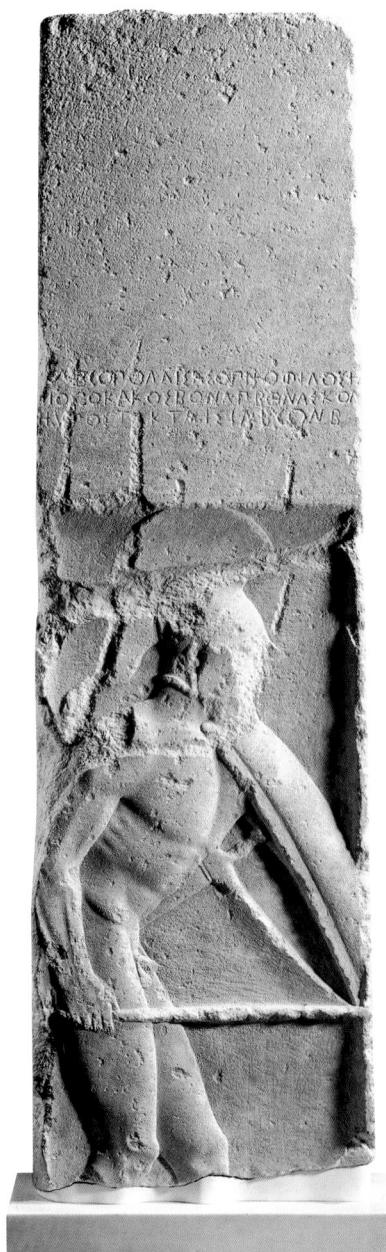

STATUE OF A KORE (THE ELGIN KORE)

Greek, circa 475 B.C.
Marble
H: 71 cm (28 in.)
W: 28 cm (11 in.)
D: 19 cm (7½ in.)
70.AA.114

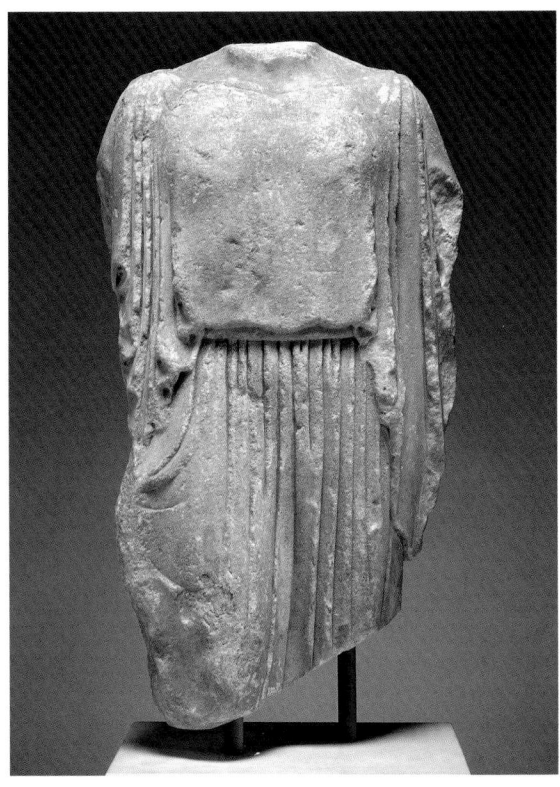

The Greek kore statue, depicting a standing or striding young woman (i.e., the female equivalent of the kouros), was the embodiment of youthful beauty and grace. Like the kouros, it was usually a religious dedication or a funerary monument. This kore wears a peplos and steps forward with her right leg. A peplos was a one-piece woolen garment belted at the waist and pinned at the shoulders with long, metal, decorative dress pins. Formed from a rectangular piece of heavy woven cloth, the tunic was folded at the neckline to create an overfall on the upper body. Little of the body of this young woman is actually visible except for the contour of her right thigh, which is revealed as she pulls the peplos to one side with her now-missing right hand. This gesture is typical of the kore statue type, in which one hand was usually extended with an offering to the gods while the

other grasped the fabric of the dress below the waist.

Draped statues of women were the norm in the 400s B.C. in Greece, whereas men were often shown nude. Sculptors of korai were interested in capturing the interplay of fabric folds over the body underneath. A statue such as this one may have been offered as a gift to the gods in a sanctuary, or have served as a funerary marker, or even been used to decorate the pediment of a Greek temple.

This statue was once in the collection of Thomas Bruce, 7th Earl of Elgin. Lord Elgin, as he is commonly known, was British Ambassador to Constantinople in the late eighteenth century. He is best known as the person responsible for removing most of the sculptural decoration from the Parthenon on the Acropolis in Athens and bringing the pieces to England, where they now are displayed in the British Museum in London.

GRAVE STELE OF PHILOXENOS WITH HIS WIFE, PHILOUMENE

Greek, from Attika,
circa 400 B.C.
Marble
H: 102.2 cm (40¼ in.)
W: 44.5 cm (17½ in.)
D: 16.5 cm (6½ in.)
83.AA.378

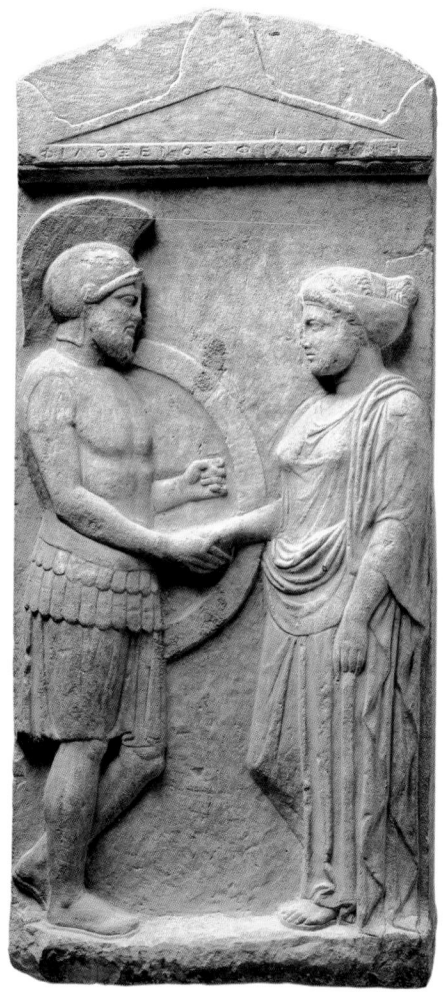

Philoxenos, wearing the armor and shield of a warrior, solemnly shakes hands with his wife, Philoumene, on this stele, or gravestone, from Attika. The names of the couple are carved above their heads, and both figures were originally elaborated with painted details. The handshake was a symbolic and popular gesture on gravestones of the Classical period. It could represent a simple farewell, a reunion in the afterlife, or a continuing connection between the deceased and the living.

The fact that it is often difficult to tell which figure represents the deceased on these gravestones further emphasizes the connection between the world of the living and the world of the dead. The living rarely display sorrow or grief on grave markers of about 400 B.C. Instead, their calm, expressionless faces reproduce the idealized features and detachment that prevailed at this time in the sculptural style of Athens and its surrounding region, Attika.

Philoxenos, here represented as a soldier, probably distinguished himself in combat. The style and the iconography of this gravestone date it to a period just after the end of the Peloponnesian War in 404 B.C. Funerary reliefs of the time reflected a renewed appreciation for family life following that disastrous war with Sparta.

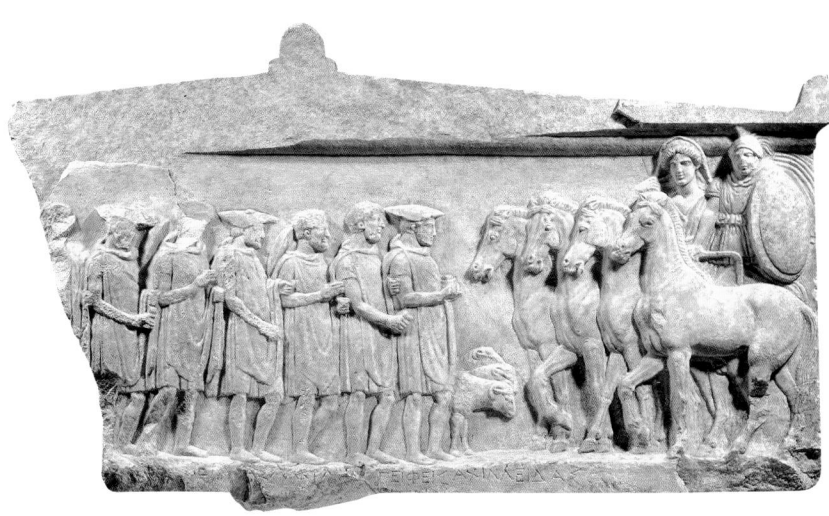

VOTIVE RELIEF TO ACHILLES AND THETIS

Greek, from Thessaly,
circa 350 B.C.
Marble
H: 78 cm (30¾ in.)
W: 132 cm (52 in.)
D: 7.6 cm (3 in.)
78.AA.264

On this relief, the greatest of the Greek heroes of the Trojan War, Achilles, rides with his mother, Thetis, in a chariot. The chariot confronts a procession of votaries, who are dressed as travelers, wearing cloaks and wide-brimmed hats. Only seven of these waiting men remain on the broken relief, but originally there must have been about ten.

In Greek religion, many heroes were honored and had religious cults associated with them. It was believed that these heroes could intercede with the gods on behalf of mortals. Achilles was certainly worshiped as a hero, and some scholars believe that in certain places he may even have been worshiped as a god. In this relief, the group of votaries brings three rams to sacrifice to Achilles. The relief may be from Thessaly, where, according to Greek mythology, Achilles was born and educated. It takes the usual form of a votive monument that was set up as an offering in a religious sanctuary. The dedicators of the votive are named in the partially legible inscription at the bottom of the relief, which gives the names of Lakrates and Gephes and refers to the religious association of the Achilleides, who claimed to be descendants of Achilles. Plaques made of marble or more perishable materials existed as religious dedications before the Classical period in Greece, but only after the completion of the Parthenon in Athens, in 432 B.C., did marble votive reliefs begin to be mass-produced.

CEREMONIAL CHAIR (THE ELGIN THRONE)

Greek, from Athens,
circa 300 B.C.
Marble
H: 81.5 cm (32⅛ in.)
W: 70 cm (27½ in.)
D: 58.5 cm (23 in.)
74.AA.12

This throne takes its name from the English aristocrat who once owned it, Thomas Bruce, the 7th Earl of Elgin. It originally functioned as a dignitary's seat in a public place, perhaps at a theater. Based on stylistic comparisons with thrones depicted on coins, the marble chair has been dated to the end of the fourth century B.C. A partial inscription preserved along the upper edge of the throne's back provides the name of a certain Boëthos, possibly the dedicator.

The throne is decorated with lion's legs in the front, two symmetrical olive wreaths in the rear, and a pair of two-figure action scenes carved in low relief on either side. On the (proper) left, Theseus raises his sword to kill the Queen of the Amazons, who has fallen at his feet and shields her head from the imminent blow. Among the mythological hero's many deeds, Theseus repelled an Amazon invasion of Athens. On the right, two nude swordsmen prepare to attack. They can be recognized as Harmodios and Aristogeiton, two Athenian noblemen who attempted to slay the tyrant Hippias in 514 B.C. Although they succeeded only in assassinating his brother Hipparchos and were themselves killed, they came to be considered founding heroes of Athenian democracy. A famous pair of bronze statues known as the Tyrannicides (Tyrant Slayers) was erected to commemorate their valor, and the swordsmen on the throne stand in the same poses. Because both reliefs on the throne celebrate the freedom of the Athenians, some scholars believe that the throne was the honorary seat of Demetrios Poliorketes, an early Hellenistic prince who "liberated" Athens from his rivals in 296 B.C.

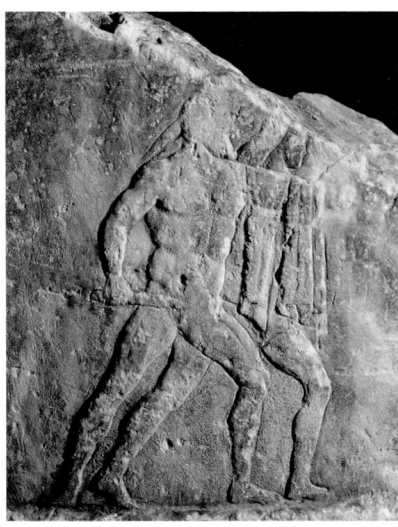
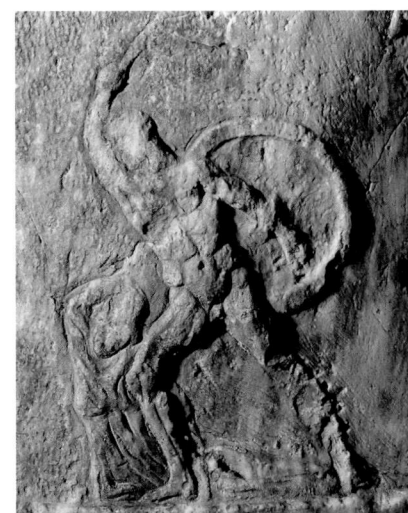

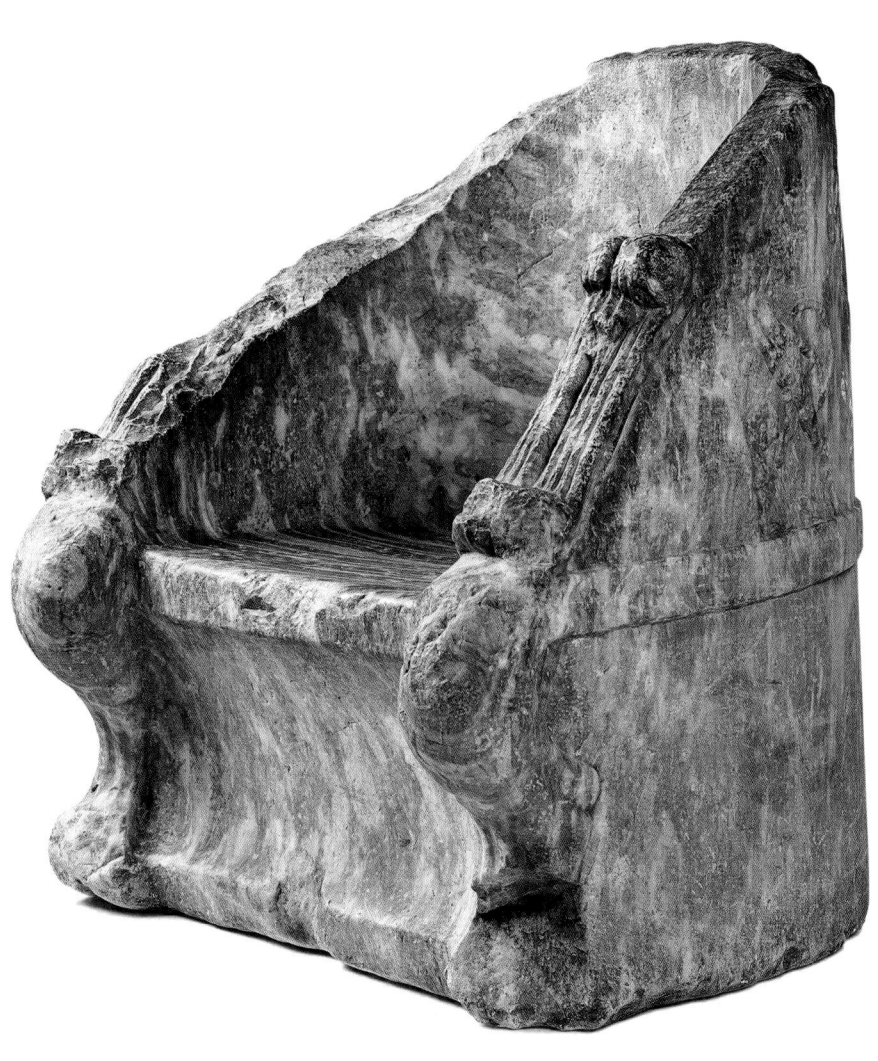

SIDE PANEL OF A GRAVE *NAISKOS* WITH A RELIEF OF A YOUNG HUNTER

Greek, from Thessaly or
Macedonia, circa 325 B.C.
Marble
H: 143.1 cm (56⅜ in.)
W: 42.7 cm (16⅜ in.)
D: 10.2 cm (4 in.)
96.AA.48

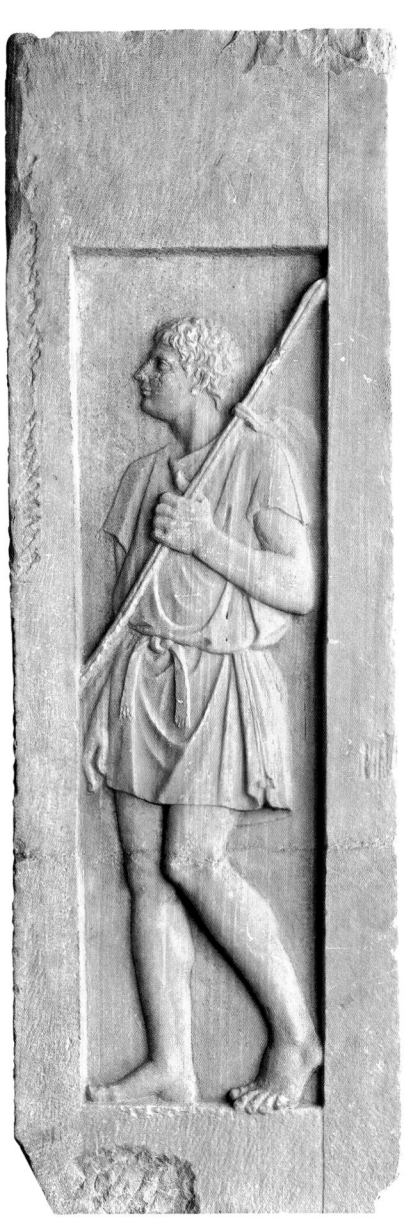

Carved in a recessed rectangular area
on this marble slab, a young hunter
wearing a short tunic tied with a belt
walks with his spears resting on
his shoulder. An indistinct object or
objects hang from the weapons. The
rounded shape at the top may represent a petasos, a broad-brimmed hat
worn by hunters and travelers, while
the baglike shape at the bottom is
likely a purse net, used in antiquity for
catching rabbits. This relief was
originally painted, and colored details
would have made it easier to identify
the objects.

A curved molding at the top right
corner indicates that this relief panel
was part of a three-sided *naiskos*,
an elaborate funerary monument
constructed in the form of a small,
open-fronted building. It would have
formed the right-hand side of the
naiskos, with the carving on the
interior and the young hunter looking
toward an image of the deceased on
the back wall.

Being shown with horse, hound,
servant, or hunting gear established
the high rank and status of the
deceased in society. The style, subject,
and type of marble of the panel point
to an origin in Macedonia or Thessaly
in northern Greece.

PORTRAIT OF ALEXANDER THE GREAT

Greek, circa 320 B.C.
Marble
H: 29.1 cm (11½ in.)
W: 25.9 cm (10¼ in.)
D: 27.5 cm (10¾ in.)
73.AA.27

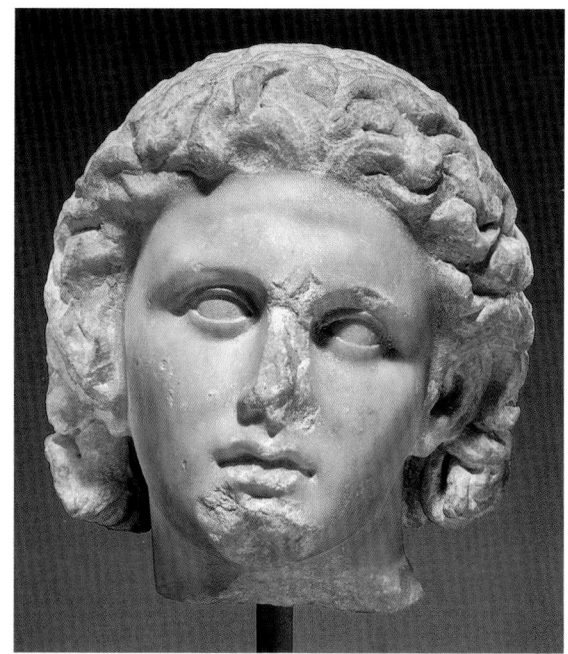

Clearly identified here by his mass of leonine hair, his young idealized face, and his deep-set upturned eyes, Alexander the Great, king of Macedon (reigned 336–323 B.C.), was the first Greek ruler to understand and exploit the propagandistic power of portraiture. According to ancient literary sources, he let only one sculptor carve his portrait—Lysippos (active ca. 370–ca. 300 B.C.), who created the standard Alexander portrait type. Ancient writers describe Alexander as handsome, energetic, charismatic, and unconventional. Brave and decisive, he had endurance, delighted in exploration, and was a founder of cities.

Surviving images of the youthful conqueror incorporate characteristics that had been used earlier for the representations of gods and heroes. Claiming descent from the Greek heroes Herakles and Achilles, and identifying himself with the gods Dionysos and Zeus Ammon (a divinity combining Zeus, king of the Greek pantheon, and Ammon, king of the Egyptian pantheon), Alexander was treated as divine even before his death.

This practice was part of Alexander's adoption of the Egyptian and Near Eastern idea of honoring rulers as if they were gods.

This posthumous portrait of Alexander was part of a multifigured composition. More than thirty fragments of the group, which might have included sacrificial elements, survive. The participants include Alexander, his companion Hephaistion, a goddess, Herakles, a flute player, and several other figures, as well as animals and birds. The ensemble to which this head belonged probably served as a votive or commemorative monument, possibly even as an elaborate funerary monument for someone who wanted to associate himself with the ruler. Alexander became the new ideal ruler, a hero on Earth, and an example to follow, even to worship after his death.

HEAD OF A YOUNG WOMAN FROM A GRAVE MONUMENT

Greek, from Athens,
circa 320 B.C.
Marble
H: 34.3 cm (13½ in.)
W: 15.6 cm (6⅛ in.)
D: 22.2 cm (8¾ in.)
56.AA.19

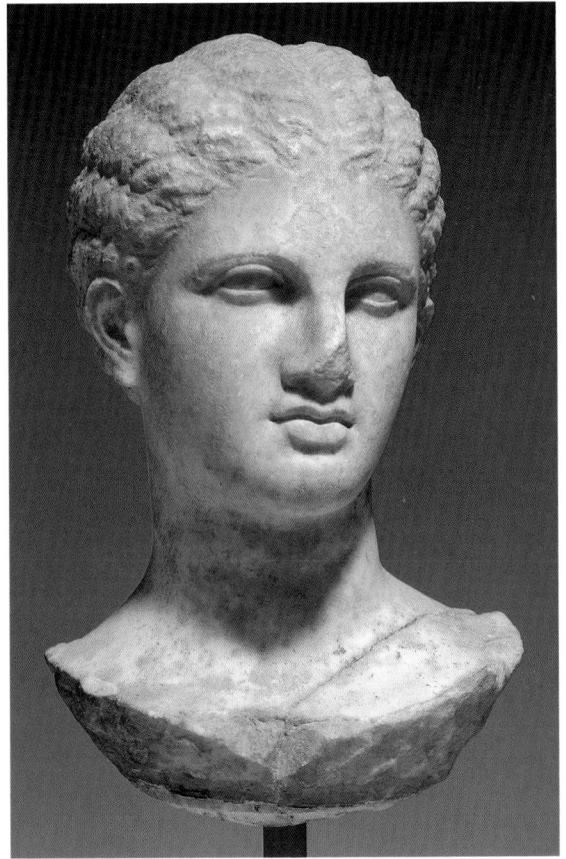

This life-size head of a beautiful young woman was carved to fit into the neck cavity of a full-length statue. Her hair is styled in what is known as a "melon coiffure," because of its resemblance to a lobed melon. A flat area on the back of the head indicates that the figure was originally placed within a roofed, three-sided *naiskos* (see p. 24), where the head rested against the back panel.

This distinctive hairstyle was introduced by Athenian sculptors in the second half of the fourth century and was used by, among others, Praxiteles (active 375–340 B.C.) and Silanion (active 360–330 B.C.). It seems to symbolize vigorous youthfulness and can be seen on such figures as those of several Muses and the virgin goddess Artemis. On funerary figures, the hairstyle emphasizes the community's loss of a young woman of childbearing age.

GRAVE STELE
OF PHANOKRATES

East Greek, from Smyrna,
circa 200 B.C.
Marble
H: 125.4 cm (49³⁄₈ in.)
W: 53.3 cm (21 in.)
D: 21.6 cm (8¹⁄₂ in.)
96.AA.50

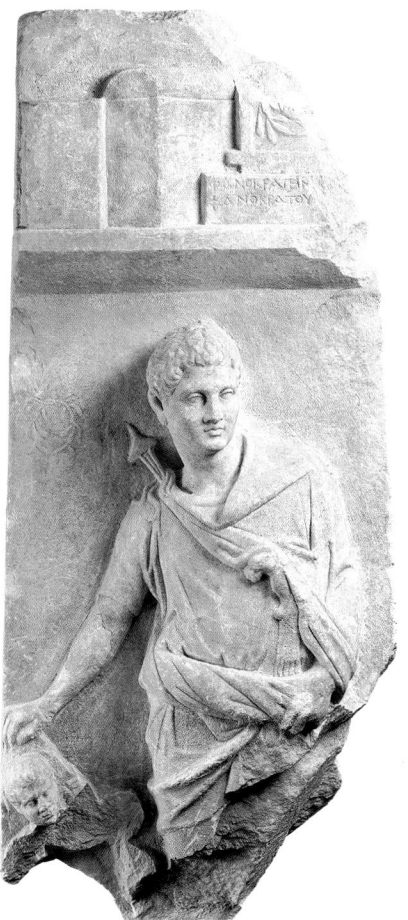

Elements from his life surround the deceased, named Phanokrates, on this fragmentary grave stele. Together with his luxurious garments, various other implements suggest an aristocratic background, commemorating him as a wealthy, learned man. Phanokrates' cloak is fastened on his right shoulder with an unusual pin in the shape of a large ivy leaf, and a short sword with an ornate eagle's-head hilt is tucked into the roll of fabric at his waist.

The head of a small attendant or slave who stood at the right side of Phanokrates appears just above the broken lower edge of the stele. Phanokrates' right hand rests upon an object, probably a herm, placed behind the servant boy. A shelf above the figures holds objects associated with the life of an educated man: on the left, a closed pair of wax writing tablets; in the middle, a chest with an arched lid that probably held book rolls; and, on the right, a framed tablet with a wreath. The inscription on the low base under the wreath names the deceased and his father: "Phanokrates, son of Phano-krates." A second honorific wreath is on the background below the shelf, next to Phanokrates' head.

The stele was freestanding; it was not a slab from a longer frieze, but it was probably set in an architectural framework. Phanokrates' pose and outfit indicate that the gravestone comes from the area around the ancient city of Smyrna (modern Izmir, Turkey).

PORTRAIT OF
A BEARDED MAN

Greek, 160–150 B.C.
Marble
H: 40.7 cm (16 in.)
W: 25 cm (9¾ in.)
D: 29 cm (11⅜ in.)
91.AA.14

Broken in antiquity into two large fragments, this head is all that remains of a larger-than-life-size, full-length statue. A furrowed brow and an intense gaze distinguish this portrait of an older man, whose face reflects serious determination. The condition and irregular shape of the subject's nose suggest that it has been broken more than once, and one can surmise that the man had endured many rigorous experiences, perhaps as a soldier or an athlete. Features such as the nose, the square jaw, and the folds between his cheeks and mouth capture the man's individual character, but his true identity cannot be determined with certainty.

The head belongs to a category of portraiture that arose in the wake of Alexander the Great (reigned 336–323 B.C.), that of portraits of Hellenistic rulers. Designed as propaganda to legitimize that ruler and emphasize dynastic connections, these portraits combined individual traits with dramatic, idealized images of their subjects. Yet this man cannot have been a king when the statue was carved, for he does not wear a diadem—a type of headband reserved for only royalty and gods. Drapery on the back of the neck indicates that the man was portrayed as a statesman, not as a warrior. The portrait's scale and the man's regal bearing, however, clearly suggest that he is a member of a royal family—but which one?

Stylistically, the head relates closely to sculpture produced at Pergamon, a city near the west coast of modern Turkey. In addition, sculptors at Pergamon frequently used the type of grayish marble from which this portrait is carved. The Attalids ruled Pergamon during the Hellenistic period, and the subject of this portrait was probably a high-ranking member of that dynasty, perhaps even Attalos II himself (reigned 158–138 B.C.), portrayed shortly before he became king.

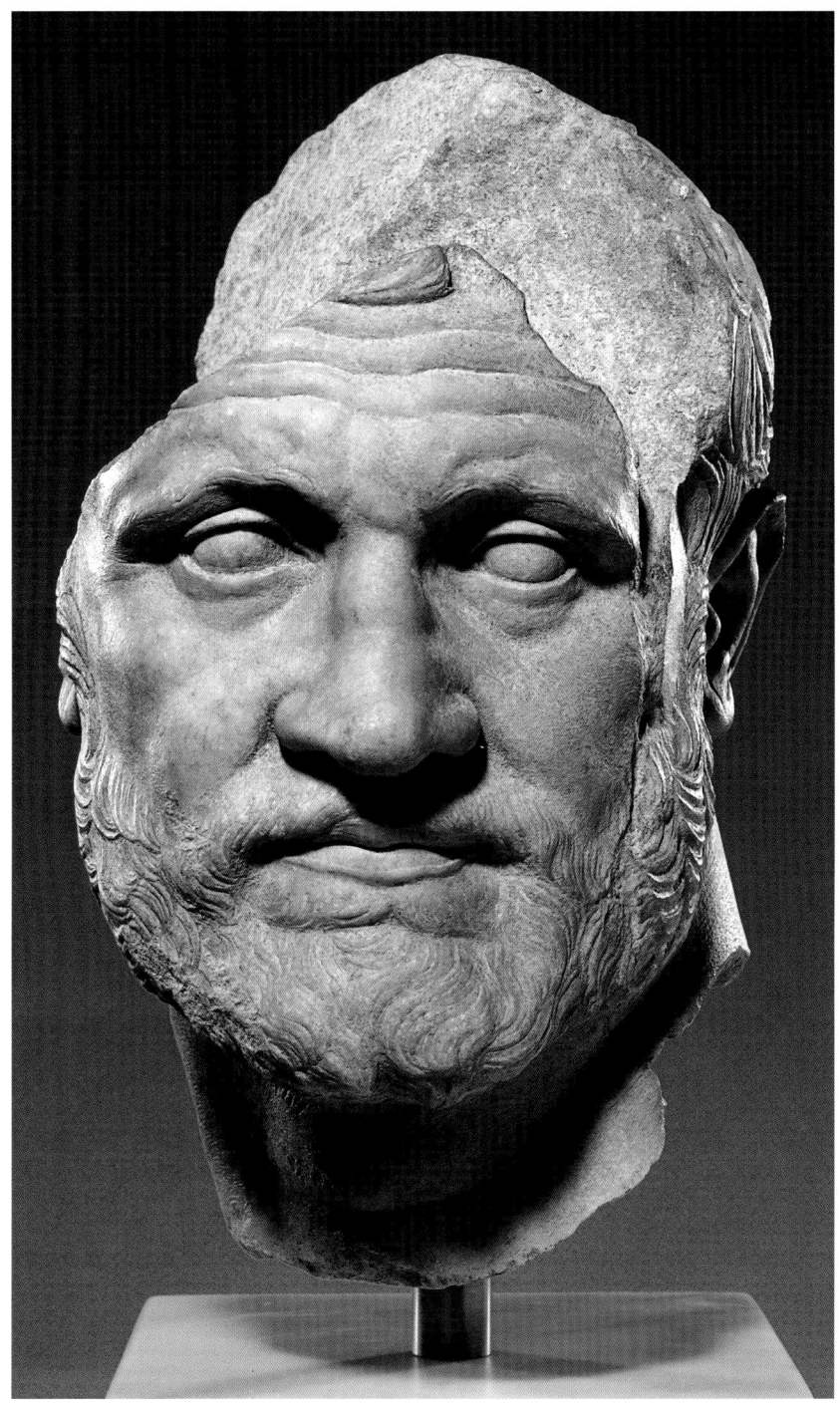

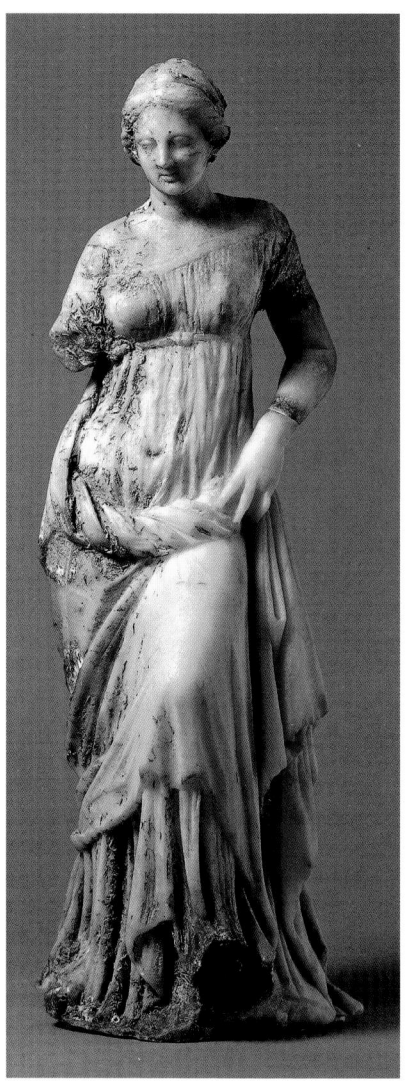

STATUETTE OF A DRAPED FEMALE FIGURE

Greek, from the Eastern
Mediterranean, 100–1 B.C.
Marble
H: 45.1 cm (17³/₄ in.)
96.AA.169

This slender young woman in a graceful undulating pose probably represents Aphrodite, goddess of love, often identified by the fleshy folds on her neck known as "Venus rings," which were considered a sign of beauty in antiquity (and which take their name from Aphrodite's Roman counterpart). She wears a gathered chiton of delicate material belted high under her breasts; with her left hand she holds a voluminous mantle that is secured at her left shoulder and has fallen from her right. Her narrow shoulders, broad hips, elongated proportions, and complex drapery folds are characteristic of the Hellenistic period, as is her hairstyle.

Like many small-scale Hellenistic sculptures, especially those from the island of Delos, this piece employs the technique of piecing small sections, such as the arms, feet, and parts of the head, to the main body of the statuette. Small statues like this one were produced for private use and widely exported all over the ancient world.

STATUETTE OF A HORSE

Greek, from Lakonia,
750–700 B.C.
Bronze
H: 7.9 cm (3⅛ in.)
W: 3.5 cm (1⅜ in.)
D: 5.5 cm (2⅛ in.)
85.AB.445

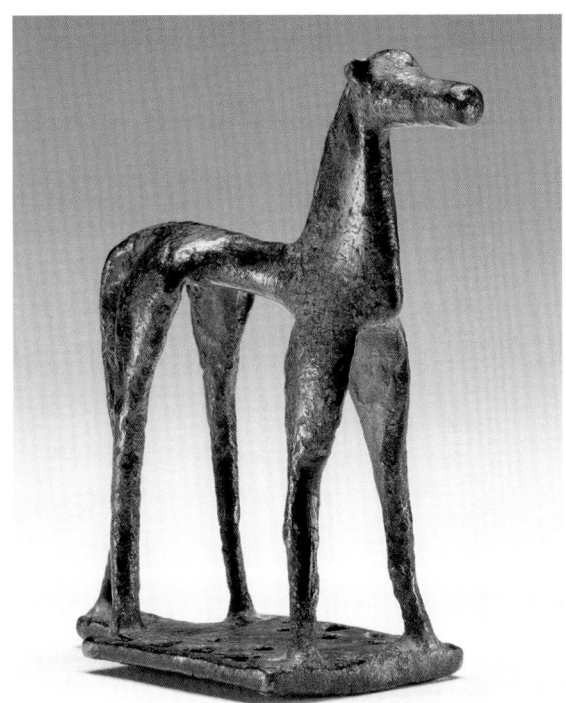

This diminutive bronze horse was made during the late Geometric period of Greek art (900–700 B.C.), when the naturalistic rendering of a subject was not as important to artists as capturing its essence by emphasizing distinctive features. Thus the horse is defined by its exaggeratedly long legs, which call attention to its speed and mobility, and its large haunches and shoulders, which serve to denote its strength and agility. Typical of small-scale bronzes made in Greece during this period, this schematic rendering of a horse relies upon the viewer's familiarity with the subject. The artist has not intended to produce an exact likeness.

Since horses require extensive land for grazing and are expensive to own, they denote wealth and power. Bronze statues of both horses and cattle are thus suitable offerings to the gods, and examples are found in almost every sanctuary of the period. The perforations on the rectangular base of the sculpture and the rendering of the horse suggest that it was made in southern Greece, perhaps Lakonia, at a time when the great sanctuaries, such those at Olympia and Delphi, were beginning to emerge. Many of the Geometric bronzes discovered in Lakonia in this period, which present a great cohesion of style and technique, come from the sanctuaries of Artemis Orthia and Athena Chalkiokos at Sparta.

STATUETTE OF A LYRE PLAYER WITH A COMPANION

Greek, perhaps from Crete,
690–670 B.C.
Bronze
H: 11.5 cm (4½ in.)
W: 8.5 cm (3⅜ in.)
D: 4 cm (1⅝ in.)
90.AB.6

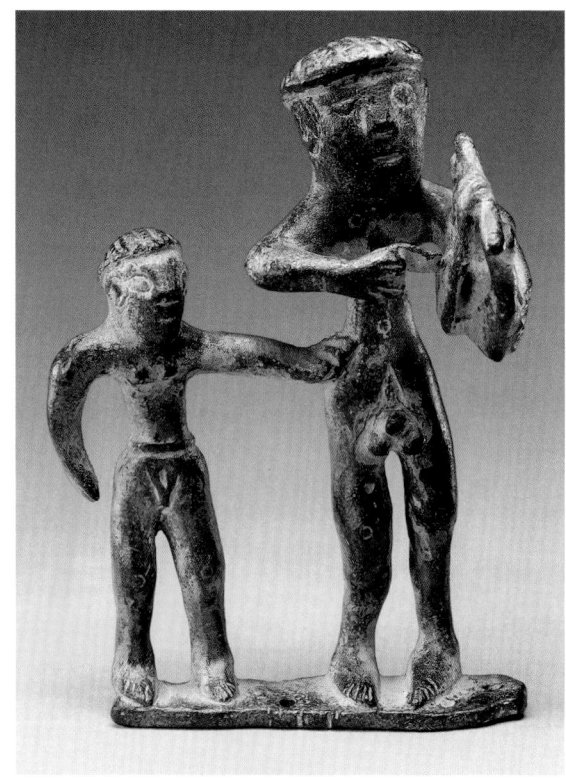

Cast in solid bronze, this small statuette of a standing lyre player and a smaller companion was originally attached by the holes in its base to another object, probably a large bronze vessel. Both figures are male, with fluid limbs and thin, tapering trunks. Caplike hair tops their oversized heads, with rows of braids marked with parallel lines radiating from the crown. The larger figure is nude and plays a stringed instrument—perhaps the Homeric *phorminx* or kithara—evidently with a plektron (pick) held in his right hand. One of his eyes is rendered differently from the other. The smaller figure wears a loincloth and belt, attire typical for those from the island of Crete.

Group compositions such as this one are rare in Greek art of the late eighth and seventh centuries B.C., and groups of two or more human figures are rarer still. It is also very unusual to find three-dimensional musicians from this period. Although certain deities, such as Apollo, are later depicted as musicians, this bronze bard, along with his companion, must be mortal. He is an *aoidos*, or minstrel, like Demodokos, the blind singer at the court of King Alkinoos described by Homer in the *Odyssey*. The date of this small bronze is roughly contemporary with that of Homer himself. The fact that Homer was said to be blind, and that the sightless Demodokos was assisted by a herald, suggests that this lyre player—with his unusual eyes—is also a blind bard, like Homer or Demodokos, assisted by a young companion or apprentice.

GRIFFIN PROTOME

Greek, circa 650 B.C.
Bronze
H: 28.5 cm (11¼ in.)
W: 10.7 cm (4¼ in.)
D: 9.3 cm (3⅝ in.)
96.AC.44

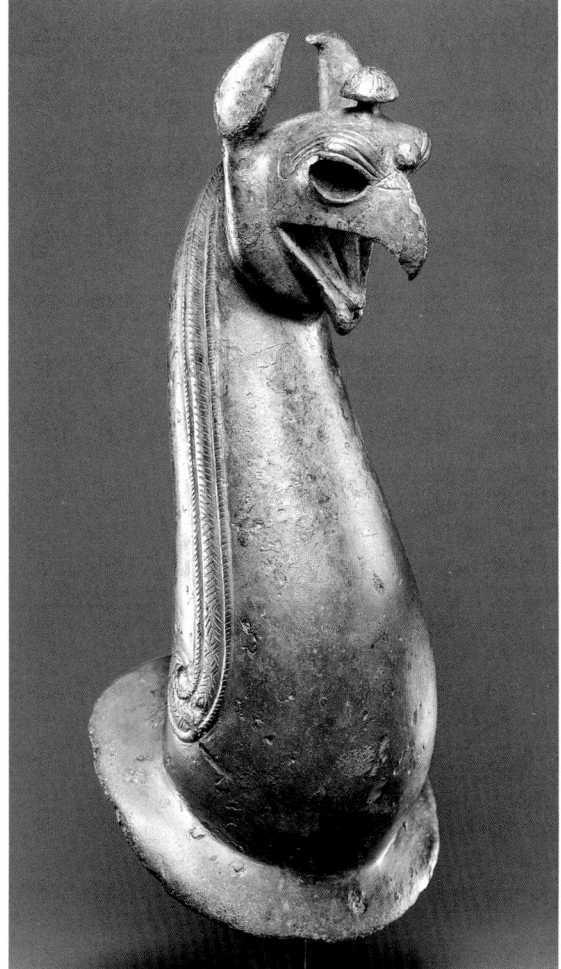

Griffins, hybrid creatures combining characteristics of a lion, bird, and snake, were often chosen to decorate the large bronze cauldrons that were popular votive offerings in temples of the early Archaic period. This cast image of a griffin was one of several that were attached to the shoulder of such a vessel by means of the holes in its flanged base. The creature is represented with upright ears, a gaping mouth, and wide-open eyes that were once inlaid—an apt visage considering its role as a sentinel for a valuable vessel. Griffins in general are appropriate guardians of prized possessions because they were the creatures that guarded the god Apollo's gold and were known for their unwavering vigilance. These griffin cauldrons are found in particularly great numbers at the sanctuaries of Zeus at Olympia, Apollo at Delphi, and Hera at Samos. They were placed on tall stands and presented by, among others, victors in athletic games.

SHIELD STRAP FRAGMENT

Signed by
Aristodamos of Argos
Greek, from Argos,
circa 575 B.C.
Bronze
H: 16.2 cm (6³⁄₈ in.)
W: 8 cm (3¹⁄₈ in.)
84.AC.11

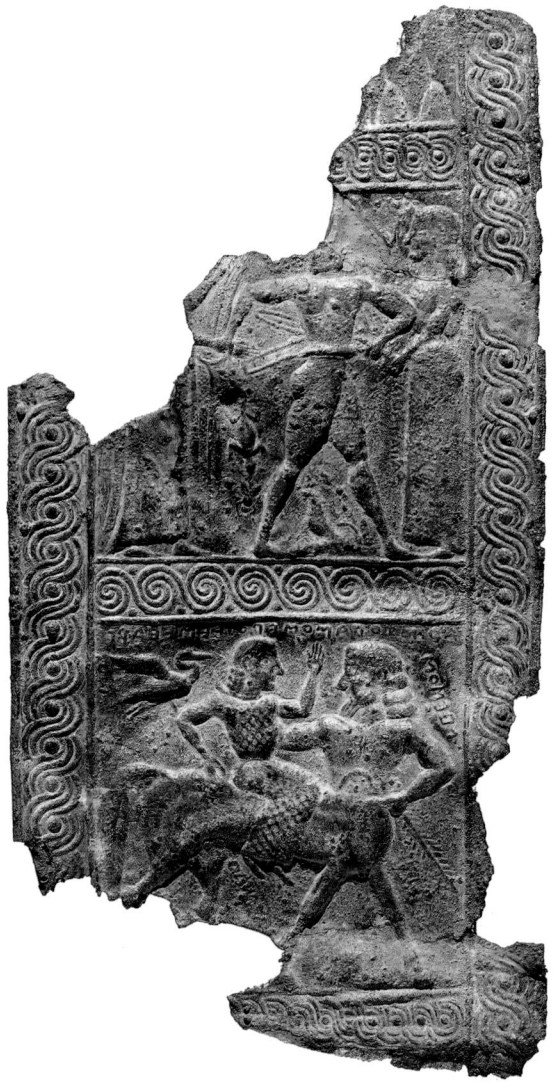

This small bronze relief fragment once decorated the inside of an Argive warrior's shield. It is an especially significant piece because it contains the earliest surviving signature of an ancient Greek metalworker. At the top edge of the lower square, the signature of the bronzeworker is written retrograde (from right to left): "Aristodamos the Argive made [this]."

Ancient Greeks considered shields to be valuable dedications, and shield straps are often found in the excavations of sanctuaries, particularly at the Sanctuary of Zeus at Olympia. Because

Aristodamos names himself as an inhabitant of Argos, this work can be taken as important evidence for the style of Argive art in the early Archaic period. Indeed, this strap represents two myths that were favored there. The lower square shows the Centaur Nessos abducting Deianeira, the wife of Herakles. The scene above it represents the recovery of Helen of Troy by her Greek husband, Menelaos, an Argive king. Athena, protectress of the Greeks, stands watching to the right. The names of the figures are inscribed beside them.

STATUETTE OF A RIDER

Greek, from Corinth,
circa 550 B.C.
Bronze
H: 8.3 cm (3¼ in.)
W: 4 cm (1⅝ in.)
D: 3.4 cm (1⅜ in.)
96.AB.45

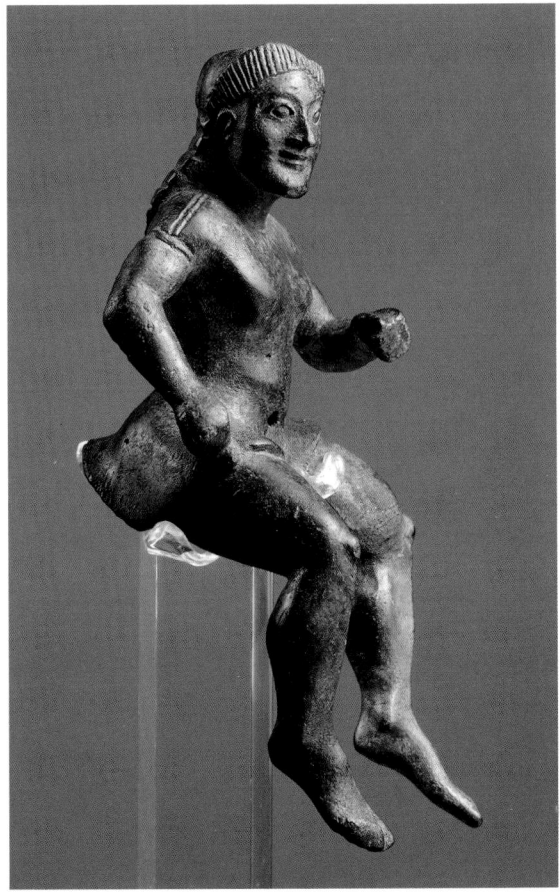

Virtually all ancient Greek bronzes served as devotional gifts to gods and were therefore dedicated in sanctuaries. The valuable material and spirited execution of a youthful, exuberant horseman distinguish this small bronze rider. The matching horse he rode has been lost, but horses from similar contexts are known. The Getty figure is dressed in a short tunic enlivened by a zigzag pattern around the neck; he probably originally wore a petasos, or traveler's hat, atop his flattened head. His leg muscles arch in response to the movement of the horse as he guides the reins to his right.

Details of this work's manufacture may link it to a bronze workshop in Corinth, but the patina, or surface corrosion, suggests that it may have come from the Sanctuary of Zeus at Dodona, in northern Greece. This situation reflects the trade movement of art in antiquity, where a popular workshop would produce quantities of figures that could be destined for any number of sanctuaries. Corinth was an important center for bronzeworking in the middle of the sixth century B.C., and it was a likely place for an aristocrat to commission a votive piece that would reflect his energy and status as a horseman. The ancient Greeks would have associated horsemen, especially those grouped in pairs, with the Dioskouroi, Kastor and Polydeukes, the twin sons of Zeus and Leda and the brothers of Helen of Troy.

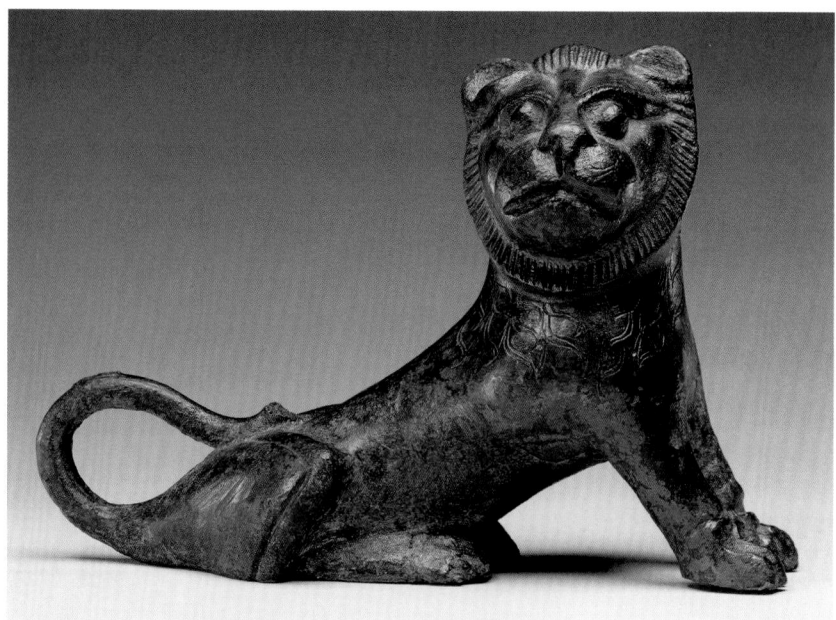

STATUETTE OF A SEATED LION

Greek, from Lakonia,
circa 550 B.C.
Bronze
H: 9.3 cm (3⅝ in.)
D: 5 cm (2 in.)
L: 13.3 cm (5¼ in.)
96.AB.76

In contrast to more common depictions of lions as fierce and menacing, this small whimsical figure seems somewhat bemused. He sits back on his haunches with his front paws outstretched, turning his head to look straight at the viewer. His tail makes a graceful S-curve up the center of his back. The style of the piece suggests that it was made in the region of Lakonia in southern Greece, an area once controlled by the ancient city of Sparta. The treatment of the lion's ruff as short and incised, the flamelike lines incised on the body to indicate the patterns of fur, and the rounded face and ears are all hallmarks of the Lakonian style.

In antiquity lions were seen as guardian beasts. Statues of lions were placed on the corners of funerary plots or atop graves to guard the deceased. They were a popular subject during the Archaic period of Greek art (about 700–480 B.C.) even though they probably no longer existed in Greece at that time.

This statuette was once attached to another object, perhaps the rim of a large metal vessel. The remnants of an attachment pin are preserved on the bottom of the lion's left front paw. The figure was hollow cast, and much of the ancient core material remains inside.

HANDLE OF A VESSEL

Greek, circa 500 B.C.
Bronze
H: 23.5 cm (9¼ in.)
W: 14.4 cm (5¾ in.)
D: 9 cm (3½ in.)
96.AC.79

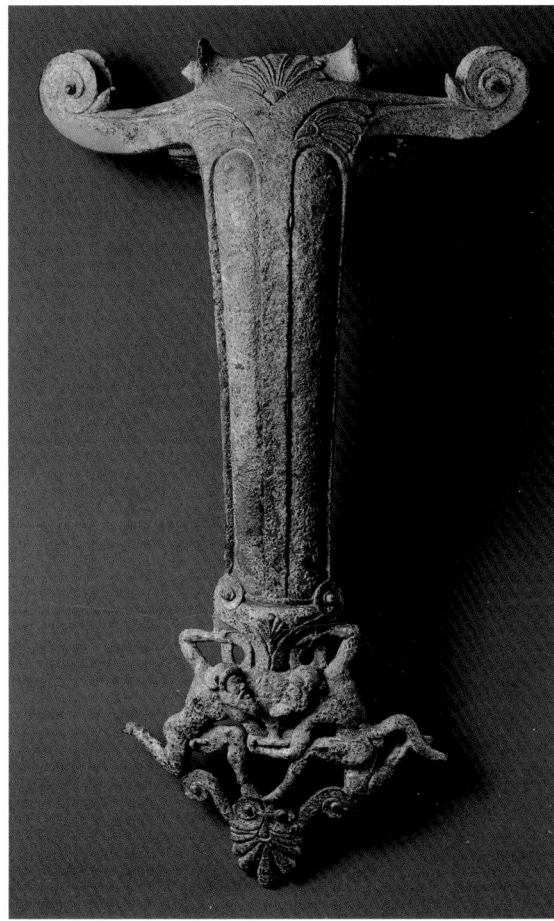

This handle once belonged to a large bronze serving vessel. The image of a pair of satyrs holding up a large two-handled drinking cup, or kantharos, at the base of the handle suggests that this vessel was probably intended to hold wine. The wine god Dionysos is often pictured holding this type of cup, and he is accompanied in his revelry by satyrs, hybrid creatures combining human traits with those of horses or goats. On this handle, these playful beings balance carefully atop a palmette; they mirror one another across the large cup, striking the same pose, despite its different orientation with respect to the viewer. The satyr on the right is turned so that his back faces toward the viewer, while the one on the left is shown in frontal perspective, exposing his chest and erect phallos; the long tail he once had is now missing. The remainder of the handle appears to grow out of the kantharos. A double volute rises out of its mouth to form the base of the shaft, and the palmettes and volutes at the top of the handle continue the organic theme. This decoration encompasses the fertility connotations of the satyr's phallos as well as Dionysos's additional role as god of the vine, vegetation, and rebirth.

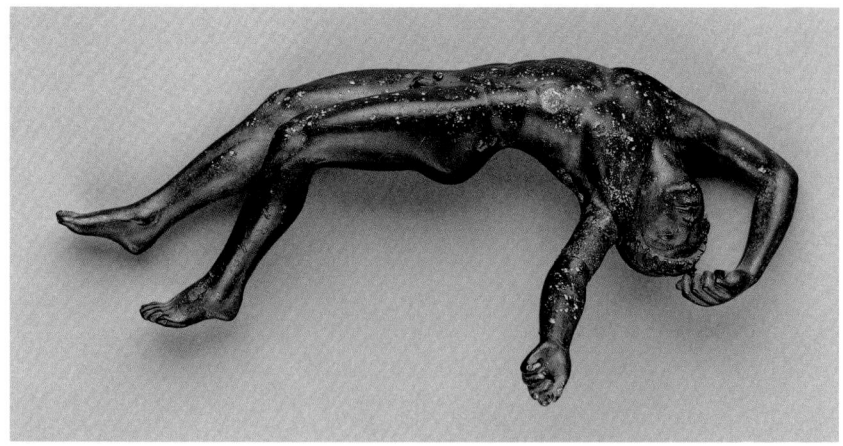

STATUETTE OF A FALLEN YOUTH

Greek, 480–460 B.C.
Bronze with copper inlays
L: 13.5 cm (5¼ in.)
W: 7.3 cm (2⅞ in.)
86.AB.530

This figure is unique among surviving bronzes of the early Classical period. The evocative pose is a clue to the figure's identity, for it suggests either sleep or death, which the Greeks believed to be closely related. In this case the figure is posed on his back; the angle of the chest, combined with lolling head, splayed arms, and dangling legs, completes a pose that evokes death more than sleep. For these reasons, he may be identified as a fallen Niobid. A Greek myth tells the story of Niobe, a mortal who boasted to the goddess Leto of her own seven sons and seven daughters. In a jealous rage, Leto's son and daughter, Apollo and Artemis, hunted down and slaughtered all Niobe's children. The tale was a favorite mode of expressing the dangers of boastful pride (see also Statue of a Collapsing Niobid, p. 152). The Fallen Youth's original context is uncertain, for there are no attachment marks to indicate how the statuette may have been used.

STATUETTE OF A KNEELING SATYR

Greek, 480–460 B.C.
Bronze
H: 10 cm (3⅞ in.)
W: 4.3 cm (1⅝ in.)
D: 5.6 cm (2¼ in.)
88.AB.72

Completely focused on his activity, a kneeling satyr drinks from an upraised *keras*, or drinking horn. The elements that identify him as a satyr are his hoof, pointed ears, and the remains of a tail in the small of his back. The finely incised strands of his hair and beard along with the detailed and anatomically correct musculature mark the statuette as a piece of out-standing quality. The satyr's developed anatomy and projecting, complex pose serve to date the piece to the early Classical period. At this time, artists were breaking away from the rigid confines of earlier styles to make their figures more complicated and three-dimensional. This satyr needs to be seen from all sides to be fully understood and appreciated: he supports himself on one bent and one upraised knee (a pose that also exposes his erect phallos); his left arm braces

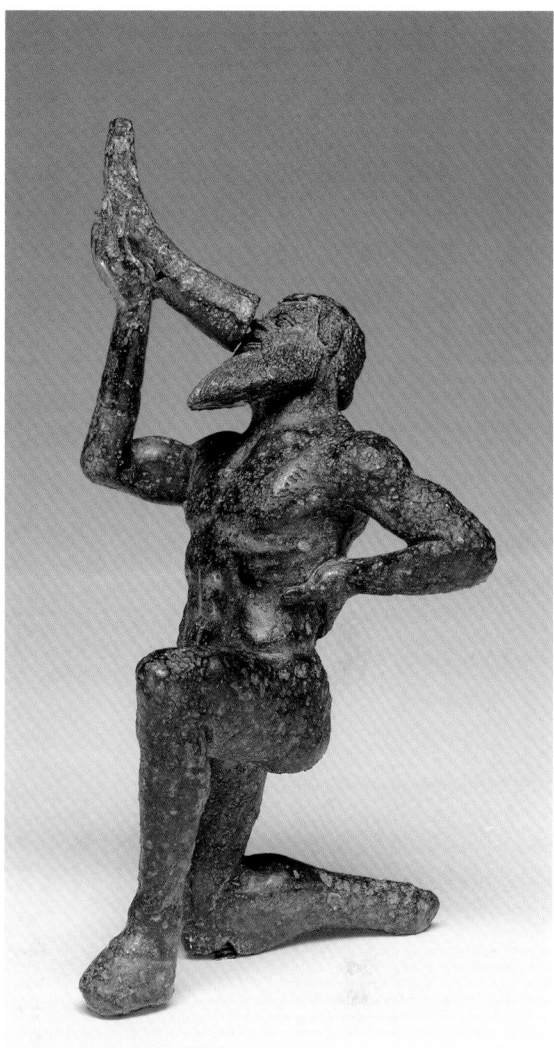

his torso as he puts his hand against his hip to balance himself; and his right arm and *keras* extend upward.

Satyrs were the companions of Dionysos, god of wine, and accompanied him on his drunken revels. In keeping with satyrs' part-human, part-animal nature, their behavior is usually bestial and uncouth, and they symbolize man's uncivilized urges. The vessel from which this satyr drinks, the *keras*, was used to drink unmixed or undiluted wine, which led quickly to drunkenness.

Appropriate to his pose, this small figure may have decorated a large metal vessel used to mix and serve wine at a banquet. A lumpy area below his left hoof may be the remains of an attachment pin. Alternatively, the statuette may have been given as a gift to the god at a sanctuary of Dionysos.

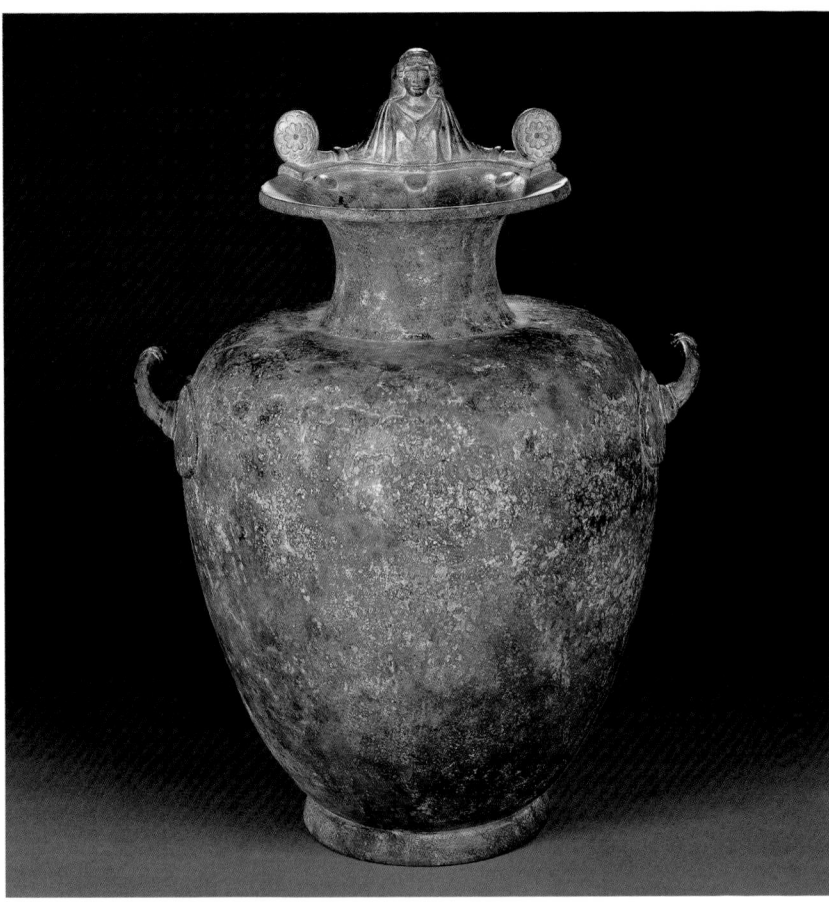

HYDRIA

Greek, circa 460 B.C.
Bronze
H: 47 cm (18½ in.)
DIAM (body): 28.2 cm
(11⅛ in.)
73.AC.12

Hydriai are among the few types of vessels pictured and named in ancient Greek vase-paintings. From images showing their shape and function, it is clear that these three-handled vessels were designed primarily to be water containers, and that they were essential wares in the daily life of the ancient Greeks.

The two horizontal handles on the sides of the vase were used to lift it, while an upright handle on the back made filling it or pouring out its contents easier. The only ornamentation on this vase appears on its handles. Palmette motifs enhance both attachment plaques of the two side handles and the lower plaque of the upright handle. The handle at the rim has a sculptural adjunct in the form of the upper body of a female. Her garment, a peplos, is somewhat altered to cover her outstretched arms and to reveal, instead of hands, two *rotellae* (disk-shaped ornaments) decorated with floral petals in relief.

Most hydriae were made of terracotta, a relatively inexpensive material that was within the means of ordinary households. In addition to carrying water,

STATUETTE OF A WOMAN WEARING A PEPLOS

Greek, perhaps from Argos,
460–450 B.C.
Bronze
H: 16.1 cm (6 3/8 in.)
96.AB.47

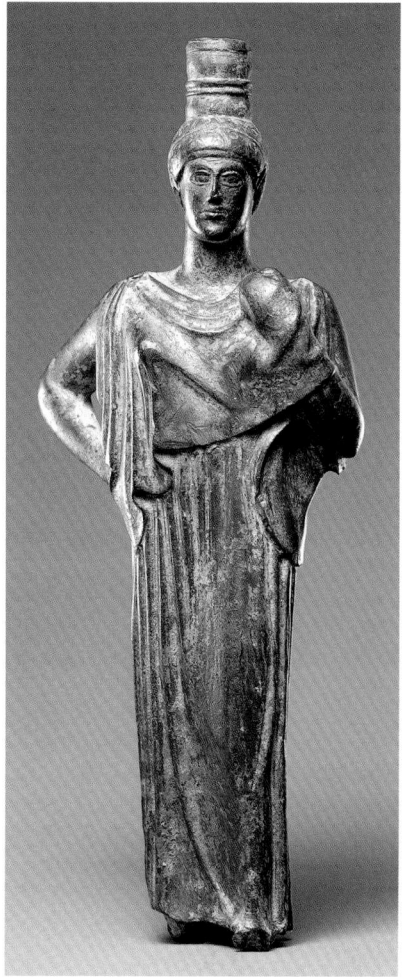

This austere, peplos-clad female probably served as a support for a thymiaterion (incense burner) or a candelabrum, as suggested by the cylindrical attachment on her head, the upper part of which is hollow. Standing in repose, she rests her weight on her right leg and extends her more relaxed left leg slightly forward, breaking the columnar folds of the peplos. Her right hand rests on her hip; her left arm is bent sharply at the elbow and held beneath the overfold of her garment, with the hidden hand raising the fabric near the neckline. Her face is rather somber, with heavy features, a prominent jaw, and a broad neck. The soft fabric of the *sakkos*, or head-dress, that covers her head is patterned with circles and zigzags and forms a series of soft ridges down the back.

This statuette's distinctive pose recalls one of the figures in a famous painting of the *Nekyia* (Descent into the Underworld) by the celebrated Classical painter Polygnotos (active ca. 475–447 B.C.) According to the Greek writer Pausanias, Polygnotos showed Eriphyle, an Argive heroine, reaching under her garment to finger the necklace for which she had betrayed her husband. The Getty figure's stance, dress, and heavy facial features are associated with larger works created by Argive sculptors and, according to tradition, Eriphyle.

these vessels occasionally functioned as ballot boxes or even as cinerary urns. Those of more costly bronze, which had the color of gold when new, were highly valued and thus were sometimes used for special purposes, such as dedicatory offerings to deities or prizes for victors in competitions. The practice of reuse is exemplified by this particular hydria. When found, it contained the skeletal remains of a child, who, at death, must have been about two years of age.

KALPIS

Greek, circa 350 B.C.
Bronze
H: 48 cm (18⅞ in.)
DIAM (body): 31.5 cm
(12⅜ in.)
79.AC.119

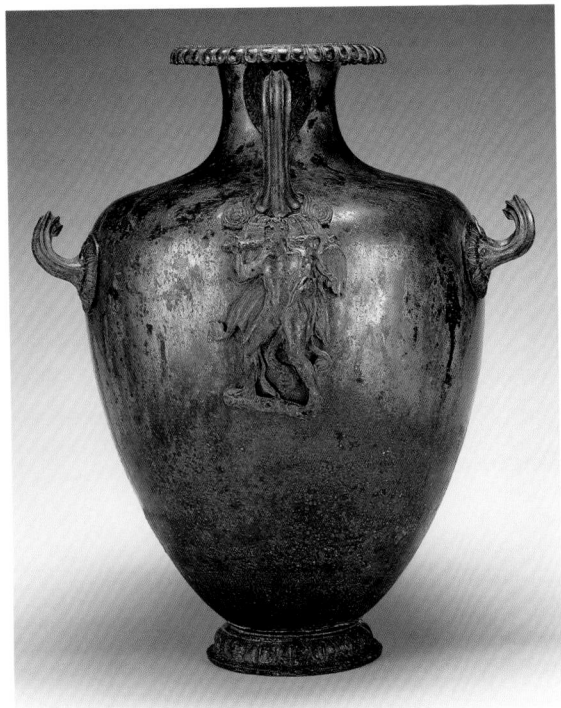

Although used to describe a vessel very similar in shape to the hydria, the term *kalpis* refers more generally to a pitcher. Whereas the hydria (see p. 40) is distinguished by a sharp division at the juncture of the neck and body, the contours of the kalpis are smooth and slightly elongated. From several sources, including inscriptions, we know that kalpides and hydriae were often awarded as prizes in competitions held at different festivals throughout the Greek world. These valued objects were offered at sanctuaries as dedications, and many of them served as cinerary urns for the ashes of the owner or a member of the family. They could also be used to hold ballots cast in voting. The decoration of bronze hydriae and kalpides was usually limited to the rim, foot, handles, and the relief at the base of the vertical handle.

The body of this kalpis was hammered from a sheet of bronze, while the ornate attachments, such as the handles, were cast and hammered separately and then added. A variety of floral patterns decorate the rim, the foot, and the base of the fluted handles. The separately hammered relief plate below the vertical handle shows the hero Herakles carrying both his club and the infant Eros. The vessel's shape and decoration belong to a class of vessels that developed in the course of the fourth century B.C., one characterized by the complex relief plates that replaced the earlier cast finials. Popular figures at this time include Eros, either alone or with another figure; later, the scope of subjects widened to include Dionysos and other deities. This depiction of Herakles carrying the infant Eros in an affectionate manner is the earliest known representation of these two figures alone in Greek art.

KALPIS

Greek, 350–325 B.C.
Bronze
H: 40.6 cm (16 in.)
DIAM (body): 26 cm (10¼ in.)
73.AC.15

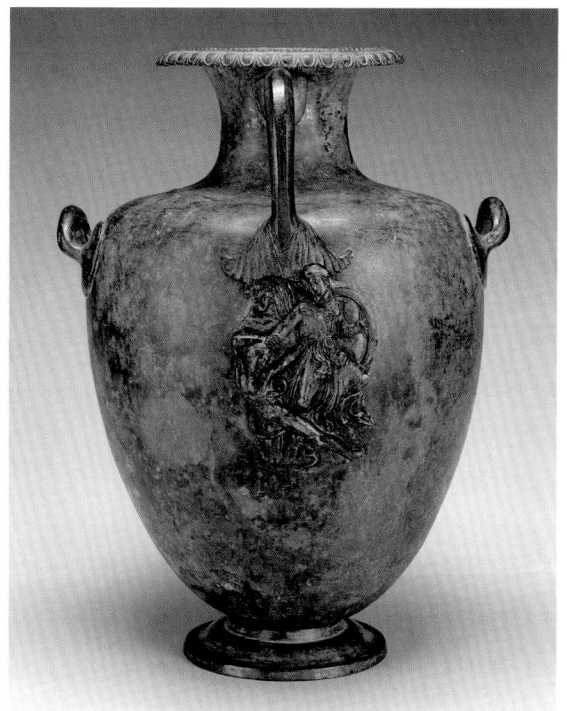

This kalpis displays little ornamentation except for the relief plate and the carefully chased pattern on the rim. The subject of the handle relief is a scene from the Gigantomachy, a battle won by the Olympian gods over the Giants, a mythological race of monsters who had previously ruled the earth. Athena, identified by her helmet, shield, and aegis (her scaly breastplate, bearing a central Gorgon head and outer fringe of snake heads) defeats a naked Giant who has fallen on his right knee and is being attacked by the snake encircling his body. He tries in vain to ward off the victorious goddess. The terrain on which the combat takes place is stippled and has several flowers seen as if from above. The vase's shape, decorative subject, and style suggest that it was produced in the third quarter of the fourth century B.C.

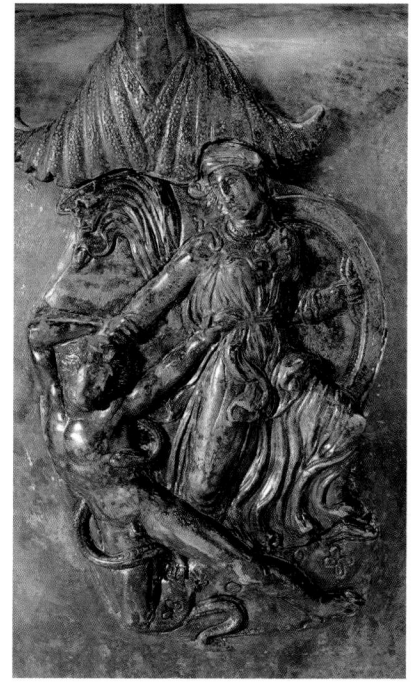

STATUE OF A VICTORIOUS YOUTH

Greek, 300–100 B.C.
Bronze with copper inlays
H: 151.5 cm (59⅝ in.)
77.AB.30

Standing in a relaxed pose, this nude youth crowns himself with an olive wreath (now mostly missing) in the traditional gesture of a victorious athlete. This kind of statue is typical of the extravagant votive offering that victors in athletic games often commissioned and dedicated after a significant success (the bronze Charioteer in Delphi is a famous example). The Getty's bronze can be dated by its stylistic resemblance to the work of the court sculptor of Alexander the Great, Lysippos (ca. 370–300 B.C.), whose lengthy career encompassed most of the fourth century B.C. Perhaps created by a pupil of Lysippos, the figure's slim proportions, including a relatively small head, are characteristic of the Lysippan style. According to the Roman writer Pliny, Lysippos was famous for representing men, not as they really were, but as they appeared to be. The characterization well describes this statue, for the polished surface of this bronze was carefully modeled in order to evoke the appearance of well-developed musculature, while naturalistic color contrasts were achieved by inlaying the eyes with colored stone or glass paste (now missing) and the nipples with copper. The suggestion of circular torsion in the posture that invites the viewer to walk around the statue is characteristic of the early Hellenistic period, during which the piece was cast.

Bronze was the favorite medium for sculpture in ancient Greece, particularly in the fifth and fourth centuries B.C. Yet only a fraction of the thousands of votive and commemorative statues that adorned the public and private spaces of cities and sanctuaries have survived, making this bronze especially important. That any original Greek monumental bronzes remain at all is primarily due to the Roman passion for them, and many Greek sculptures were brought to Rome to adorn the Roman forum as well as public and private buildings and gardens. The Victorious Youth was found in the Adriatic Sea, incrusted with shells, corals, and mud. Presumably it had been taken from a sanctuary such as Olympia or the hometown of the dedicator and was no doubt in transit on its way to Rome when the ship floundered.

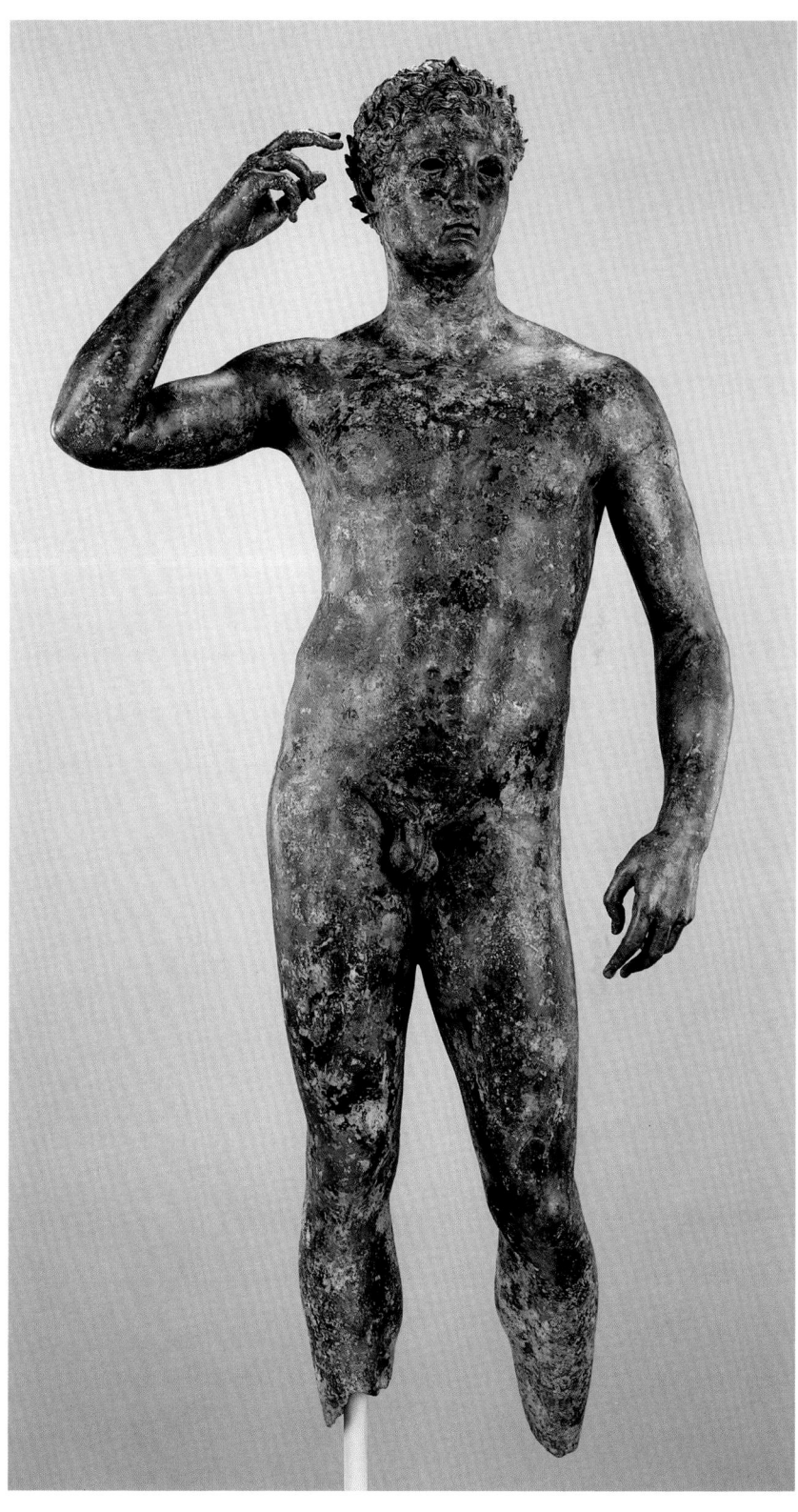

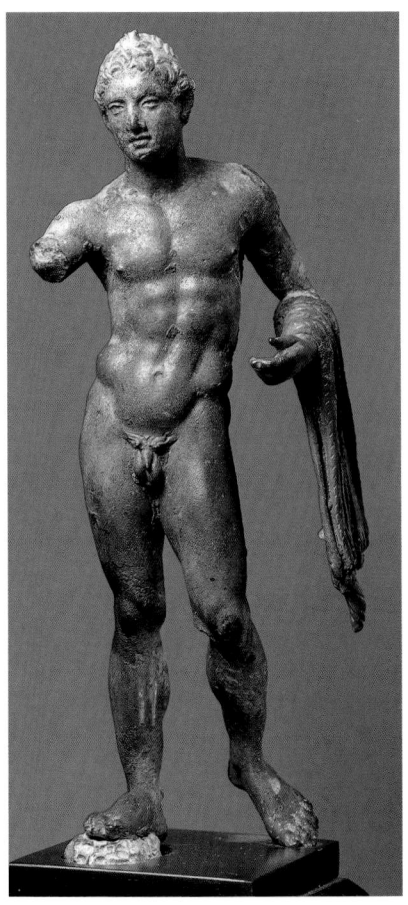

STATUETTE OF THE YOUTHFUL HERAKLES

Greek, 300–200 B.C.
Bronze
H (without tang): 17.4 cm
(6⅞ in.)
96.AB.148

Because the Greek hero Herakles is perhaps more commonly recognized as a bearded and heavily muscled older man carrying a club, this slender figure might be mistaken for an ordinary young man. But what at first glance appears to be only drapery over the left arm is actually the skin of a lion, indicating that the statuette represents the youthful Herakles, who had killed the Nemean Lion as one of his Twelve Labors. It is a small-scale version of a statue created in the fifth century B.C., perhaps by the sculptor Polykleitos (active 460–415 B.C.)

In his now-missing right hand, Herakles probably held a cup or drinking horn. In Greek art, the hero is often shown in a drunken state or in the company of Dionysos, god of wine, with whom he shared a fondness for wine and engaged in drinking contests. The depiction of Herakles as a drinker, here and in other similar examples, is termed *Bibax* (Latin for "addicted to drinking").

The diadem, which is often associated with royalty, and the central lotus leaf that crowns this figure's head raise an alternate possibility: that he represents not Herakles but a young ruler in the guise of the hero. Ancient rulers, both Greek and Roman, embraced the practice of being portrayed with the attributes of the mighty Herakles. This figure's peaked diadem is a type associated particularly with the dynasty of the Ptolemies, who assumed the rule of Egypt after the death of Alexander the Great in 323 B.C. However, the facial details seem too nonspecific to merit consideration as a portrait.

STATUETTE OF A GIANT HURLING A ROCK

Greek, 200–175 B.C.
Bronze
H: 14 cm (5½ in.)
W: 6.9 cm (2¾ in.)
92.AB.9

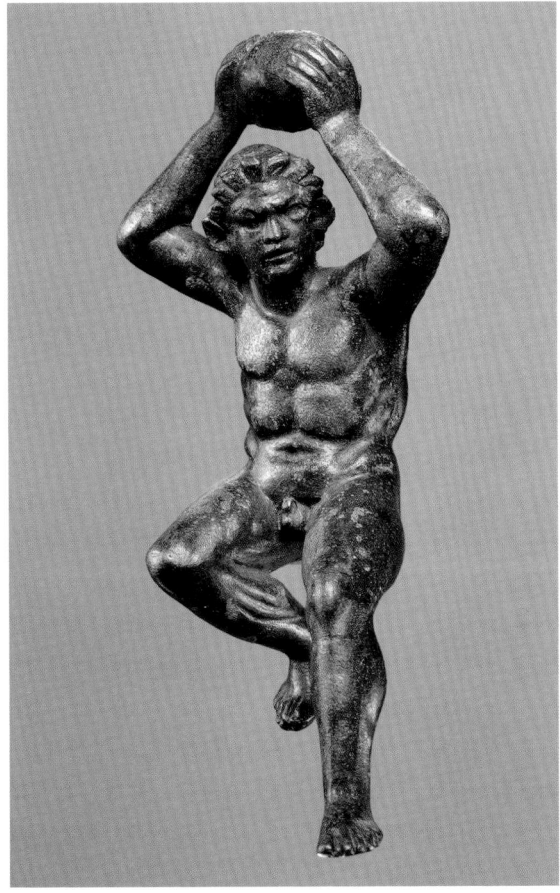

A muscular Giant, half standing with knees bent and right leg pulled up beneath him, is poised to hurl the rock that he holds over his head. This statuette was most likely part of a larger group composition depicting the Gigantomachy. In antiquity, the Gigantomachy was a popular artistic subject for both small- and large-scale compositions. It symbolized the triumph of the Greeks (as represented by the gods) over the barbarians (the uncivilized Giants). The most famous Gigantomachy was carved in marble on the Great Altar of Zeus at Pergamon. The only physical indications of this Giant's wild, inhuman nature are his pointed ears and coarse, tufted hair; the rest of the beautifully modeled figure appears quite human. The pose of this statuette is very similar to the pose of a Giant named Klytios carved on the east facade of the Gigantomachy frieze from the Great Altar of Zeus. Like the Getty Giant, Klytios holds a rock over his head.

Groups of mythological figures were frequently used as decorative attachments on candleholders, thrones, large vessels, and ceremonial chariots. A small hole under the Giant's left thigh may indicate the figure's original point of attachment to another object, perhaps a larger rock or landscape setting. Another small statuette of a Giant in the Museum's collection (see p. 195) served a similar function.

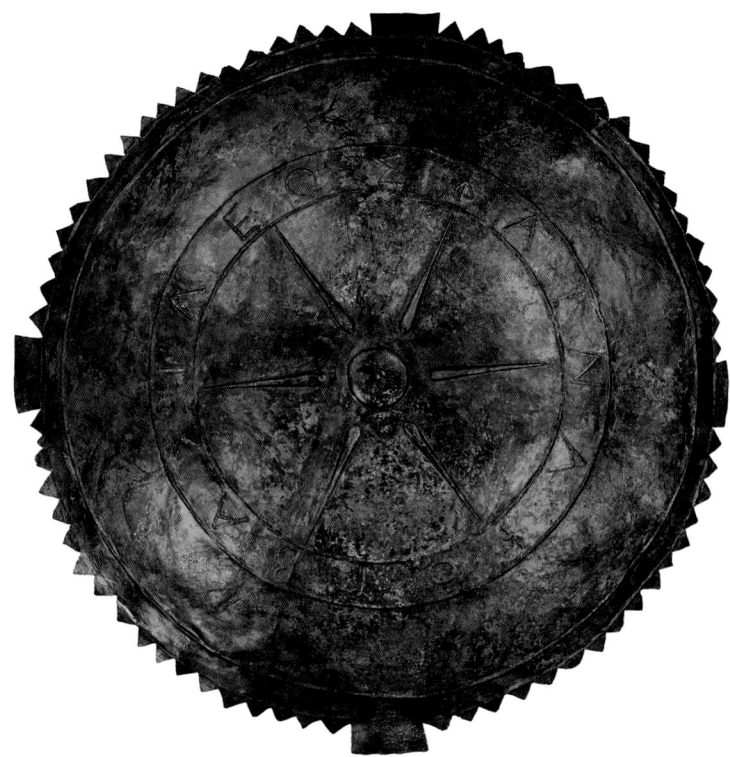

Shield of King Pharnakes

Greek, from Pontus,
185–160 B.C.
Bronze
H: 79.7 cm (31 3/8 in)
W: 81.4 cm (32 in.)
D: 11.8 cm (4 5/8 in.)
80.AC.60

The sun shield is one of the earliest and most enduring symbols of universal kingship. The motif can be traced back to Urartu (ancient Armenia) and Assyria; it reached the Greek world around the sixth century B.C. This bronze shield, with a central star pattern representing the sun, is inscribed in Greek "King Pharnakes," a reference to Pharnakes I of Pontos (in present-day northern Turkey). Such solar imagery also appears on his coinage as well as on that of his predecessor, as it served to strengthen the association between royal power and the sun. Pharnakes' name too linked him to the sun, as it is formed from the root of a word conveying resplendence. Significantly, the other rulers of his dynasty likewise had names related to solar themes.

Created from a single large sheet of metal, the shield is so thin and light that it must originally have been strengthened by a core of wood or leather. Its sharp, serrated edges would have been folded back over this inner core and thus would not have been visible. The appearance of a similar shield in a tomb mural of around 200 B.C., and the discovery of another in a Macedonian mausoleum, suggest that this shield may have been intended for funerary use in a royal burial chamber, or perhaps was a gift dedicated at a shrine.

HERM OF DIONYSOS

Attributed to the
Workshop of Boëthos
Greek, 100–50 B.C.
Bronze with ivory inlay
H: 103.5 cm (40⅜ in.)
W (base): 23.5 cm (9¼ in.)
79.AB.138

A herm is a statue in the form of a
square pillar surmounted by a bust or
head. In antiquity, herms stood at
crossroads, served as boundary or
distance markers, and were thought to
protect travelers. They also guarded
the entrances of homes to ward off
evil. Herms also were used as decorative sculpture in the *palaistra* (exercise
arena) and in gardens. Originally, the
heads of herms represented Hermes,
god of travelers and commerce (hence
the name of this kind of sculpture), but
herms came to be topped by the heads
of other gods and mythological figures,
and later by portrait busts of athletes
and prominent citizens. Offerings
of floral wreaths were draped over the
stubby arm bosses on the herm's sides.

The Getty herm depicts Dionysos,
god of wine, wearing a turban. The
eyes, only one of which survives, were
inlaid with ivory to give a naturalistic
impression. This herm is remarkably
similar to one discovered in a Roman
shipwreck near the town of Mahdia in
Tunisia. The herms are nearly identical in size, and their sculptural features
are strikingly close. The bronze alloy
used to cast both herms is also quite
similar, indicating that they were likely
manufactured together in the same
workshop. The signature of Boëthos of
Chalkedon (in modern Turkey) appears
on the right arm boss of the Mahdia
herm; no such signature appears
on the preserved arm boss of the Getty
herm, but it may have been placed
on the missing boss. If the Getty herm
was not made by Boëthos himself,
it was probably the work of one of his
colleagues or apprentices.

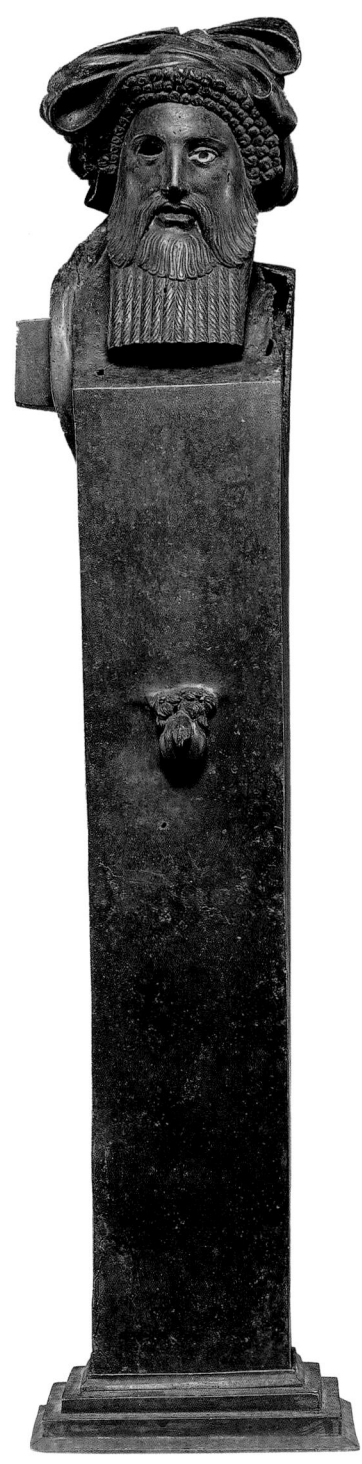

STATUETTE OF AN OLD WOMAN

Greek or Roman, 100–1 B.C.
Bronze
H: 12.6 cm (5 in.)
96.AB.175

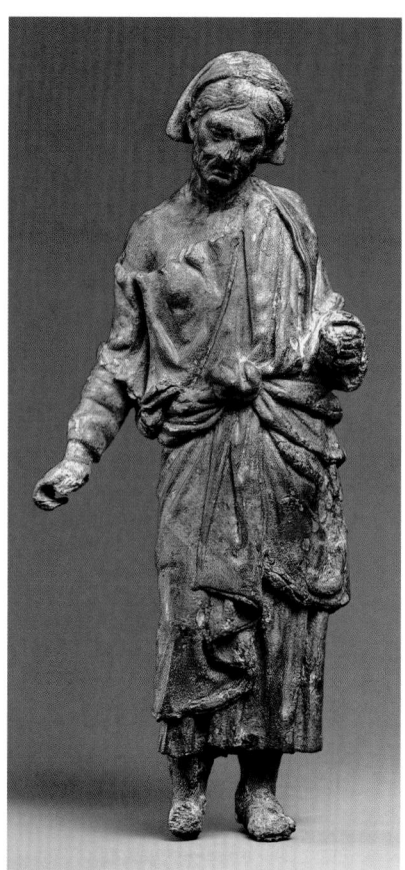

This statuette of an elderly woman poignantly depicts old age. Her wrinkled neck with visible tendons, along with her sagging cheeks and sunken eyes, all attest to a long, hard life. The garments she wears and the scarf on her head indicate that she is most likely a household servant, and her fatigue is evident in the tilt of her head and her drooping shoulders. The objects she once held in her hands are now missing, leaving us to guess at her occupation. But the positioning of her hands and her downward gaze have led some scholars to propose that she may have been spinning thread. She would have held the unworked distaff of wool in her left hand and the spindle of spun thread in her lowered right hand. It has also been suggested that she is Klotho, one of the three Fates, who spins the thread of life.

A number of similar images of domestic servants involved in household activities exist, including one that is essentially a replica of this figure in the Kunsthistorisches Museum in Vienna. Depictions of the elderly, along with an interest in portraying people with physical deformities, came into fashion during the late Hellenistic period, from about 200 B.C.

LEBES

Greek, 50–1 B.C.
Bronze with silver and copper inlays
H: 58 cm (22⅞ in.)
96.AC.51

Springing from a pattern of flowers, leaves, and spiraling tendrils on the front of this *lebes* (cauldron), an intoxicated satyr exuberantly denotes this vessel's purpose. Throwing back his ivy-wreathed head, flashing a roguish grin, and gesturing backward to the lebes with one hand while gripping a drinking cup in the other, he invites the spectator to share in the delights of the contents—strong wine that, in the custom of the Greeks, had been diluted with water. As a follower of Dionysos, who not only was the god of wine but also represented the regenerative powers of nature, the satyr's presence here, together with the vegetal motifs, indicates that the *lebes* may have been used in cult rituals or festivals honoring the god.

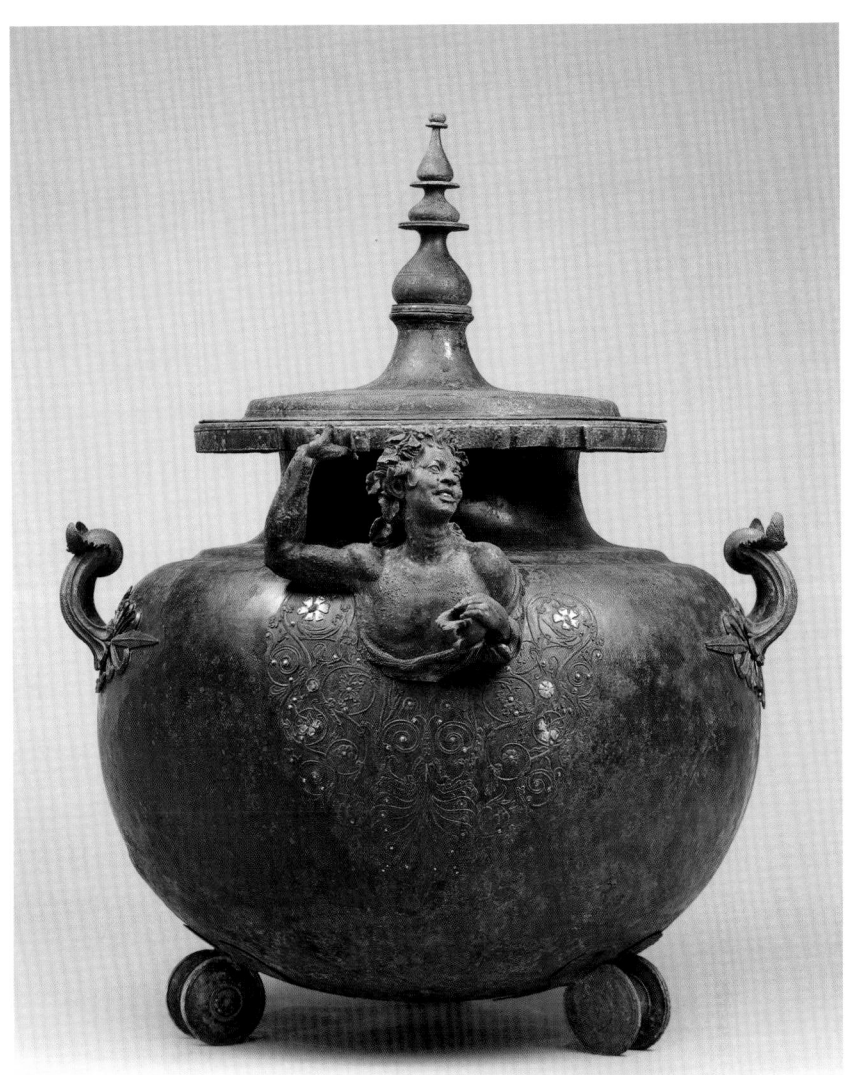

Resting upon spool feet, the *lebes* seems to sag beneath its own weight. On two sides, fluted handles with leaves at their centers are fixed to the body by plaques shaped like palmettes. Atop a large repoussé vine leaf at the back, an acanthus-leaf handle twists up from the shoulder to the mouth. The tall, conical lid is hinged to the mouth by another leaflike element. Silver enhances the eyes and teeth of the satyr as well as the floral motif on the front. A brilliant and richly ornamented example of metalworking, this *lebes* signaled the affluence and status of its owner.

LION PROTOME

Greek, from Crete, circa 650 B.C.
Terracotta
H: 7.6 cm (3 in.)
DIAM: 7 cm (2¾ in.)
91.AD.24

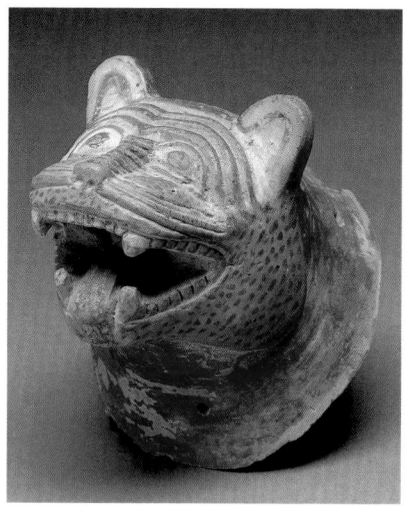

With its open, roaring mouth filled with sharp teeth, this lion appears ready to attack. Six holes around the base of the neck were used to attach the protome to another object, probably a terracotta shield. In Crete in the eighth and early seventh centuries B.C., bronze shields decorated with elaborate three-dimensional animal heads were dedicated in sanctuaries as gifts to the gods. The bronze votive shields copied real shields used for battle in the Near East. Likewise, this protome appears to have been part of a terracotta reproduction of such a votive offering. Such adaptation of Near Eastern elements was common on the island of Crete during this period as new artistic ideas flowed into Greece from the Near East, and Cretan artists took a leading role in the creation of a new Greek style.

The protome was made by pressing wet clay into a two-piece mold and then joining the two halves of the figure while the clay was still slightly damp. Next, details of the face were carved with a cutting tool. The same mold that was used to make this lion was used to produce two other surviving lion's heads: one a protome like this, the other an attachment added to a vessel. Although the maker of this lion protome is unknown, fingerprints were left in the clay on the inside of the object and in the red paint behind the lion's left ear.

CLAZOMENIAN SARCOPHAGUS

Attributed to the
Albertinum Group
Greek, from Ionia,
480–470 B.C.
Terracotta
L: 221.5 cm (87¼ in.)
W: 101 (23⅝ in.)
D: 60 (23⅝ in.)
77.AD.88

During the Archaic period in Greece, a most distinctive and unusual type of sarcophagus was produced in the eastern Greek colonies of Ionia (present-day western Turkey). A workshop centered in the settlement of Klazomenai fashioned these sarcophagi from clay. With dark figures painted on a light ground, their design harks back to an earlier era of black-figured vases produced in Corinth and Athens. Interestingly, the artisans used vase design as a stylistic inspiration rather than a technique. Since figural details were painted rather than incised into the clay, many features have been lost.

The headpiece is decorated with a frieze consisting of a traditional hoplite duel flanked by *bigas* (two-horse chariots) and drivers. Since this mode of fighting was long out of fashion at this time, the manner of battle and the presence of chariots suggest a reference to heroes and legends of the past.

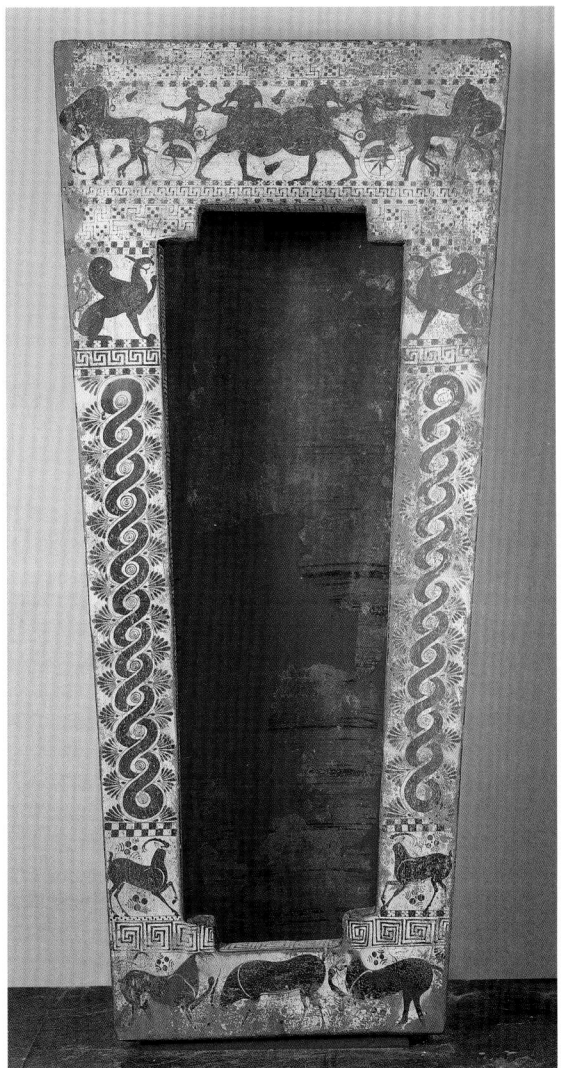

The extensive and colorful elaboration of the sarcophagus is a riot of Archaic Greek ornament: framing the top and bottom of the headpiece are meander cross and quincuncial designs; the upper-side panel squares are filled with mirrored single griffins facing inward. These Archaic hybrid monsters have open mouths, lifted paws, and curled wings and tails. Beneath the griffins are long cable and palmette ropes stretching down the length of the side panels, halted by a checkerboard frieze that introduces the boxes filled with goats with elegantly arched horns facing inward, complementary to the griffins above. The principal frieze at the bottom is another popular motif: a large goat flanked by two panthers, their forepaws lifted to strike.

PROTOCORINTHIAN ARYBALLOS IN THE SHAPE OF A RECUMBENT RAM

Greek, from Corinth,
640–625 B.C.
Terracotta
H: 9.1 cm (3⅝ in.)
L: 14 cm (5½ in.)
86.AE.696

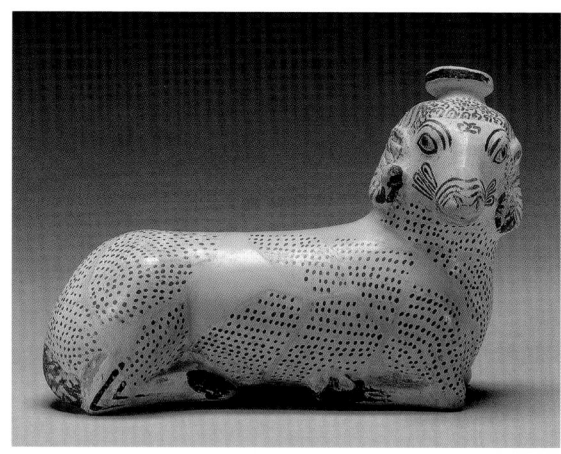

Plastic vases (molded vessels made in the form of human, animal, or mythological beings) first appear in the eastern regions of the Greek-speaking world during the late eighth century B.C. and were popular from about 650 B.C. on. Among the many Greek cities that produced such vases, Corinth and Rhodes were the leading manufacturing centers. This Protocorinthian aryballos is a combination wheel-thrown and moldmade vessel fashioned in the shape of a mature ram resting on legs tucked up under its body. Large horns curve behind the ears and frame a carefully detailed face, with stylized locks of wool falling between the eyes and curling around both corners of the mouth. Dots scattered randomly over the body represent the fleece, perhaps cut short, and black is used to accentuate the hooves and the thick, stubby tail. The vessel's comparatively large body is surmounted by a short neck and rim, with a narrow opening.

Plastic vases such as this appear to have been used for the export of specific precious liquid commodities, whether cosmetic or medicinal. The value of such vessels derived in part from their contents, which were themselves enhanced by the container. Widely distributed throughout the Mediterranean, perhaps through intermediaries such as the Phoenicians, such vases were important to the economy of Corinth.

OINOCHOE

East Greek, from Miletos,
circa 625 B.C.
Terracotta
H: 35.7 cm (14 in.)
DIAM (body): 26.5 cm
(10⅜ in.)
81.AE.83

Herds of wild goats and spotted deer arranged single file in two discrete registers surround this oinochoe. The trefoil mouth perfectly suits its use as a pitcher for wine. On the shoulder of the vase, pairs of dogs, enormous water birds, and sphinxes flank a floral ornament. The cream-colored background is neatly filled with various patterns including rosettes, some of which are brought to life by small birds perched on their petals. In whimsical touches, the painter placed a bird on the tail of a sphinx and broke the monotony of the lower frieze by having a deer turn its head.

The goats have given their name to this kind of pottery decoration: the Wild Goat style. It was popular in the Greek settlements on the coast and offshore islands of Ionia (west coast of modern Turkey and

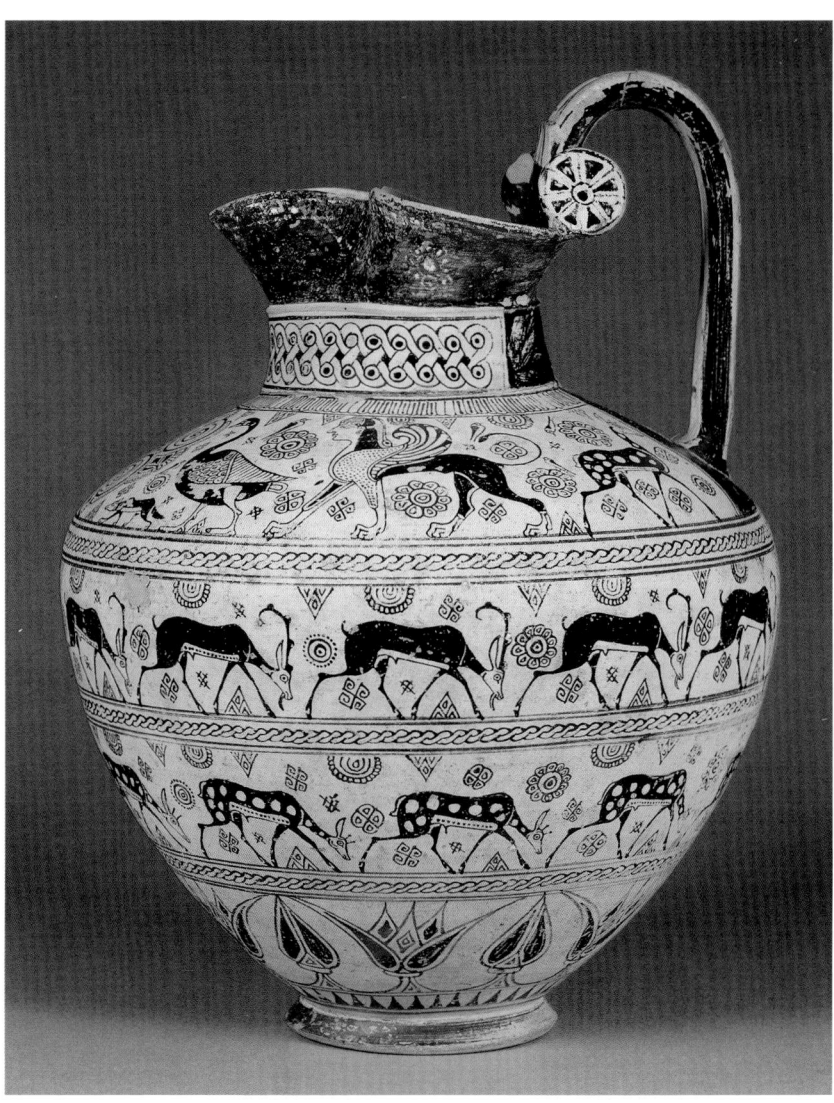

nearby islands) in the seventh and sixth centuries B.C.
The island of Rhodes was once thought to have been
the main producer of Wild Goat pottery, but excavation and clay analysis have since established the
importance of workshops based in the ancient city
of Miletos. Animals arranged in friezes appear
frequently in Greek art of the Orientalizing period.
At this time, Greeks came into closer contact with
their neighbors in the Near East, where repetitive
bands of animal decoration were common. The
highly ornate Wild Goat style is thought to have been
patterned after textile designs, but ivory and bronze
objects may also have provided sources of inspiration;
the disks applied to the rim of this oinochoe are
clearly derived from metalwork.

CORINTHIAN OLPE

Name-vase of the Painter
of Malibu 85.AE.89
Greek, from Corinth,
650–625 B.C.
Terracotta
H (with rotellae): 32.8 cm
(12⅞ in.)
DIAM (body): 17 cm (6¾ in.)
85.AE.89

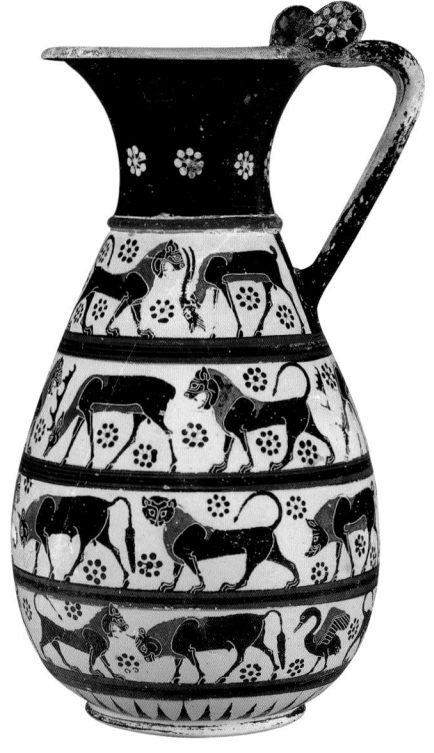

The body of this elegant pouring vessel, or olpe, is decorated in the manner most frequently used on Archaic Corinthian vases, a combination of floral and animal designs in neatly defined friezes or registers. This was a style strongly influenced by the ancient Near East. The four superimposed friezes repeat many of the animals that form the Corinthian vase-painter's standard repertoire: lions, panthers, goats, deer, bulls, boars, swans. Dot-rosettes surround and separate the animals. Both the creatures and the filling ornaments are carefully laid out and meticulously drawn. Individual animals are depicted as if slowly moving forward in their distinct rows, although not all move in the same direction. Certain details, such as the animals' manes and underbellies or the birds' wings, are highlighted with the use of added red paint. The close-set nature of the animals and rosettes, combined with the superimposed rows, suggest that the overall design may imitate textiles, which, according to ancient literary sources, were highly valued.

This olpe was made early in the Corinthian period and displays stylistic traits often called "transitional" by scholars. The neck, lip, and handle of the vase are painted in solid black, for example, while dot-rosettes in added white enhance each of the two roundels that flank the tall handle and encircle the neck. A slightly raised collar-ring, highlighted in added red, separates body from neck, and the characteristic ray pattern encircles the lower body above the foot. The olpe, the aryballos, the pyxis, and a number of other Corinthian shapes were widely distributed throughout the Mediterranean. The distinctive design of such vessels was closely copied in a number of local pottery workshops, particularly in Ithaca, Etruria, and South Italy.

CORINTHIAN ARYBALLOS

Greek, from Corinth,
600–575 B.C.
Terracotta
H: 11.2 cm (4 3/8 in.)
DIAM: 11.7 cm (4 5/8 in.)
92.AE.4

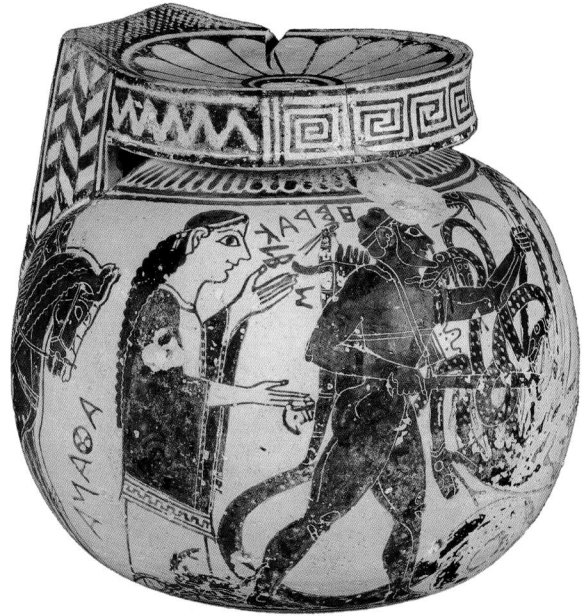

The black-figure technique—in which figures are painted in black silhouette, with details incised and added in white and red paint—was invented in Corinth before spreading to Athens, Sparta, and other Greek centers. Corinthian vase-painters exploited the technique to produce some of the earliest narrative scenes in Archaic Greek art, as on the small vase pictured here. They excelled, in particular, in mastering the miniature picture frieze, where complex mythological stories were artfully rendered in great detail on the surfaces of small vessels. Here, the greatest of all Greek heroes, Herakles, battles the Lernean Hydra, a monster whose multiple heads took the form of snakes. Required to destroy the fierce creature as the second of the Twelve Labors assigned to him by King Eurystheus, Herakles grasps one of the snaky heads while stabbing the creature with his sword. On the side of the vase shown here, one of the Hydra's heads is about to bite Herakles'

shoulder, and a crab, sent to help the Hydra, approaches the hero's ankle from behind. Herakles' protectress, the goddess Athena, stands behind him, gesturing her support. Both Herakles and Athena are identified by inscriptions written retrograde, or right to left, in the distinctive Doric alphabet of Corinth. Likewise, on the other side of the vase, inscriptions identify Iolaos, Herakles' nephew and faithful companion, and Iphikles (written as Wiphikledas), Herakles' twin brother. One holds the Hydra; the other (under the handle) is shown as a charioteer, head turned back to face the action while keeping the four-horse chariot at the ready to carry off the victorious hero. The handle itself is decorated with a female head resembling that of Athena. Although aryballoi, small jars for perfumed oils, were mass-produced and widely distributed, few are as elaborately decorated or as well made as this example.

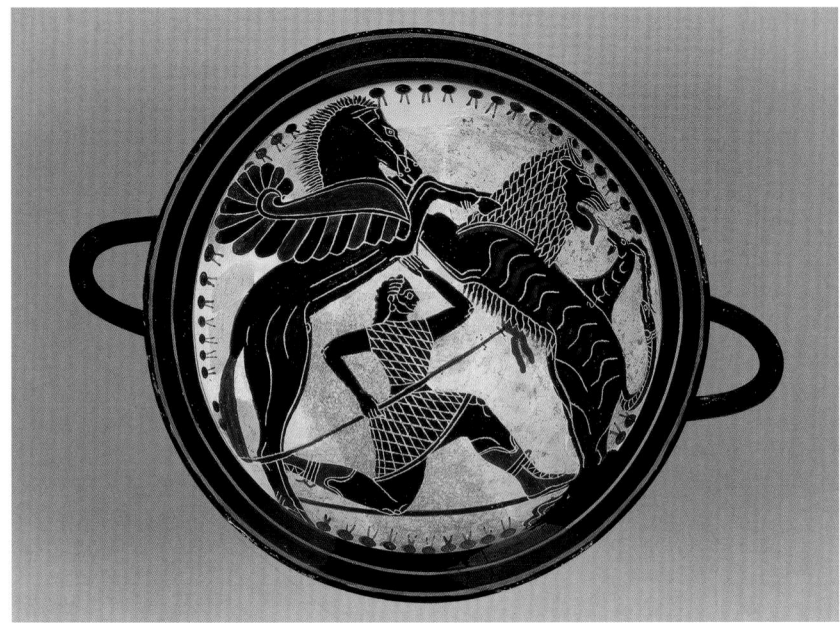

LAKONIAN BLACK-FIGURED KYLIX

Attributed to the
Boreads Painter
Greek, from Sparta,
570–565 B.C.
Terracotta
H: 12.5 cm (4⅞ in.)
DIAM: 18.5 cm (7¼ in.)
85.AE.121

In the sixth century B.C., several regions of ancient Greece followed the Corinthian model and decorated vases in the black-figure technique, with details rendered in incision and added red paint. Stemmed drinking cups like this one were a specialty of Lakonia, the region around Sparta, from whence they were exported to a number of centers in the Mediterranean.

Lakonian vase-painters developed different ways of adapting narrative scenes to the circular space, or tondo, of a cup's interior. Here, the triangular composition almost seems to burst the frame, and the groundline bends under the foot and knee of Bellerophon, a hero more often associated with Corinth rather than Sparta or Lakonia. With his right hand, he thrusts a spear into the chest of the lion-bodied Chimaera; with his left, he holds the reigns of the winged horse Pegasos rearing behind him. Bellerophon has dismounted to attack the monster—an unusual tactic. He is shown in the kneeling pose used to characterize quick movement in Greek art of the Archaic period. Squeezed against the border of the cup, the Chimaera cannot fully display its terrifying features: the snarling lion's face, the fire-breathing goat's head growing from its back, and the tail turned into a snake. The painter of this vessel has been identified as one of two influential masters of the first generation of Lakonian vase-painters. As he did not sign his name, he has been called the Boreads Painter after one of his tondo designs, which shows the Boreads, the sons of the North Wind.

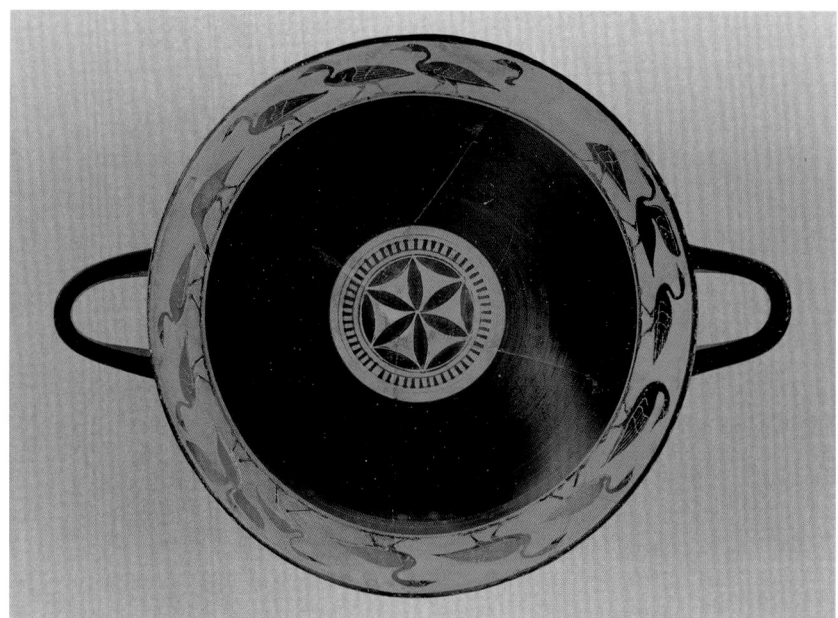

EAST GREEK BLACK-FIGURED LIP CUP

Attributed to the
Osborne House Painter
East Greek, from Samos,
circa 550 B.C.
Terracotta
H (as restored): 9 cm
(3½ in.)
DIAM: 14.2 cm (5⅝ in.)
86.AE.57

Fine miniaturist painting matches the delicate potting of this wine cup. Made around the middle of the sixth century B.C., it is similar in form to the so-called Little Master cups made in Athens, but its painted decoration is more typical of Ionia (west coast of modern Turkey and nearby islands). Features such as the ivy vine on the exterior lip and the rosette in the center of the cup suggest that it was made on the Greek island of Samos. The waterfowl marching around the interior of the lip are another common motif on Ionian pottery: here, two birds flap their wings, another turns its neck, and yet another reaches down with its beak to the black surface below. When the cup was filled to the lower edge of the lip, the birds would have appeared to be wading in shallow liquid as if on the shores of the sea or a lake. In a similar play with design and contents, other cups show dolphins instead of birds. The idea of a sea of wine inside a cup or bowl, perhaps meant to play on the common Homeric epithet referring to the "wine-dark sea," was also taken up by pot-painters in Athens, who depicted fleets of ships inside the rims of kraters and dinoi (mixing vessels; see, for example, the dinos on p. 64).

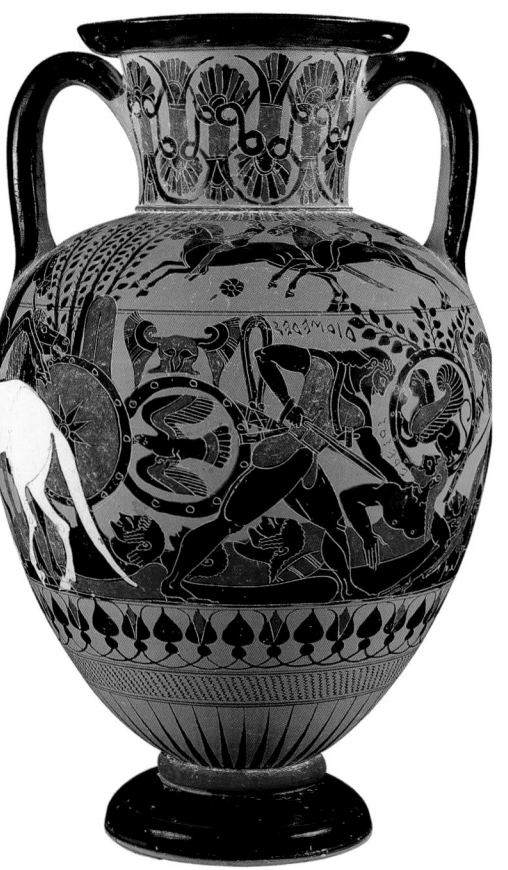

CHALKIDIAN BLACK-FIGURED NECK-AMPHORA

Attributed to the
Inscription Painter
Greek, from Rhegion,
South Italy, circa 540 B.C.
Terracotta
H: 39.6 cm (15⅝ in.)
DIAM (body): 24.9 cm
(9¾ in.)
96.AE.1

According to Homer's epic poem the *Iliad*, the Thracian king Rhesos and his troops came to Troy to fight on the side of the Trojans against the Greeks. Arriving late at night and exhausted from the journey, they had to camp outside the city walls. In the middle of the night they were attacked by the Greek heroes Odysseus and Diomedes, who coveted their immortal horses. Odysseus and Diomedes killed twelve of the sleeping Thracians and their king, Rhesos, before they led the horses away. Remarkably, many details of the written epic recur in the colorful painting on this amphora. The Thracians are depicted wrapped in their robes and with their armor and weapons hanging in the landscape around them. Odysseus and Diomedes are identified by inscriptions, as is King Rhesos, who is about to be stabbed by Diomedes. Under the handles of the vase, the horses that Homer described as "fast as the wind and white as snow" are shown rearing in panic, with a striking white stallion in the foreground.

Bold use of added red and white paint highlights the composition. This vase has been attributed to the so-called Inscription Painter, who did not sign any of his surviving works and has therefore been named for his practice of labeling the figures in his drawings. The local variant of the Greek alphabet used in these inscriptions is one of the features suggesting that his home was Rhegion (modern Reggio) in South Italy, a colony of the Greek city of Chalkis. There he appears to have set up a workshop producing the type of black-figured pottery known today as Chalkidian.

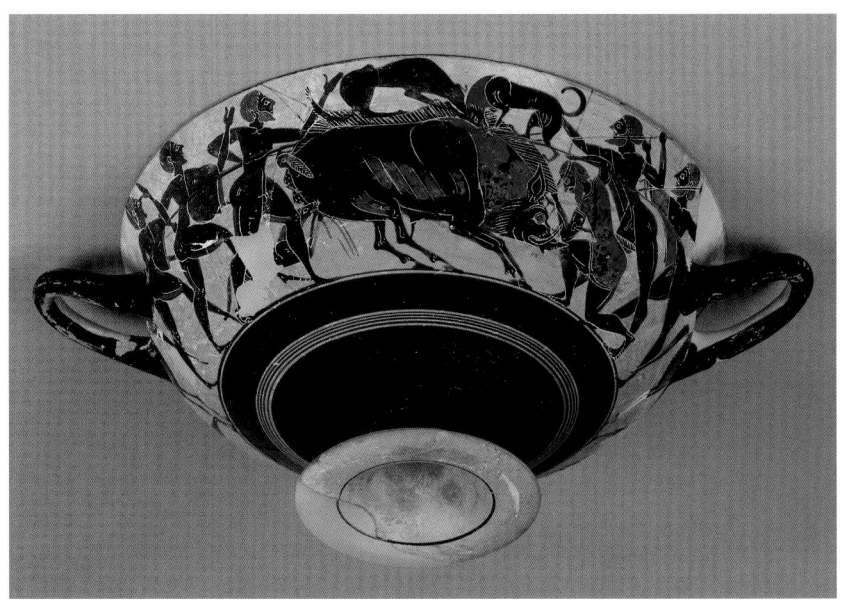

ATTIC BLACK-FIGURED SIANA CUP

Attributed to the
Painter of Boston C.A.
Greek, from Athens,
circa 560 B.C.
Terracotta
H: 12.9 cm (5⅛ in.)
DIAM: 26.2 cm (10⅜ in.)
86.AE.154

The Siana cup was one of the most popular black-figure cup shapes from early in the sixth century B.C. until about 540 B.C. It was named after a cemetery on the Greek island of Rhodes, where two examples of the shape were found. These cups are distinguished by an offset lip, which could be either decorated separately from or, as in this case, painted in unison with the composition on the body. Heroic and mythical exploits decorate the exterior of this vase. The Kalydonian boar hunt, one of the favorite adventures of the early Archaic age, seems to be the subject of one side (pictured here), although without inscriptions to identify the figures, one cannot be certain. According to myth, Peleus, Meleager, and the huntress Atalanta were among the notable heroes who helped to kill the enormous boar sent by Artemis to ravage Peloponnesian Kalydon. Here, six nude men and three dogs are shown energetically attacking a giant boar. On the other side, an episode from the Battle of Lapiths and Centaurs is represented. The marginally civilized Centaurs, half-horses and half-men, had become drunk and unruly at the wedding of Perithoös, the prince of the Lapiths. In the center of the composition, the Lapith hero Kaineus is being beaten into the ground with stones by two Centaurs, for this was the only way he could be destroyed. The interior of a Siana cup is typically black, with a simply designed tondo. This cup's tondo depicts a mounted rider of the aristocratic Athenian class, the type of man who may have purchased and drunk from a cup like this.

ATTIC BLACK-FIGURED AMPHORA, TYPE A

Attributed to Lydos
(as painter) or a painter
close to him
Greek, from Athens,
550–540 B.C.
Terracotta
H: 45.5 cm (17⅞ in.)
DIAM (body): 32.6 cm
(12⅞ in.)
86.AE.60

On two vases, Lydos (active 565–535 B.C.) signed his work "the Lydian," so, although he spent a long career in Athens (and may even have been born there), he linked himself to Lydia (modern Turkey). A master of Athenian black-figure vase-painting, Lydos was one of the first to depict certain tales and legends on vases in the middle of the sixth century B.C. Among these were Herakles' fight with the triple-bodied Geryon (seen on the red-figured krater by the Kleophrades Painter, p. 72), many of the Trojan War episodes, and the battle of Theseus and the Minotaur. This scene was a favorite because it represented the most heroic exploit of the first great hero of Athens.

On the principal side of this amphora (shown here), the Athenian youths and maidens whom Theseus saved from the Minotaur watch the battle. Lydos's style is typified by robust male forms with beefy thighs and articulated musculature that resemble the sculpted Archaic kouroi (see pp. 16 and 17). Many black-figured neck-amphorae have necks constructed at sharp divisions to the body (see opposite page). In contrast, on Type A amphorae (also called belly-amphorae), that transition is smooth.

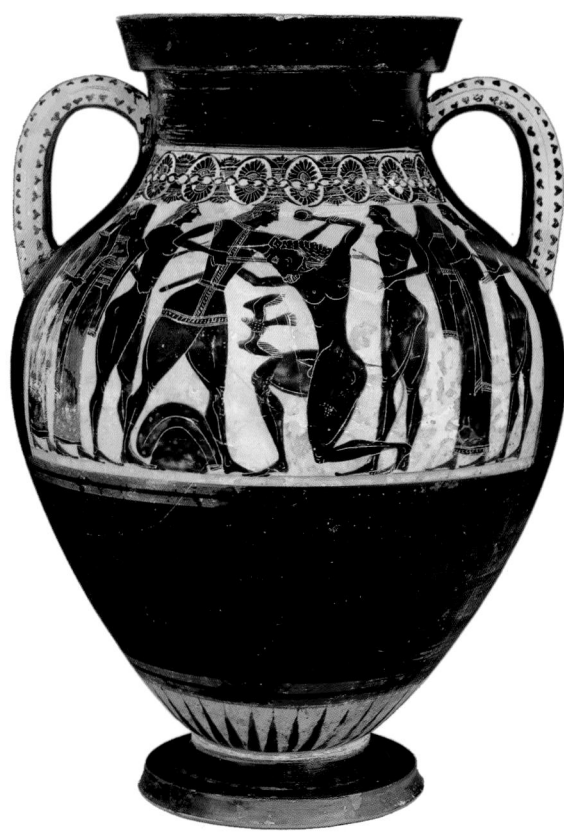

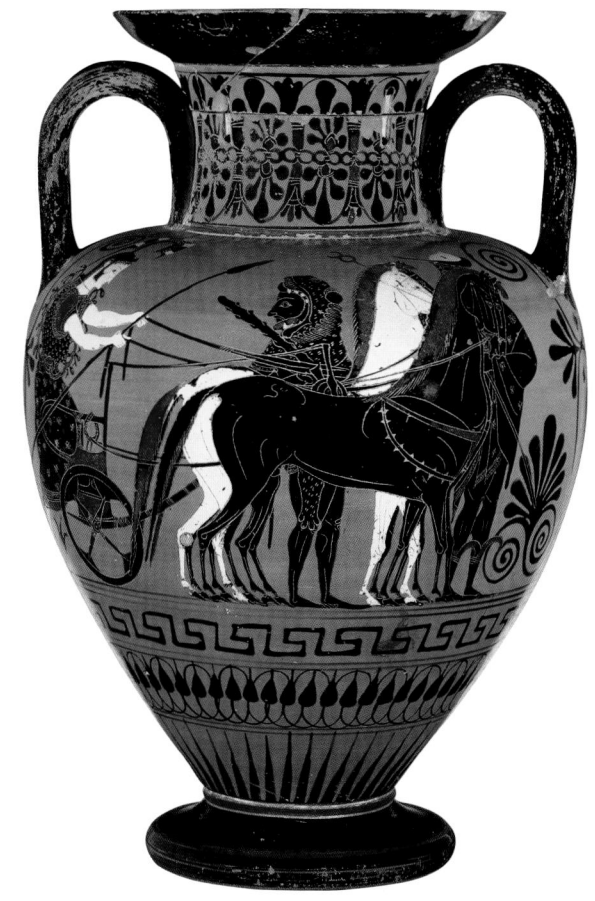

ATTIC
BLACK-FIGURED
NECK-AMPHORA

Name-vase of the
Bareiss Painter
Greek, from Athens,
530–520 B.C.
Terracotta
H: 32.8 cm (12⅞ in.)
DIAM (body): 21.9 cm
(8⅝ in.)
86.AE.85

One of this vase's interesting features is its physical condition. At some point the entire mouth and upper area of the neck were damaged so seriously that they had to be replaced. The broken edge was leveled, and a neck from a different amphora of slightly later date but almost exactly the same dimensions was substituted for the first neck. The still-evident drill-holes would originally have received bronze pins (and, later, lead clamps) to hold the two pieces together. The skillful repair work is nearly seamless, and clearly indicates the value placed on this vessel in antiquity.

This vase has been identified as the name piece of the Bareiss Painter, an artist who worked within a group of painters of similar style called the Medea Group. Because so few Greek vase-painters signed their work, scholars assign names to them based on noteworthy features of individual vases or painting styles. In this case, the name of the collector who owned the vase was used.

The scenes on this vase are typical of favorite subjects on pots of the last third of the sixth century B.C. The Apotheosis of Herakles is represented on the principal side (seen here), which shows him about to join Athena in a quadriga (four-horse chariot) that will take them to Mount Olympos. The opposite side shows mounted hoplites in combat over a fallen warrior. To the vase's ancient owner, this combat scene may have recalled heroic battles such as those Homer described in the *Iliad*.

ATTIC BLACK-FIGURED DINOS

Attributed to the Circle
of the Antimenes Painter
Greek, from Athens,
520–510 B.C.
Terracotta
H: 35.5 cm (14 in.)
DIAM (rim): 33 cm (13 in.)
92.AE.88

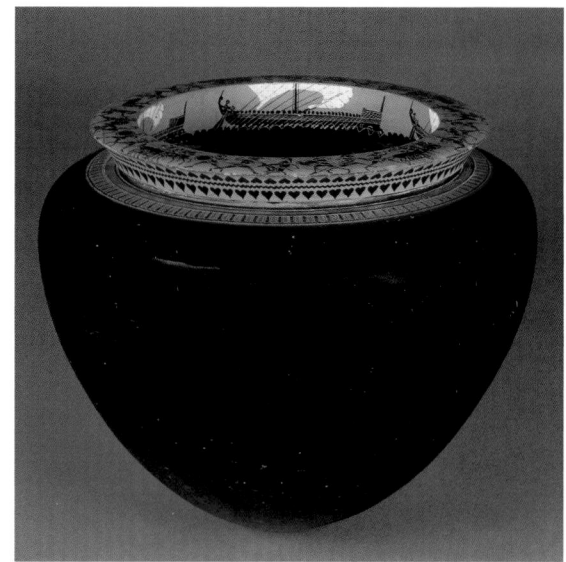

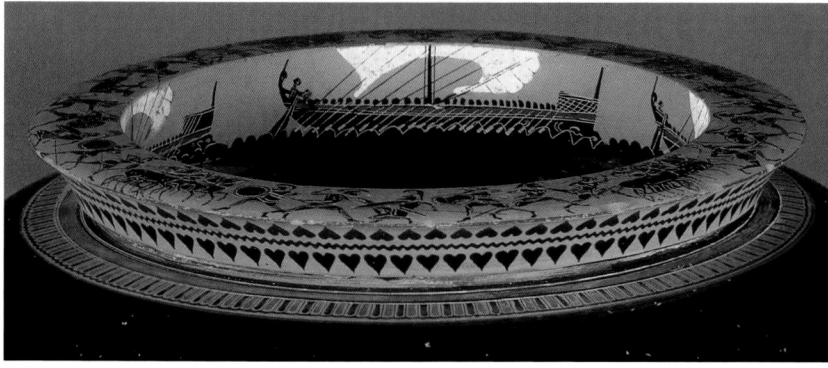

During the sixth century B.C., the black-figured dinos was the centerpiece of the men's wine-drinking ritual called the *symposion*. This vase was originally made to fit a separate stand. Its mouth is wide to accommodate a variety of functions: at times another vessel was placed inside it to chill the wine; the dinos could also serve as a mixing vessel for wine and water. Small pitchers were dipped into the wine, which was then poured into drinking cups.

The strong influence of the Antimenes Painter, the most prolific of the late sixth-century black-figure painters, is evident in this vase's clean and uncluttered style of painting, as well as its legible, straightforward narrative.

The top of the rim is decorated with battles of hoplites, or foot soldiers, interspersed with four quadrigae (four-horse chariots) in one continuous battle frieze that has been carefully calculated to fill the circular space. Four large ships are under sail on the rim's interior. Ranks of oarsmen and a helmsman are visible on each ship, which have swan's heads carved on their sterns and battering rams shaped like boar's heads. In a wittily designed and executed comment on Homer's "wine-dark sea," these ships would have seemed to those who peered inside to be sailing directly on the surface of the wine itself.

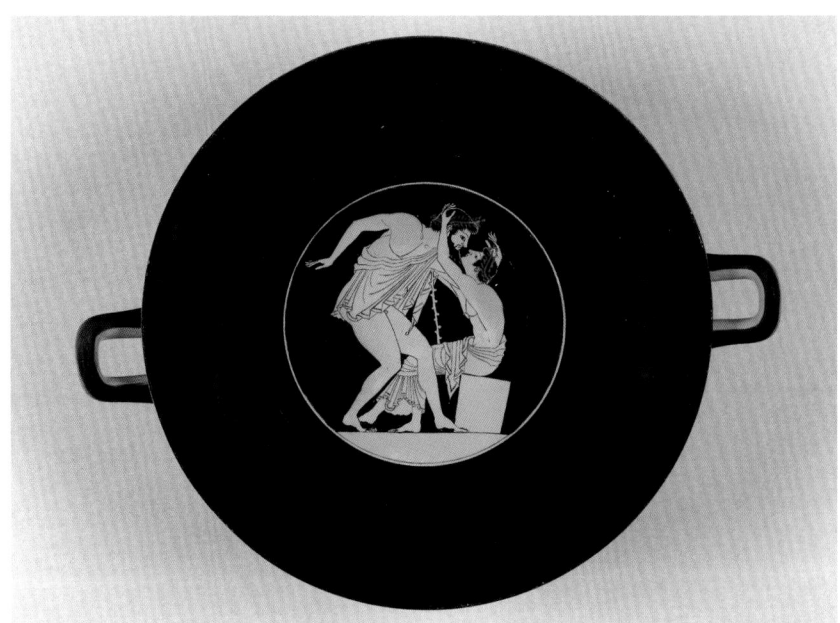

ATTIC RED-FIGURED KYLIX, TYPE B

Attributed to the
Carpenter Painter
Greek, from Athens,
510–500 B.C.
Terracotta
H: 11 cm (4⅜ in.)
DIAM: 33.5 cm (13⅛ in.)
85.AE.25

Drinking cups intended for banquets were frequently decorated with scenes depicting their users' favorite activities, such as athletics, feasting, entertainment, and amorous adventures. Thus, on the exterior of this cup, men and youths participate in athletics. On the interior, a seated youth, with his long chiton lowered to his hips and draped across his legs, reaches to embrace and draw his older friend toward him for a kiss. Dressed in a short chlamys, the man leans forward somewhat tentatively on his toes, his left arm reaching behind the youth's head. Among the upper classes in Athens during the time when this kylix was painted, the erotic aspect of relationships between older and younger men was considered fundamental to the education of adolescents in preparation for adult status in Greek society. It is interesting to note that the painter neglected to complete a minor element in the picture on the interior of the cup. He had meant to show the older man leaning on his walking stick, but forgot to draw it all the way down to the ground behind the legs of the seated youth.

Activities in the gymnasium decorate the exterior of the cup: depictions of youths and older men practicing discus hurling, javelin throwing, and the long jump to the musical accompaniment of a flute played by another youth illustrate another important component of the socialization of Athenian youth. Near the handle, an altar completes the picture; religion and the gods were central to all facets of life, including the outcome of any athletic contest.

ATTIC RED-FIGURED KYLIX, TYPE B

Greek, from Athens,
510–500 B.C.
Terracotta
H: 11.2 cm (4 3/8 in.)
DIAM: 27.5 cm (10 7/8 in.)
86.AE.280

This drinking cup is decorated entirely with figures of dancing revelers. One, shown here, is framed in the tondo of the cup's interior, while ten more stretch and pose in attitudes around its exterior. This cup's most remarkable feature is the rich red color used to glaze the interior. Most Athenian vases were produced in either the red-figure technique, as were the exterior and tondo of this cup, or the black-figure technique (see the neck-amphora on p. 63). Some workshops produced a coral-red glaze, named for the red sea coral it resembles. The production of coral red, also known as intentional red, is still not fully understood, but the iron content of coral red is slightly different from that of traditional black gloss, suggesting that the color was achieved through the addition of particular minerals to the black glaze, which then turned red in the firing process. It was first and most often practiced around 510 B.C. on cups like this, where the red color would richly enhance the appearance of the wine held within. Later, coral red was used on larger vessels (see the volute-krater on p. 73), but it never gained widespread production or popularity. Though extraordinary in effect, the technique was gradually abandoned, perhaps because the reddish glaze was fragile and easily flaked off from the surface of the clay.

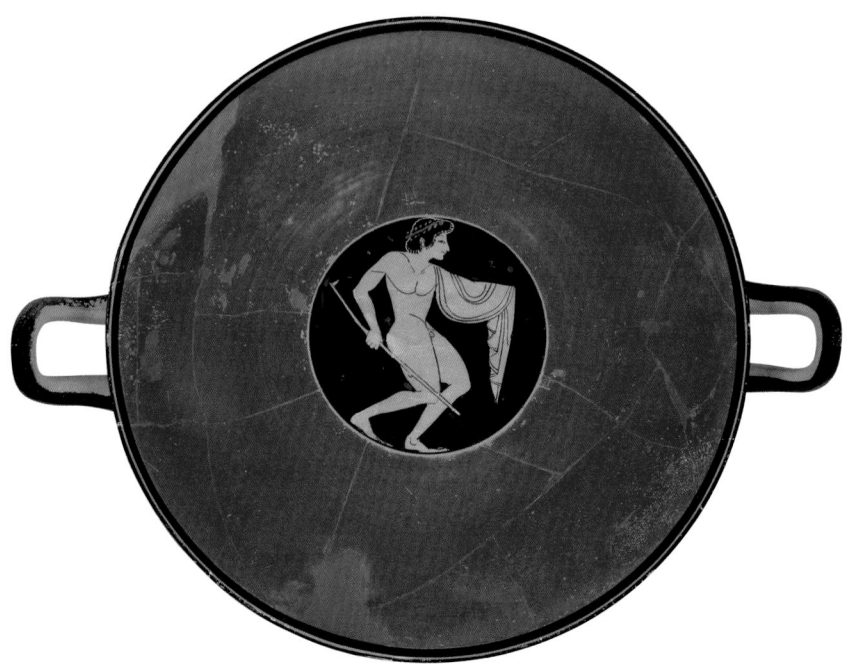

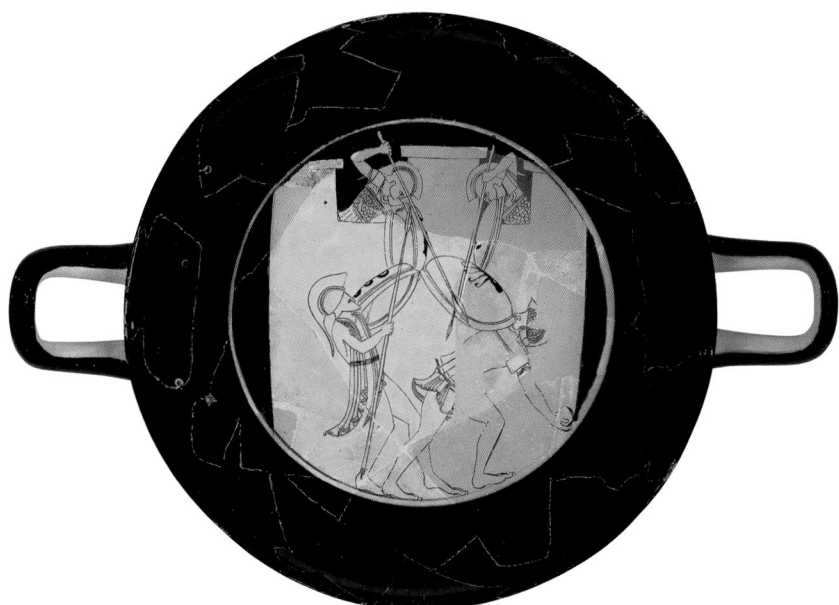

ATTIC RED-FIGURED KYLIX, TYPE C

Attributed to Apollodoros
(as painter)
Greek, from Athens,
circa 500 B.C.
Terracotta
H: 7.7 cm (3 in.)
DIAM: 18.8 cm (7⅜ in.)
84.AE.38

Cityscapes are rarely seen in Greek art. While the exterior of this cup was left black, the interior shows one of the very few extant representations of late Archaic city walls. The scene is a city under siege, succinctly represented by two attacking and two defending warriors. Interestingly, no one hits his mark; this is a picture of an anonymous battle, not a conquest. The artist demonstrates an understanding of spatial extension in the way the walls disappear behind the frame of the tondo. In contrast, the attacking warriors are solidly balanced on the curve of the tondo frame itself. To combine a fictional space with the viewer's own physical space in this way is characteristic of Greek Archaic art. The swallow-tailed folds of the chiton worn by the warrior on the right, which move somewhat unrealistically in response to his action, are also typical. The holes visible on the left side of the cup are evidence of an ancient repair in which lead clamps were used to hold the fragments together. This suggests the cup was highly valued by its owner.

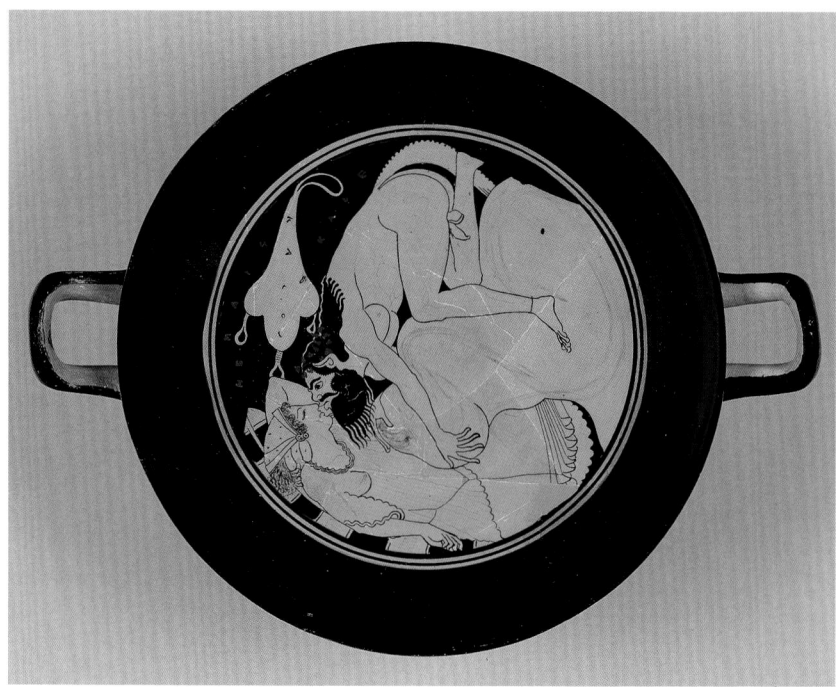

ATTIC RED-FIGURED KYLIX, TYPE B

Attributed to Onesimos
(as painter)
Greek, from Athens,
500–490 B.C.
Terracotta
H (restored): 8.3 cm (3¼ in.)
DIAM: 23.5 cm (9¼ in.)
86.AE.607

The antics of satyrs, companions of Dionysos, were
a popular subject for the drinking cups of Athenians.
In the interior of this kylix, a satyr creeps up on a
nymph who naps on a large striped cushion beneath
a rocky outcropping. The Greek inscription above
them tells why the satyr is so smitten: "the girl is
beautiful." The cup's painter, Onesimos (active
510–480 B.C.), seems to take particular delight in
juxtaposing the lovely profile of the sleeping girl with
the brutish, pug-nosed face of the satyr about to
steal a kiss. Echoing contemporaneous philosophical
and poetic interests in sleep and wakefulness, beauty
and ugliness, and tamed and untamed nature, the
artist has expressed these contrasts with clarity
and sensitivity in this scene, which is meant to both
amuse and arouse. On each side of the exterior a
single satyr dances. The figures' robust physicality
combined with the use of short groundlines helps
to identify this kylix as an early work by Onesimos,
a pupil of Euphronios (active 520–470 B.C.) and
considered among the greatest of Attic red-figure
cup-painters.

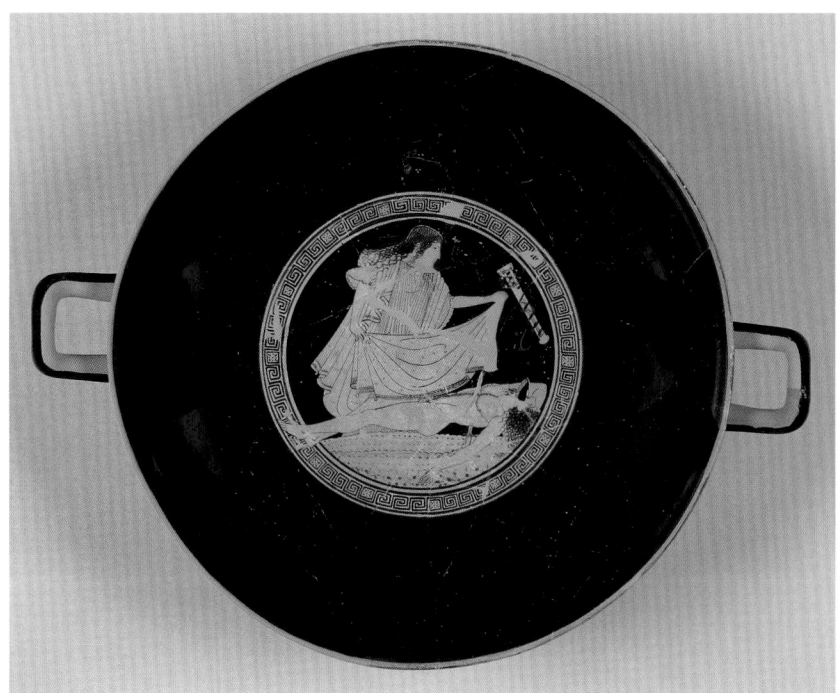

ATTIC RED-FIGURED KYLIX, TYPE B

Attributed to the
Brygos Painter
Greek, from Athens,
circa 490 B.C.
Terracotta
H: 11.2 cm (4³⁄₈ in.)
DIAM: 31.4 cm (12¹⁄₄ in.)
86.AE.286

On this cup, the Brygos Painter tells the tragic story of Ajax, one of the greatest Greek heroes at Troy. The essential parts of the narrative are shown on the three painted areas of the cup. On one side of the exterior, the Greeks cast their votes to award the arms of Achilles to either Odysseus or Ajax; on the other, after Odysseus wins by a single vote, a fight breaks out between the opponents. Finally, on the cup's interior, one sees the tragic outcome: driven to despair by the madness that had come over him, Ajax commits suicide on the beach by throwing himself onto his sword. The painter has chosen to represent not Ajax's moment of death (a popular scene in Greek art) but the tenderness of his companion, Tekmessa, who rushes to cover the body and restore to it the respect due a great hero. The Brygos Painter has emphasized the event and the figure of Ajax by draping the hero's feet over the border of the tondo and placing him on his back, so that he looks as if he has been stabbed from behind. Ajax's story is particularly poignant, for he had risked his own life to retrieve the body of Achilles from the Trojans. The rightful inheritor of Achilles' arms, he had been tricked out of them by Odysseus's skillful tongue.

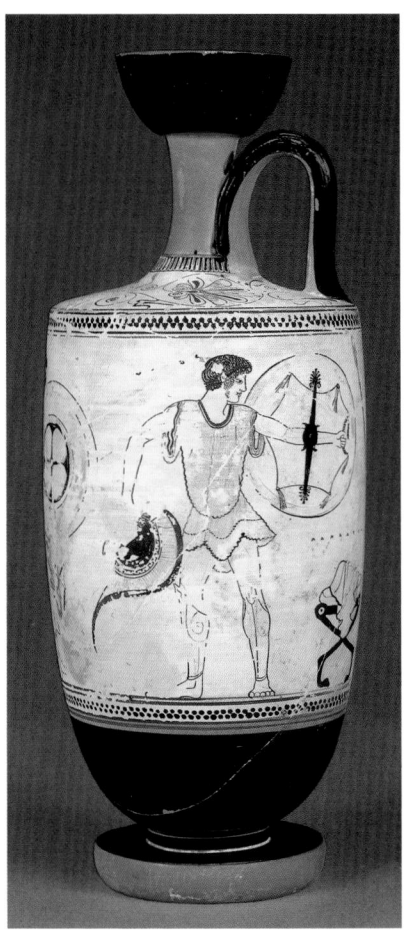

ATTIC WHITE-GROUND LEKYTHOS

Attributed to Douris
(as painter)
Greek, from Athens,
circa 500 B.C.
Terracotta
H: 33.4 cm (13⅛ in.)
DIAM (shoulder): 12.6 cm
(5 in.)
84.AE.770

Two young Athenian aristocrats arm themselves in the presence of a boy and a woman on this lekythos painted by Douris (active 500–475 B.C.), one of the most skilled and productive artists of late Archaic Athens. The youths are dressed in short chitons; one puts on his greaves, while the other, pictured here, proudly holds out his helmet and shield. *Kalos* (meaning "beautiful" in Greek) inscriptions painted in the field between the figures praise the beauty of two youths, Nikodromos and Panaitios.

Some of Douris's best draftsmanship appears on white-ground lekythoi, although he was primarily a cup-painter. The application of a white slip to the outside of the red-clay body enabled the artist to draw his figures with a very precise, clean outline while using a dilute glaze to delineate the interior lines of muscles and drapery folds. The lekythos was designed for holding precious oils; its slender neck and sharply rimmed mouth were especially suited to controlling the flow of the expensive material inside. This lekythos was painted in a developmental phase, before the shape became exclusively used for funerary purposes. Clues to its dating are the inscription naming Panaitos (which places it early in the artist's career), the encircling figural frieze, and the maenad running amidst the floral pattern on the shoulder. The latter two features are derived from the earlier black-figure technique, which Douris may also have practiced.

ATTIC RED-FIGURED NECK-AMPHORA WITH DOUBLE HANDLES

Attributed to the
Berlin Painter
Greek, from Athens,
circa 480 B.C.
Terracotta
H: 30.6 cm (12 in.)
DIAM (body): 17.2 cm
(6¾ in.)
86.AE.187

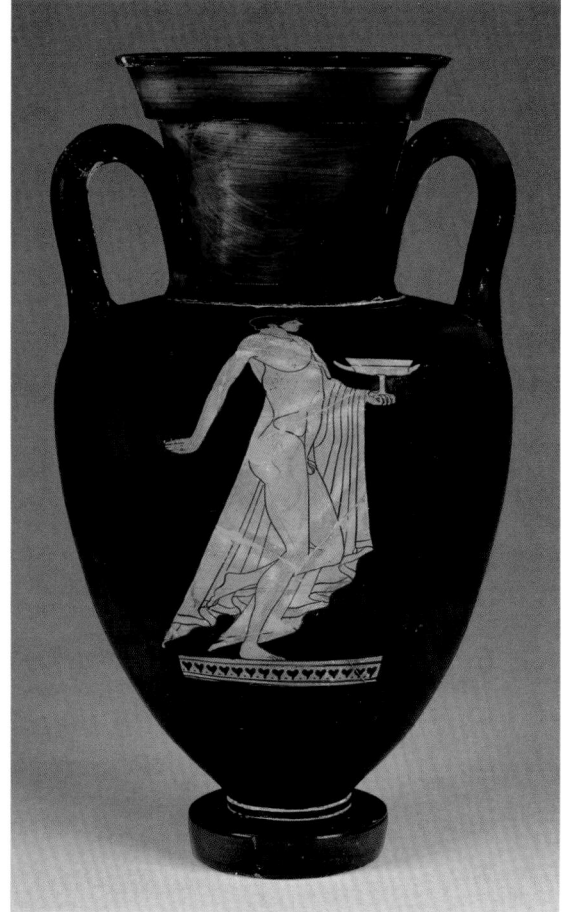

The Berlin Painter is considered to be among the foremost draftsmen of late Archaic Athens. Building on the experiments of earlier painters, in some of whose workshops he was trained, the Berlin Painter took full advantage of the possibilities for anatomical rendering and expression that the red-figure technique offered. He did not paint cups, preferring larger shapes, usually closed ones (such as amphorae), although at times he painted open shapes (such as calyx-kraters). His style is immediately recognizable by its finely drawn single figures or small groups on a groundline, silhouetted against a black expanse. This amphora is a classic example. Crowned with an ivy wreath and holding a drinking cup by the foot,

the youthful dancer seen here on the front of the vase moves in a similar way to the old, foreign-looking man on the reverse, yet the contrast between them is striking. The Berlin Painter has juxtaposed youth to old age and beauty to ugliness, but there is also a contrast of class, for the pug-nosed man on the reverse is probably a slave accompanying his master, the youth, at an initiation ritual or a *symposion.*

ATTIC
RED-FIGURED
VOLUTE-KRATER

Attributed to the
Kleophrades Painter
Greek, from Athens,
circa 490 B.C.
Terracotta
H (as restored): 56.9 cm
(22 3/8 in.)
DIAM (rim): 41.1 cm (16 1/8 in.)
77.AE.11

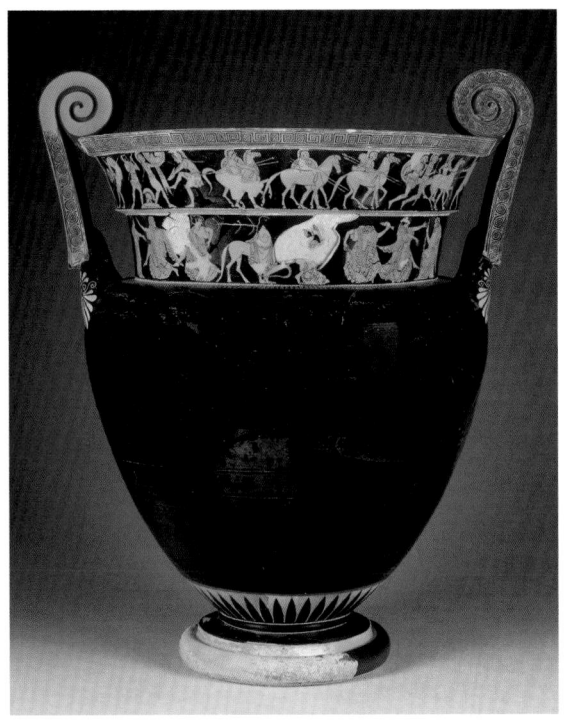

The volute-krater is named for the shape of the decorative handles that rise in spirals over the rim of the vase like architectural Ionic volutes; other types of kraters have similarly straightforward names—calyx, column, or bell—reflecting the shape of the handles or body. As large vessels used for chilling and mixing wine and water, red-figured kraters served the same function in the fifth century B.C. as black-figured dinoi (see p. 64) in the sixth century B.C. The shape became more popular than dinoi around 500 B.C. This krater, from the same workshop as the volute-krater opposite, was decorated with a double-frieze design that provided the Kleophrades Painter enough space to accommodate his interest in painting myth and legend with actively striding figures in energetic poses.

The entire upper frieze of this krater is painted with an Amazonomachy, a battle between the Greeks (here aided by Herakles) and the fierce female warriors. The lower frieze on the side shown here shows the Capture of Thetis by Peleus, watched at left by her parents, Doris and Nereus, and by the wise Centaur Cheiron, who would later tutor Achilles, the son of Thetis and Peleus. On the other side, the lower frieze is filled with three of the Labors of Herakles: the Battle with the Lernean Hydra; the fight with the triple-bodied monster Geryon; and the last Labor, in which Herakles picks the Apples of the Hesperides.

ATTIC RED-FIGURED VOLUTE-KRATER

Attributed to the
Kleophrades Painter
(as painter and potter)
and a pupil (as painter)
Greek, from Athens,
480–470 B.C.
Terracotta
H (to top of volutes):
56.9 cm (22⅜ in.)
DIAM (rim): 41.1 cm (16⅛ in.)
84.AE.974

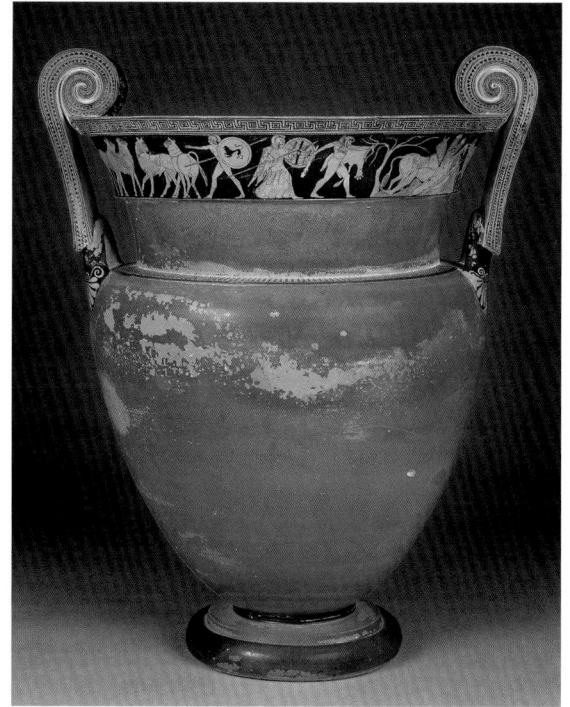

This volute-krater was potted and painted in the
same workshop as the previous entry, as evidenced
by its nearly identical size, shape, and proportions.
The principal side also appears to be the work of
the same artist, the Kleophrades Painter, who was
among the greatest pot-painters of late Archaic
Athens. The body of the krater was decorated with
the earliest known use of the coral-red technique on
the exterior of a large vessel (see also p. 66). Four
of the Labors of Herakles have been represented
around the rim. On the principal side (shown here),
Herakles, with assistance from his patron goddess,
Athena, creeps up on the sleeping Giant Alkyoneus,
who had stolen the magic cattle of Helios. The Giant's
deep slumber is personified by a tiny winged figure
of sleep (Hypnos) crouching on his chest. As Herakles
prepares to engage Alkyoneus in battle, his nephew
Iolaos drives off the cattle. The complexity of this
narrative composition and the stylistic inventiveness
of a foreshortened cow point to the hand of the
Kleophrades Painter, while the more straightforward
representations of three other Labors on the opposite side (the battles with the Keryneian Hind, the
Hydra of Lerna, and the Nemean Lion, respectively)
suggest a pupil's work.

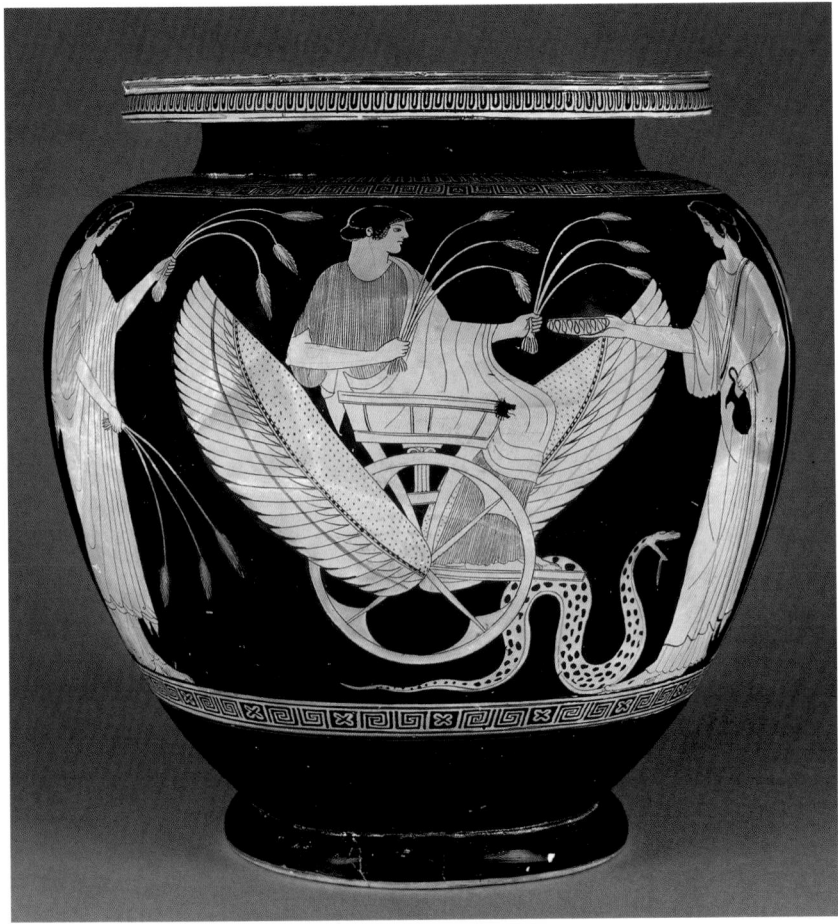

ATTIC RED-FIGURED FOOTED DINOS

Attributed to the
Syleus Painter
Greek, from Athens,
circa 470 B.C.
Terracotta
H: 36.8 cm (14½ in.)
DIAM (body): 35.7 cm (14 in.)
89.AE.73

Demeter and Kore flank Triptolemos on this red-figured dinos from the early Classical period. The scene presents the heroes and deities of Eleusis, a city outside Athens that was home to the highly secretive cult of Demeter, goddess of agriculture. Triptolemos first appears as an Eleusinian hero in Greek art around 500 B.C. Demeter, who stands behind him holding stalks of grain, gave him a fabulous winged chariot so that he could spread the knowledge of grain cultivation across the world. This vase shows him departing on that journey. To wish him good fortune, Kore, Demeter's daughter (inscribed "Pheraphatta," an alternative form of her usual name, Persephone), offers him a libation bowl that she has just filled from the jug in her left hand. Other figures on the vase include Theos (Hades), god of the Underworld, his wife, Thea, and the personification of the city of Eleusis itself, all identified by inscription.

ATTIC WHITE-GROUND LEKYTHOS

Attributed to the Painter
of Athens 1826
Greek, from Athens,
470–460 B.C.
Terracotta
H: 24.7 cm (9¾ in.)
DIAM (shoulder): 8.9 cm
(3½ in.)
86.AE.253

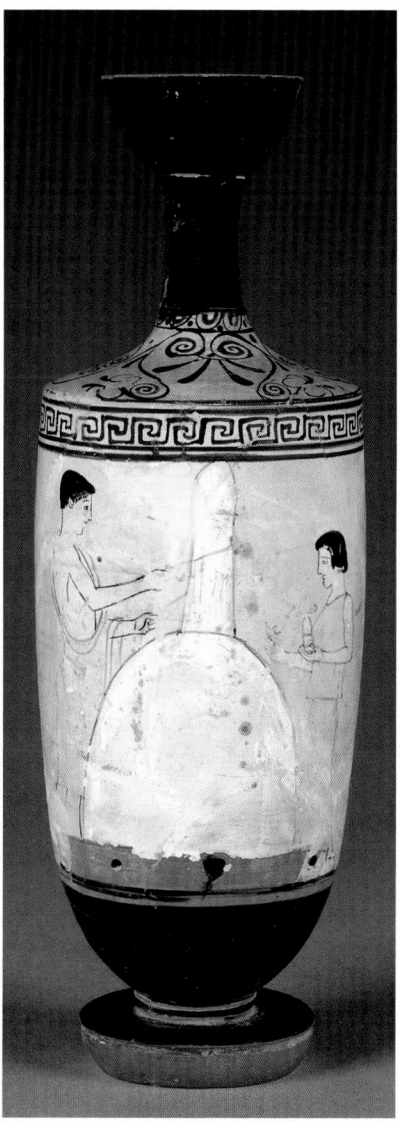

Intended as a tomb offering, this
Athenian white-ground lekythos
depicts family members visiting a
loved one's burial site. The grave is
shown as a high earthen mound
marked by a tall, thin stele, or gravestone. A youth, standing at the left,
ties fillets, or ribbons, around the stele
as a sign of respect and commemora-
tion. On the right, a girl, her hair
cut short as a gesture of mourning,
holds an alabastron (a small oil vessel)
and a flower. The oil contained in
the alabastron was used to anoint the
gravestone, with the container itself
and the flower left as offerings. The
two visitors conducting these grave
rituals are presumably the children
of the person buried under the
mound, whose name would have been
inscribed on the stele above.

Many white lekythoi were made
specifically as containers for the oil
that was used in funerary rituals
and for burial with the deceased. The
scenes most frequently depicted on
them are visitations to a tomb or the
preparations for such a visit. In actual
practice in ancient Greece, care of
tombs began when all the rituals of
burial were completed and continued
frequently and indefinitely. It was
an important responsibility usually
performed by the women of the family.

The Painter of Athens 1826
decorated vases in the white-ground
technique in Athens around 470 to
460 B.C. He (or she) painted primarily
lekythoi and was one of the earliest
artists to focus on their production.
The true name of the Painter of Athens
1826 is unknown; the name used
by scholars comes from a vase of that
inventory number in the National
Archaeological Museum in Athens.

ATTIC RED-FIGURED LEKYTHOS

Attributed to the Painter
of the Frankfort Acorn
Greek, from Athens,
420–400 B.C.
Terracotta
H: 18.4 cm (7¼ in.)
DIAM (body): 10.6 cm (4⅛ in.)
91.AE.10

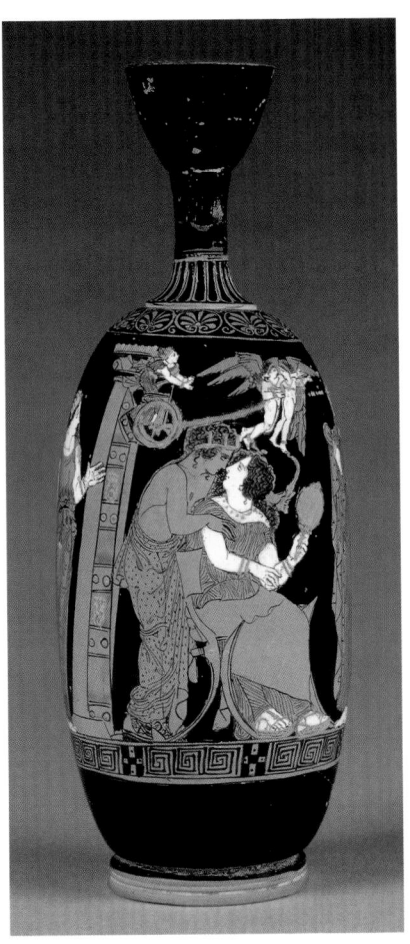

The setting of this dramatic encounter
is the palace of Menelaos at Sparta,
indicated by the doors at the left.
The visiting Trojan prince, Paris, has
encountered Helen gazing at herself
in her mirror, and, as she turns,
their eyes meet. Aphrodite, her work
accomplished, flies above them in a
tiny chariot drawn by two tiny erotes
(companions of Eros). To the left,
one of Helen's companions reacts in
astonishment as she watches the
chariot fly by. The opulent painting
style, with its applied gilding, added
white pigment, and attention to
sumptuous fabrics and jewelry (also
evident on the volute-krater opposite),
was popular during the late Classical
period. It follows in the manner of the
Meidias Painter, whose work typifies
the tastes of the age. This vase, like
most lekythoi, probably once contained perfumed oil. In contrast to
those used by their owners, this vase
was most likely a funerary gift, as
indicated by its extremely fine state of
preservation.

ATTIC RED-FIGURED DINOID VOLUTE-KRATER AND STAND

Attributed to the
Meleager Painter
Greek, from Athens,
390–380 B.C.
Terracotta
H (krater): 54 cm (21¼ in.)
DIAM (krater): 40 cm
(15¾ in.)
H (stand): 16.5 cm (6½ in.)
87.AE.93

This vase is a sumptuous combination of late Classical
relief decoration, gilding, and highly refined red-figure
painting. That it was produced to intentionally imitate
metal vessels is partly indicated by the fluted body,
gilded olive wreath around the shoulder, and floral
and figural decoration limited to the neck and base.
On the front of the krater's neck (shown here), Adonis,
the consort of Aphrodite, goddess of love, lies on a
couch covered with elaborately embroidered textiles.
As Adonis binds a fillet around his head, Eros offers
him a plate of food. Because Adonis spent part of each
year living with Aphrodite on Mount Olympos and
part with Persephone in the Underworld, the goddesses are placed with their attendants on either side

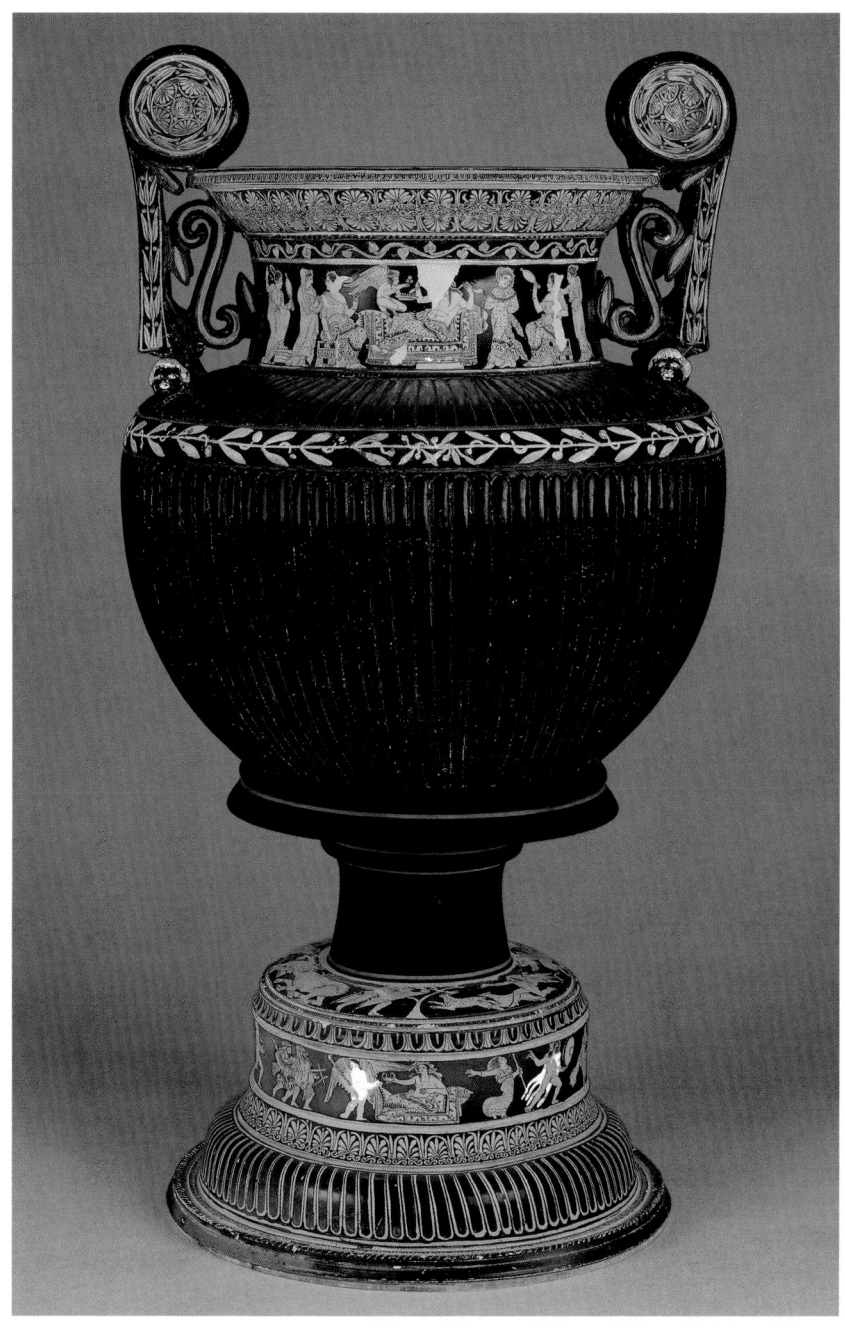

of him. The *symposion* scene on the reverse side of
the neck shows a mortal (and less luxurious) version
of this scene. Each couple engages in the pleasures
of the revel. The stand too is richly decorated with
hunters and mythical figures on top and Dionysos, his
companions, and other divinities on the side.

ATTIC RED-FIGURED PELIKE OF KERCH STYLE

Attributed to the Painter
of the Wedding Procession
Greek, from Athens,
circa 360 B.C.
Terracotta
H: 48.3 cm (19 in.)
DIAM (body): 27.2 cm
(10¾ in.)
83.AE.10

The front of this tall pelike, a storage jar for olive oil and other commodities, shows the Judgment of Paris. Dressed in rich oriental attire, Paris, the young prince of Troy, sits on a rock and looks toward Athena, goddess of war. Behind Athena, Aphrodite, goddess of love, holds a veil to her face in feigned modesty, while Eros tugs at her himation. To Paris's proper right stands Hera, queen of the Greek deities, followed by Hermes, the messenger god, who has escorted the goddesses to Paris so that he can decide which is the most beautiful. Bribed by all three goddesses, Paris chose Aphrodite because she had promised him the love of the world's most beautiful woman, Helen. The Trojan War would be precipitated by Paris's abduction of Helen; thus this Judgment is considered to be its cause.

The colorful dress, white female skin, and golden highlights create an air of luxury and beauty typical of the so-called Kerch vases of the later fourth century B.C. These vessels represent a late stage of Attic red-figure vase-painting named after the city of Kerch, an ancient Greek colony in the Crimea where many examples have been found.

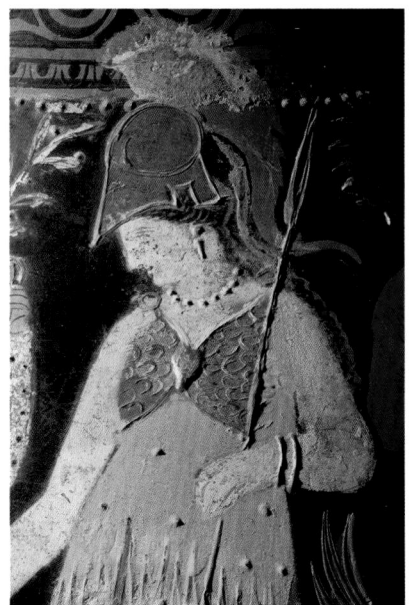

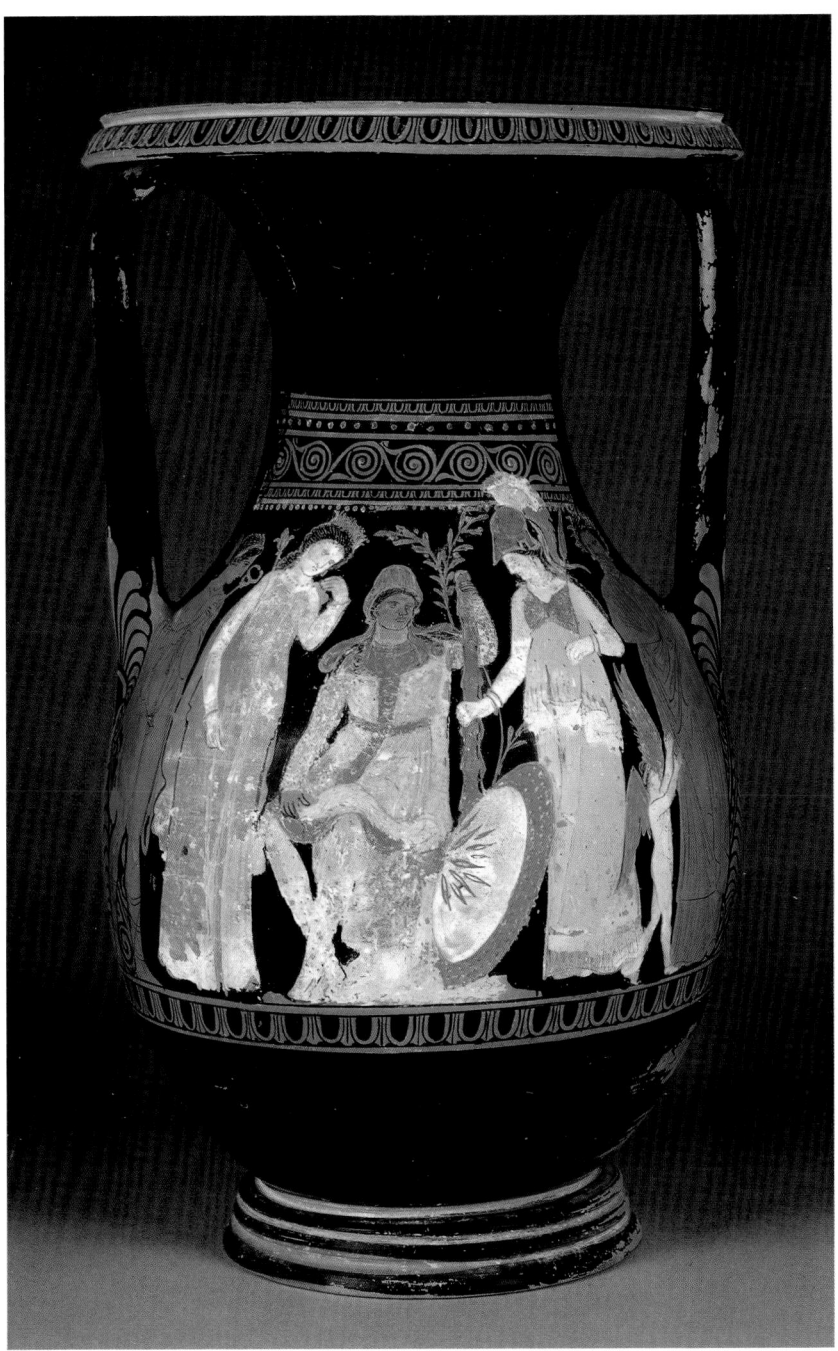

ATTIC PANATHENAIC PRIZE AMPHORA

Attributed to the Painter
of the Wedding Procession;
signed by Nikodemos
(as potter)
Greek, from Athens,
363–362 B.C.
Terracotta
H (with lid): 89.5 cm
(35¼ in.)
DIAM: 38.3 cm (15⅛ in.)
93.AE.55

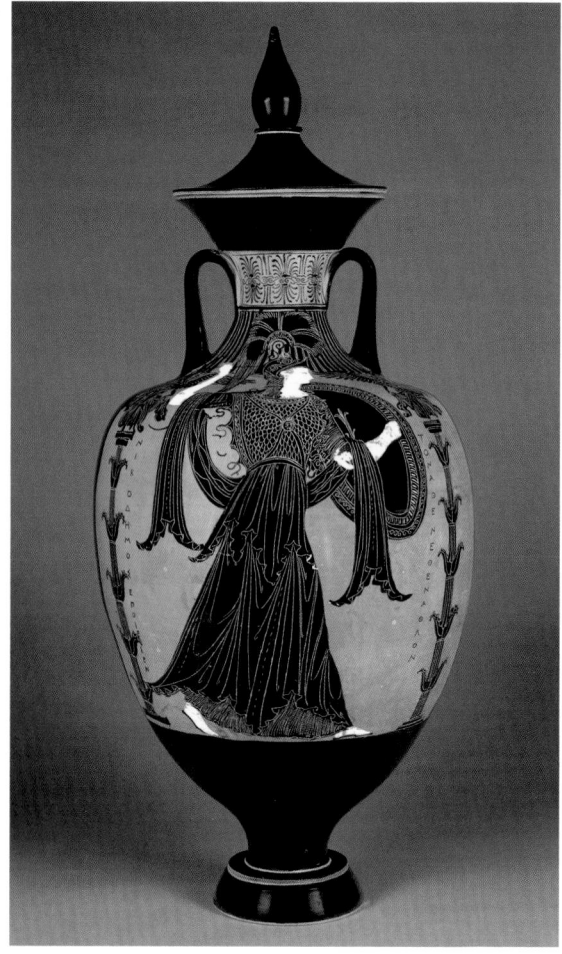

Every four years the Athenians celebrated the Great Panathenaia festival
held to honor Athena, goddess of war
and patron deity of Athens. The festi-
vities included a procession, sacrifices,
and games similar to those held to
honor Zeus at Olympia. The winners
of the athletic contests were rewarded
with olive oil in two-handled pottery
jars, the so-called Panathenaic
amphorae. The amount of oil awarded
to victors changed over time and
depended on the particular event, with
some victors taking home hundreds
or even thousands of liters of oil. Like
all other such amphorae, this one is
decorated with a representation of an
armed Athena, and identified as "from
the games at Athens" by an inscription
running along a column flanking the
goddess, here decorated with acanthus
leaves. The back of the vase, which
shows Nike, winged personification
of victory, crowning a victor, indicates
the sport: the long straps held by
the contestants were wrapped around
their hands and wrists to serve as
boxing gloves. The vase's imagery
is unusual in illustrating the victory
ceremony rather than the boxing
match itself.

This example, which was made to
hold more than 37 liters of oil, pro-
claims in Greek along the left column
on the front: "Nikodemos made (me)."
It can be dated to a specific Panathenaic festival by the figures of Nike that
crown the columns.

ATTIC PANATHENAIC PRIZE AMPHORA

Attributed to the Marsyas
Painter
Greek, from Athens,
340–339 B.C.
Terracotta
H (with lid): 99.5 cm
(39⅛ in.)
DIAM (body): 39.2 cm
(15⅜ in.)
79.AE.147

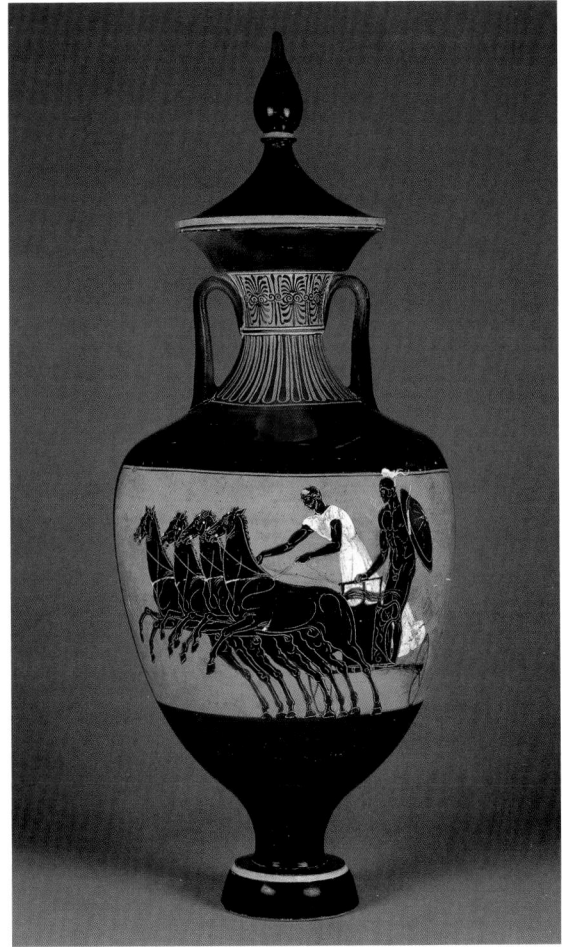

Like the preceeding vase, this amphora was made as a container for high-quality olive oil from Athens, to be awarded to one of the winners of the Panathenaic games. The goddess Athena is depicted on the front. The back (seen here) shows the contest for which it served as a prize. A charioteer wearing a long white garment stands in a chariot moving to the left; next to him is a nude man with a helmet and a shield. This is a scene from the race of the *apobates*, literally, "the dismounters": the warrior is about to leap from the chariot and continue running on foot. This contest also appears on the Parthenon frieze; it was held at few places other than Athens.

The inscription "Theophrastos was archon" on the front names the magistrate responsible for collecting the olive oil. Because that official was appointed annually, this amphora can be dated precisely to the year 340 or 339 B.C. With their highly conventional decoration, Panathenaic amphorae had over generations become specifically associated with the Athenian games. To underscore the venerable history of the Panathenaic tradition, Athena is deliberately rendered in an old-fashioned manner, wearing a garment with swaying, swallowtail folds that echo Archaic dress styles. Likewise, these prize amphorae were painted in black-figure long after the technique had otherwise gone out of fashion.

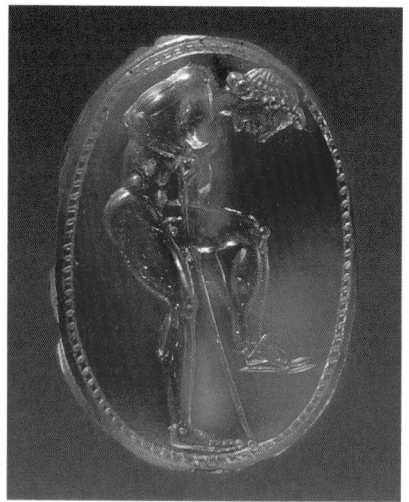
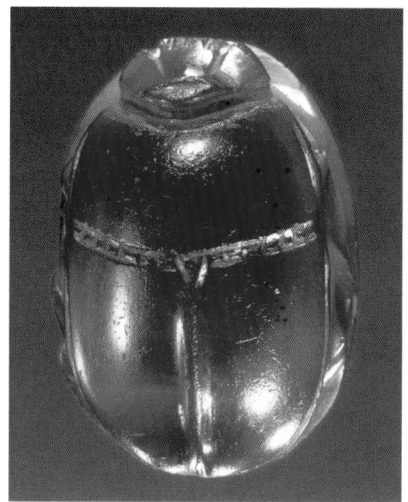

ENGRAVED SCARAB DEPICTING A YOUTH

Attributed to Epimenes
Greek, from the Cyclades,
circa 500 B.C.
Carnelian
H: 1.6 cm (⅝ in.)
W: 1.1 cm (⅜ in.)
D: .8 cm (⁵⁄₁₆ in.)
81.AN.76.22

Carved on the flat surface of this gem is a youth leaning forward to adjust the heel strap of his sandal while supporting himself on a staff. The precise identification of this figure is unclear: the youth may represent someone from mythology for whom sandals are meaningful, such as Theseus or Jason, or he may be a generic youth shown in an everyday activity. The figure's pose, standing but leaning over to engage in an activity, was a favorite for carved gems in the late 500s B.C. Yet the skill of the carver sets this gem apart. Epimenes (active around 500 B.C.; the scaraboid in the next entry is likewise attributed to him) has depicted a three-quarter view of the youth in which the musculature is carefully rendered in great detail.

In the mid-500s B.C., Greek gem carving changed dramatically in form, materials, and technique. The scarab, with its convex back carved like a beetle and its flat surface decorated with an intaglio scene, was introduced. The scarab form ultimately derives from Egypt, where it had been used for seals and amulets for centuries. Certain features of Greek scarabs, however, such as the form of the beetle and the hatching surrounding the intaglio motif, show the influence of Phoenician models, which the Greek gem carvers probably saw on Cyprus. Scarabs were pierced and generally worn as rings or pendants. When attached to a metal hoop and worn as a ring, the beetle side faced out and the intaglio surface rested against the finger. When serving as a seal, the ring was removed, the scarab could be swiveled, and the intaglio design was pressed into soft clay or wax placed on an object to identify its sender or owner and to secure it.

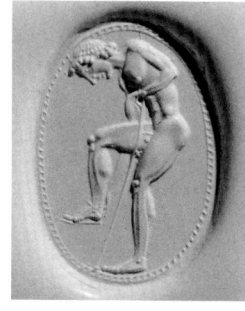

ENGRAVED SCARABOID DEPICTING A YOUTH

Attributed to Epimenes
Greek, from the Cyclades,
circa 500 B.C.
Obsidian
H: 1.62 cm (⅝ in.)
W: 1.29 cm (½ in.)
D: .7 cm (¼ in.)
85.AN.370.6

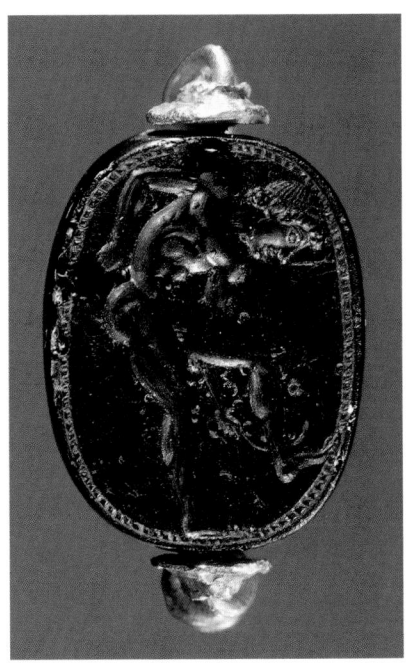

On this gem, a youth bends over to
scrape his shin with a curved blade
called a strigil. After training, Greek
athletes coated themselves with oil
and used a strigil to scrape off the
sweat, oil, and dirt. The pose of this
figure, bending over in an activity
quite similar to that seen on the scarab
in the previous entry, was a favorite
for carved gems in the late 500s B.C.,
in part because it fills the oval space
well. However, the difficult three-
quarter view of the youth, the rendering of the musculature, and details
such as the duck's head decorating the
end of the strigil display the unique
skills of the artist Epimenes. Epimenes
worked in the period about 500 B.C.
in the Cyclades, the group of islands in
the Aegean Sea between Greece and
Turkey that surround the island
of Delos. He carved both scarabs and
scaraboids in a distinctive manner,
often depicting nude youths with
the musculature clearly defined and
naturalistically rendered. The
scaraboid shape is a simplified scarab,
ultimately influenced by Egyptian
prototypes. While many oval gems
were carved on their reverse side to
resemble convex beetles, on this
gem the reverse is plain while the
flat side is decorated with an intaglio
design. In the 400s B.C., the scaraboid
form gradually replaced the scarab
in Greece. Scaraboid gems were
pierced, worn as rings or pendants,
and used in the same manner as
scarabs (see previous entry).

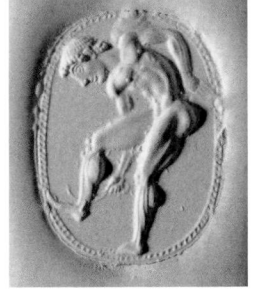

CAMEO OF
BERENIKE II

Greek, perhaps made
in Alexandria,
210–200 B.C.
Rhodolite garnet
H: 1.8 cm (¾ in.)
81.AN.76.59

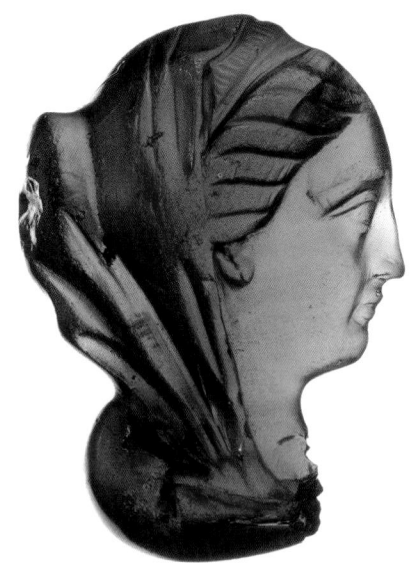

Carved in relief, this tiny but exquisite head and bust
of a veiled woman probably depicts Queen Berenike II,
wife of King Ptolemy III Euergetes, who ruled Egypt
from 246 to 221 B.C. She is shown with her hair rolled
in a bun and bound by a fillet. Berenike was powerful
and independent: ancient historians report that she
rebelled against her mother, who wished her to marry
a Macedonian prince. After her husband's death,
she became joint ruler with her eldest son, Ptolemy IV,
but was murdered by him soon after his ascension.

Garnet is harder than carnelian and most other
stones carved into intaglios in the Archaic and
Classical periods, and its use became common in the
Hellenistic period, when trade with Egypt and India
increased. Writing around 300 B.C. the Alexandrian
poet Theophrastos called garnets "virtually the most
valuable of stones." A relief (cameo) such as this
was probably meant to be mounted in a ring, but
unengraved cabochons were also inserted as accents
on vessels (see p. 93), diadems, earrings, and other
items of jewelry (see pp. 90–91, 204–5).

ENGRAVED GEM INSET INTO A HOLLOW RING

Greek, 100–1 B.C.
Carnelian and gold
H (gem): 2.2 cm (⅞ in.)
W (gem): 1.3 cm (½ in.)
D (gem): .3 cm (⅛ in.)
DIAM (hoop): 2.82 cm (1⅛ in.)
85.AN.124

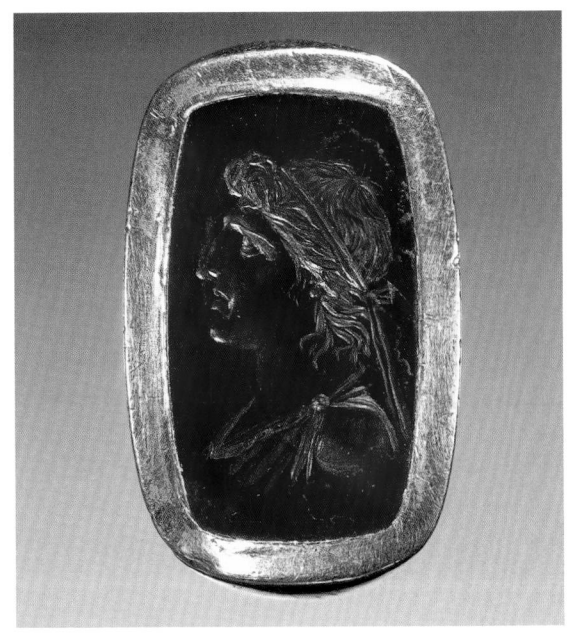

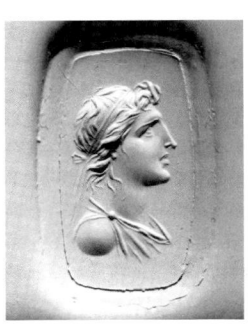

Engraved on the gem is the draped bust of a young man wearing a diadem. His long hair flows in a manner often ascribed to Alexander the Great; the diadem in his hair indicates his royal status, and the upward curl of the locks of hair on the forehead resembles Alexander's well-known *anastole.* It is possible that the charismatic young ruler is depicted here. According to Pliny the Elder (*Natural History* 7.37.125), Pyrgoteles was the only engraver whom Alexander would allow to carve his image into gems during his lifetime. Gem portraits like this were popular after Alexander's death in 323 B.C., however, and were used also by late Hellenistic rulers, most notably Mithridates VI (reigned 120–63 B.C.) and other Pontic kings. Mithridates VI formed a famous collection of gems, which was taken to Rome after his defeat at the hands of Pompey the Great (106–48 B.C.). The popularity of gems engraved with portrait busts continued into the Roman period.

GOLD RING

Greek, circa 350 B.C.
Gold
H (bezel): 2.23 cm (⅞ in.)
W (bezel): 1.76 cm (¾ in.)
DIAM (hoop): 2.07 cm (¾ in.)
85.AM.277

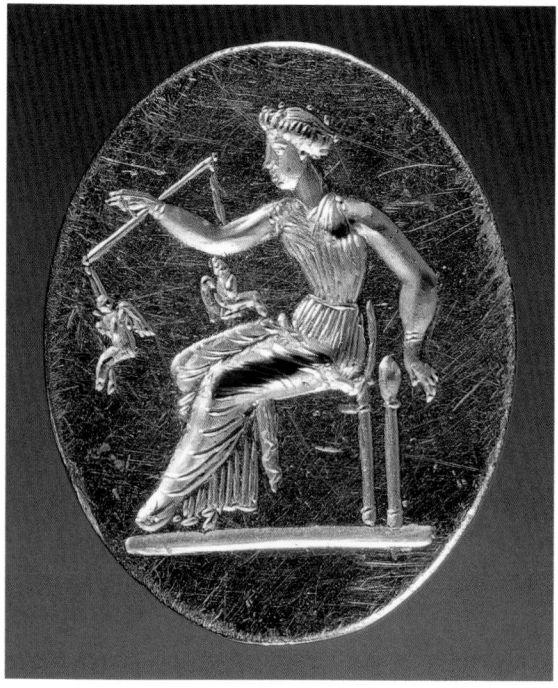

On the oval face of this gold ring, an elegantly clad woman sits on a stool, delicately balancing a scale with two erotes. This is the *erotostasia*, or weighing of love, which appears also on Athenian and South Italian vases. It was later copied by eighteenth-century Neoclassical painters, who specialized in scenes of love derived from the models of antiquity. Although the true meaning of the scene is unclear, it may symbolize some aspect of love related to the Homeric weighing of souls, the *psychostasia*. Because the only woman capable of judging weight in the realm of love is the goddess Aphrodite, her identity in this context seems certain.

PAIR OF DISK EARRINGS WITH NIKAI PENDANTS

Greek, 225–175 B.C.
Gold with glass beads
H (.1): 9.7 (3⅞ in.)
H (.2): 9.3 cm (3⅞ in.)
96.AM.159.1–.2

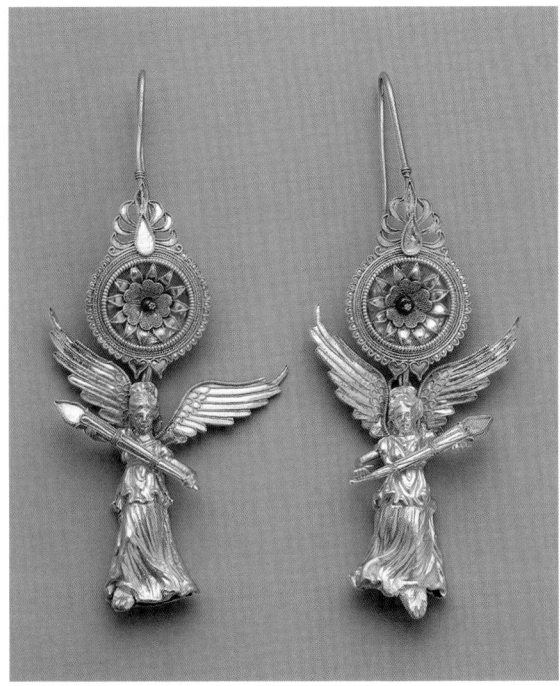

Tiny golden sculptures for the ears, these earrings with Nikai (plural for Nike, the goddess and personification of victory) are prime examples of the flamboyant taste for jewelry that is characteristic of the Hellenistic age. Erotes and Nikai were popular pendants for earrings because they would appear to be flying when suspended from the wearer's ear. Their billowing garments and slightly twisted torsos are reminiscent of the famous Nike of Samothrace and the Nike of Paionios from the Sanctuary of Zeus at Olympia, to which they are stylistically related. Like those monumental statues of Nike, these miniatures seem about to touch the ground, their drapery billowing in the wind. Their torches (a common attribute for Nike), and wings were added separately and are articulated by filigree. The feathers and flames were originally filled with colored enamel. The Nikai are suspended from elaborate disk rosettes punctuated by a petal-within-petal design constructed from dense granulation. The rosettes themselves dangle from flame-shaped palmettes, the hearts of which may have been inlaid with garnets or colored glass.

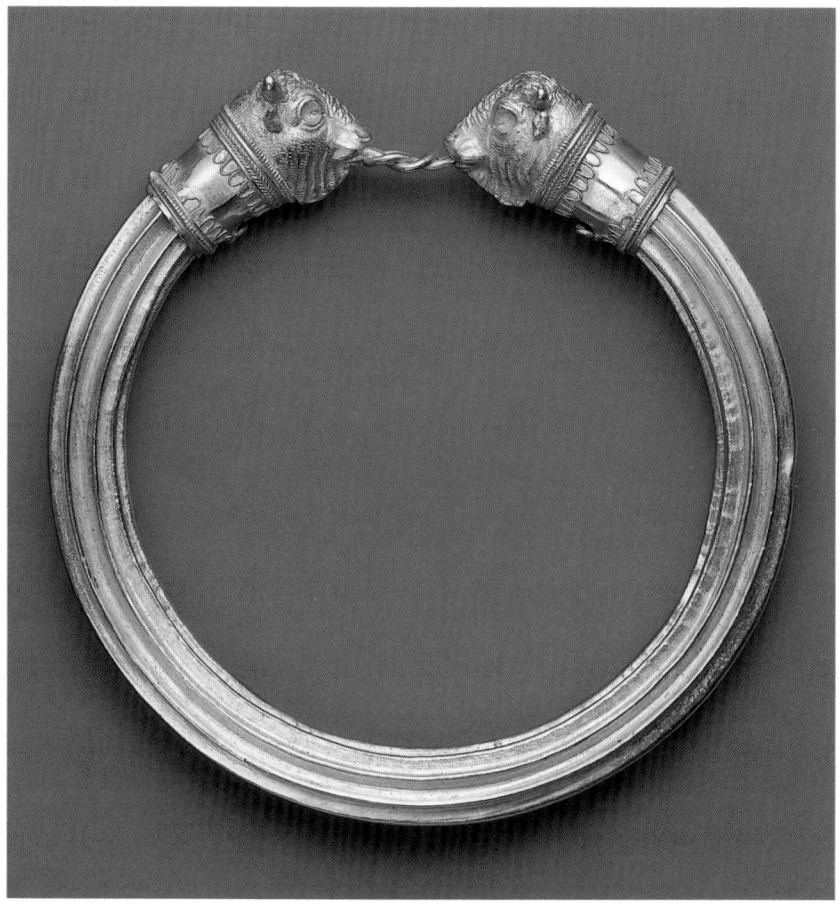

BRACELET WITH BULL'S-HEAD TERMINALS

Greek, 250–200 B.C.
Gold
DIAM: 8.5 cm (3³/₈ in.)
96.AM.158

The hoop of this solid-gold bracelet was made by fluting a sheet-gold tube and curving it to connect two bull's-head terminals with a gold Herakles knot. The Herakles knot was never intended to be loosened, as it was a magical knot with amuletic significance (see also the diadem in the ensemble of Ptolemaic jewelry on pp. 90–91), and this one cannot be detached from the bracelet. For this reason, as well as the ornament's ample diameter, this piece of jewelry may have been designed to be worn on the upper arm rather than on the wrist. The repoussé gold bull's heads were worked in fine detail from both the interior and exterior. The eyes were recessed to hold enamel filling, which has been lost. The tiny horns and ears were made separately and attached by soldering into small holes punched in the heads.

Despite its apparent visual simplicity, this bracelet contains more than one hundred separate items fashioned together. The assembly of many parts is typical of Hellenistic jewelry, distinguishing it from other styles of ancient ornament. The Greeks

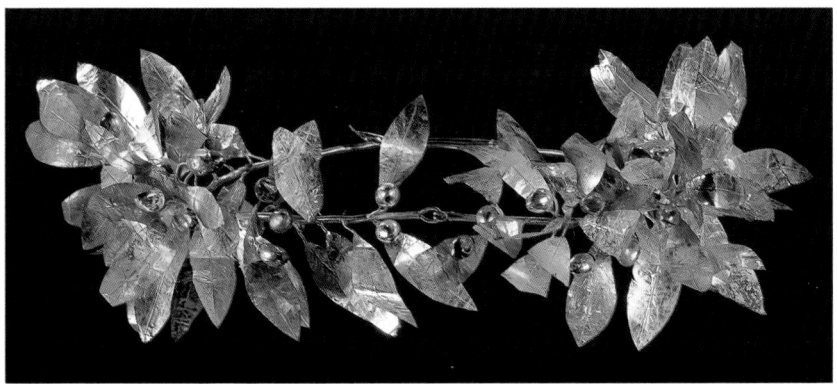

FUNERARY WREATH

Greek, 300–100 B.C.
Gold
DIAM: 21.7 cm (7½ in.)
92.AM.89

Ancient authors describe the various uses of wreaths, both those made from natural leaves as well as ones made from materials imitating nature. The gold laurel leaves comprising this wreath are specifically associated with the god Apollo. Laurel was his attribute, and laurel wreaths were awarded to victors at the athletic and musical contests held in his honor every four years at his sanctuary at Delphi. Wreaths were also presented as engagement gifts or gifts to war heroes, dedicated at temples, worn at banquets, and used as funerary offerings. The fragility of this wreath suggests that it was not worn frequently, although some similar pieces do bear signs of ancient wear and repair. Most such wreaths probably formed part of the grave contents of the wealthy.

borrowed from the Near East the popular fashion of wearing bracelets with animal- and bull's-head terminals; bracelets such as these can be seen on Assyrian reliefs and are one example of the influence on jewelry styles that resulted from eastern contact even before the campaigns of Alexander the Great (356–323 B.C.). Bull's-head terminals, however, are somewhat rare. Generally symbolic of power, bulls were associated with Apis in Egypt and specifically connected to the realm of the god Dionysos in Greece, where they were considered the most prestigious form of sacrifice.

ENSEMBLE OF PTOLEMAIC JEWELRY

Greek, possibly from Alexandria, 220–100 B.C.
Gold with various inlaid and attached stones, including garnet, carnelian, pearl, and glass paste
92.AM.8.1–.11

This spectacular collection of gold jewelry was likely the prized possession of a woman of high social rank. Signs of ancient repair show that the jewelry had been worn and was therefore not made specifically as a funerary offering. The style and iconography of the pieces indicate that they were probably made by goldsmiths in Alexandria, Egypt, during the reign of the Ptolemies, the rulers of Egypt descended from Ptolemy I Soter, one of the Macedonian generals of Alexander the Great. The imagery conveys the importance of magic and ritual at the Ptolemaic court.

The group's centerpieces are a hairnet (upper left) and a diadem (center right). On the hairnet, one of the few surviving from antiquity, a central medallion displays an image of Aphrodite, goddess of love, with a tiny Eros tugging at her neck. The Ptolemaic queens often presented themselves as descendants of Aphrodite; here the goddess's features and hairstyle are similar to those of Queen Arsinoë II. At the front of the diadem, a magical Herakles knot (once inlaid with garnets or red glass) marks the hinge. A torch motif, with flames made of twisted ribbons of gold wire, adorns the diadem's sides. The torches may refer to Nike, Greek goddess of victory (see the earrings on p. 87), or to Eros, for whom they symbolize passion. Erotes appear also on the disk earrings that are part of this ensemble (below the hairnet).

Wearing arm ornaments like the ones here, which are fashioned in the shape of snakes, was not an Egyptian custom; rather, it was a trend that Ptolemaic women brought to Egypt from Greece. Cobras, in particular, indicated power over death. When worn on the arms, a snake motif was intended to communicate a magical control over life and fertility.

The style of the massive gold and carnelian rings is particularly characteristic of Hellenistic Egypt. One shows Artemis, goddess of the hunt, while the other depicts the figure of Tyche, goddess of good fortune. Tyche's identifying attribute, the cornucopia, symbolizes her function as a provider of abundance, fertility, and wealth. On this gem, Tyche holds a double cornucopia, a symbol created specifically for Queen Arsinoë II by her husband and brother, Ptolemy II. The scepter Tyche holds is also significant, for it was widely used on coinage of the Ptolemies to indicate the divine status of the dynasty.

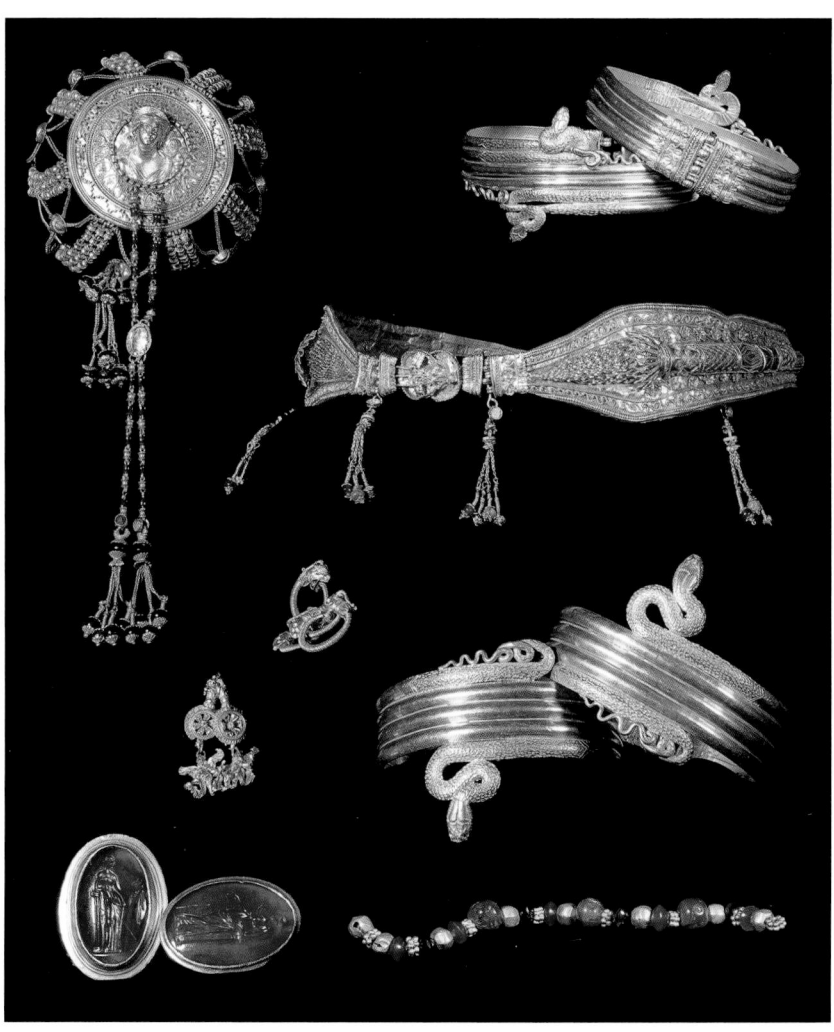

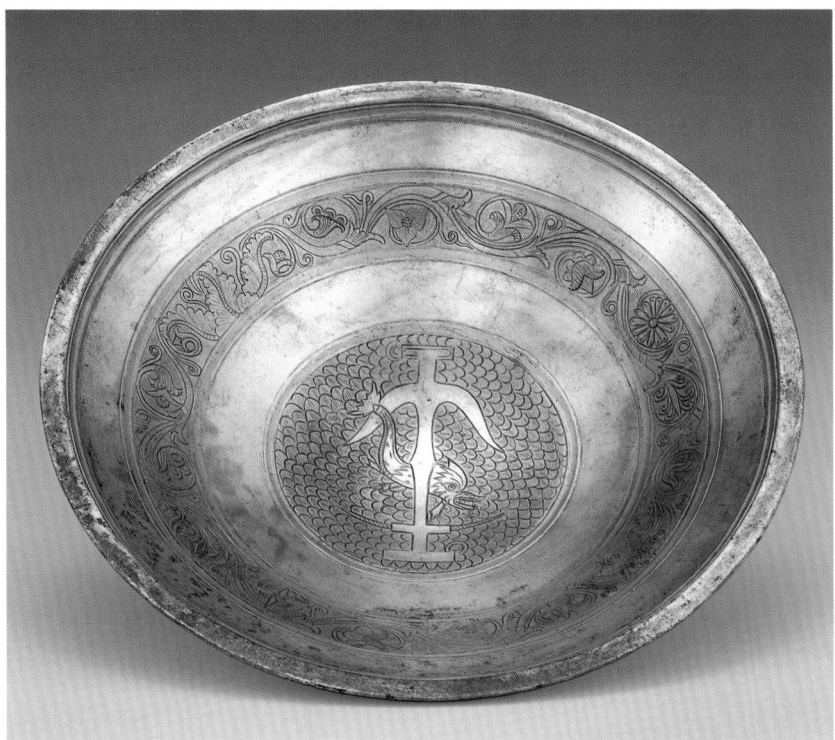

BOWL WITH ANCHOR AND DOLPHIN MEDALLION

Parthian, 200–100 B.C.
Silver
H: 4.3 cm (1⅝ in.)
DIAM: 18.6 cm (7⅜ in.)
81.AM.84.1

This elegant silver bowl is one of a group of twenty-five that range in height from 2.9 to 8.4 cm (1⅛ to 3⅝ in.) and together offer evidence for the kinds of luxury objects produced in the Parthian Empire. In about 238 B.C., the Parni, a nomadic or seminomadic people later known as the Parthians, took control of the area from eastern Turkey and Syria to the border of India. Their cultural influences were derived from both the Achaemenid (Persian) and Hellenistic Greek traditions.

The silver bowls that make up this treasure are for the most part the widely distributed calotte type, a hemispherical shape with no foot that resembles earlier Achaemenid bowls. Only the interiors are decorated, usually with a small ornamental motif in the center framed by decorative friezes. The inverted anchor on this bowl is found also on coins minted by Seleucus (358–281 B.C.), Alexander the Great's general, who had previously ruled this territory.

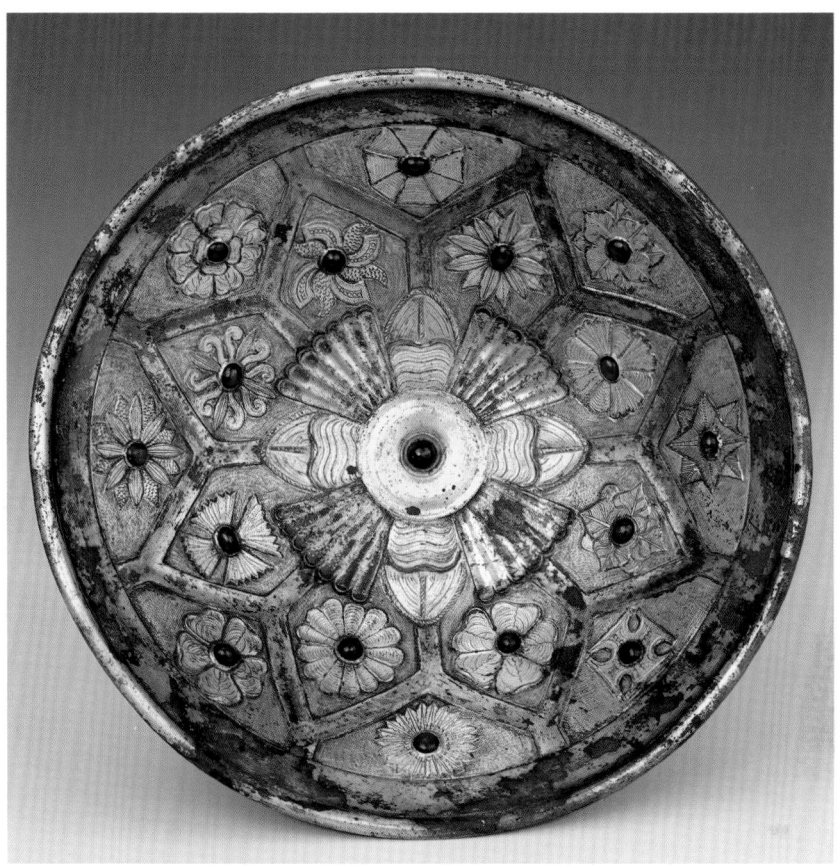

NET-PATTERN BOWL

Parthian, 100–1 B.C.
Gilt silver with garnets
H: 5.1 cm (2 in.)
DIAM: 20 cm (7⅞ in.)
86.AM.752.3

Since the time of Alexander the Great's conquest of parts of the Near East and India in the fourth century B.C., the Greek world had become increasingly familiar with and fond of exotic materials and ornate patterning. This bowl is a rare and beautiful example of the type of elaborately decorated vessel that an affluent collector of the first century B.C. would obtain to enrich his set of table silver.

The net pattern decorating the bowl's interior is composed of fourteen staggered pentagons, a design typically seen in Hellenistic Greek pieces. Within each pentagon, a different type of gilt flower is inset with a garnet. In the center of the bowl, a single garnet forms the heart of a floral calyx. Although the floral calyx motif was often incorporated into Near Eastern pieces, its use in Greek work is quite rare and adds to the bowl's value.

HANDLE OF
AN OINOCHOE

Greek, 100–50 B.C.
Gilt silver
L: 27 cm (10⅝ in.)
W: 9.5 cm (3¾ in.)
85.AM.163

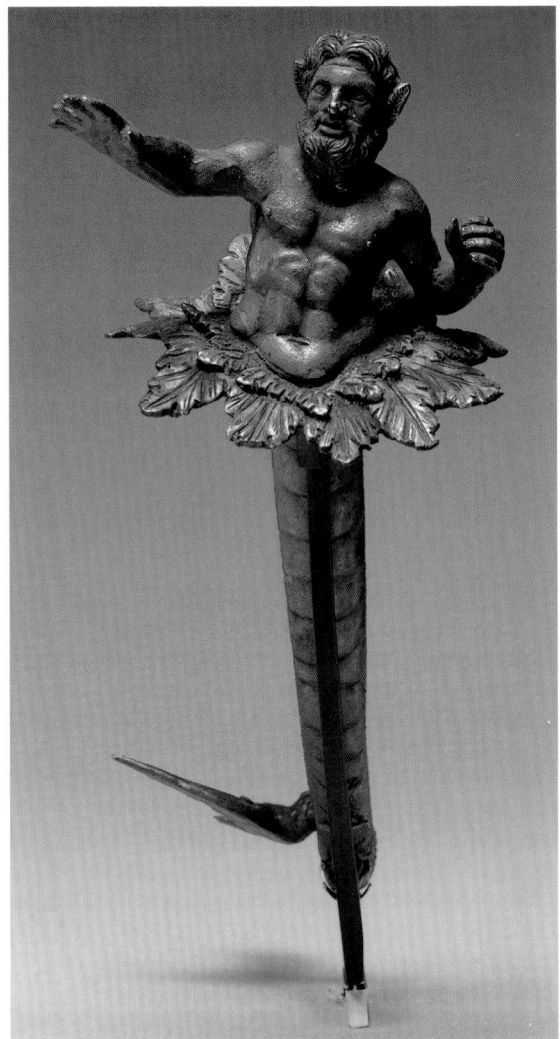

Elegantly modeled in silver, this figure represents a triton, a mythological hybrid of a human and a sea serpent. Originally, this triton served as the handle of a silver or gold oinochoe, or pouring vessel; as a deity of the sea, his powers were well suited to protecting a container's precious liquid contents. The figure reaches out with his right hand in a dramatic gesture; his other hand presumably once held a trident. This creature's large eyes, swirling shaggy beard and hair, and horselike ears all recall his untamed nature.

As is typical in much fine Greek metalwork, the unusual aspects of the subject are used to great advantage in the design. While the tail itself arcs to serve as the handle, its end is delicately curled and distracts the viewer from its practical function as an attachment to the body of the oinochoe.

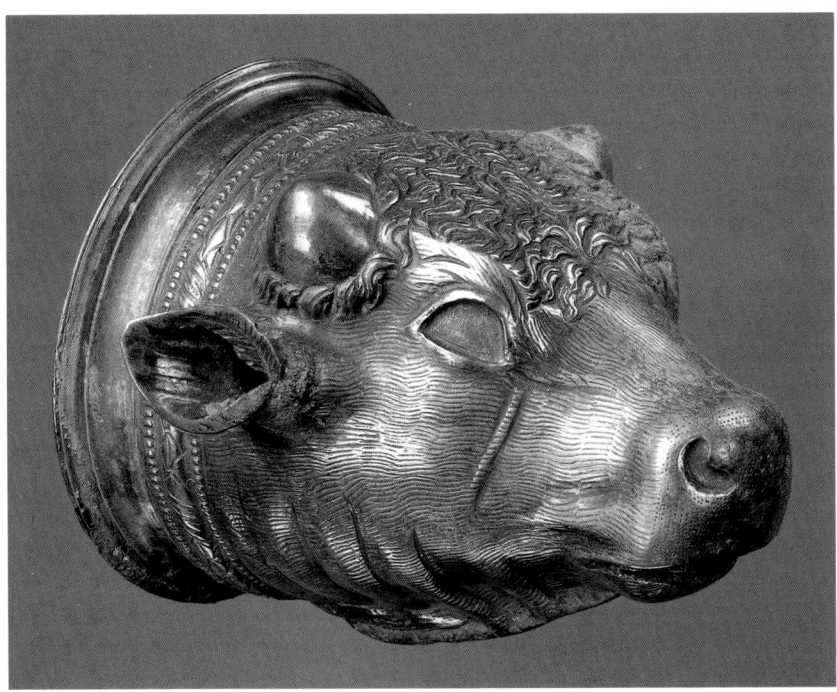

Bull's-Head Cup

East Greek,
100 B.C.–A.D. 100
Gilt silver
H (head): 12.1 cm (4¾ in.)
W (head): 9.1 cm (3⅝ in.)
DIAM (head): 7.8 cm (3⅛ in.)
H (bowl): 5.9 cm (2⅜ in.)
DIAM (bowl): 9.5 cm (3¾ in.)
87.AM.58

This unique Hellenistic drinking cup in the form of a bull's head is a superb example of the type of luxurious metalwork created for religious occasions. Small budding horns and vigorous curls with a prominent whorl of fur on the forehead indicate the young age of this calf. The horns, mouth, garland, and tear ducts are gilt, adding opulence to the piece and suggesting that it represents a sacrificial animal. The cup itself may have been used for drinking ceremonial wine or for pouring libations to the gods when a bull was sacrificed. The cup was hammered into a mold from a single sheet of silver. Naturalistically rendered with repoussé designs and stamped details, the calf has ears, which were made separately and inserted, and wide-open eyes, which were once inlaid with glass paste to give a lively expression.

A Greek inscription on the rim of the cup gives the weight of the piece as 67 drachmas. This indicates that one practical measure of the cup's value was the weight of the bullion, 276.71 grams.

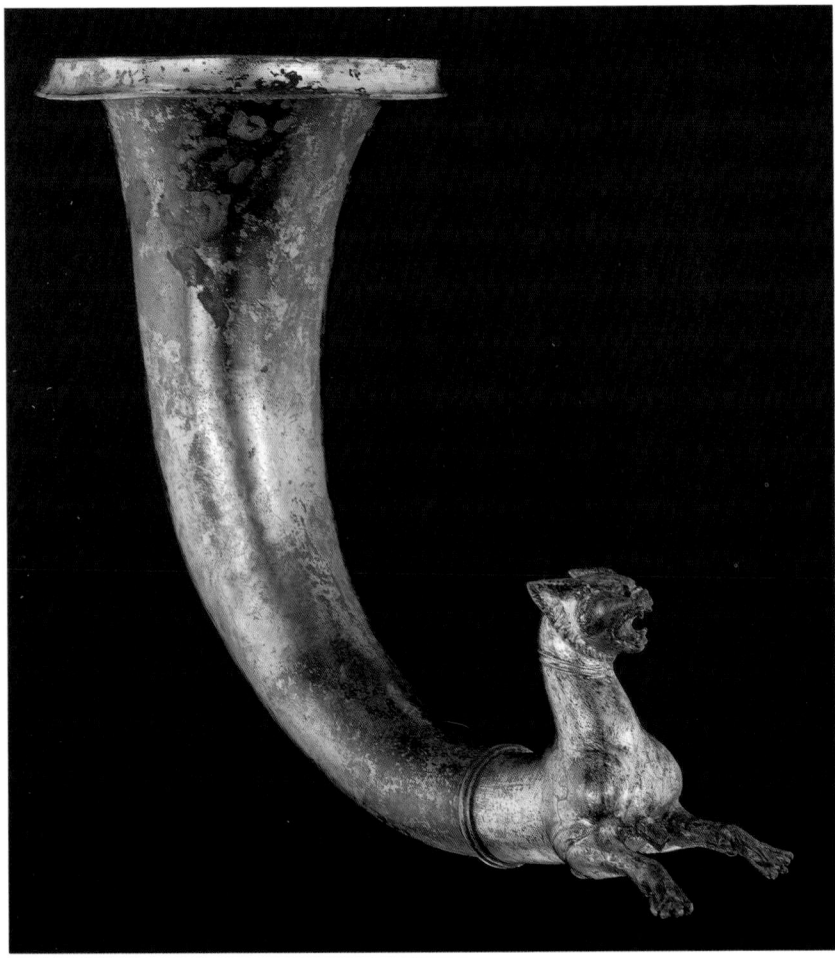

Lynx Rhyton

Parthian, 50–1 B.C.
Gilt silver
H: 24.5 cm (9⅝ in.)
L: 41.9 cm (16½ in.)
DIAM (rim): 12.2 cm (4¾ in.)
86.AM.752.1

This elegantly shaped rhyton (pl. rhyta), or drinking horn, terminates in the protome of a snarling lynx. It is one of a pair that are so close in style they must have been made as a set. Each animal is dynamically represented with outstretched paws, open mouth, bared teeth, and laid-back ears, all of which ferociously emphasizes its wild nature. Rhyta, which often take the shape of human or animal protomes (as here), could also be made of horn or terracotta, and were used to pour wine into a cup or directly into the drinker's mouth, in this case through a spout between the forelegs of the lynx. The vessels are raised from single sheets of silver with only the legs of the animal cast separately. Dotted inscriptions in Aramaic on the rim of each rhyton provide the (indecipherable) name of the silversmith who made them. Also incised on the lip is *zwzyn*, a unit of weight corresponding most likely to the Parthian drachma; the inscription indicates the amount of silver used to produce the vessel.

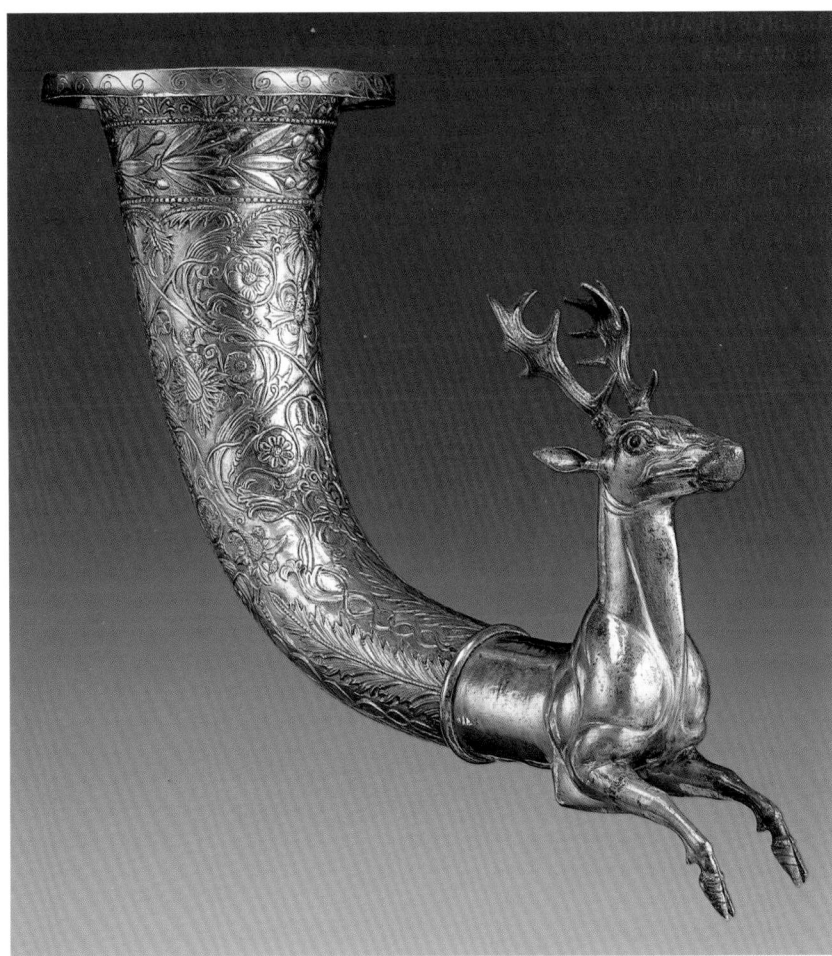

STAG RHYTON

Eastern Mediterranean,
50 B.C.–A.D. 50
Gilt silver, garnet, glass
H: 27.4 cm (10 3/4 in.)
L: 46 cm (18 1/8 in.)
DIAM (rim): 12.6 cm (5 in.)
86.AM.753

The horn of this gilt-silver rhyton is elegantly
decorated with floral patterns and ends in the protome
of a stag. The artist captures the animal's natural
grace and power by carefully rendering its taut
muscles, its protruding veins, and the gentle sweep of
its antlers and legs. The spirited nature and alertness
associated with a stag are expressed in the wide-open
eyes, which are inlaid with glass paste and black
stones, and the way the animal holds his head upright.

A spout, now lost, was once attached to the hole
between the stag's legs. Wine could be poured through
the spout into a drinking cup or directly into the
mouth of the drinker. An inscription in finely dotted
Aramaic letters (possibly Persian) is on the belly of
the animal.

DOUBLE-HEADED ARYBALLOS

East Greek, from Rhodes,
circa 550 B.C.
Faience
H: 5.6 cm (2¼ in.)
DIAM: 6 cm (2⅜ in.)
91.AI.25

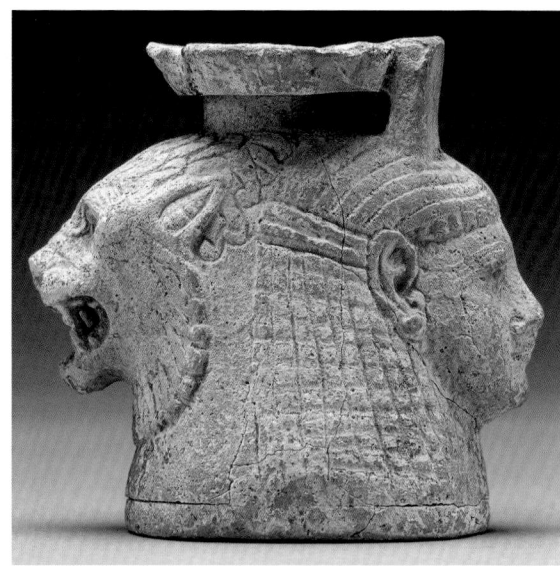

Two heads placed back-to-back form this delicate aryballos, a vessel used to hold perfumed oil. One head is that of a woman, the other a snarling lion. The style of the piece indicates that it was most likely made on the island of Rhodes. Because of its location linking the Aegean with the greater Mediterranean, Rhodes was a crossroads for commercial travelers. The so-called East Greek style prevalent in this region shows the influence of a variety of artistic sources: Egypt, the Mesopotamian kingdoms, and Greece. The woman's head, in particular, shows a strong influence from Egyptian art, especially in the treatment of her hair as a solid mass, parted at the center of the head. Incised lines emphasize strands of hair, and the "checkerboard" pattern of the lower locks may be an indication that she wears a wig. The style of the lion, with its incised, flamelike locks and laid-back ears, is closer to the arts of the eastern Mediterranean.

The aryballos is made of a composite material known as faience, which consists primarily of crushed quartz or some other silicate material. This is combined with lime and the mineral natron and mixed with water to form a claylike paste that can be pressed into a mold or thrown on a wheel. Once the piece is formed, it is allowed to air-dry prior to firing. Faience was a material used for centuries, primarily in Egypt but also in Mesopotamia and later in Greece.

The body of this aryballos was constructed by pressing the damp faience into a mold. The mouth and handle were added after the body was removed from the mold, and finer details were incised into the faience before firing. This method of combining separately made pieces is a typical technique used to construct objects made of faience.

OINOCHOE DEPICTING BERENIKE II

Greek, from Alexandria,
Egypt, 243–221 B.C.
Faience
H: 22.2 cm (8 ¾ in.)
DIAM: 14 cm (5 ½ in.)
96.AI.58

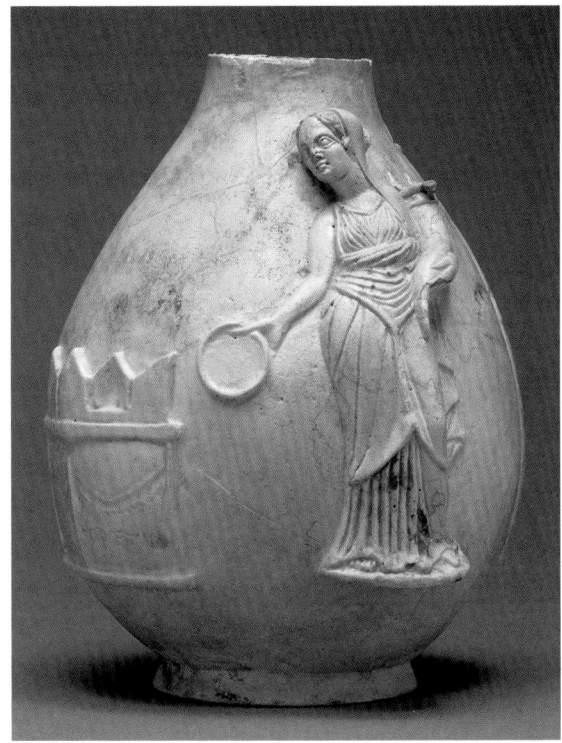

Despite the loss of its trefoil mouth and handle, this faience wine jar is a fine example of a class of vessels that demonstrates the fusion of cultures that occurred in Egypt under the rule of Alexander the Great's successors, the Ptolemies (323–30 B.C.). The shape of the vase is Greek, but the material is Egyptian—faience, a blend of ground quartz and natron, with copper oxide added to provide the light blue color.

Standing between an altar and a tall pillar is a female figure, elegantly swathed in a chiton and himation, with a veil covering the back of her head. A channel in her hair above the forehead may once have been gilded, in order to depict a golden headband. Supporting a cornucopia that contains grain and grapes, she pours a libation from the phiale in her right hand. An inscription on the shoulder of the vase reads "for the good fortune of Queen Berenike," and the identity of the woman on this vase as Berenike II (273–221 B.C.) can be supported by comparable portraits on coins and elsewhere (see p. 84) and by the inscription on the altar, "of the bene-factor gods." This is a reference to the epithet that her husband, Ptolemy III (reigned 246–221 B.C.), received on returning successfully from his campaign in Asia in 243 B.C.

Faience oinochoai with this type of relief decoration, called Queen's vases, were probably used for the pouring of libations at a royal cult festival. The practice was first introduced for Berenike II's predecessor, Arsinoë II (316–270 B.C.). See also pages 90–91.

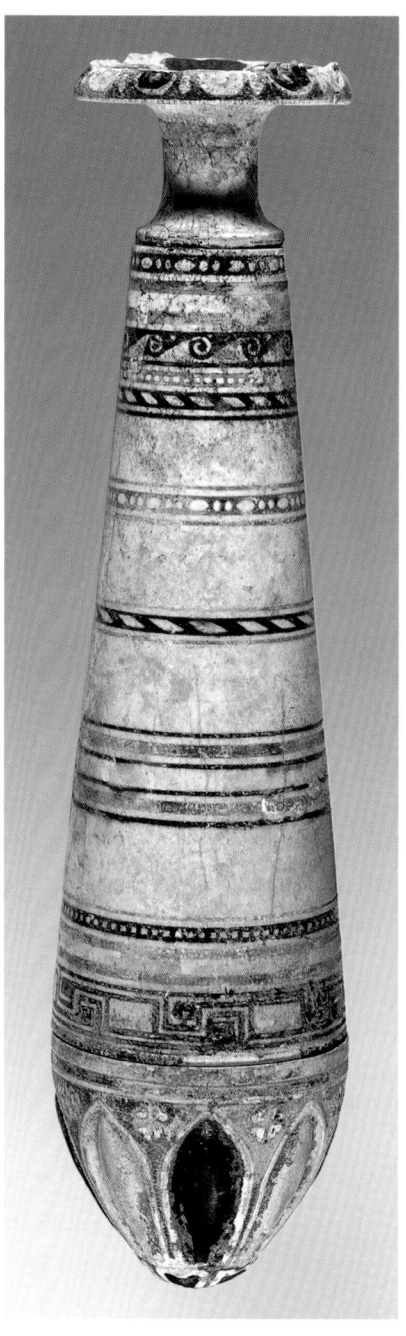

ALABASTRON

Eastern Mediterranean,
200–100 B.C.
Faience
H: 23 cm (9 in.)
DIAM: 5.5 cm (2½ in.)
88.AI.135

The name given to this shape of vessel, alabastron, originates from objects of the same shape made first in Egypt using precious alabaster. An alabastron contained perfumed oil, and the flat rim may have aided in the application of oil to the skin. This alabastron is made of faience (see p. 98) and was made in three parts: the base, the body, and the neck and rim. These parts were formed in separate molds and then attached to one another before firing.

Various ornamental patterns decorate all parts of the alabastron. Rosettes line the edge of the rim and petals descend down the throat. The rim's base color is blue, and the rosettes are alternately yellow and brown with white edges. The shaft of the body contains eight brown or blue ornamental patterns intermixed with solid bands of blue, all set on a white ground perhaps meant to imitate more costly alabaster or ivory. The base is decorated with a rosette from which petals ascend. The patterns help to date the vessel to the second century B.C.

APPLIQUÉ DEPICTING THE HEAD OF PAN

Greek, circa 100 B.C.
Ivory
H: 8.6 cm (3⅜ in.)
W: 6.9 cm (2¾ in.)
87.AI.18

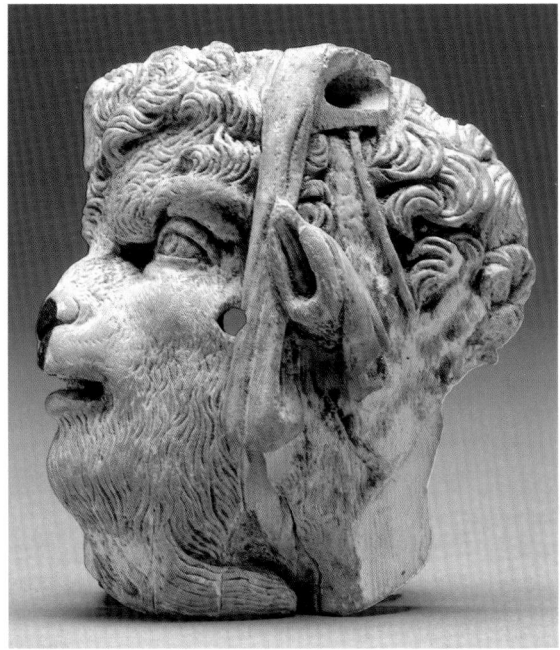

This small disk is carved in low relief with the head of the god Pan. A woodland god native to the region of Arcadia in Greece, Pan is associated with fertility, particularly the fecundity of animal herds. He is half-human and half-goat in appearance. In myth, he often joins the wine god Dionysos in his drunken escapades. Pan accompanies the revelry by playing music on his syrinx (panpipes).

The animal qualities of the god are evident in this relief profile portrait. Here, Pan is nearly all goat, with a flattened nose, facial hair and goatee tucked under his chin, and curling locks that resemble a fleece on top of his head. His alert ear is also goat-like and follows the direction of his piercing gaze. The god's mouth is slightly open and a row of small, short teeth are visible below his upper lip. In his hair he wears a flat ribbon, or fillet, an item associated with revelry. The ribbon's knot is missing, and one loose end hangs in front of his ear. His profile goat's horn is also missing, but a hole carved at the top of the head behind the flap of the fillet's loose end indicates its placement; it was probably carved from a separate piece of ivory and attached with a pin or adhesive. The hole in the god's cheek-bone indicates that the relief roundel was once attached to another object, perhaps a piece of furniture. The circular shape of the appliqué suggests that it may have been an inlay used to decorate the fulcrum (armrest) of a banqueting couch. Ancient literary sources describe luxurious couches that were inlaid with ivory and other precious materials. The ivory used for this piece came from an elephant's tusk; ivory from both African and Indian elephants was imported into the ancient Mediterranean at this time.

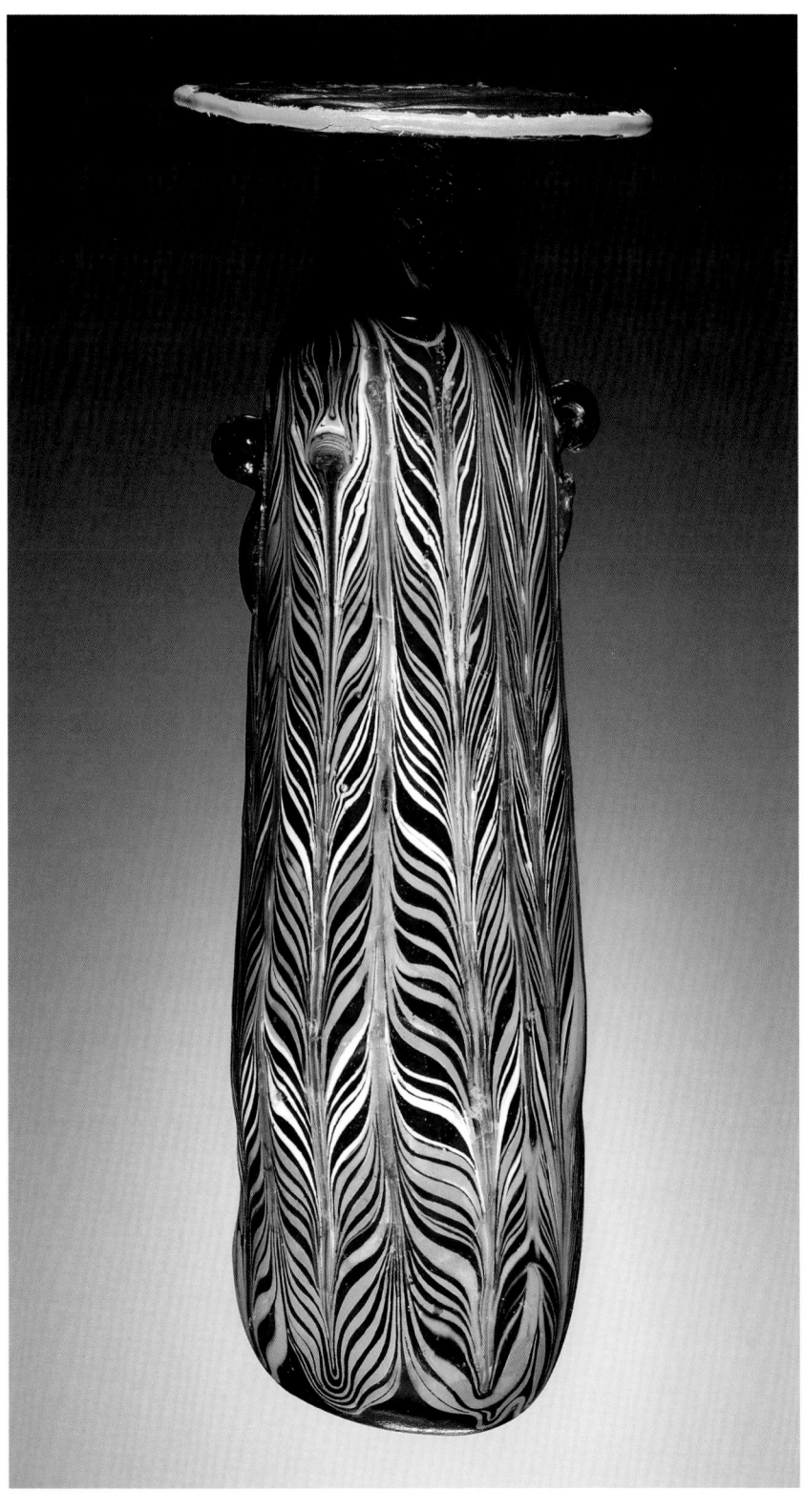

CORE-FORMED ALABASTRON

Greek, 400–200 B.C.
Glass
H: 16.5 cm (6½ in.)
2003.193

Elongated glass vessels such as this one were used to hold perfume, much like their counterparts in clay, stone, faience, and metal. This alabastron was constructed by encasing a dried core of some composite material, probably clay or dung, in a dark blue glass. Additional trails of white, yellow, and turquoise glass were wound around the vessel's body and then dragged with a pointed tool to create a featherlike pattern. The pinched neck and flattened rim were formed by pincers; the tool's marks can still be seen. Small handles were added onto the shoulder as a means of attaching a leather cord or bronze chain used to suspend the vessel.

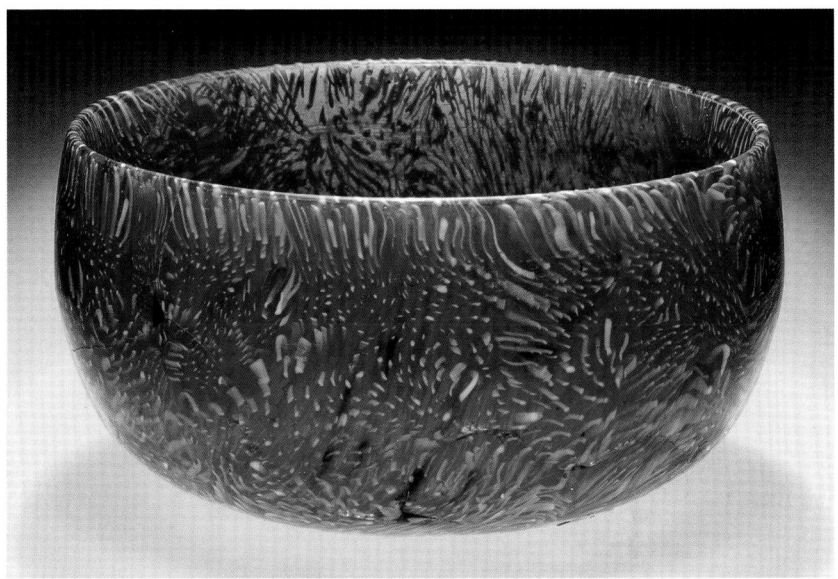

BLUE AND WHITE HEMISPHERICAL MOSAIC BOWL

Greek or Roman, 100–1 B.C.
Glass
H: 5.2 cm (2 in.)
DIAM: 10.2 cm (4 in.)
2004.24

A spectacular example of late Hellenistic or early Roman mosaic glass, this bowl was constructed from segments of a blue cane (rod) with a central white dot. When reheating the cane segments over a hemispherical mold in the glass kiln, the glassmaker allowed the glass to heat up enough to allow the white dot to run slightly, creating a vessel that almost resembles white sea anemones moving under Mediterranean blue water.

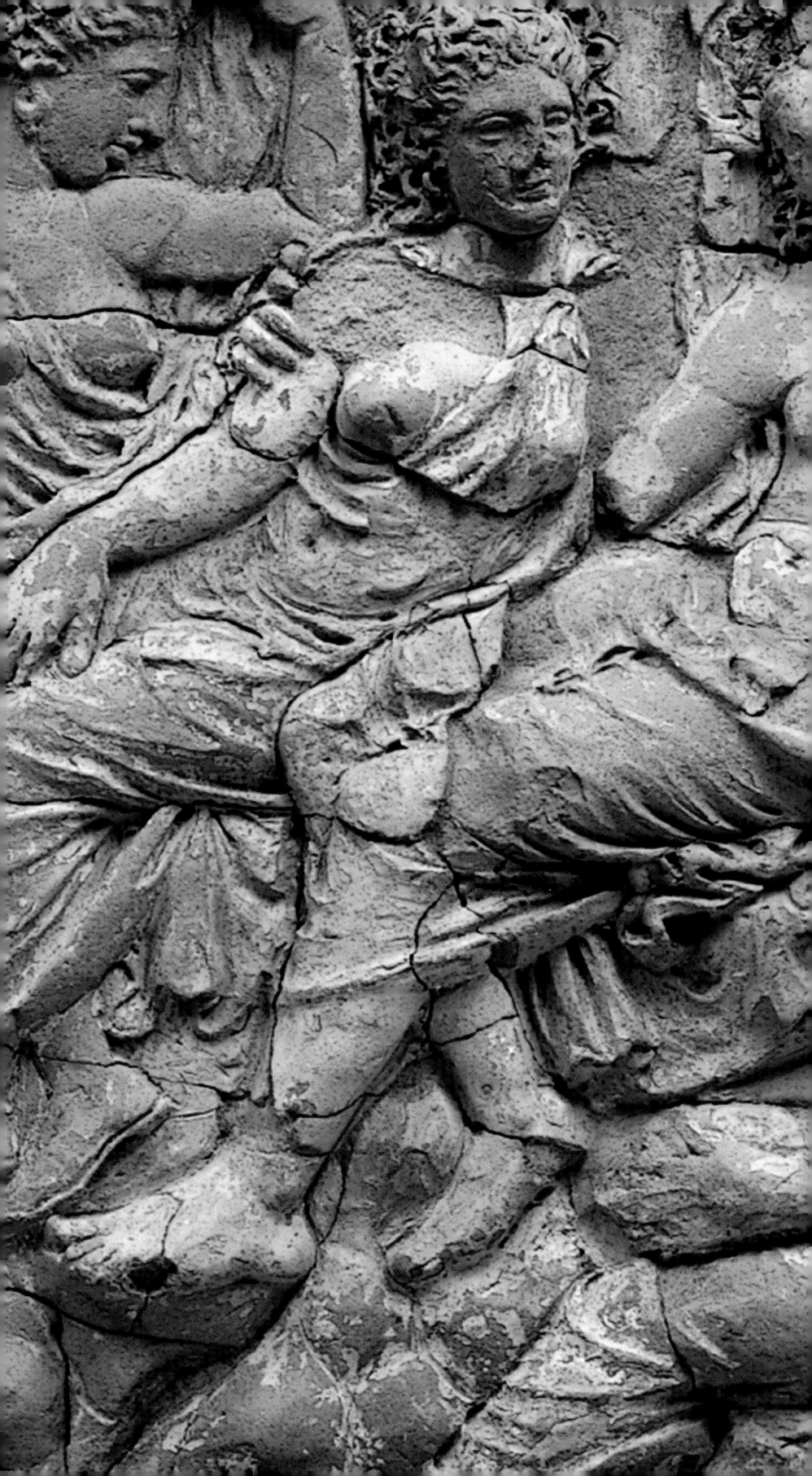

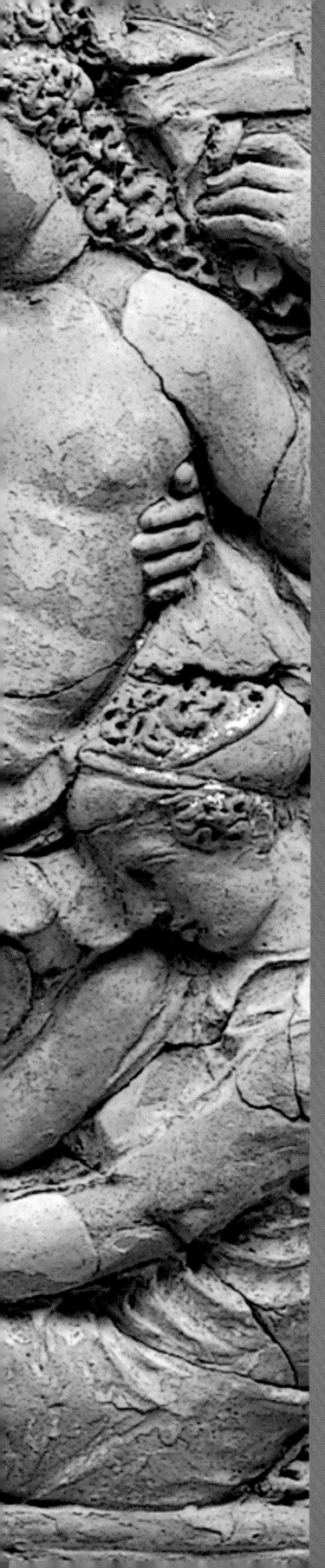

South Italian

FRAGMENT OF A RELIEF OF A HORSEMAN AND COMPANION

Greek, from Taras,
South Italy, 290–250 B.C.
Limestone with polychromy
H: 37.5 cm (14¾ in.)
W: 34 cm (13⅜ in.)
D: 7 cm (2¾ in.)
74.AA.7

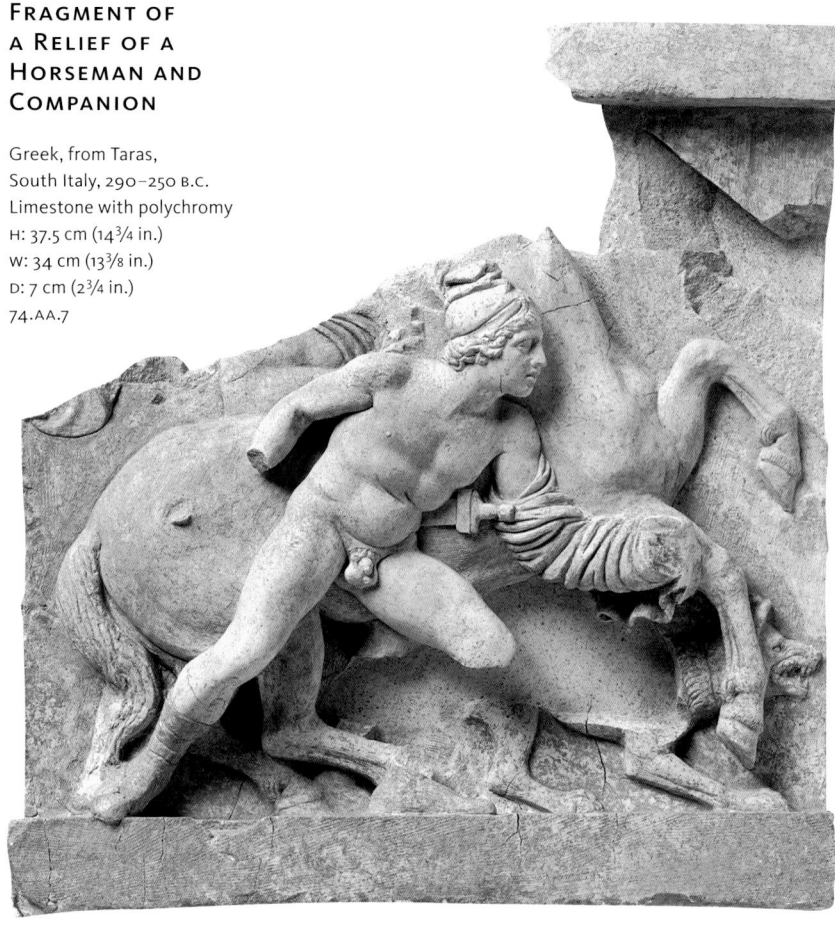

A cloaked horseman pulls back his rearing mount while his companion on foot, naked except for a soft peaked cap and a cloak wrapped around his left arm, leans forward to attack with a spear (now missing) in his right hand. Although only the chest and parts of the animated cloak of the horseman remain, they reveal his muscled physique, and two creases indicate that his torso turns at the waist. The man on foot is beardless with long, curly hair. He wears high boots and carries at his left side a sword suspended from a strap that was originally added in paint. From beneath the horse, a snarling dog menaces the unseen foe. The dog indicates that the opponent is actually prey and that this is a hunting scene.

At Taras, a Greek colony in South Italy, the dead were honored with small, ornate funerary monuments, often decorated with sculpture carved from soft local limestone. This fragment of relief sculpture probably comes from a funerary monument made in the shape of a small temple, and it was once part of a long frieze that ran across its front. The missing sections would have shown the hunter's quarry, probably a boar or a lion. When used on a funerary relief, the theme of hunting refers to the pleasures of the afterlife. Traces of preserved paint hint at the original vibrant appearance of the relief: red on the cloaks, the hilt of the sword, the horse, and the hunter's boots; brown on the dog; blue on the background.

Hand Mirror

Greek, from South Italy,
500–480 B.C.
Bronze
H: 20.2 cm (8 in.)
DIAM (disk): 15 cm (5⅞ in.)
96.AC.109

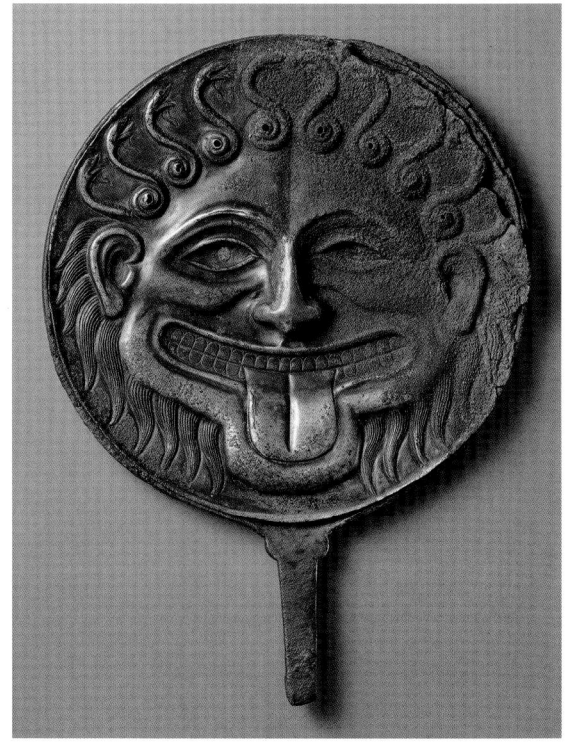

In antiquity, modest utilitarian objects, whether household or personal, were often treated by craftsmen with the same creative attention and skill as monumental art. The reflective side of this hand mirror was initially highly polished and protected by a raised beaded flange around it. The tondo itself is edged by a simple *kymation* pattern bordering two incised concentric circles. A support for the now-missing handle has an Aeolic capital with simple incised volutes. But it was the cover over the back of the disk (seen here) on which the artisan lavished attention. It is a separately made repoussé relief of the head of Medusa, the monstrous Gorgon whose face could turn anyone who gazed upon it into stone.

Because Medusa's head could unnerve and paralyze an enemy with fear, the Greeks deployed its image on everything from military armor and public architecture to household furnishings and personal amulets, believing that its apotropaic power would safeguard them from their adversaries and any potential threat. Thus, while the user was busy viewing his or her own reflection on the interior of the mirror, any onlooker would be confronted by the protective head of Medusa on the outside. Despite the typical Gorgon features—the locks of spiraling snakes capping her head, the wide, grinning mouth with its long rows of teeth, the protruding tongue, and the flamelike beard—this decorative Medusa lacks the fangs of most of her predecessors and seems more benign than sinister.

HEADPIECE FOR A HORSE

Greek, from South Italy,
circa 480 B.C.
Bronze; ivory and
amber inlays
H: 45 cm (17¾ in.)
W: 17.2 cm (6¾ in.)
83.AC.7.1

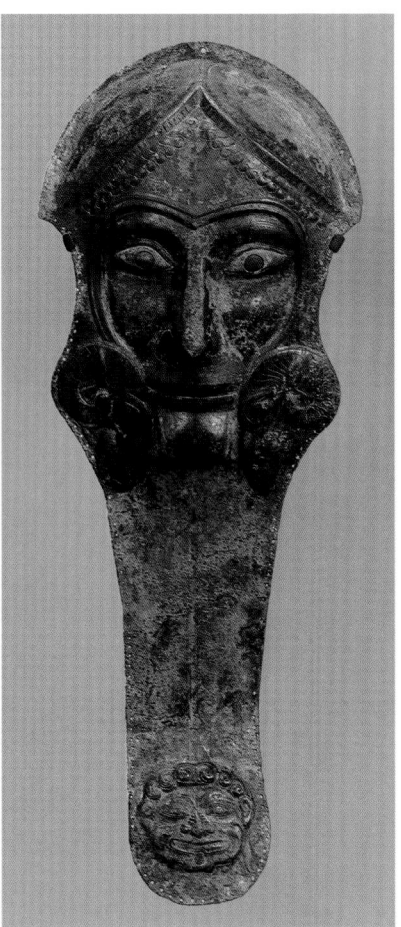

Although equine armor commonly
was used to protect the chest and
forehead of a horse in battle, the
precious amber and ivory materials
embellishing the decorative work
on this elaborately detailed headpiece
(*prometopidion*) distinguish it as
ceremonial armor. It is decorated at
the top with the face of a warrior,
symbolizing the armor's ability to
protect its wearer, and at the bottom
with the head of the Gorgon Medusa,
a symbolic device used to ward off
evil. The warrior wears a helmet
with ram's-head cheekpieces, which,
like most of the details of his face,
is delineated with elaborate incision;
his eyes are inlaid with ivory for
the whites and amber for the irises.

Two equine breastplates and a
second headpiece are associated with
this one. The breastplates are incised
with a frontal view of a quadriga, or
four-horse chariot, and flying figures
of Nike, goddess of victory, who carry
wreaths for the charioteer standing
in the chariot box. This motif suggests
that the trappings had perhaps been
made for a champion chariot team that
had brought glory to its owner.

HELMET

Greek, Apulo-Corinthian,
from South Italy,
400–375 B.C.
Bronze
H: 19.3 cm (7⅝ in.)
W: 22.5 cm (8⅞ in.)
92.AC.7.1

One of the numerous forms of military headgear used
throughout the Greek world, the so-called Corinthian
helmet covered almost the entire head and had
openings for only the eyes, nose, and mouth. When
not used in battle, it could be pushed up and worn on
top of the head like a cap. In Greek art, both warriors
and Athena Promachos (the goddess fighting in the
front line, or first in battle) are often shown wearing
the helmet that way (compare p. 78). Although the
Corinthian helmet eventually fell into disuse in
Greece, it survived in the Greek colonies in South
Italy where, in time, the openings in the face of
the helmet grew so small in size that they no longer
served any real function.

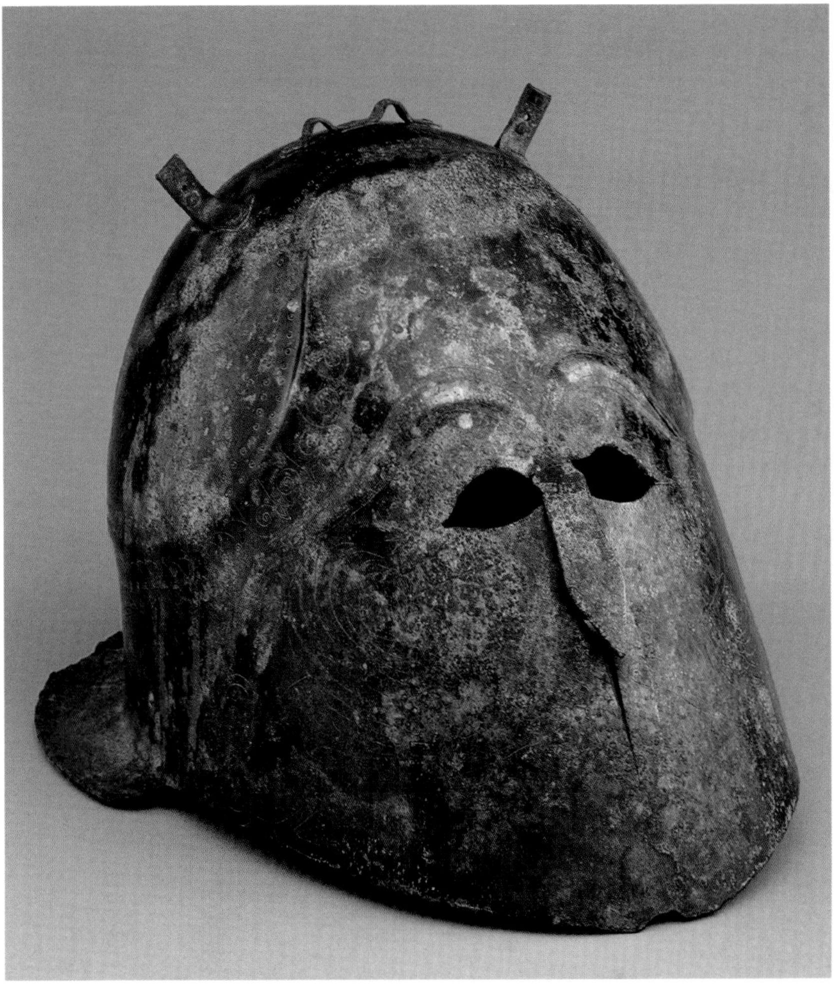

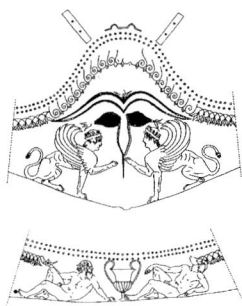

Drawings by Beverly Lazor-Bahr

As it evolved in Apulia and other parts of Italy, the Apulo-Corinthian helmet became a decorative piece of armor worn atop the head in the style of Athena herself and intended only for ceremonial purposes or as a dedication in the tomb.

This helmet is ornamented with incised patterns representing curling locks of hair across the forehead and, between the repoussé brows, a lotus bud. Chevrons border the nose and eyes, and seated heraldic sphinxes decorate the cheekpieces. The attachments on the crown originally held either horsehair crests or feathers. Two lounging satyrs are incised on the back.

HELMET OF CHALKIDIAN SHAPE

Greek, from South Italy,
350–300 B.C.
Bronze
H (without cheek flaps):
27.9 cm (11 in.)
W: 16.2 cm (6⅜ in.)
93.AC.27

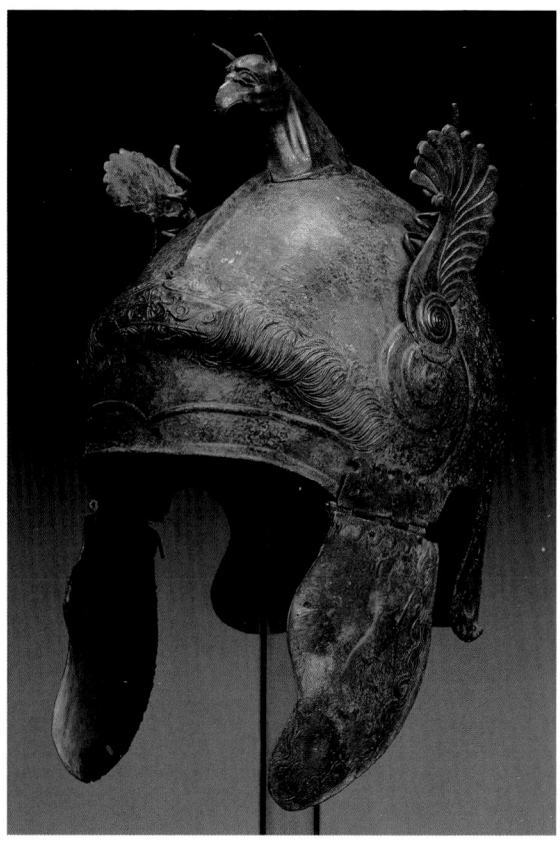

Like the Apulo-Corinthian helmet (see previous entry), this type of helmet derived from those originally developed in Corinth on the Greek mainland. It slid completely over the warrior's head, with openings for the eyes and mouth and a protective guard for the nose. In Chalkis, a city located on the island of Euboia that was well known for its metalwork, a significant improvement was made by opening up the areas over the ears, enabling warriors to hear what was going on around them. It was this variant—hinged cheekpieces but no protection for the nose—that came to be widely used throughout Italy and beyond. It remained a common part of the military panoply even in the time of the Roman Empire.

In relief on the front of this helmet, above the embossed lines mimicking eyebrows and as if set over the wearer's hair, there is a diadem with a central rosette and surrounding spiraling tendrils. Carefully arranged locks of hair curl up and over it from beneath. The cheekpieces are embellished with the side-whiskers of a beard, through which a quadruped climbs as if scrambling up a mountainside. Ornamental attachments include the protome of a griffin on the crest and stylized griffin wings concealing coils that once held feathers. These were meant to make the wearer appear particularly imposing and frightening and to impart some of the mythological creature's potency.

Because helmets with griffin protomes are almost always appropriate to gods and heroes alone, this helmet probably served not for actual battle but for ceremonial rites, used at a funeral to heroize a dead mortal warrior.

STATUETTE OF A GRIFFIN DEVOURING AN ARIMASP

Greek, from South Italy,
300–1 B.C.
Bronze
H: 7.9 cm (3⅜ in.)
96.AB.152

Among the barbarian races that inhabited the northern steppe regions of Skythia was the legendary tribe of one-eyed Arimasps. In the poem *Arimaspea* by the seventh-century-B.C. author Aristeas, Arimasps waged war against griffins (winged lions with an eagle's beak) that guarded Apollo's hoard of gold. Scenes of Grypomachy (Battle of the Griffins) illustrate the Arimasps' incessant quest to steal gold nuggets. Here a griffin mauls a lifeless warrior, wrenching the victim's arm upward while forcing his head down with its paw. Traces of a broken element between the wings indicate that the statuette probably functioned as a decorative fitting or as part of a larger composition.

Beginning about 400 B.C., Greek artisans portrayed heroic Grypo-machies with male and female Arimasps dressed in boldly patterned Asiatic costume. Wearing only a helmet, this youth probably represents an Arimasp, who in ancient Italy were conventionally depicted naked. The griffin's archaizing recurved wing resembles the wings on a South Italian helmet (see previous entry); its jagged crest and elongated proportions point to a date later in the Hellenistic period. Grypomachy scenes on Tarentine and Etruscan sarcophagi symbolize the passage to immortality. Reflecting a long visual tradition of beasts devouring humans, the violent death of the Arimasp may be connected with Pythagorean beliefs in the transmigration of the soul. Historical accounts of a cult of Aristeas in Metaponton, where Pythagorean philosophy took root, offer a suggestive context for this unusual depiction of the myth.

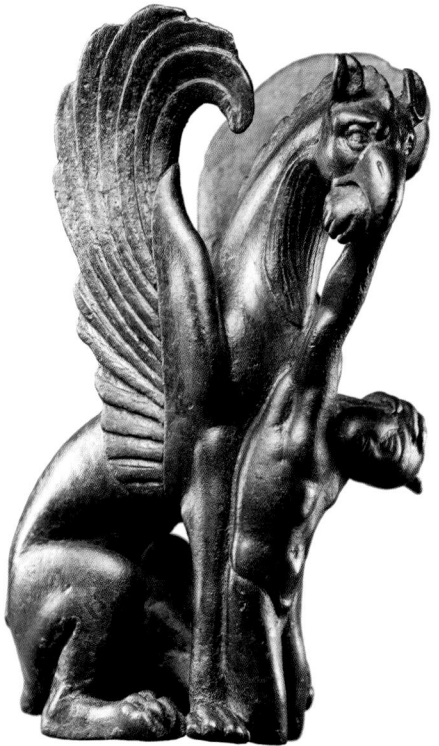

THYMIATERION SUPPORTED BY A STATUETTE OF NIKE

Greek, from Taras, South
Italy, 500–480 B.C.
Terracotta with polychromy
H: 44.6 cm (17½ in.)
DIAM (incense cup): 7 cm
(2¾ in.)
86.AD.681

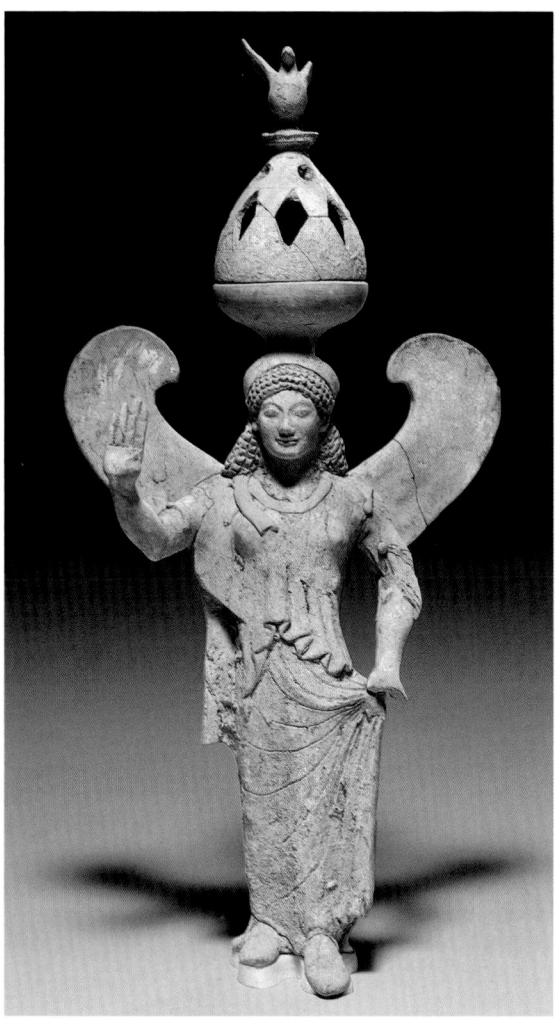

This figure of Nike, winged goddess of victory, conveys an impression of monumentality. She is, in fact, a statuette functioning as a caryatid, or support, for the shallow bowl of an incense burner and its egg-shaped openwork lid, on which a dove perches. This thymiaterion may have been intended for use in the performance of religious rituals. However, because it preserves traces of its original vibrant pink, purple, red, and blue pigments and the incense bowl shows no evidence of use, it more likely was placed in a tomb as a grave offering.

The exquisitely detailed features of this figure—the crimped hair that frames the forehead and falls gracefully over the shoulders, the finely pleated chiton beneath the heavier folds of the himation, and the pose, in which the goddess stands with her left leg advanced while she draws the fabric of her garments to one side, revealing the contours of her limbs—all find parallels among the large-scale marble korai (maidens) found in Greek sanctuaries of the late Archaic period (e.g., on the Acropolis in Athens; see also the kore on p. 19, and the statuette on p. 41, which may have supported a thymiaterion).

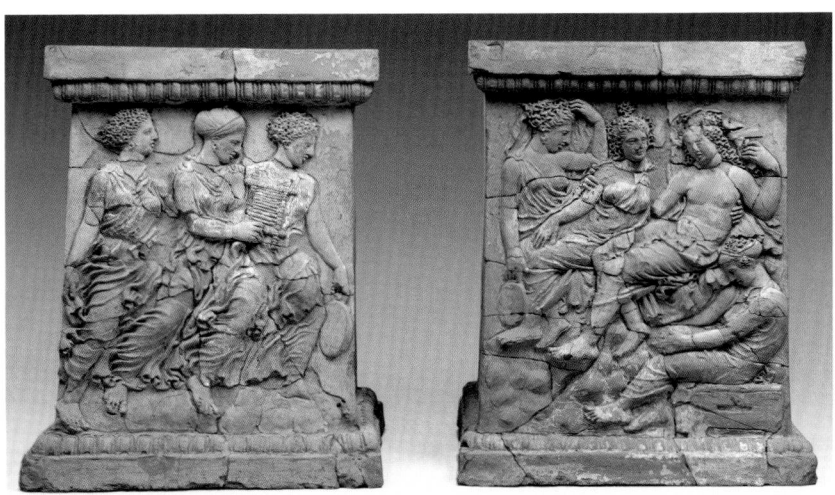

PAIR OF ALTARS

Greek, probably from Taras,
South Italy, 400–375 B.C.
Terracotta
H: 41.8 (16½ in.)
W (top): 31.5 cm (12⅜ in.)
D (top): 27 cm (10⅝ in.)
86.AD.598.1

H: 41.8 cm (16½ in.)
W (top): 31.5 cm (12⅜ in.)
D (top): 27.8 cm (11 in.)
86.AD.598.2

The scenes on these two altars together form a single composition in which the altar on the right provides the primary narrative. In the rocky landscape at its center, Aphrodite, goddess of love and sexuality, sits in the embrace of her lover Adonis. A beautiful youth associated with vegetation and fertility, Adonis was also the lover of Persephone, consort of Hades in the Underworld. To appease both deities, Zeus decreed that Adonis spend half the year with one goddess and half with the other.

While most of the other figures, including the dancing figures on the left altar, are perhaps the nymphs who are common to the mythology of both Aphrodite and Adonis, the identity of the dejected figure seated at the bottom right is unclear. Although she does not carry a musical instrument (such as the tympanum [hand drum] held by her counterpart in the upper left corner), she too may be a nymph, one whose attitude of mourning foretells the doomed nature of the relationship. Alternatively, she may be Persephone, mourning her loss of Adonis to Aphrodite. In either case, the altars could have served for the burning of offerings or incense in a private shrine dedicated to these deities. The third, though least likely, possibility is that the seated woman represents a deceased mortal bride who, unlike Aphrodite and Adonis, will never again enjoy the companionship and love of her husband. In such an instance, the altars could have been made as funerary offerings to be deposited in the bride's grave.

SEATED POET
AND SIRENS

Greek, probably from Taras,
South Italy, 350–300 B.C.
Terracotta with polychromy
H (poet): 104 cm (41 in.)
H (sirens): 140 cm (55⅛ in.)
76.AD.11

Once brightly painted, these large clay figures, often
identified as the mythological characters Orpheus
and the Sirens, are unique among extant South Italian
terracottas in both size and iconography. According
to myth, the half-human, half-bird Sirens used their
sweet, seductive songs to lure sailors to their deaths
upon a rocky shore somewhere in the south of Italy.
They met their match, however, in Orpheus, the
mythical musician and singer. He saved Jason and the
Argonauts during their quest for the Golden Fleece
by singing so beautifully that the Sirens not only
stopped their own singing to listen but threw themselves into the sea, allowing the ship to pass safely.
Orpheus charmed even Hades, the king of the
Underworld, when he ventured there to rescue his
wife, Eurydice.

Here, the seated man is singing, as shown by his
slightly open mouth. He uses the object in his right
hand, the plektron (pick) to strike the strings of his
now-missing kithara (harp) that once rested on his
lap. Each Siren stands on a small, rocklike base. With
her chin resting on her hand, one appears to listen
attentively, while the other sings, lips parted and one
arm outstretched.

The fact that the man is singing and playing the
kithara suggests that he may be Orpheus, whose cult
was widespread in South Italy. Yet, Sirens are often
found in funerary contexts as figures who sing to
mourn the dead, lead them to the Underworld, or help
fulfill the promise of life after death. Thus, the seated
man may be a mortal, perhaps even a poet, who,
for his funerary monument, is depicted as Orpheus.

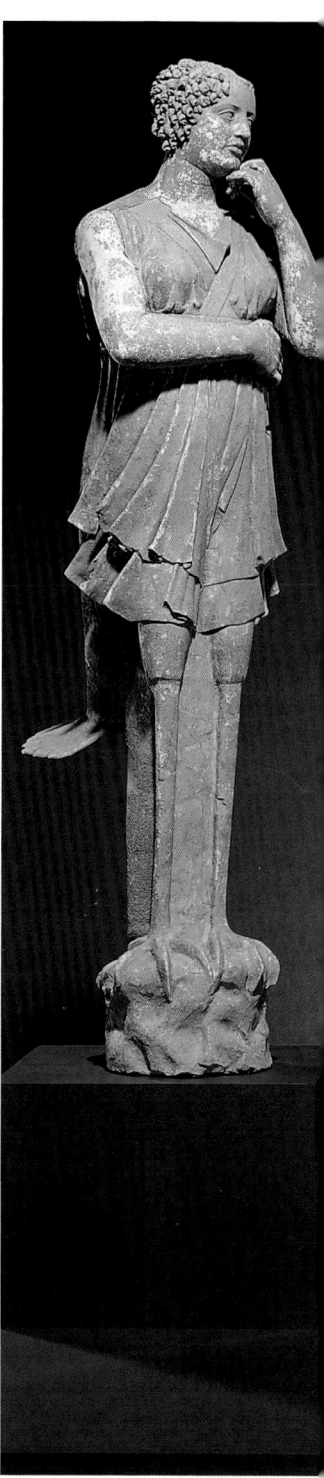

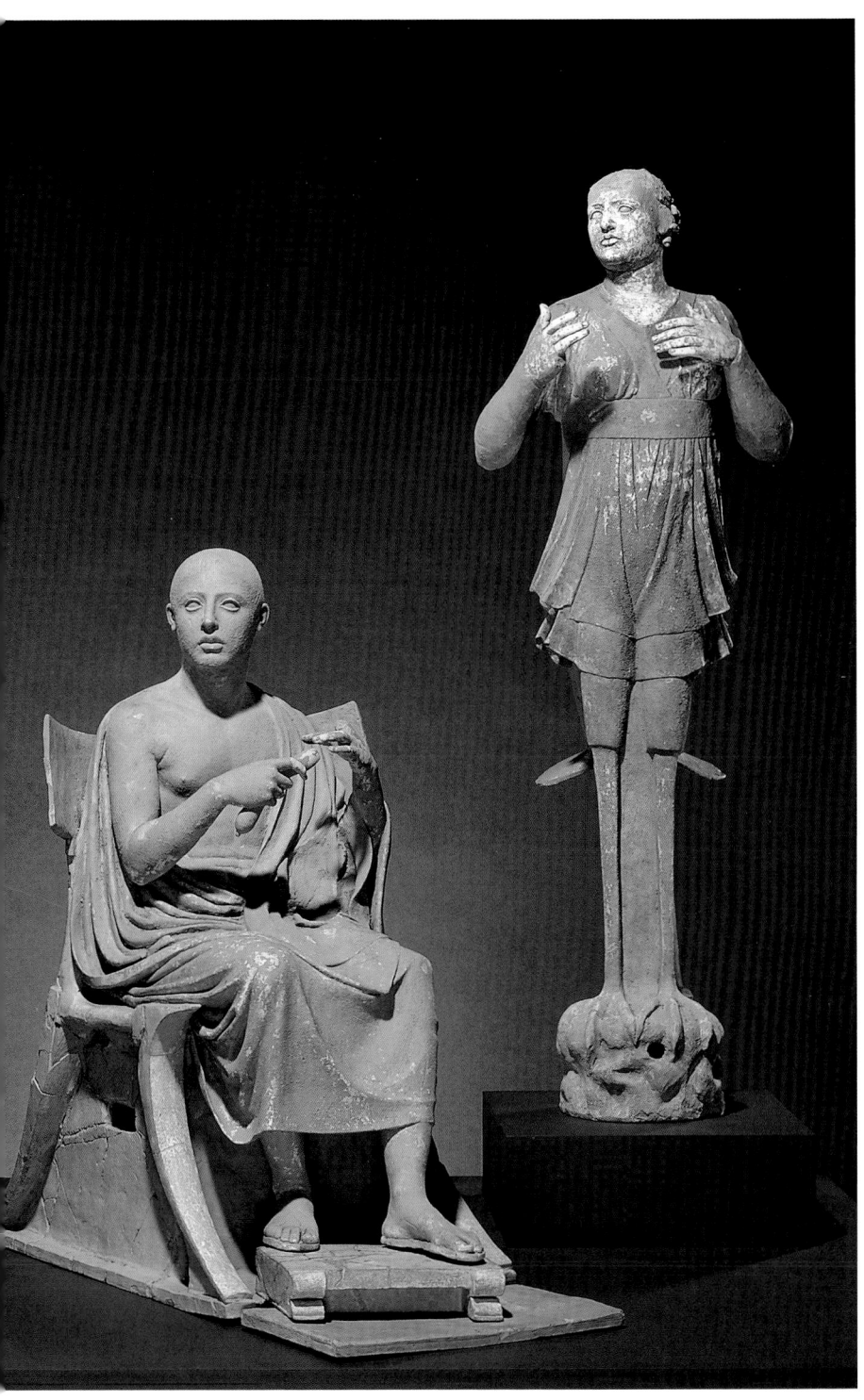

BEARDED HEAD, PERHAPS OF A GOD

Greek, from South Italy or
Sicily, 350–300 B.C.
Terracotta with polychromy
H: 27.3 cm (10 3/4 in.)
W: 20.5 cm (8 1/8 in.)
D: 18.5 cm (7 1/4 in.)
85.AD.105

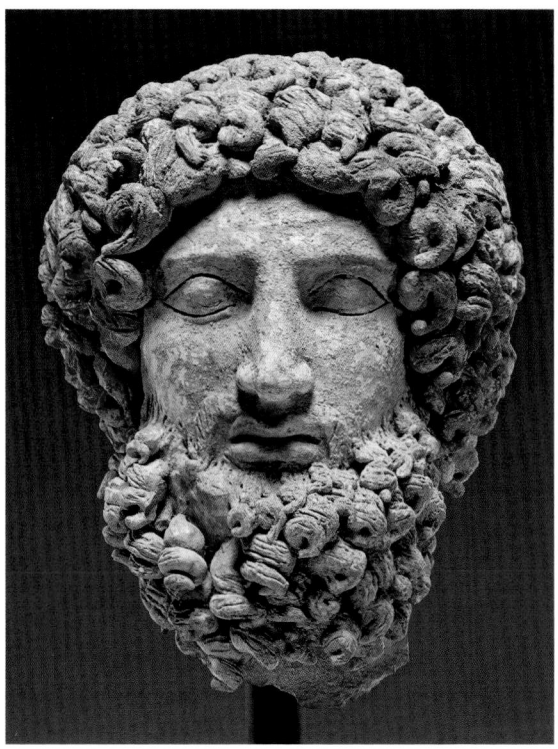

The identity of this head remains uncertain, but it could be Hades, king of the Underworld, who snatched Demeter's daughter Persephone to be his wife. He was persuaded to release her, but since he had tricked her into eating pomegranate seeds, she had to spend part of her time beneath the earth. Her annual re-emergence, with its connotations of fertility and rebirth, is intrinsic to the cult of Demeter and Persephone. The head might also be identified as another typically bearded male divinity, such as Zeus, who himself can be associated both with fertility rites (Zeus Meilichios) or the Underworld (Zeus Katachthonios). The break at the neck indicates that this head was part of larger whole, most likely a bust. A significant quantity of votive busts and other terracottas of similar date have been found at a number of sanctuaries in Sicily, and it is likely that this head had a votive function.

Each of the thick locks on the head was handmade, incised to give a sense of texture, and painted— reddish-brown for the curls of hair, blue for the beard. There are also traces of a rose color, most clearly on the lips and the right side of the face, which would once have covered the whole face and neck. Short incisions on the cheeks indicate the emergence of the beard, as well as on the added strip of clay for the mustache. A deep incision delineates the almond-shaped eyes and probably held inserted metal lashes.

STATUETTE OF A DANCER

Greek, from Taras, South
Italy, 300–200 B.C.
Terracotta
H: 23.5 cm (9¼ in.)
96.AD.246

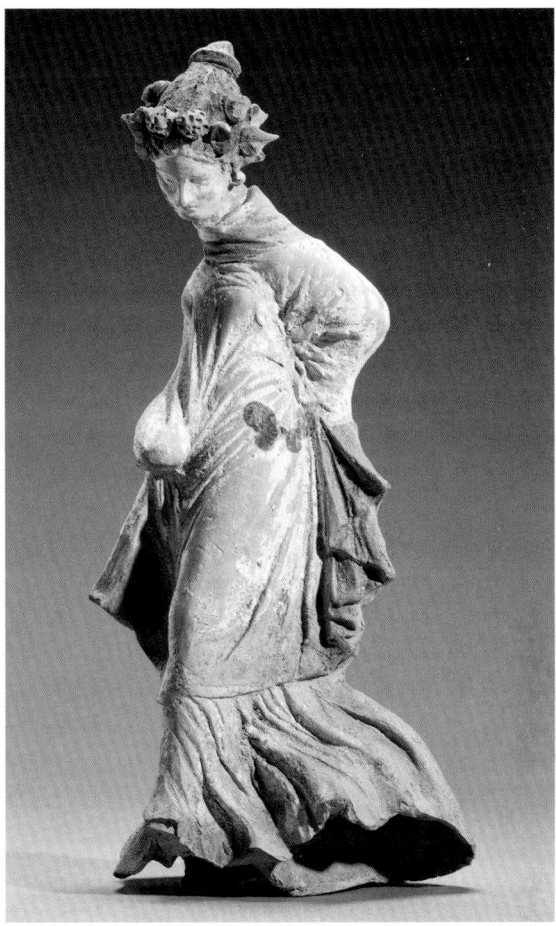

Hellenistic sculpture is characteris-
tized by an interest in movement,
a feature embodied by this dancing
figure. She steps forward, looking
down to her left, with one arm across
her abdomen and the other behind her
back at her hip. The resulting spiral-
like form is emphasized by her
clothing: the himation clings tightly
to her body, its creases amplifying
her gestures, while the lighter chiton
beneath billows out at her feet.

Another typical detail of the period
is her ivy-wreathed hairstyle, the
so-called melon coiffure, where the
hair is pulled back tightly behind
the head to form lobes (see also p. 26).
The red-brown color of her hair
is well preserved, and there is much
white remaining on the body. This

would have served as an undercoat for
the application of color; other figurines
of this type are painted with red, pink,
yellow, or brown, or more rarely, blue
and green.

Terracotta statuettes such as this
are commonly termed Tanagras, after
the site in Boiotia where examples
were first discovered in the early 1870s.
Although most have been found in
cemeteries, others come from domestic
contexts or were dedications at sanctuaries. The figurines are moldmade,
and although the basic types were
originally developed in Athens, they
came to be produced throughout the
Greek world. This example may have
been made in Taras (modern Taranto),
in southern Italy.

CAMPANIAN RED-FIGURED NECK-AMPHORA

Attributed to the Caivano
Painter
Greek, from Campania,
South Italy, circa 340 B.C.
Terracotta
H: 63.5 cm (25 in.)
DIAM (body): 25 cm (9⅞ in.)
92.AE.86

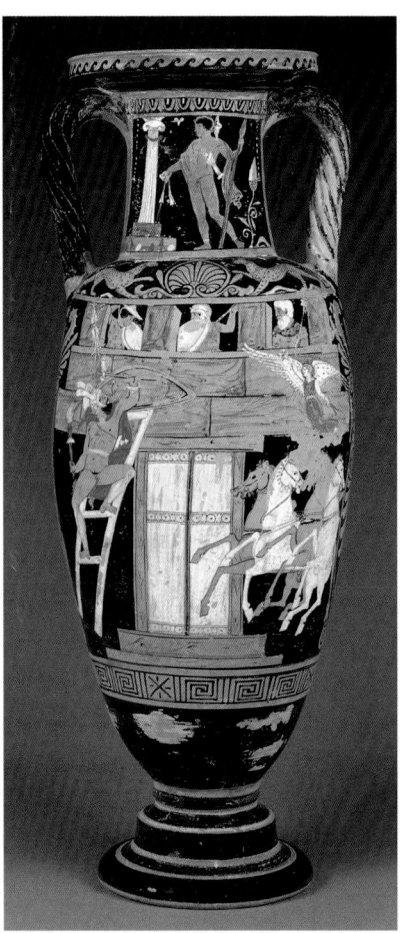

The development of South Italian vase-painting continued the traditions of red-figured Attic pottery, with many of the first artists probably migrating from Athens to southern Italy around the end of the fifth century B.C. New generations of artists helped to create a distinctly South Italian style, often with quite large vases, decorated with multiple added colors. Subject matter was often taken from mythology and Greek drama, as on this piece, which seems to have been inspired by a production of Aeschylus's tragedy, the *Seven Against Thebes*. In that tale, the warrior Kapaneus was the only one of the seven attacking leaders to reach the walls of Thebes in an effort to reinstate the rightful king. His boasting that he did not require the help of the gods in this undertaking led to his downfall. Zeus could no longer endure the warrior's arrogant claims and destroyed him with a lightning bolt.

As on many of his other large vases that are decorated with subjects drawn from drama, here the artist known to us as the Caivano Painter has transferred the essential elements of the tragedy to this amphora. Holding a firebrand and shield, Kapaneus climbs a ladder toward the top of the battlements. Two defenders and a bearded, white-haired man holding a scepter, probably Kreon, the usurping ruler of Thebes, watch him. Just as the doomed Kapaneus reaches the top, the fatal lightning bolt flashes down. On the right side of the city gate, a winged figure of Nike, holding a wreath and

fillet, hovers over a four-horse chariot. The vase documents a highly dramatic event rarely shown in ancient art, particularly in vase-painting. The depiction of the city wall and gate, detailing the grain of the wood and metal attachments, most likely copies a stage set for the play. The way in which Kapaneus climbs the ladder suggests that he is posed as an actor who wants to face the audience in order to be heard when he speaks.

The local Oscan-style helmet with an upright feather on either side, as worn here by Kapaneus, is characteristic of the warriors depicted by the Caivano Painter. This vase-painter also makes extensive use of added white, yellow, and purplish red, giving his ﹍﹍sels a bright and colorful aspect.

APULIAN RED-FIGURED LOUTROPHOROS

Attributed to the Painter
of Louvre MNB 1148
Greek, from Apulia, South
Italy, circa 330 B.C.
Terracotta
H: 90.1 cm (35½ in.)
DIAM (rim): 26 cm (10¼ in.)
86.AE.680

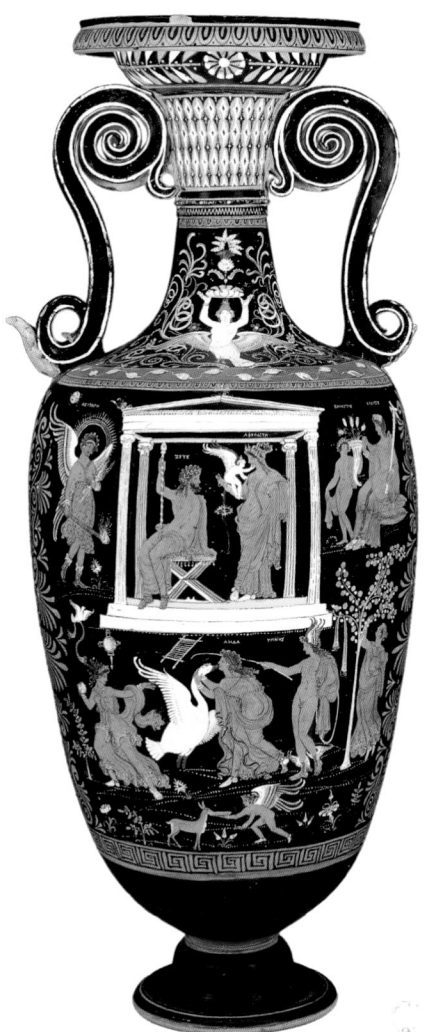

Even though vase-painters of the fifth century B.C. in South Italy at first imitated the shapes, subjects, and style of the Attic pottery of mainland Greece, they soon developed an independent style and expanded their repertoire with novel shapes and subjects. The maker of this loutrophoros with spiraling handles, a uniquely Apulian shape, is considered to be an important South Italian vase-painter, both for the large number of vases attributed to him (or her), and for the innovative treatment of their subject matter. Here, on two different levels, the painter has shown two scenes relevant to the myth of Leda and the Swan (see also the Roman statue on pp. 150–51). The upper register depicts Zeus, Aphrodite, and Eros inside an Ionic building. The king of the gods may be asking for Aphrodite's help in seducing Leda and using Eros to help plead his case. In the lower scene, in one of the guises Zeus adopted while seducing mortal women, he appears as a white swan leaping into Leda's embrace, while Hypnos, a personification of sleep, showers them with drowsiness. One of the children of this union was Helen, the cause of the Trojan War. Other mythological figures, also identified by their incised names— Astrape, a personification of lightning; Eniautos, the personification of the calendar year; and Eleusis, the personification of an important sanctuary —are not clearly connected to this tale. The depiction of the story in two registers, the dual appearance of Zeus as both god and bird, and the inclusion of inscribed names and secondary figures suggest that this painter's representation of the myth may have been inspired by a theatrical performance.

APULIAN RED-FIGURED LOUTROPHOROS

Attributed to the Painter
of Louvre MNB 1148 and the
Circle of the Darius Painter
Greek, from Apulia, South
Italy, circa 330 B.C.
Terracotta
H: 98 cm (38⅝ in.)
DIAM (rim): 21.9 cm (8⅝ in.)
82.AE.16

According to ancient sources, vases of this shape were used for carrying water to nuptial baths and also as funerary offerings for those who had died unwed. Thus their painted scenes are usually relevant to marriages and funerals. The main scene on this vase depicts the conclusion of the story of Niobe. Although there are differing accounts of the tale, the most common relates that, as the mother of six (or seven, as some legends have it) sons and an equal number of daughters, she was excessively proud and mocked Leto, the mother of Artemis and Apollo, for having only two children. To avenge this insult, Leto directed Apollo and Artemis to slay all Niobe's children, although in some versions two survive (for a sculpture of one of the wounded sons, see p. 152). Grief stricken, Niobe lamented for nine days and nine nights at the tomb, imploring Zeus to change her into stone.

Here, her wish granted, Niobe stands inside a *naiskos*, or small shrine, with her head covered and in an attitude of mourning. The added white paint on the lower part of her garment indicates the onset of the process of her petrification. The two loutrophoroi shown within the shrine—one closely matching the shape of the very vessel on which it is painted—as well as the women making offerings outside it serve to emphasize this vase's funerary significance. The loutrophoroi are painted in white, perhaps in imitation of marble. One may represent an offering to Niobe's slain sons, the other to her daughters. In the scene below, Pelops and his bride, Hippodameia, appear in a four-horse chariot. Because he was Niobe's brother, Pelops may be arriving at the tomb in order to plead with her to desist.

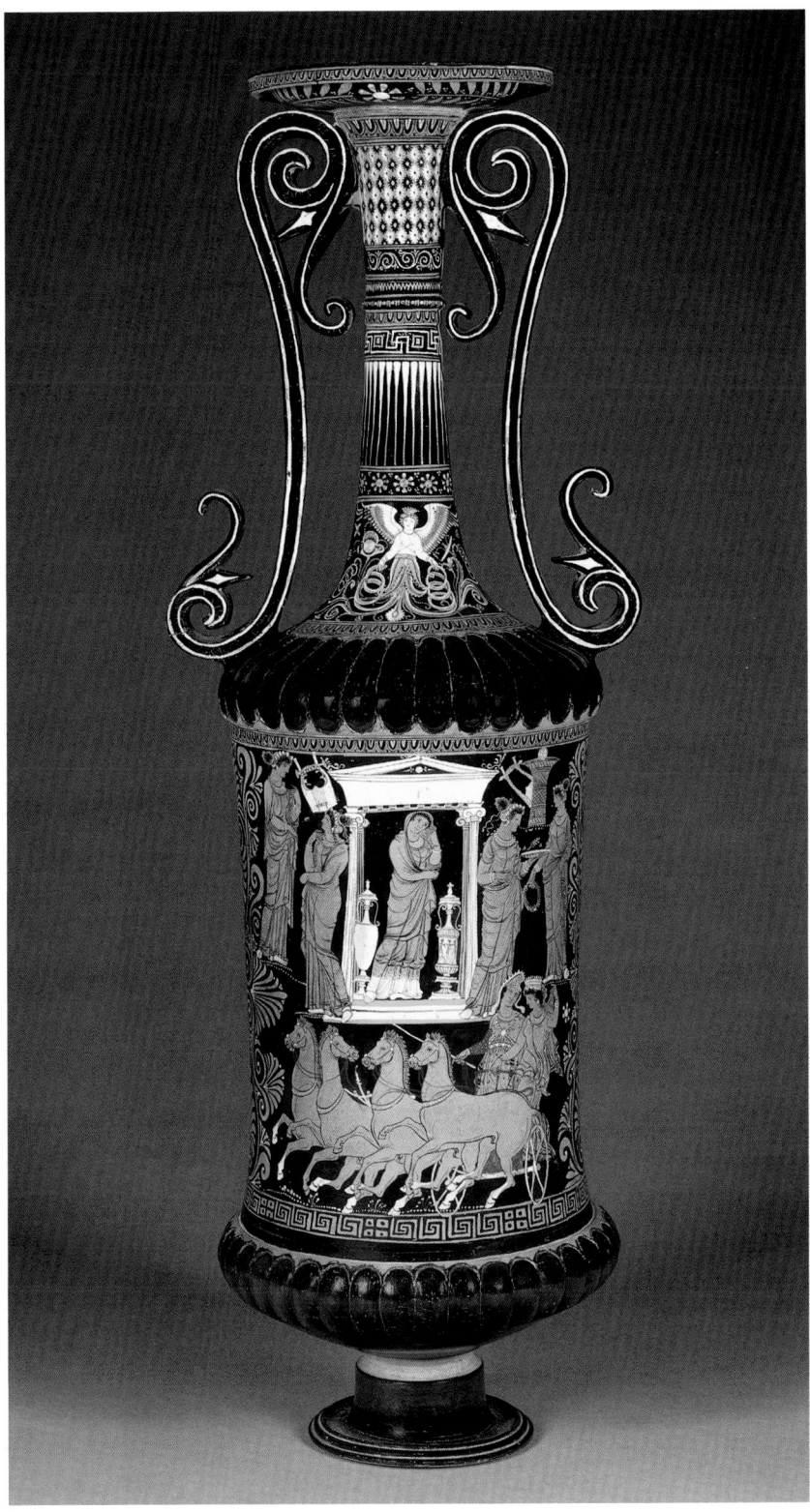

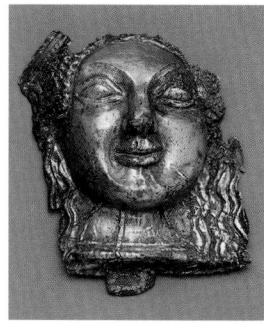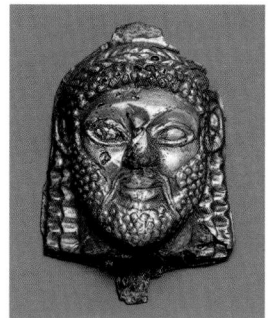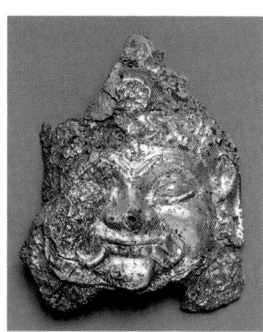

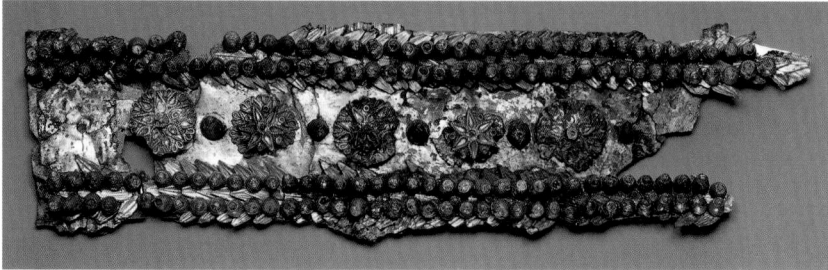

THREE APPLIQUÉS AND ONE BAND WITH FOLIATE ORNAMENT

Greek, from South Italy,
525–500 B.C.
Gilt silver and bronze
Various dimensions
96.AM.110

The illustrated objects are representative of a larger set of ornaments once used for personal adornment. The three heads pictured here are part of a group of eleven, which were formed by hammering thin sheets of silver into molds. Details were highlighted with gilding. A kore, her hair falling onto her shoulders, wears a diadem and necklace. A wreath of pointed leaves crowns the bearded male (center). The monstrous Gorgon Medusa has the furrowed brow, broad nose, protuding tongue, and fangs that typify her portrayal in the Archaic period. Because there are no traces of holes for either sewing or nailing the heads to a background, it is likely that an adhesive fastened them to whatever that background may have been.

The most impressive element in the assemblage is a broad band of gilt silver preserving an elaborate decoration of schematized floral forms. The background sheet is plain except for a tongue pattern along the top and bottom edges. Applied over this is a triple row of overlapping cutouts in the shape of laurel leaves. On each laurel garland is a super-imposed double line of small buds or acorn-shaped finials. Against the plain background of the middle zone, large bud-shaped finials alternate with stylized blossoms made in two layers. Too fragile to be worn, the band was probably part of a belt or a ceremonial crown that may have adorned a cult statue or the garments of a deceased woman.

The group also includes four pairs of pins, the head of another pin that may have been used as a perfume dipper, a D-shaped object (perhaps part of a belt), and four finials.

BOX-BEZEL RING

Attributed to the
Santa Eufemia Master
Greek, from South Italy,
340–320 B.C.
Gold
H (bezel): 2.04 cm (¹³/₁₆ in.)
W (bezel): 1.42 cm (⁹/₁₆ in.)
D (bezel): .77 cm (⁵/₁₆ in.)
DIAM (hoop): 2.31 cm (¹⁵/₁₆ in.)
88.AM.104

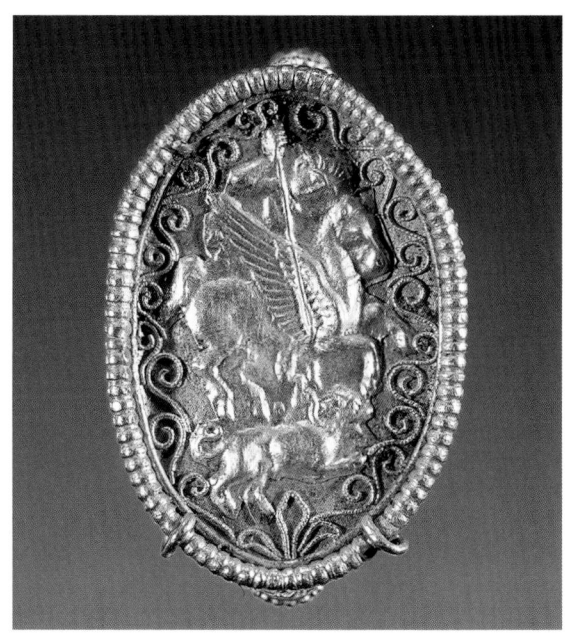

Elaborate ornamentation is the distinguishing feature of this ring, one of the few ancient rings that can be attributed to a particular goldsmith. It is called a box-bezel ring because the bezel is formed in the shape of an oval box. On the top, the Greek hero Bellerophon, mounted on his winged horse Pegasos, thrusts his spear downward to kill the Chimaera, a hybrid monstrous lion with the head of a fire-breathing goat emerging from its back and the tail of a serpent. This legend often had funerary associations and was popular throughout the ancient world, from Archaic Greece and Etruria to the Greek cities of South Italy, where this ring was made.

The figural group is embossed on a thin gold sheet, which was then cut around the edges and fixed as an appliqué to the surface. Filigree spirals and floral devices surround it. Though it is not visible when the ring is being worn, the underside of the box is decorated with filigreed back-to-back palmettes with a tendril spiral and a bellflower. The manufacture of these motifs seems to identify the artist, one of whose stylistic traits was the use of

a corkscrew coil of gold wire that lies flat on the surface of the object. This method has been observed on other pieces of jewelry found in a female burial in southern Italy and given the name of the Santa Eufemia Treasure (now in the British Museum in London); hence the artist who made them is now called the Santa Eufemia Master.

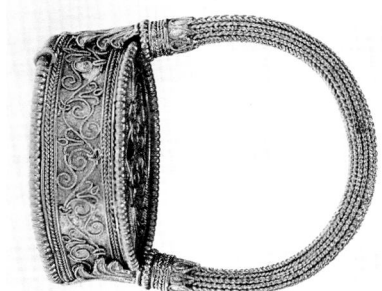

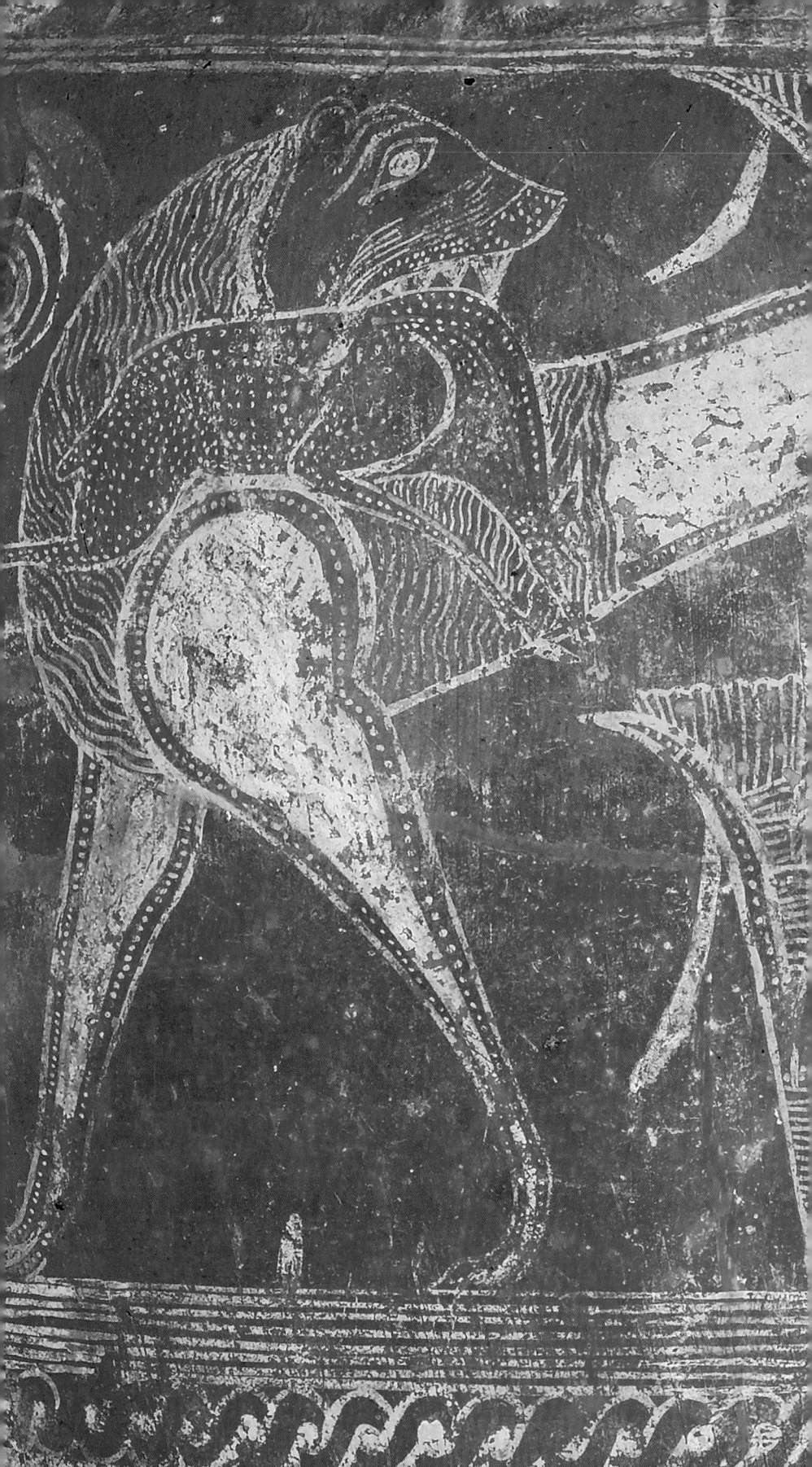

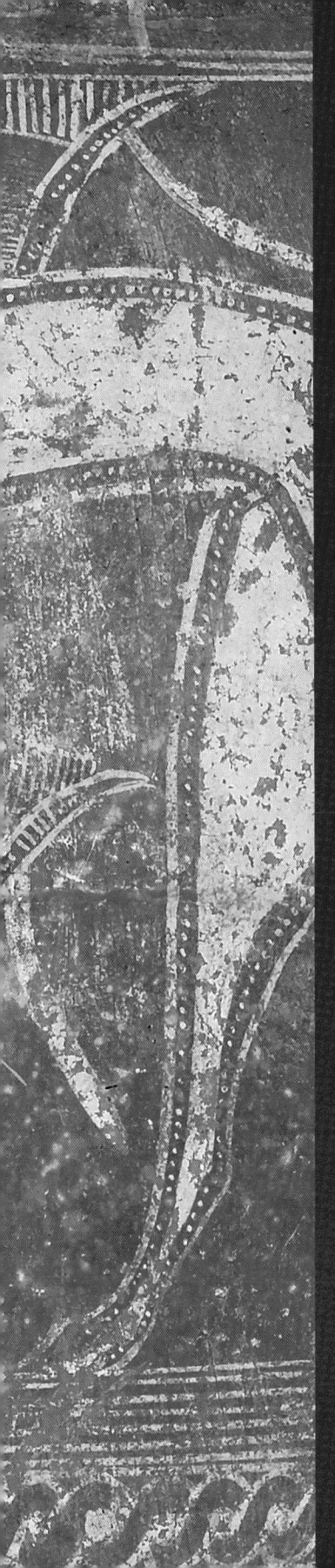

Etruscan

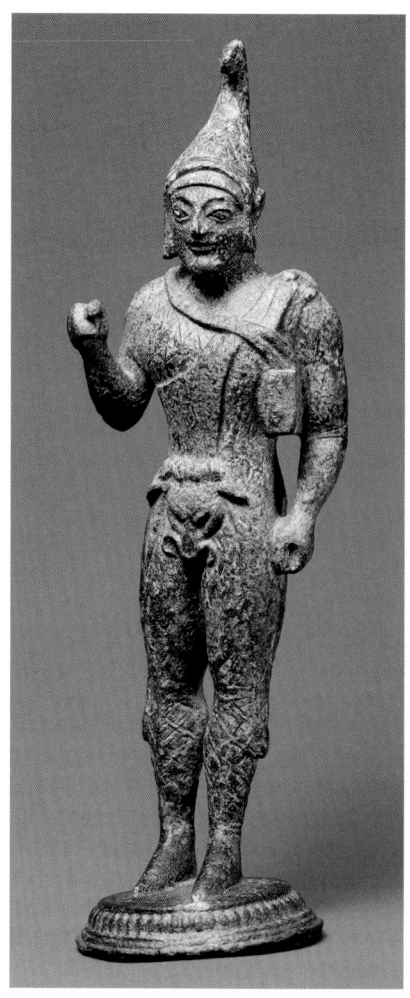

STATUETTE OF
HERCLE AS A HUNTER

Etruscan, 510–490 B.C.
Bronze
H (with base): 11.5 cm
(4½ in.)
96.AC.124

This statuette of Hercle as a young hunter, cast solid together with its base, once topped a candelabrum, a tall, footed stand meant to hold candles. Such pieces were quite common throughout Etruria, the region of the Etruscans located between modern Florence and Rome. The figure is similar in style to statuettes found at Vulci, the famous Etruscan bronze-casting center. He shares with them large almond-shaped eyes, a short nose, a gently smiling mouth, and a heavy chin. The body type is that of the Greek kouros, often used as a model by Etruscan sculptors at this time (see opposite page). Typically, a kouros stands with one leg advanced; in this early example, however, the feet are parallel and the weight is distributed evenly. This figure once held his bow in his upraised right hand; his quiver and bow case (*gorytos*) are slung beneath his left arm. His distinctively pointed archer's helmet is decorated all over with a zigzag pattern and lined with a soft material that hangs free in two lappets, one in front of each ear. He wears pointed boots, tight leggings with incised patterns, and a close-fitting upper garment also completely covered with rows of zigzags. This is the typical costume of an archer, which is worn also by Amazons but with a significant variation: Here the figure has draped a deerskin over his traditional costume, which identifies him as a hunter. Its forelegs are knotted on the left shoulder and its head hangs protectively over his groin. The skin is dappled with incised almond-shaped spots, suggesting a fallow deer. Hercle, the Etruscan Herakles, often wears a lionskin, but several Etruscan statuettes depict him clad in a deerskin. This seems to represent a local variant of his labor relating to the Kerynian Hind. Although in Greek myth Herakles was told to capture the golden horn of the hind without harming it, in the Etruscan version the hero seems to have slain the beast. Moreover, as Pindar notes in his third Olympian ode, the hero traveled to the far north to visit the Hyperboreans immediately after his encounter with the hind in Arcadia. Thus this figure of Hercle wears not only the skin of the mythical beast but also the costume of exotic northerners, the Skythians.

STATUETTE OF A KOUROS

Etruscan, circa 490 B.C.
Bronze
H: 22.5 cm (8⅞ in.)
W: 9 cm (3½ in.)
85.AB.104

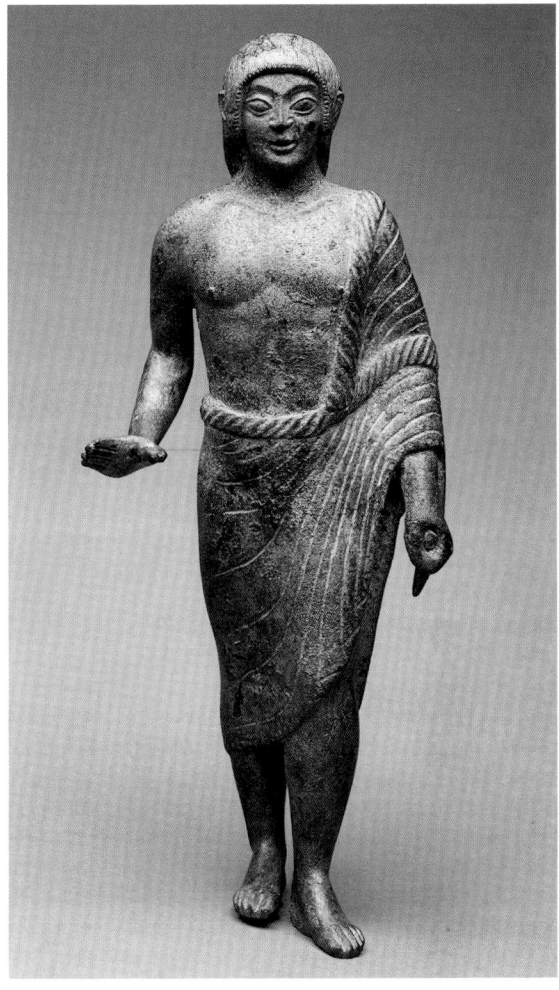

This statuette of a kouros, or young male, is based on a type widely known in sixth-century-B.C. Greece. In its form and intention it is very similar to the bronze on p. 129. Like that work and its Greek prototypes, this figure was originally intended to serve as a votive offering in a sanctuary to an important god, in this case most likely Apollo. The Etruscan statuette stands with his left leg projecting slightly forward. Unlike the typically nude Greek kouros, however, this one is clothed in the Etruscan costume of status, the *tebenna*, precursor to the Roman toga. The long garment is wrapped around his right hip, with one end pulled over his left shoulder from behind and the other thrown over his left forearm. The decorative patterns at the edges of the cloth made by diagonal and dotted incisions indicate areas that would have been embroidered if this cloth were real. A hole in his lowered left hand suggests that he originally may have held a staff. The authenticity of this kouros was once questioned because the drapery's arrangement and thickness is inconsistent with other examples. However, extensive analysis of the statuette's patina, or surface corrosion, has proved that it is authentic. The uncharacteristically thick band at the edge of the *tebenna* therefore probably reflects a misunderstanding on the part of the artist.

FOOT OF A *CISTA* IN THE FORM OF A WINGED GOD, PROBABLY USIL

Etruscan, circa 490 B.C.
Bronze
H (with base): 15.2 cm (6 in.)
W: 10.3 cm (4 in.)
96.AC.127

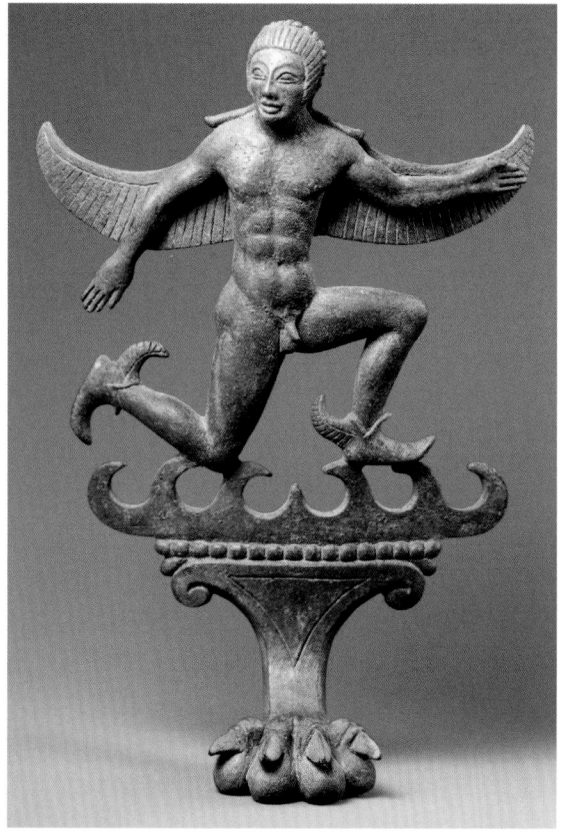

The youth's outstretched arms and wings, his twisted torso, and the undulating waves below his feet all serve to convey the idea of movement. The position of the legs is an artistic convention used throughout the Archaic period to represent running or rapid motion, while the strain of the muscles is evident in both the arms and legs. Such liveliness of pose characterizes images of the Etruscan sun god Usil, identified with the Greek Helios, who was believed to traverse the course of the heavens every day as he brought light to the Earth. Images of Usil were considered to be appropriate decorations for women's toiletry objects, on which winged deities of both sexes often appeared (see also the Etruscan patera handle, p. 130).

This piece once belonged to a *cista*, or round cosmetic box. The slightly curved back of the figure and the outstretched wings indicate that it was attached to the side of the box, while the feline paw below functioned as one of the *cista*'s three feet. It has been suggested that this type of figural foot was an invention of the bronze-casting workshops in the city of Vulci, located in southwestern Etruria.

STATUETTE OF A BEARDED MAN, PROBABLY TINIA

Etruscan, circa 480 B.C.
Bronze
H: 17.2 cm (6¾ in.)
W: 9 cm (3½ in.)
D: 4 cm (1⅝ in.)
55.AB.12

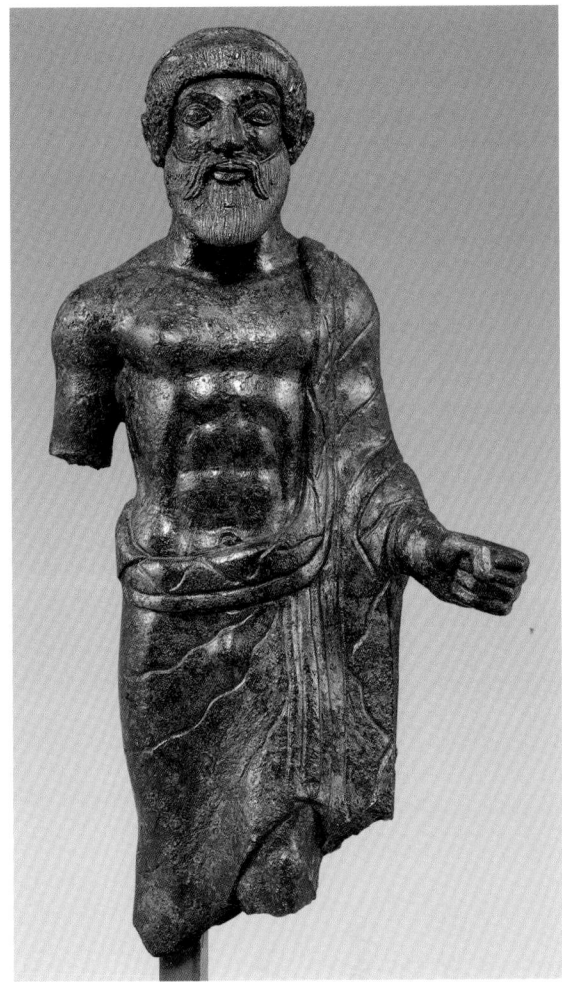

This stately bearded figure once held an object—perhaps a trident or a scepter—in his clenched left hand. If he held a trident, then the figure would represent either the Etruscan sea god Nethuns or his Greek counterpart Poseidon; if a scepter, as the position of the arm suggests, then he can be identified as the god Tinia, the Etruscan equivalent to Zeus, king of the Greek gods. This small bronze was probably intended to be a dedicatory offering. Tinia is clothed in a *tebenna*, the Etruscan togalike garment, which falls in zigzag folds down his left arm and across his lap.

The rigid frontality of his pose and his advanced left leg recall the Archaic sculptural style and the pose of a typical Greek kouros. Yet the relatively naturalistic treatment of the torso and face place this work stylistically in the early Classical period. This juxtaposition of stylistic traits is characteristic of Etruscan art.

PATERA HANDLE IN THE FORM OF A WINGED GODDESS, PROBABLY LASA

Etruscan, 350–300 B.C.
Bronze
H (with base): 21 cm (8¼ in.)
W: 14.7 cm (5¾ in.)
96.AC.34

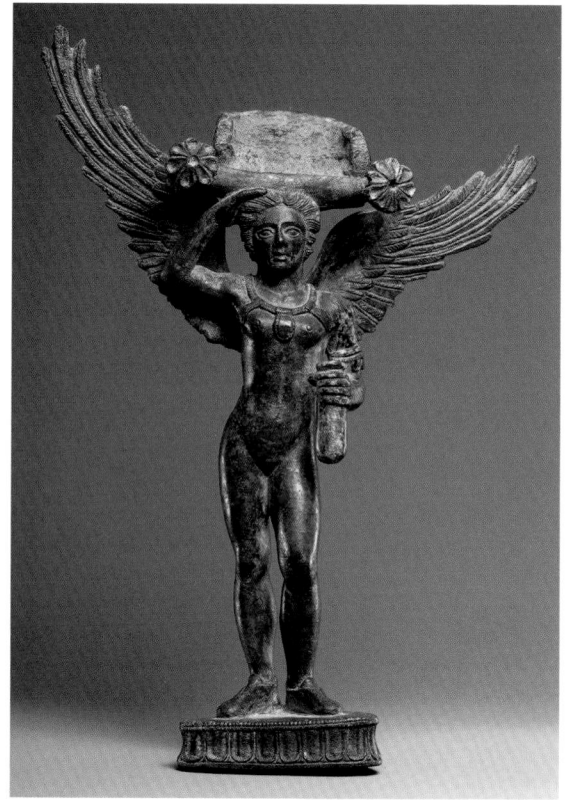

Etruscan artists often fashioned human figures as handles for vessels; this nude girl once served as the handle for a patera, or shallow libation dish. She supported the edge of the dish on the top of her head, in a manner similar to ancient mirror handles. She stands on a triangular base with her left leg slightly advanced and her right arm raised, the hand resting on her head. She wears only a pair of soft slippers, a necklace, and, on her upper arm, a bracelet. The relaxed S-curve of the girl's body and her nudity belong to the style of fourth-century-B.C. Greek sculpture. Unlike many Greek works, however, this figure is not depicted in the fleshy, sensual manner used for contemporaneous nude females; rather, the girl's lean muscularity echoes the aesthetic generally used for figures of young men. The figure's nudity, her wings, and the perfume flask (alabastron) in her left hand suggest that she is Lasa, an Etruscan divinity who corresponds to Greek nymphs and is frequently associated with Turan, the Etruscan goddess of love. Although her wings recall those of another Etruscan deity, Vanth, the two are distinct, for Vanth is always clothed and is a divinity of death and passage, whereas Lasa belongs to the world of life and love.

STATUETTE OF A NUDE YOUTH

Etruscan, 325–300 B.C.
Bronze
H: 19.7 cm (7¾ in.)
96.AB.35

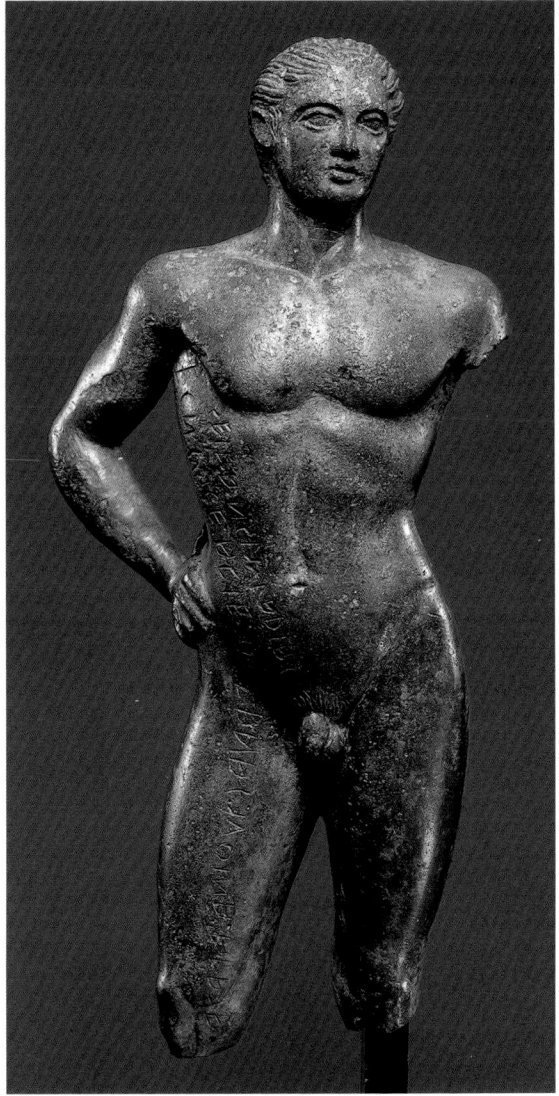

This youth may have held either a votive offering or a piece of athletic equipment in his now-missing left hand. The inscription incised along the right side of the figure immediately marks the statuette as a votive object that was dedicated to a god. Translated from the Etruscan it reads: "Avle Havrnas gave this [for *or* in the] tuthina of the father to Selvans of the boundaries." The word *tuthina* likely refers to a rural area or village, and the family name Havrna is known from inscriptions incised on a set of banqueting vessels found in a tomb at Bolsena (in central Etruria, southwest of Orvieto). Selvans, an Etruscan deity associated with the protection of crops and field boundaries, was worshiped particularly in the area of Bolsena.

The figure's proportions, with a relatively small head surmounting a lean and muscular frame, recall the style of the famous fourth-century-B.C. sculptor Lysippos (active ca. 370–ca. 300 B.C.). This type of athletic build was popular in Etruscan sculpture of the last quarter of the fourth century B.C.

Votive Statuette of Hercle

Etruscan, 320–280 B.C.
Bronze
H: 24.3 cm (9⅝ in.)
96.AB.36

Hercle is the Etruscan version of the immensely popular Greek hero Herakles. Of the many ways that Herakles could be represented, this type, with the lion's skin worn over the head and shoulders like a cape, originated in Archaic Cyprus and was actually more popular in outlying areas influenced by Greece, such as Etruria, than it was in mainland Greece itself. The perked ears of the lion's skin and the collarlike way that it frames Hercle's face are typically Etruscan, as is the delight in textural embellishment, particularly in the treatment of the lion's skin across the back. The type was especially popular during the age of Alexander the Great (356–323 B.C.), when this statue was created. Alexander, who claimed Herakles as his ancestor, often had himself portrayed in the guise of the young hero, helping to spread the heroic imagery throughout the ancient Mediterranean world. For that reason, the modeling of this figure, with its mixture of broad faceted planes used for the muscles of legs and buttocks combined with anatomically detailed attention to the working of the torso, is similar to the style of Alexander's court sculptor Lysippos (active ca. 370–ca. 300 B.C.). The sculptural result is a powerfully modeled yet fluid and elongated figural type. This Hercle probably held the Apples of the Hesperides in his left hand. Representing the last of his Twelve Labors, the apples were proof that, despite his mature age, Hercle had completed his deeds and was now prepared to take on immortality, as suggested by his youthful and godlike physique.

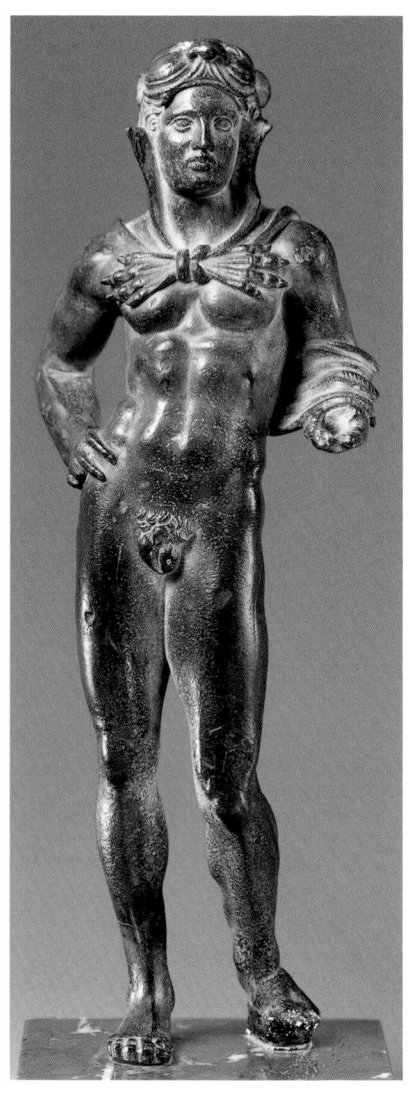

STATUETTE OF A MAN

Etruscan, 300–280 B.C.
Bronze
H (without casting tangs):
31.6 cm (12⅜ in.)
96.AB.37

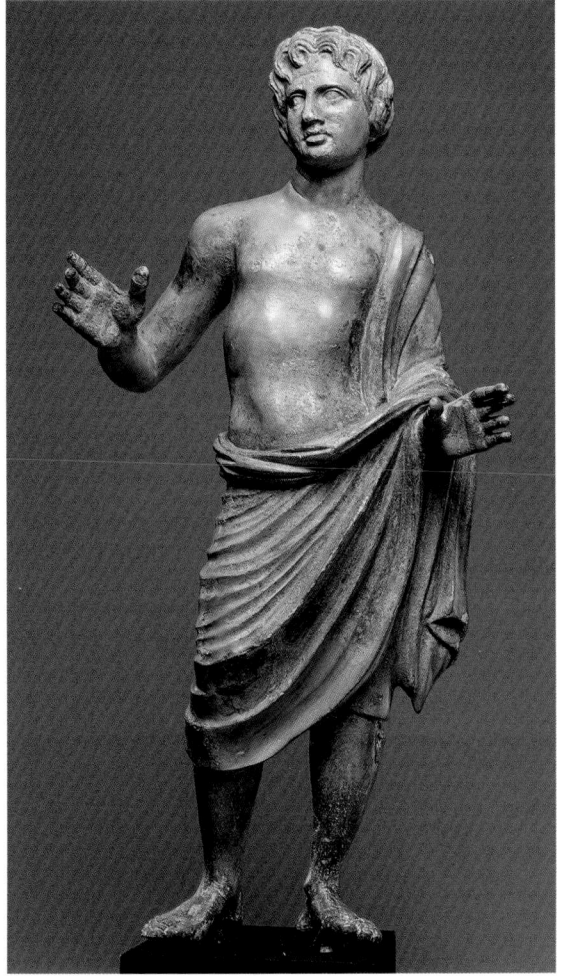

The pose of this nude figure, with its sinuous torsion and shifting of weight, is typical for the Hellenistic period and is enhanced by the arms raised in an *orans*, or praying, position. The expressively modeled face twists to follow the lead of the gesturing right hand. The upturned eyes, furrowed brow, and wavy locks of hair are all traits seen on the portraits of Alexander the Great (356–323 B.C.).

A votive inscription is engraved on the mantle in two parts. The first runs along the edge of the cloth from behind the left wrist: *VEL MATUNAS TURCE* (Vel Matunas dedicated); the rest follows the slanting folds of drapery across the buttocks: *LUR : MITLA : CVERA* (precious/sacred gift to Lur). Lur is the name of an Etruscan divinity, and Matunas is a noble South Etruscan family name, recorded both at Caere (modern Cerveteri, Italy) and Tarquinia. The letter forms, however, are typical for the region of Orvieto.

PITHOS DEPICTING THE BLINDING OF POLYPHEMOS

Etruscan, 650–625 B.C.
Terracotta
H (with lid): 100.7 cm
(39⅝ in.)
DIAM: 33.5 cm (13⅛ in.)
96.AE.135

This large pithos, made for storing grains or wine, is an example of early Etruscan white-on-red impasto ware and an early illustration of the compelling influence of Greek tales, legends, and religion on the Etruscans. It features one of the most popular stories of the time: the escape of the Greek hero Odysseus and his men from the cave of the cyclops Polyphemos, as told in Book IX of Homer's *Odyssey*. This is the earliest known surviving representation of the legend in Etruscan art. In a visual approximation to Homer's account of the adventure, three men have picked up a long stake and are shoving it toward the Cyclops's single eye. These are the best of Odysseus's remaining men (the monster having eaten the rest of them), and the hero himself is likely first among them as they approach the giant. The painted cream-slip amphora in front of Polyphemos signifies his drunkenness, for in order to lull him to sleep Odysseus served him strong wine. On the opposite side of the vase are a pair of horses and a lion with its prey parading in a magical landscape filled with conical flowers. Friezes of rays ascend from the bottom of the vase to augment the pictorial zone.

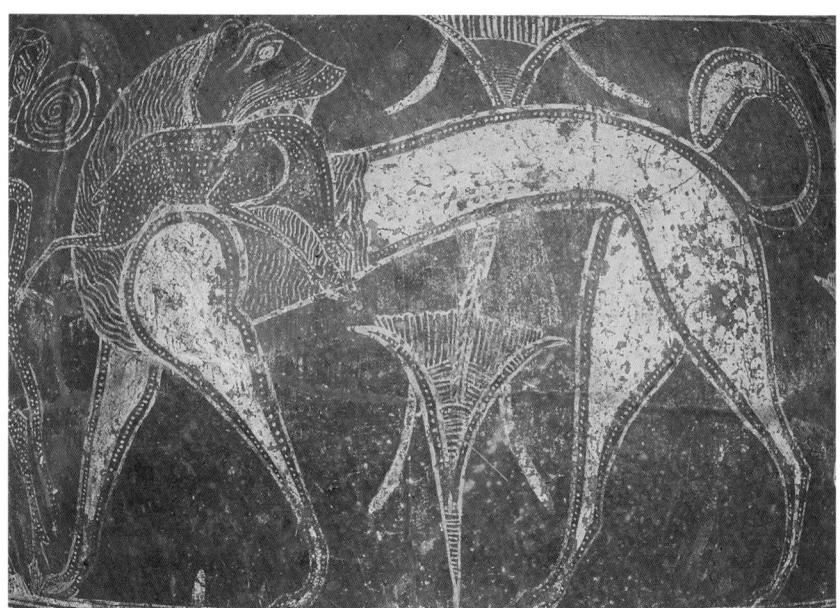

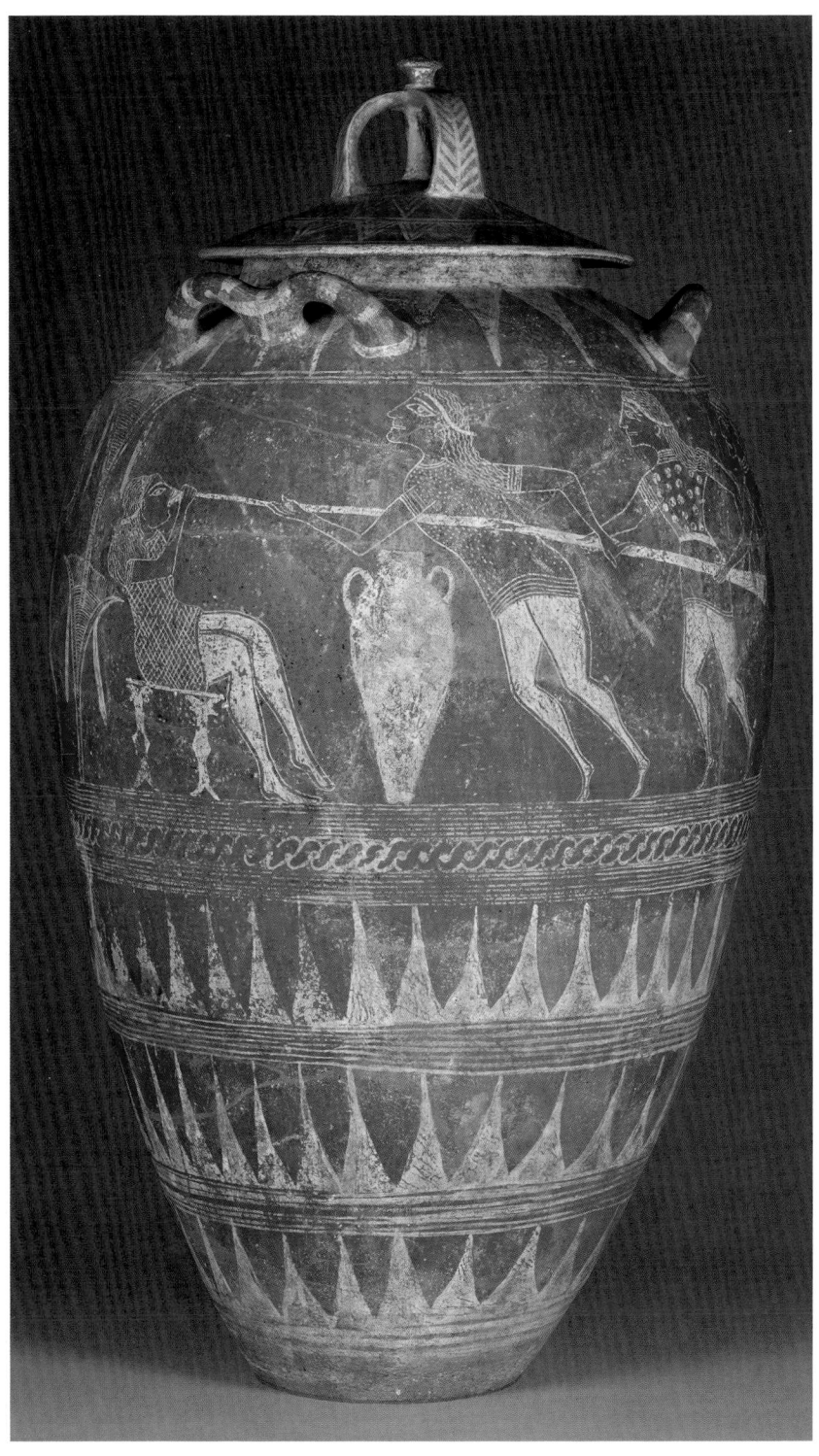

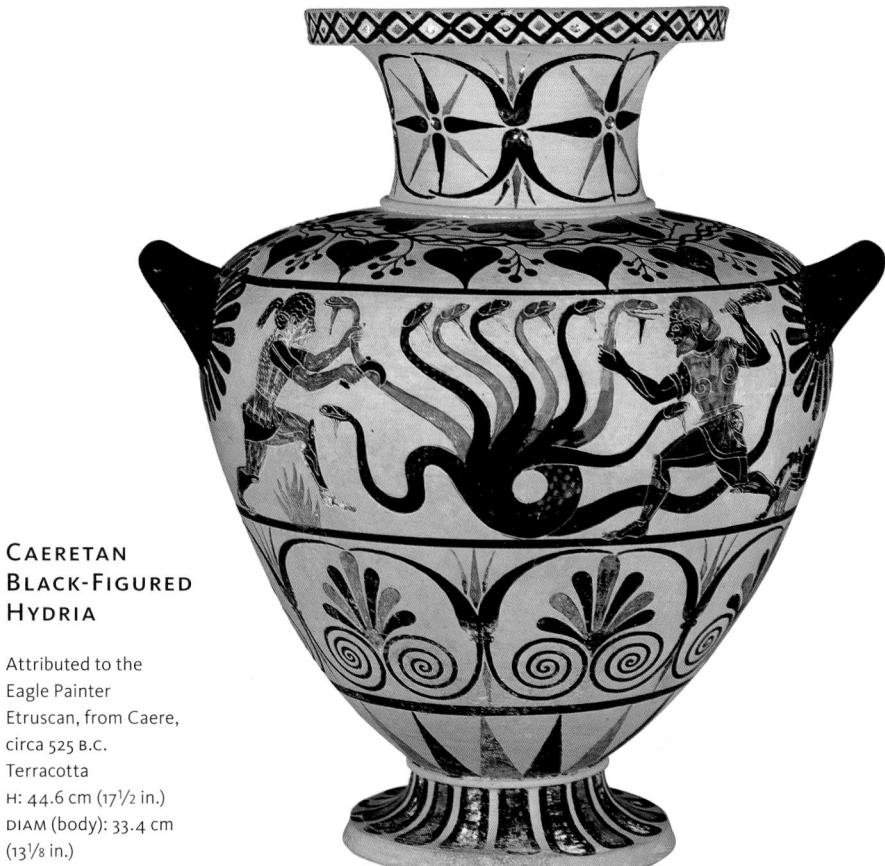

CAERETAN BLACK-FIGURED HYDRIA

Attributed to the
Eagle Painter
Etruscan, from Caere,
circa 525 B.C.
Terracotta
H: 44.6 cm (17½ in.)
DIAM (body): 33.4 cm
(13⅛ in.)
83.AE.346

Etruria was an important market for Attic black-figured pottery in the sixth century B.C., and it is not surprising to find that a few Greek or Greek-trained potters and painters actually set up businesses there. The workshop of the Eagle Painter at Caere seems to have lasted only one generation, with most of the vases the products of only two artists and their assistants. Some of the most original and lively compositions of the time are to be found on their wares, which regularly combined Greek and Etruscan elements.

The most numerous products of the Eagle Painter's workshop were hydriai, water jars with two horizontal handles for carrying and a vertical one for pouring. On this, as on other examples, the artist lavished attention on precise drawings of large floral ornaments, but the main focus is a snakelike monster with its multiple heads painted alternately red and black. This is the legendary Hydra, which lived in the swamps of Lerna in the Peloponnese and was killed by Herakles. The hero can be seen to the right, attacking with his club and wearing a cuirass and greaves instead of the lion's skin. As seen on other surviving representations of the labor, a giant crab helps the Hydra by attacking Herakles from behind. Herakles, in turn, receives support from his nephew Iolaos, who is equipped with a sickle. In contrast to Greek vases, where the convention is to have the victorious hero move from left to right, on this, and other Caeretan pieces, Herakles moves to the left.

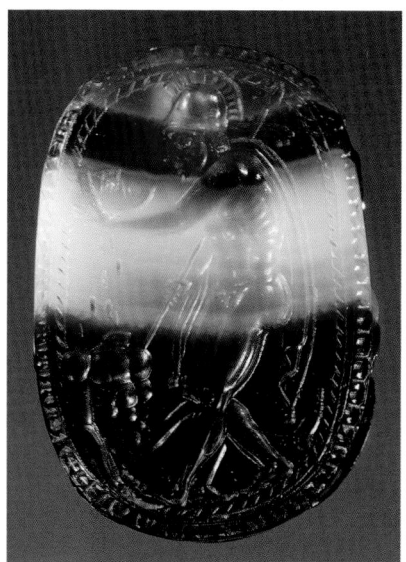
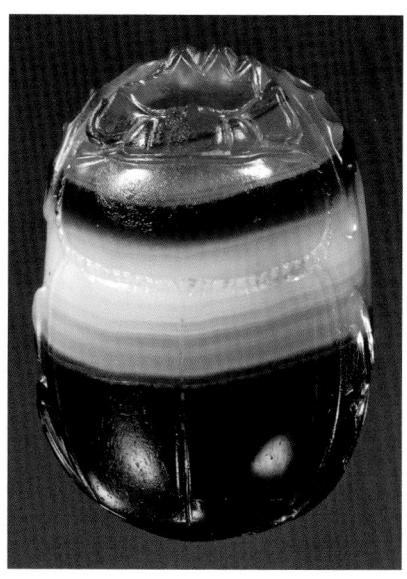

ENGRAVED SCARAB
DEPICTING
TWO WARRIORS

Etruscan, 400–380 B.C.
Banded brown and
white agate
H: 1.65 cm (⅝ in.)
W: 1.13 cm (⁷⁄₁₆ in.)
D: .86 cm (.40 in.)
92.AN.85

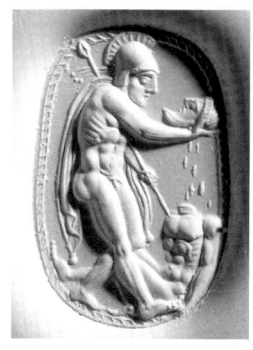

A helmeted warrior with his cloak thrown over his
shoulder clutches his spear with one hand while
holding a severed head dripping with blood in the
other. The body of a decapitated warrior lies at his
feet. These two figures probably represent an episode
in the story of the *Seven Against Thebes*, in which
Oedipus's sons fought against each other for control
over their father's kingdom (see p. 118). According
to myth, Tydeus, an exile from Kalydon in western
Greece, slew Melanippos, one of the Theban champi-
ons, but was himself mortally wounded in combat.
As he lay dying, he asked his ally Amphiaraos to
bring him the head of his enemy. Although sometimes
described in Greek literature, mutilation of the dead
enemy (*maschalismos*) was rarely depicted in Greek
art. A notable exception is a pivotal scene from
the *Iliad* in which Achilles drags the body of Hektor.
The Etruscans, in contrast, often depicted scenes of
maschalismos in gem carving.

    The other side of this gem is carved as a scarab
beetle, a form that reached Etruria in the late sixth
century B.C. and was introduced through Greek and
Phoenician imports and by immigrant artisans. The
scarab ultimately derives from Egypt, where the shape
had been used for seals and amulets for centuries.
Etruscan scarabs were typically carved with great
detail, with delicately incised wings and mottled heads,
and the beetles often sit on elaborate plinths. The
scarab remained popular in Etruria into the second
century B.C., long after it had gone out of fashion in
Greece and was replaced by less elaborate scaraboids.

GEM ENGRAVED WITH A YOUTH AND DOG INSET INTO A RING

Italic, 300–100 B.C.
Carnelian and gold
H (gem): 1.81 cm (³/₄ in.)
W (gem): 1.32 cm (¹/₂ in.)
DIAM (hoop): 2.8 cm
(1¹/₈ in.)
85.AN.165

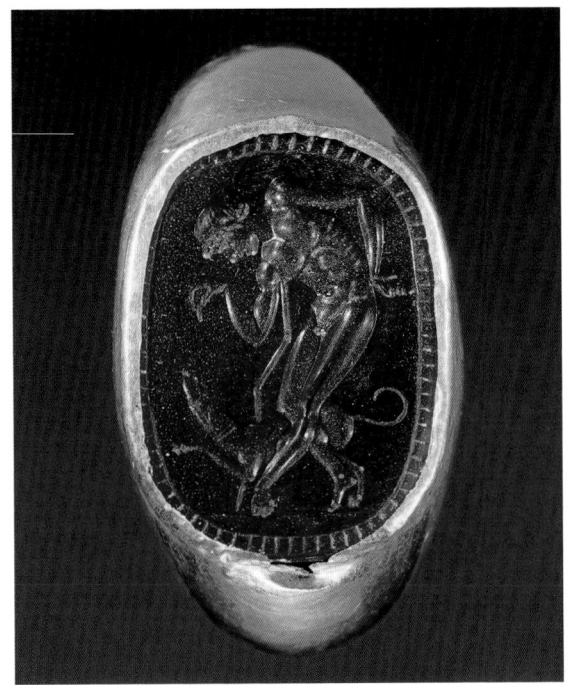

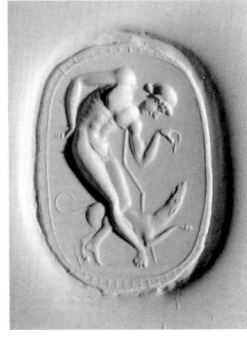

Carved on the surface of this gem is a scene of a nude youth leaning on a crooked staff, bending over to feed his dog. The young man delicately balances himself on the balls of his crossed feet as the dog lifts his snout toward the scrap of food held in the youth's left hand. The dog is long and lean with a smooth coat; called a Lakonian hound, it was a breed commonly used in ancient Greece for hunting. A hatched border surrounds the pair, enclosing them in a tight composition. The poses of the youth and the dog have been arranged in a manner perfectly suited to the elongated shape of the gemstone. Even on this small scale, the unknown gem carver has carefully modeled both figures, depicting the anatomical proportions and musculature in a naturalistic manner.

The theme of a youth and his dog was very popular in ancient art in all media from the 600s B.C. onward. It is found on both Archaic Greek gems and Etruscan scarabs. The use of the motif on this gem, as well as the style of the figure, is archaistic, or intentionally old-fashioned. The native Italic people and the Romans, like the Greeks before them, admired the styles of earlier times, and traditional styles could elevate the importance of an object. The original setting, the type of border surrounding the scene, the use of small drilled holes for details, and the shape of the ring itself are typical for Italic gems of this period.

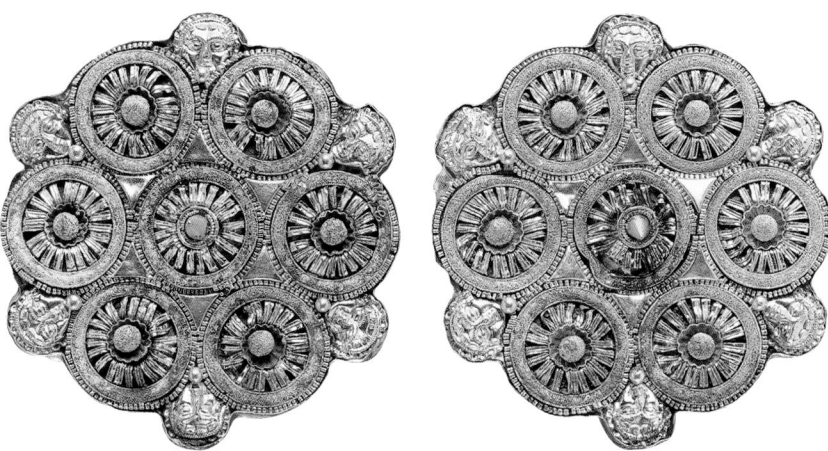

PAIR OF DISK EARRINGS

Etruscan, 525–500 B.C.
Gold
DIAM: 4.8 cm (1⅞ in.)
83.AM.2.1

The Etruscans are considered by many modern scholars to have been the finest goldsmiths in the ancient world. At the end of the Archaic period, when this pair of earrings was made, the Etruscans seem to have favored highly elaborate ornaments whose form followed Near Eastern models. The rosettes that make up these disk earrings, for example, are a typically Near Eastern motif. Three of the best-known Etruscan gold-working techniques were used to make these earrings: repoussé, filigree, and granulation. The tiny masks that fill the interstices of the small rosettes, each unique, are made using the traditional repoussé technique, in which the sheets of gold are hammered into a mold to create the relief features, then finished from the front. Filigree, the manipulation and soldering of wires of gold, and granulation, the melting of small golden beads into patterns, are employed to further embellish the earrings.

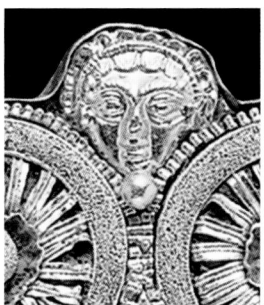
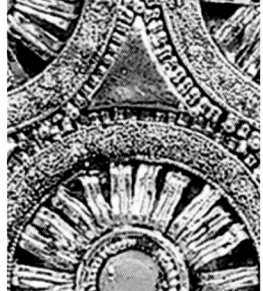

PENDANT CARVED AS A KORE

Italic, from South Italy, or
Etruscan, 525–500 B.C.
Amber
H: 7 cm (2¾ in.)
76.AO.77

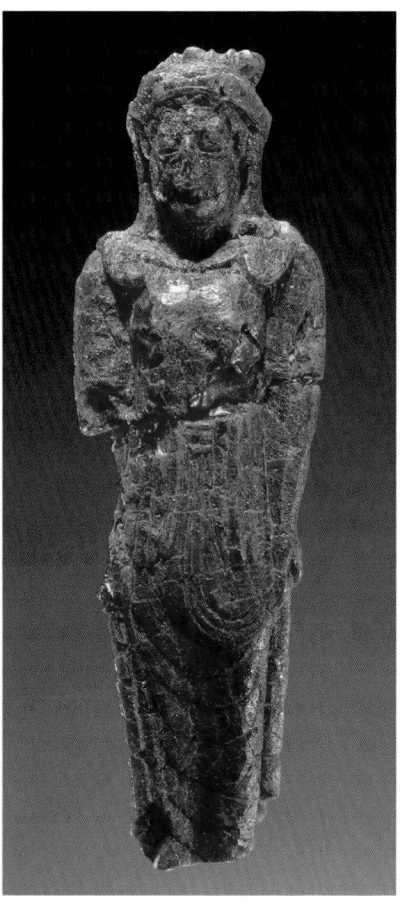

In antiquity, amber, the fossilized remains of tree sap, was considered a luxury object with special powers and purpose. Most of the ancient amber carved in the central and eastern Mediterranean is Baltic in origin, gathered on the shores of the Baltic Sea. It was traded as a commodity along the merchant routes from northern Europe southward, and its physical qualities and rarity made it a precious commodity in the Mediterranean. It was associated with the sun, fecundity, and regeneration. It was also believed to ward off evil and to guarantee a safe passage to the Underworld.

This small pendant figure of a girl comes from southern Italy or Etruria, but was carved by a craftsman from the eastern Mediterranean, perhaps from Miletos. She stands facing frontally, with her left arm held stiffly, pulling her drapery to the side. Her right arm is lost below the elbow. Her eyes are shallow and were probably inlaid with another material that is now lost. Atop her head is a flange carved as a bead; the hole bored through the bead served as the pendant's suspension point. The girl's pose and clothing are characteristic of the kore figures created on the Greek islands during the latter part of the Archaic period. These figures are found in larger scale in marble and terracotta throughout the Greek world and served both votive and funerary functions. The style of this kore's belted chiton, with its long overfold and vertical emphasis, her hair covering, and her facial characteristics compare most closely with marble kore sculptures from Miletos and Didyma, cities along the Ionian coast of the Aegean Sea. In antiquity, this area (now Turkey) was populated by migrants from the Greek mainland.

The pendant was probably designed as a grave gift. Amber was believed to have regenerative powers and these, combined with the normal funerary or votive function of a kore, made it doubly acceptable as a gift for the deceased.

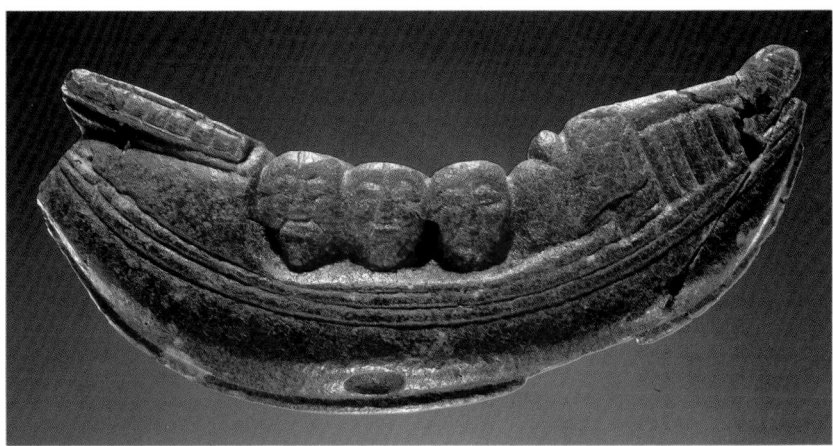

Pendant Carved as a Ship with Passengers

Italic, from South Italy, or
Etruscan, 500–400 B.C.
Amber
H: 4.5 cm (1¾ in.)
L: 11.9 cm (4⅝ in.)
76.AO.76

This curving piece of amber was originally part of some larger ensemble. There are multiple holes drilled on either side for attachment to another object, a pin, pendant, or pectoral. The amber is carved as the curving body of a cargo or merchantman ship, carefully rendered with details like the rails, *aphlaston* (terminal above the stern), and other ship's parts incised into the material. No mast or sail is indicated, however, which suggests that the vessel sits at anchor rather than being on the open sea.

The heads of three passengers peer over each side of the ship. A seventh head of a bearded man is carved in front of the stern castle; in front of him is a tied sack or some other cargo. It is tempting to identify this scene as one related to Greek or Etruscan myth or epic. The sketchiness of the carving, however, makes it difficult to associate with any known imagery; it might be Odysseus and his men, or Jason and the Argonauts, or Theseus and his fellow Athenians sailing to Crete to face the Minotaur.

PENDANT CARVED AS TWO FIGURES AND A BIRD

Italic, from South Italy, or
Etruscan, 500–400 B.C.
Amber
H: 8.3 cm (3¼ in.)
77.AO.85

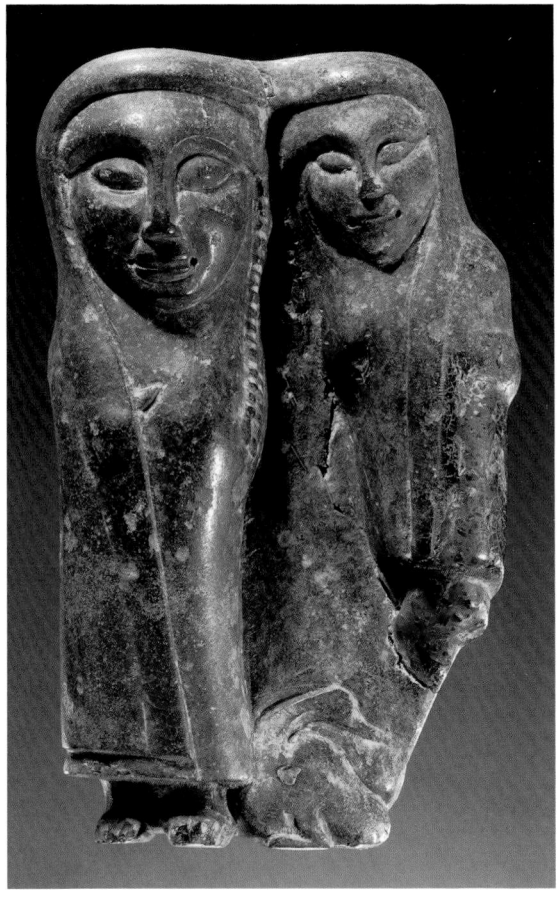

Two female figures are carved side by side on this pendant. The woman on the left is larger and appears to be holding the smaller figure next to her. Both are enveloped in the same cloak-like garment, and their heads are at the same level. The difference in their sizes may indicate a difference in age; they might be mother and daughter, perhaps Vei (Greek Demeter), goddess of vegetation and rebirth, and her daughter Phersipnai (Greek Kore or Persephone). As amber is associated with rebirth and regeneration, a depiction of these goddesses carved in amber would be appropriate. Near the figures' feet sits a small waterfowl, perhaps an egret. If the two figures are deities, it is likely that the bird is their attribute; it is meant to help identify who they are.

In style, the pair compares most closely to Etruscan bronze votive statuettes that depict cloaked women. The proportions, facial features, and costumes are all similar. What is dissimilar, however, is the way the two figures are grouped together and the presence of the bird with them. Images of gods defined by animal attributes are very rare in early Etruscan art, and it is possible that the pendant is not Etruscan but rather Italic, a product of other indigenous peoples of Italy who inhabited the regions south of Etruria.

PAINTED WALL PANEL

Etruscan, 520–510 B.C.
Terracotta with pigment
H: 88 cm (34 5/8 in.)
W: 52.5 cm (20 5/8 in.)
D: 4.5 cm (1 3/4 in.)
96.AD.140

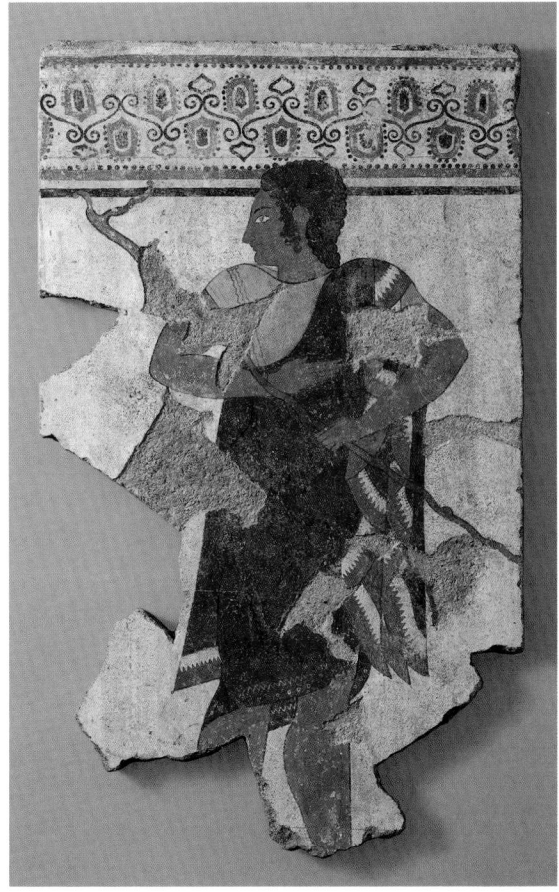

The Etruscans frequently decorated tombs, temples, and secular buildings with brightly painted panels and terracotta figures. On this panel, a poised and dignified youth carries a crooked stick with a forked top, probably a symbol indicating that he holds a specific office. The youth wears a light-colored tunic and a darker mantle with a decorated border. His figure is rendered in the composite manner characteristic of the late Archaic period, with his chest shown frontally and the rest of his body in profile. Forked staffs like the one depicted here seldom appear in Etruscan painting. In a scene of athletic competition in the Tomba delle Bighe in what is now Tarquinia, forked staffs are held by three men wearing bordered mantles who address athletes. In painted representations on Greek vases, forked staffs are often held by officials charged with the education and training of athletes. Athletic competitions were frequently convened in honor of the dead, and a figure such as this was perhaps in a scene of an athletic competition that decorated the interior of a tomb. It was undoubtedly once part of a larger scene: the frieze at the top of the panel is interrupted at both ends, and the youth looks back over his right shoulder toward the missing portion of the composition.

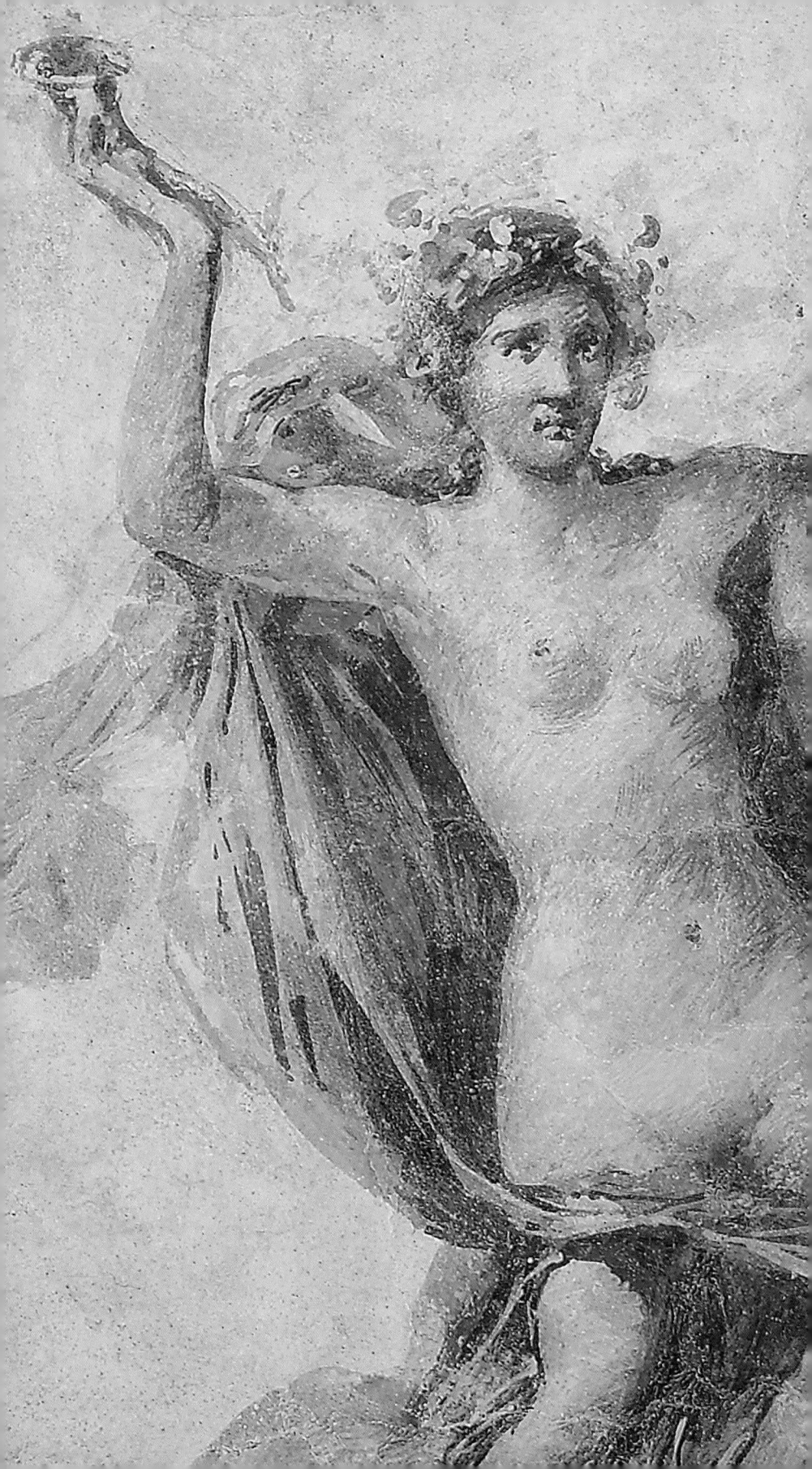

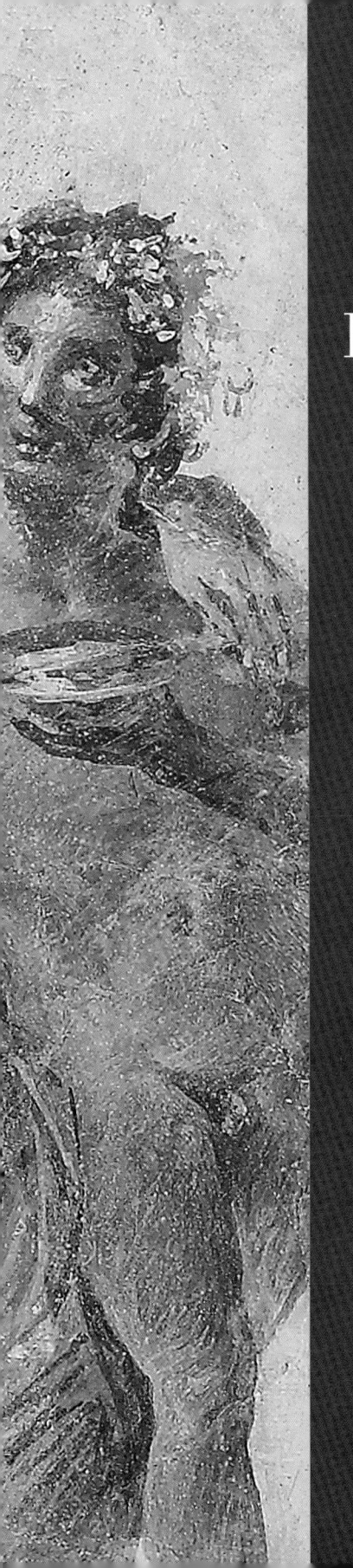

Roman

GRAVE RELIEF OF A SILVERSMITH

Roman, A.D. 1–25
Marble
H: 79.9 cm (31½ in.)
W: 58.5 cm (23 in.)
D: 31.7 cm (12½ in.)
96.AA.40

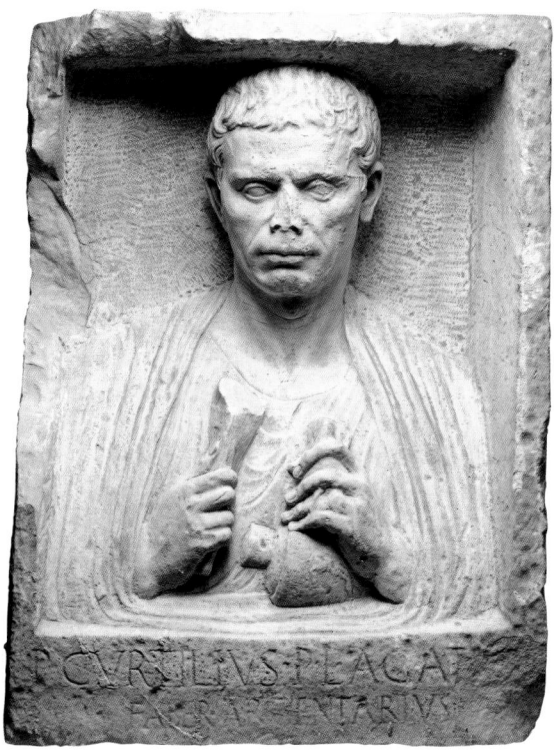

As the Latin inscription on the bottom of this commemorative relief, *P[ublius] CURTILIVS P[ublii] L[ibertus] AGAT[US] / FABER ARGENTARIVS,* tells us, it was made for "P. Curtilius, freedman of Publius, silversmith." The subject is expressively depicted without idealization. His prominent cheekbones, sunken cheeks, slack jaw, and wrinkled neck indicate his age. The pride in his profession is shown not only by the inscription but also by the fact that he chose to be represented with his tools. He works, using a chasing tool with his left hand and what is probably a mallet with his right. Remnants of lead on the top of the stone indicate that this piece was likely set into a larger architectural funerary monument. Such tributary structures lined the roads out of Rome and other cities. In addition to being memorials they also advertised the social and professional status of the deceased.

The class of *libertini*, or freedmen, was originally made up of freed slaves who were brought to Rome as captives in the second century B.C. Generally, they were educated and possessed valued skills that they could eventually exchange for their freedom, after which they often continued to work for their former masters. Although they were restricted by certain legal exclusions, such as not being allowed to place ancestral portraits in their household shrines, and were for the most part less wealthy than the patricians, some were able to amass large fortunes. The Getty's silversmith proudly wears his toga on his expensive funerary monument meant as a tribute to the prosperity he achieved through his skill.

PORTRAIT BUST OF
L. LICINIUS NEPOS

Roman, A.D. 1–25
Marble
H: 37.5 cm (13/4 in.)
W: 26 cm (10¼ in.)
D: 17.5 cm (67/8 in.)
85.AA.111

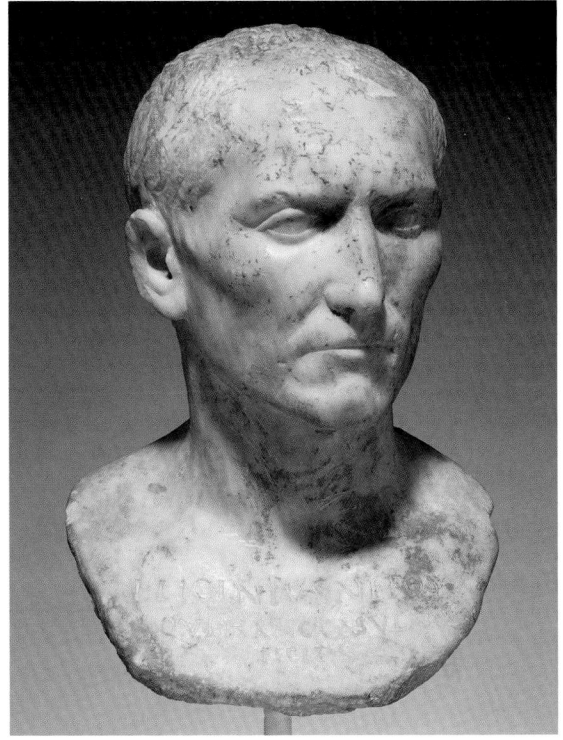

The man represented in this portrait is identified by
an inscription written across the bust: *L[ucius]
LICINIVS NEPOS / QVI HANC CASVLAM / FECIT*
("L. Licinius Nepos who made this little house"). The
term *casula* refers to a family tomb, probably of the
columbarium type, in which several niches housed
the cinerary urns of the deceased. Licinius, as the
founder of the tomb, would have his funerary bust
placed in a central niche among those of his relatives
and friends. The fact that the inscription was carved
on the bust itself and not on a separate tablet that
would have required additional space beneath the
niche suggests that the tomb was a modest structure.

A tradesperson named L. Licinius Nepos is the
subject of an extended funerary inscription carved on
a travertine block that was found in Rome near Porta
Pinciana in 1756. The personal name on both the bust
and the inscription employ the same exceptional term
casula in describing Licinius as the builder of the
tomb. Peculiarities in the form of the lettering further
confirm that the individual portrayed in the bust and
the one mentioned in the long inscription are the
same. Both the portrait bust and the inscribed block
were originally placed inside the same tomb, probably in a necropolis outside the Aurelian Wall along
the Via Salaria in Rome.

STATUE OF JUPITER (THE MARBURY HALL ZEUS)

Roman, found at Tivoli,
A.D. 1–100
Marble
H: 207 cm (81½ in.)
W: 100 cm (39⅜ in.)
D: 62.5 cm (24⅝ in.)
73.AA.32

Discovered in the 1700s in Italy, this colossal statue of the king of the gods, called Jupiter by the Romans and Zeus by the Greeks, probably once belonged to the emperor Hadrian (reigned A.D. 117–38), who had a villa very near the findspot. Seated on a throne, Jupiter originally held a scepter in his left hand and a lightning bolt in his right, symbolizing both his authority and the powerful natural forces at his command.

Although carved in a Roman workshop in the first century A.D., the inspiration for this image of Jupiter was a Greek sculpture of the 430s B.C., the monumental gold and ivory statue of Zeus created by the sculptor Pheidias (active 470–420 B.C.) for Zeus's temple at Olympia. Pheidias's Zeus was renowned in antiquity; as one of the Seven Wonders of the Ancient World, many ancient writers praised it and numerous sculptors copied it. At 12 meters (39.4 feet) high, the Greek statue was so large that the seated Zeus almost touched the ceiling of the temple, giving the impression that if he stood up he would go through the roof.

After this Roman Jupiter was discovered on the grounds of the Villa d'Este at Tivoli in Italy, it was used as the decorative centerpiece in one of the villa's elaborate fountains (as documented in an eighteenth-century etching, see below). Subsequently, Gavin Hamilton, a well-known art dealer who obtained antiquities for wealthy British collectors, sold the statue to James Hugh Smith Barry, who displayed it in his stately home, Marbury Hall, in Cheshire, England. The antiquities in the Marbury Hall collection were eventually dispersed, and J. Paul Getty purchased the Jupiter in 1973.

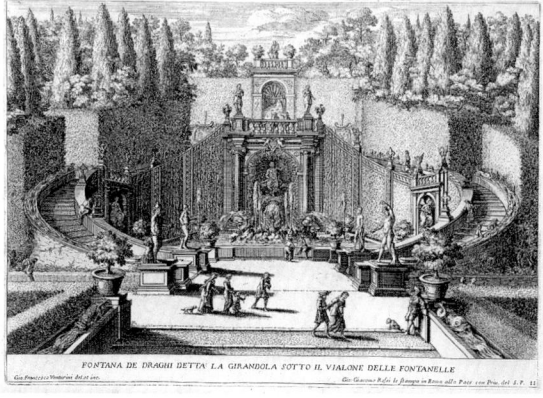

FONTANA DE DRAGHI DETTA LA GIRANDOLA SOTTO IL VIALONE DELLE FONTANELLE

From Gio. Francesco Ventvrini, *Le fontane del giardino Estense in Tivoli, con li loro prospetti, e vedvte della cascata del fivme Aniene*, 1691. Courtesy of the Research Library, Getty Research Institute 83-B213.

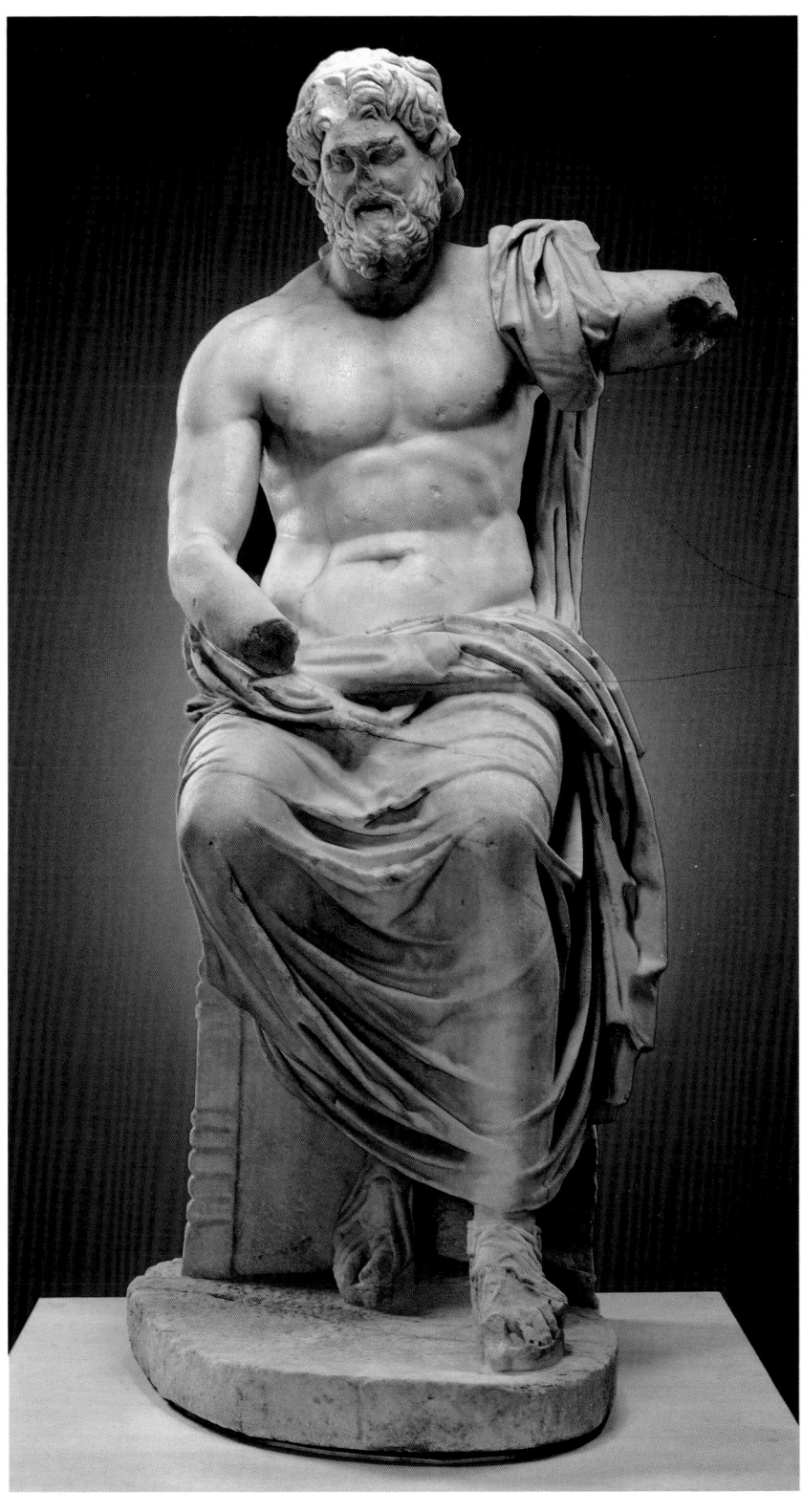

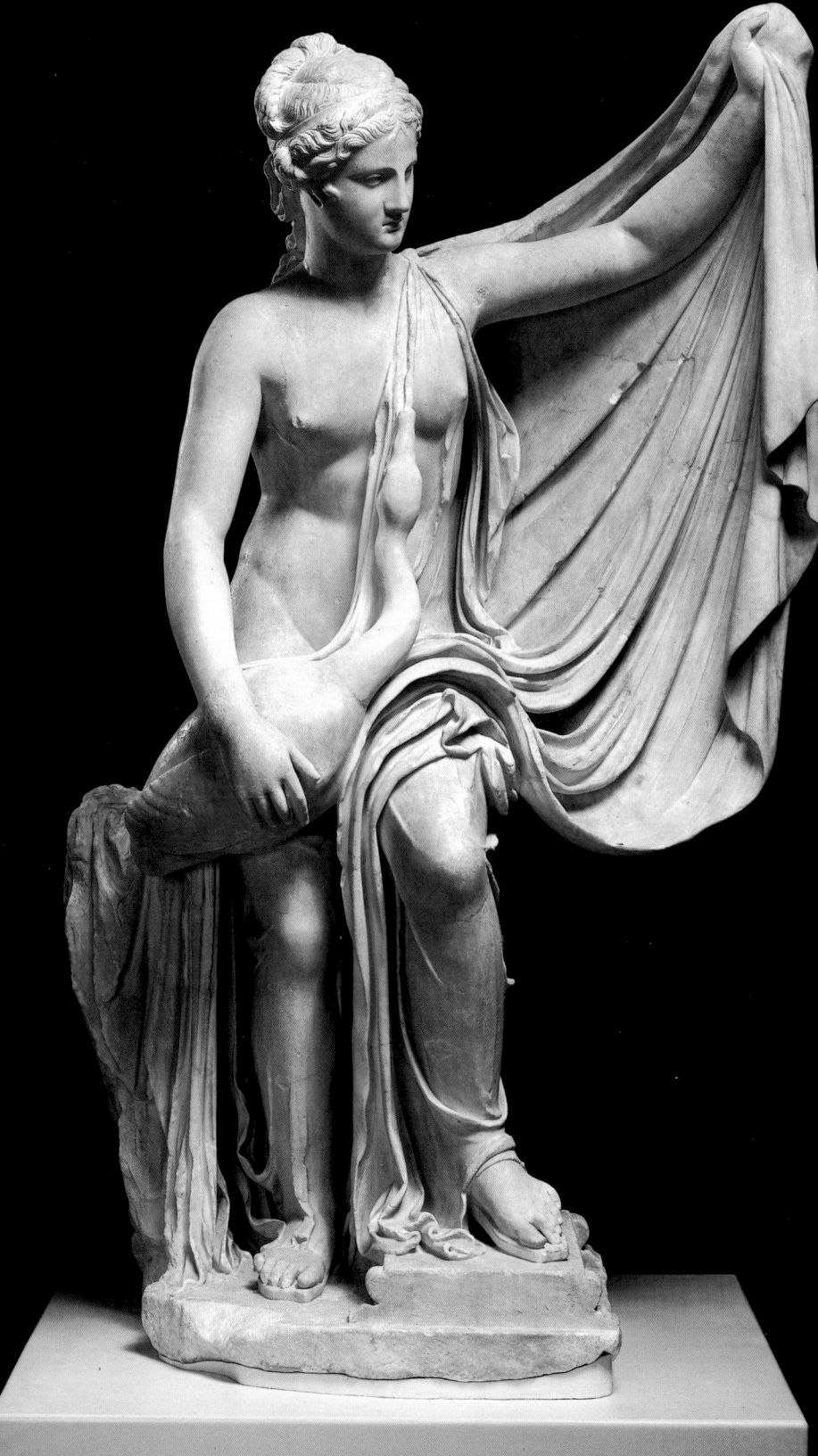

STATUE OF LEDA AND THE SWAN

Roman, from Rome,
A.D. 1–100
Marble
H: 132.1 cm (52 in.)
W: 85.3 cm (32⅞ in.)
D: 52.1 cm (20½ in.)
70.AA.110

Greek mythology tells the story of Leda, a mortal woman and queen of Sparta who caught the eye of Zeus, king of the gods. Zeus had frequent affairs with mortals but often had to disguise himself as an animal in order to avoid detection by his wife Hera, as well as angry husbands and fathers. He appeared to Leda in the form of a swan. Here, she draws the amorous bird into her lap while she holds up a sheltering cloak. After the union, Leda laid two eggs: one bore the twins Helen and Klytaimnestra; the other produced the heroic horsemen Kastor and Polydeukes. Helen grew up to be a famous beauty and queen of Sparta. It was her abduction by the Trojan prince Paris that caused the war between Greece and Troy, described by Homer in the *Iliad*.

Found in 1775 in Rome, this marble sculpture is a Roman version of an earlier Greek statue from the 300s B.C. attributed to the sculptor Timotheos (active 380–350 B.C.). More than two dozen statues modeled on Timotheos's original survive, attesting to the theme's popularity among the Romans. The contrast of the clinging transparent drapery on Leda's torso, especially over her left breast, and the heavy folds of cloth bunched between her legs characterizes Timotheos's style. The statue both conceals and reveals the female body, a tension often found in fourth-century sculpture, before actual female nudity became acceptable.

After its discovery, the piece was extensively restored and reworked. Both arms, most of the outstretched cloak, the swan's head, and the folds of cloth between Leda's legs are eighteenth-century restorations. The head, though ancient, is not original to this work, but comes from a statue of Venus.

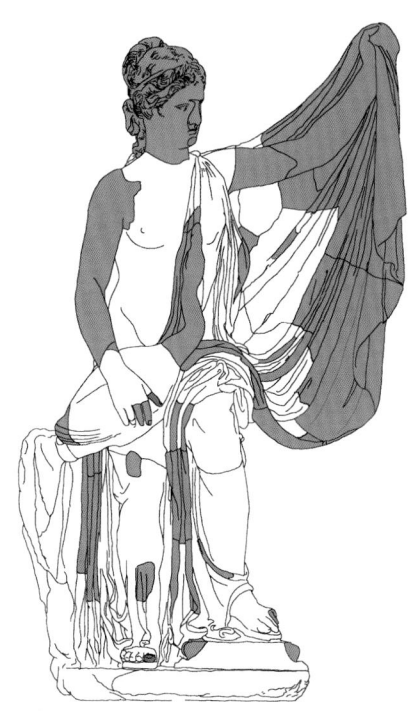

ANCIENT RESTORATION

HISTORICAL RESTORATION

1997 RESTORATION

STATUE OF A
COLLAPSING NIOBID

Roman, A.D. 1–100
Marble
H: 146.6 cm (57½ in.)
W: 81.3 cm (32 in.)
D: 52.1 cm (20½ in.)
72.AA.126

This fragmentary figure probably comes from a larger sculptural group that depicted the slaughter of the children of Niobe. Niobe, the daughter of King Tantalus of Sipylon and wife of Amphion of Thebes, had made the rash claim that she was as good a mother as Leto, the mother of the gods Apollo and Artemis. Niobe had given birth to many children, whereas Leto had only two. To retaliate for Niobe's act of hubris, Apollo and Artemis killed all her children. Niobe (see also pp. 120–21) was so grief stricken at their deaths that she pleaded with Zeus to turn her to stone.

This youth, one of Niobe's sons, has been hit with an arrow in his right shoulder blade. With his drapery wrapped around his lower legs, he collapses to his knees and reaches back to try to pull out the now-missing arrow (the hole for the arrow's insertion remains). Although the arms and head of the youth are now missing, most of his left hand is preserved on his back.

The larger sculptural group of the Niobids to which this statue belongs was made in the first century A.D. and depicted the deaths of all the children. The earliest known sculpture of the scene was a relief frieze that decorated the throne of the cult statue of Zeus at Olympia, created by the Greek sculptor Pheidias and one of the Seven Wonders of the Ancient World. Just as that statue inspired many copies (including the Marbury Hall Zeus, pp. 148–49), so too were related compositions, like the scene of Niobe's children, frequently copied by later artists. The most famous original large-scale sculptures of the Niobids, now lost, were probably the work of the mid-fourth-century sculptor Skopas.

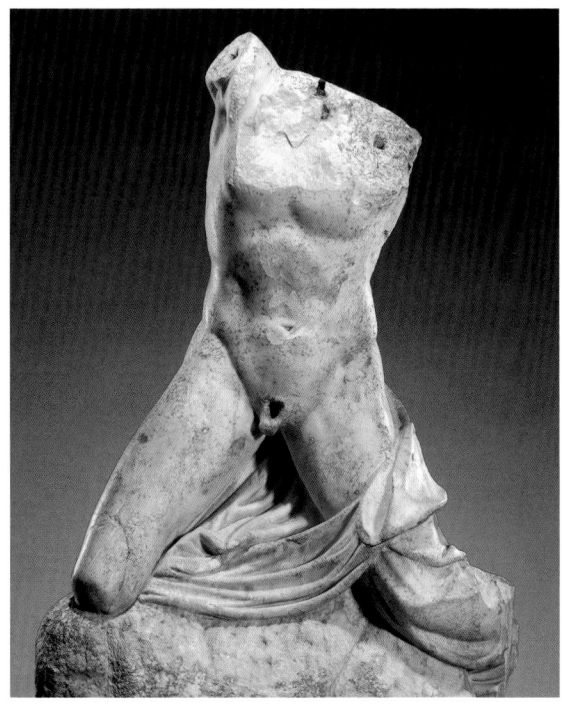

PORTRAIT HEAD OF AUGUSTUS

Roman, 25–1 B.C.
Marble
H: 39 cm (15³⁄₈ in.)
W: 21 cm (8¹⁄₄ in.)
D: 24 cm (9¹⁄₂ in.)
78.AA.261

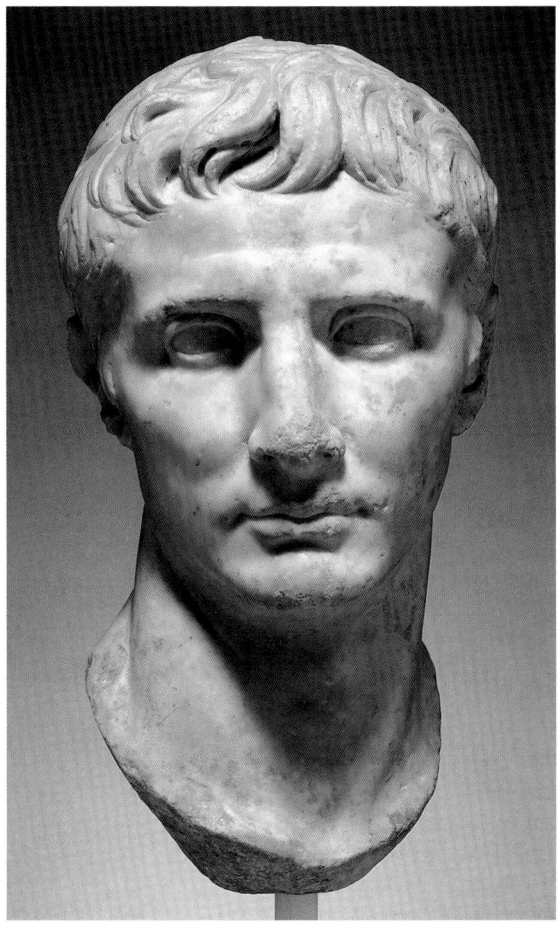

The adopted son of Julius Caesar, Augustus became the first emperor of Rome in 27 B.C. and ruled until his death in A.D. 14. During the new golden age of expansion, peace, and prosperity that followed a bloody civil war, many portraits of the emperor were erected in Rome and throughout the provinces. Augustus used art to help convey his political and social beliefs and to validate his claim to power. To contrast his rule with that of the earlier Roman Republican period, wherein age was emphasized in portraits as a sign of experience, images of Augustus always depicted him as youthful, recalling Classical Greek sculpture from the fifth century B.C. Here, his face is smooth and idealized, with a broad cranium, narrow chin, almond-shaped eyes, aquiline nose, sharply ridged eyebrows, and rounded mouth. His hairstyle is also an identifying feature in that the comma-shaped locks in the center of his forehead turn toward each other to form a pincer. The locks were reworked in antiquity, as were the forehead and the eyes. This has suggested to some scholars that the head originally represented the emperor Caligula (reigned A.D. 37–41; see next entry). At least ten other portraits of Caligula seem to have been recarved to represent Augustus. Recent research, however, indicates that the original head was not a portrait of Caligula, but rather an Augustus that was recut in antiquity to emphasize the emperor's distinctive, pincer-like locks.

PORTRAIT HEAD OF CALIGULA

Roman, circa A.D. 40
Marble
H: 43 cm (16⅞ in.)
W: 21.5 cm (8½ in.)
D: 25 cm (9⅞ in.)
72.AA.155

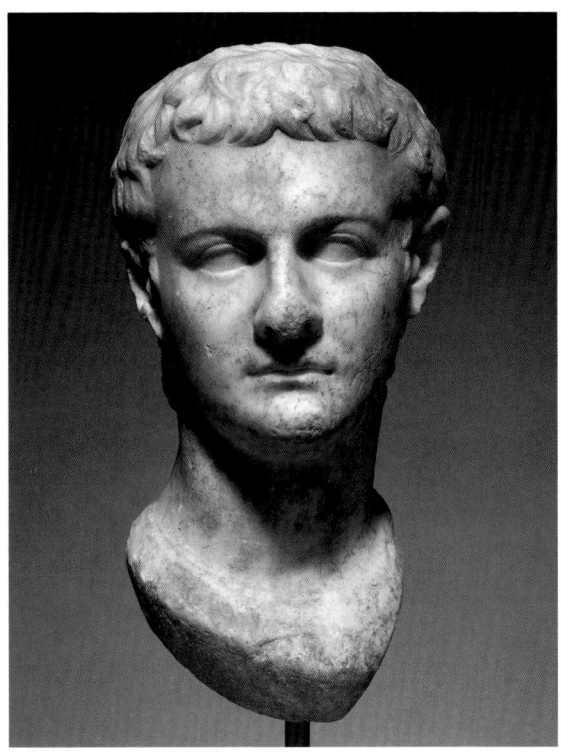

The third Roman emperor, Gaius Julius Caesar Germanicus (reigned A.D. 37–41), was known more commonly as Caligula, a nickname meaning "little boots" that was given to him during his childhood when he accompanied his father, Germanicus, to a Roman military camp in Germania. An intellectual and a skilled orator with a passion for building projects (the reconstruction of the Theater of Pompey was one among many of his plans), Caligula has become infamous for his capricious cruelty and insistence upon self-deification. He was assassinated in A.D. 41 by members of his own guard.

This head was originally made to be inserted into a *togatus* statue, a traditional form of imperial portraiture with Etruscan ancestry (see also the statuette on p. 129). The original would have been a life-size figure dressed in a toga, the distinctive mark of a Roman citizen. Although ancient authors describe Caligula's physical presence in the most unflattering terms, mentioning his pallid complexion, hairy body, bald head, and sunken eyes, the appearance of this portrait is classically ideal, following the style established by the emperor Augustus (see previous entry) that had become standard for depictions of members of the Julio-Claudian family. Nevertheless, it also incorporates Caligula's individual features, such as his high forehead, small thin mouth with drawn-in lower lip, and prominent chin. After Caligula's assassination, the senate requested a *damnatio memoriae* (official damnation of his memory), by which all images and references to him would be destroyed. Even though Claudius, Caligula's uncle and successor, prevented the enactment of the *damnatio memoriae*, the memory of Caligula's reign was so repellent that many representations of and references to him were still destroyed. Portraits are thus rare, and few survived from the city of Rome.

STATUETTE OF A SLEEPING CUPID

Roman, A.D. 50–100
Marble
H: 41.9 cm (16½ in.)
W: 26 cm (10¼ in.)
D: 13.5 cm (5¼ in.)
73.AA.95

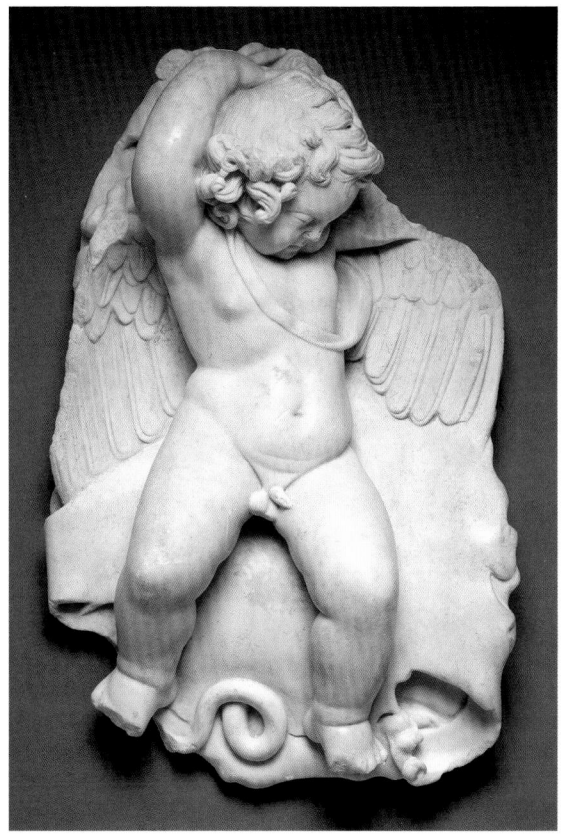

This plump-faced infant lying on his back is identifiable as Cupid by his splayed wings and the strap for a quiver across his chest. He is the son of Venus and a personification of sexual desire; his arrows and other wiles made his victims fall in love.

Here he lies with his right arm cast around his head, a typical motif to denote deep sleep. The thick curls of hair, with individual strands defined by chiseled lines, suggest a date in the late first century A.D. His missing left arm was probably limply extended. Beneath him is a lion's skin that covers a rocky surface—part of the tail is visible between his feet, and a paw to the right. The lion's skin is an attribute of Hercules, and one tale tells of Cupid stealing his club, quiver, and lion's skin, suggesting that even the mightiest are vulnerable to the playful, yet cunning, designs of love.

The motif of the sleeping Cupid is found in both poetry and art, and surviving sculptures of this type probably derive from a Hellenistic original. In this example, marks at a number of points, such as on the uppermost lock of hair lying over the right arm, may have been used for taking measurements during the copying process. Sleeping Cupids are often depicted on tomb monuments and sarcophagi. Sleep was a metaphor for death in antiquity, and the sympathetic image of the child-divinity in repose served to soften the hard fact of death. The outer edge of the underside has been carefully smoothed, but the middle protrudes and is coarsely notched, suggesting that the statue was once set into a pedestal.

PORTRAIT STATUE
OF A WOMAN
AS CYBELE

Roman, from Rome,
circa A.D. 50
Marble
H: 162 cm (63¾ in.)
W: 70 cm (27½ in.)
D: 64.5 cm (25½ in.)
57.AA.19

Seated on a throne, this life-size statue of a mature
Roman woman is surrounded by emblems of the goddess Cybele: a crown of city walls, fruits and flowers,
a tympanum (hand drum), and a lion. The cult
of Cybele, also known as the Magna Mater, the great
mother-goddess of Anatolia, was introduced to Rome
in 204 B.C. at the conclusion of the Second Punic War.
Cybele was a founder and protectress of cities, symbolized by the mural crown, and a mistress over wild
animals, represented by the lion. Her devotees performed music and ecstatic dances, and so she holds a
tympanum. Cybele acquired attributes of other divinities, represented here by a rudder from the goddess
Fortuna, and a cornucopia, which was associated with
a variety of deities and personifications responsible
for agricultural abundance.

The cult of Cybele appealed especially to women,
so it is not surprising that a Roman matron would
choose to represent herself in the guise of the goddess.
The life-size enthroned statue identifies the subject
as a woman of status and high position in Roman
society, perhaps someone of imperial stature or a
priestess of the goddess. In any case, the combination
of a body that is soft, round, and voluptuous with a
square face exhibiting a broad chin, firm mouth,
and close-set eyes produces a portrait that embodies
two traits desirable in Roman women: fecundity and
dignity. The back of the throne and the top of the
head are not fully finished, suggesting a niche as the
original setting for the statue.

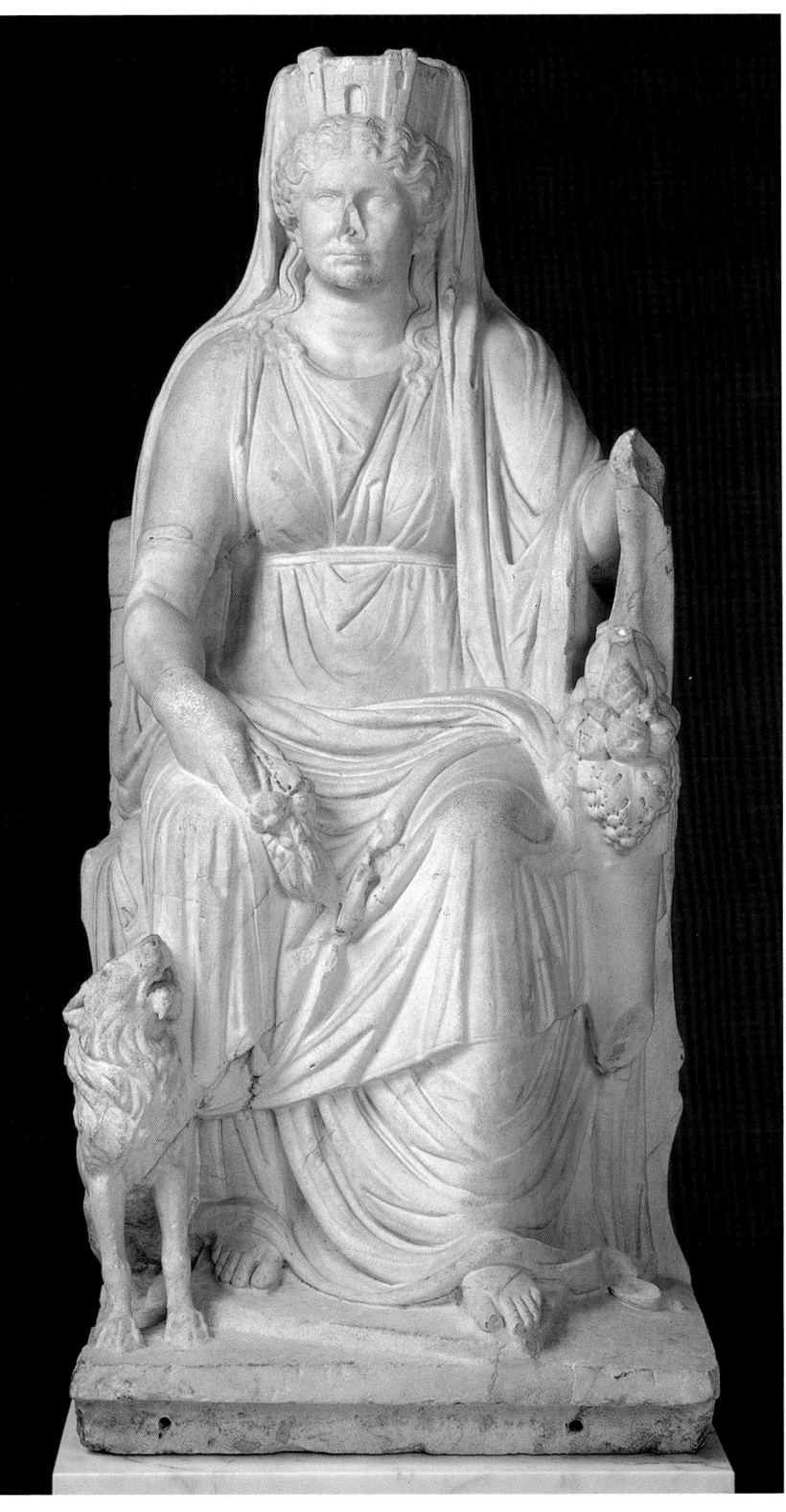

STATUE OF A POURING SATYR

Roman, found at
Castel Gondolfo, A.D. 81–96
Marble
H: 165 cm (65 in.)
W: 53 cm (21 in.)
D: 58.4 cm (23 in.)
2002.34

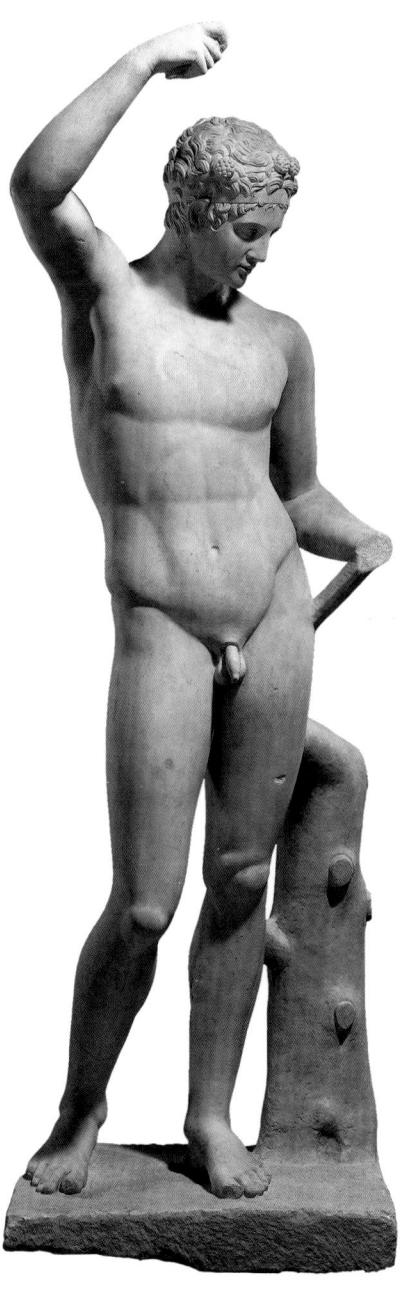

Recognizable only by his pointed ears, the satyr—traditionally a wild, lusty companion of the wine god Bacchus—is shown here as a civilized adolescent. Originally, he was pouring wine from a jug into a cup that he held in his left hand (both jug and cup are now lost). The figure is a Roman version of a statue by the Greek sculptor Praxiteles (active 375–340 B.C.), who created the first large-scale depiction of a satyr about 370 B.C.

After the statue was found in 1657 in the villa of the emperor Domitian (reigned A.D. 81–96) at Castel Gandolfo, Italy, with three identical replicas, it entered the collection of Pope Alexander VII Chigi (1655–1667). Using the other three satyr statues as models, this satyr's head and right hand were carefully restored by a seventeenth-century Italian sculptor, probably Ercole Boselli. When in 1728 the Chigi marbles were sold to Augustus the Strong, Elector of Saxony and King of Poland, the four satyrs came to Dresden. The courtly collections in Saxony eventually became state property, and after the reunification of Germany in 1990 the present statue was returned to descendants of the Saxon royal family as part of a compensation agreement.

PORTRAIT HEAD OF JULIA TITI

Roman, circa A.D. 90
Marble with pigment
H: 33 cm (13 in.)
W: 22.5 cm (8⅞ in.)
D: 24.4 cm (9⅝ in.)
58.AA.1

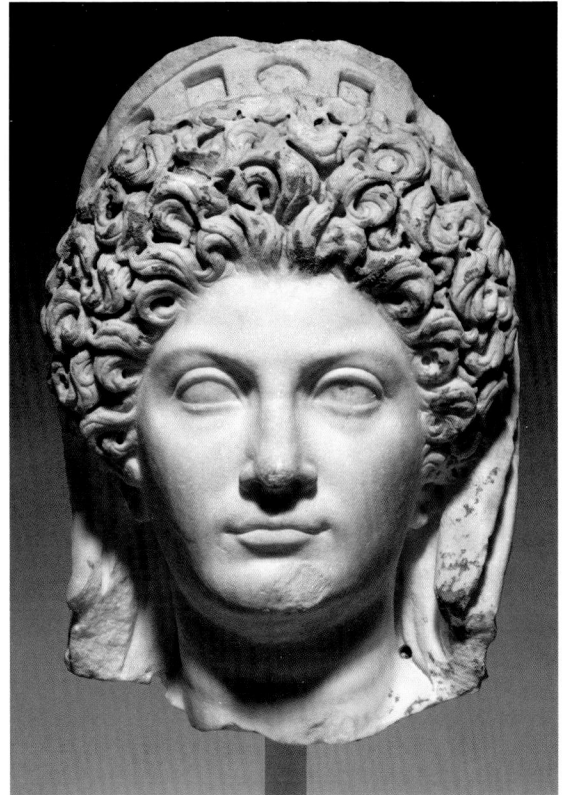

In contrast to its current appearance, this portrait originally would have been quite ornate and colorful. Traces of pigment in the hair attest to the application of paint, the square and circular depressions in the diadem were once inlaid with precious stones or colored glass, and the pierced earlobes and the drill holes on either side of the neck indicate that the head was adorned with real jewelry. The mantle pulled up over the back of the head either is an attribute of a Roman matron or points to the woman's role as a priestess.

The elaborate portrait suggests that the person depicted was a woman of power and status. The small curls typical of women in the Flavian period have led to her identification as Julia Titi (A.D. 63/4–89), the daughter of the emperor Titus (ruled A.D. 79–81) and his second wife Marcia Furnilla. But because the female members of the Flavian imperial family are not easily distinguishable from one another, there is no absolute certainty about this attribution. If it is correct, Julia Titi may be represented here as *diva*— that is, consecrated as a goddess, a status awarded to her after she died while still in her mid-twenties.

STATUE OF HERCULES (THE LANSDOWNE HERAKLES)

Roman, found at Tivoli,
circa A.D. 125
Marble
H: 193.5 cm (76⅛ in.)
W: 79 cm (31⅛ in.)
D: 47 cm (18½ in.)
70.AA.109

Hercules (known as Herakles to the Greeks) was the son of Alkmene, a mortal woman, and Jupiter, the king of the Olympian gods. He is best known for the Twelve Labors he completed for King Eurystheus of Argos. Hercules is frequently shown by ancient artists wearing or holding objects identified with these feats. Here he appears with a club and the skin of the Nemean Lion, which he killed as his first labor.

Although carved in a Roman workshop in the second century A.D., this statue was very likely inspired by a now-lost Greek statue, probably produced by the followers of the influential Greek sculptor Polykleitos working in the 300s B.C. As is typical for depictions of Greek heroes, the young Hercules is shown nude, since the Greeks considered male nudity the highest form of beauty.

Found in 1790 near the ruins of the villa of the Roman emperor Hadrian (reigned A.D. 117–138) at Tivoli outside Rome, this statue may have been one of numerous versions of Greek sculpture commissioned by Hadrian, who loved Greek culture. (Indeed, many other statues, including the Marbury Hall Zeus [see pp. 148–49], were likewise found at Tivoli.) Shortly after its discovery, the statue was restored in Rome, possibly in the workshop of Bartolomeo Cavaceppi. In 1792, it was sold to the English aristocrat Lord Lansdowne; it remained in the Lansdowne family until purchased by J. Paul Getty in 1951. One of Mr. Getty's most prized possessions, this statue inspired him to build his museum in Malibu in the style of an ancient Roman villa with a special room created for its display.

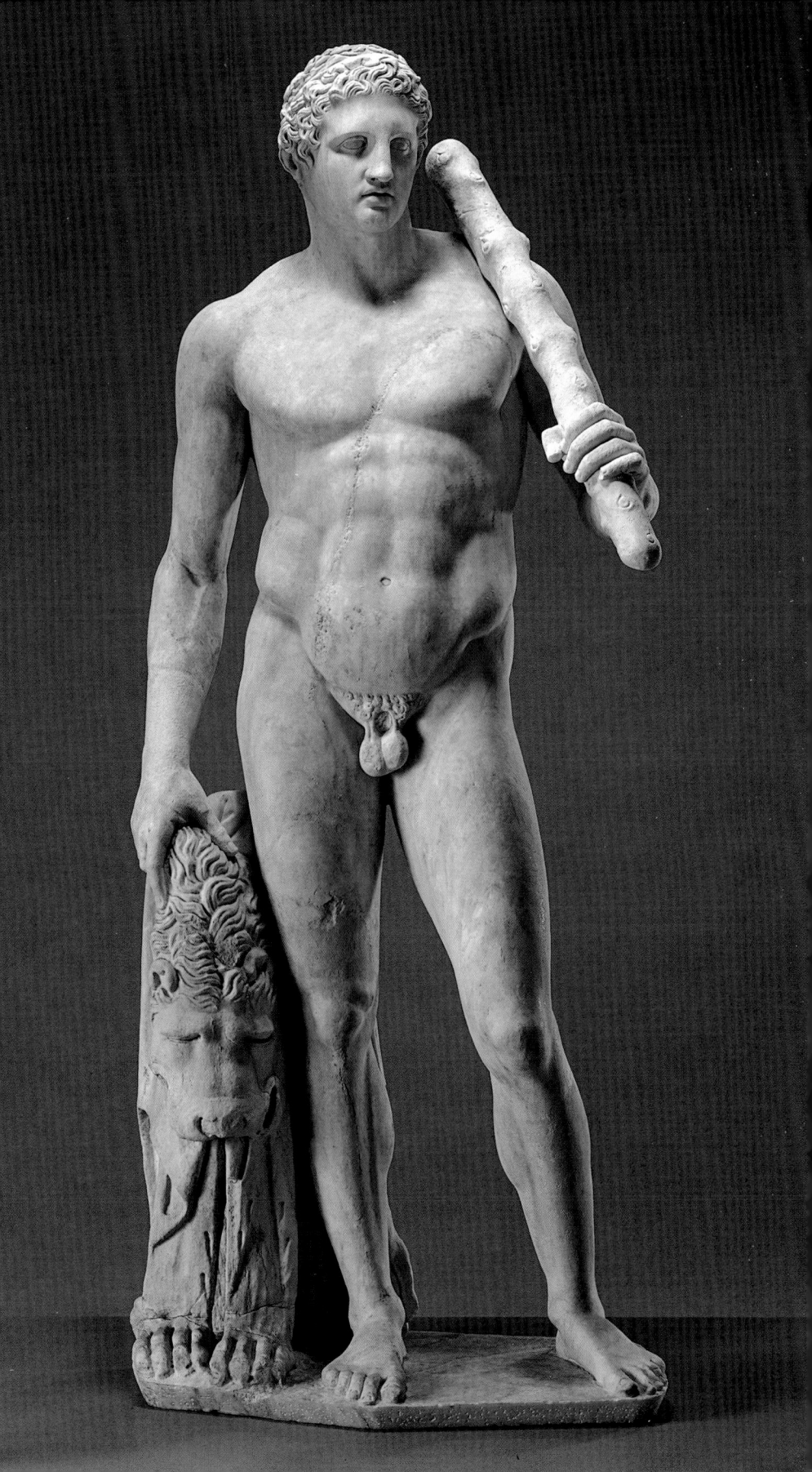

PORTRAIT BUST OF A WOMAN

Roman, circa A.D. 130
Marble
H: 43 cm (16⅞ in.)
W: 42.1 cm (16⅝ in.)
D (head): 24 cm (9½ in.)
70.AA.100

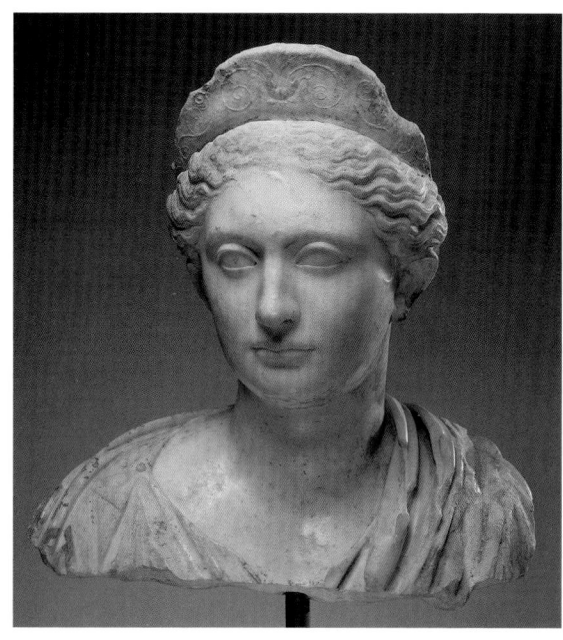

This young woman has distinct individual features: a round, somewhat pointy face with large eyes under a soft brow, a wide and strong nose, a small mouth with prominent upper lip, a short chin, and, most characteristically, protruding ears. Her wavy hair, parted in the middle and tied together in a loose bun in the back, is crowned by a tall lunate diadem adorned with tendrils in low relief. The edge of the diadem is mostly broken but it was once lined with small spheres representing pearls, one of which is visible on the right side. Although about half of the bust, including the socle, is missing, enough of the shoulders is preserved to indicate that the person portrayed wears a tunic and mantle.

The hairstyle and diadem were intended to give the woman the timeless appearance of a Greek goddess. Representing individuals in the guise of or with the attributes of divinities was common practice in Roman portraiture. In the case of this bust, these details also assimilate the likeness to the image of Sabina, the wife of the emperor Hadrian (reigned A.D. 117–138). The bust has long been interpreted as a portrait of the empress herself, yet physiognomic differences make this identification unlikely. Earlier scholars actually saw her as Livia, Augustus's wife, as did Mr. Getty when he acquired this portrait in 1939 from the art dealer Alfredo Barsanti in Rome. The form of the bust, however, and the portrait's affinity to Sabina help date the sculpture to around A.D. 130.

PORTRAIT BUST OF A WOMAN

Roman, A.D. 150–160
Marble
H: 67.5 cm (26⅝ in.)
W: 42.5 cm (16¾ in.)
83.AA.44

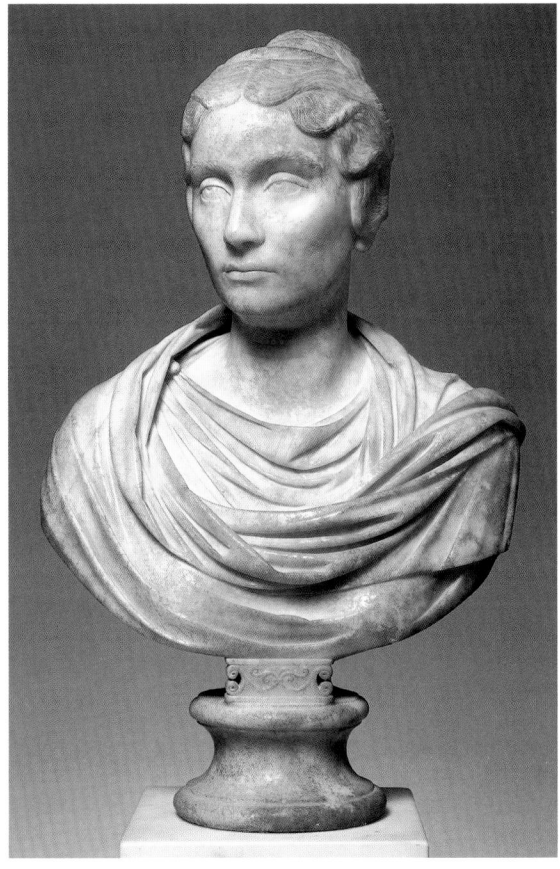

A quiet elegance radiates from this beautiful portrait of an unidentified Roman matron, carved from a single block of marble. Based upon stylistic evidence, it is possible to determine that she was sculpted during the Antonine period, a time known for widespread peace and prosperity, cultural expansion, and increased freedom for Roman women. The figure's elaborate coiffure is especially useful for dating the sculpture, for individuals often followed the fashion trends set by Roman imperial family members. Private portraits of women sculpted during the Antonine period were thus greatly influenced by those of the empress Faustina the Elder, the wife of Antoninus Pius (reigned A.D. 138–161). Faustina wore a braided bun high on her head, as this matron

does. Faustina the Younger contributed undulating waves of hair surrounding the face to Roman fashion, which have also been incorporated into this portrait. The contrast seen here between the textural treatment of the hair and the highly polished surfaces of the sitter's face is characteristic of Antonine portraiture.

Appropriately for a Roman matron, this woman wears a *stola* (a loose-fitting tunic), which is fastened with a circular brooch on the right shoulder area, and a *palla* (rectangular shawl). This bust may have been placed in the family's house as part of a shrine or it may have been incorporated into a family tomb. In either case, it was a lasting tribute to the character and image of this Roman lady.

STATUE OF VENUS (THE MAZARIN VENUS)

Roman, from Rome,
A.D. 100–200
Marble
H: 184 cm (72½ in.)
54.AA.11

This Roman image of the goddess Venus is a variation of an earlier Greek statue created by the Athenian scuptor Praxiteles. Praxiteles' statue, known as the Aphrodite of Knidos, was carved in approximately 350 B.C. and depicted the goddess of love naked, startled by an intruder while bathing. It began the tradition of the female classical nude in western European art. In this Roman version of the type, the goddess stands with her drapery wrapped around her hips, both concealing and revealing her form. A dolphin with a squid in its mouth, which serves as a support, alludes to her birth from the sea.

The modern history of the statue begins with its appearance in a 1509 engraving by Giovanni Antonio da Brescia (ca. 1460–ca. 1520) with an inscription stating it had recently been found in Rome. Its head and right arm were already restored at that time, but two drawings from the circle of Raphael, which must be slightly earlier, show it headless. Other repairs, perhaps the result of subsequent damage, seem to have been made later. The statue is said to have been purchased for the collection of French Cardinal Mazarin no later than 1643, and then to have been presented to the Louis XIV, King of France, but recent scholarship suggests that it was never in Mazarin's possession. It is known to have been in the Beaujon collection in Paris in the eighteenth and nineteenth centuries, and was acquired by Francis Cook in 1855. When the Cook collection was dispersed in 1917, the statue was bought by a private collector in France. J. Paul Getty purchased the work in 1954.

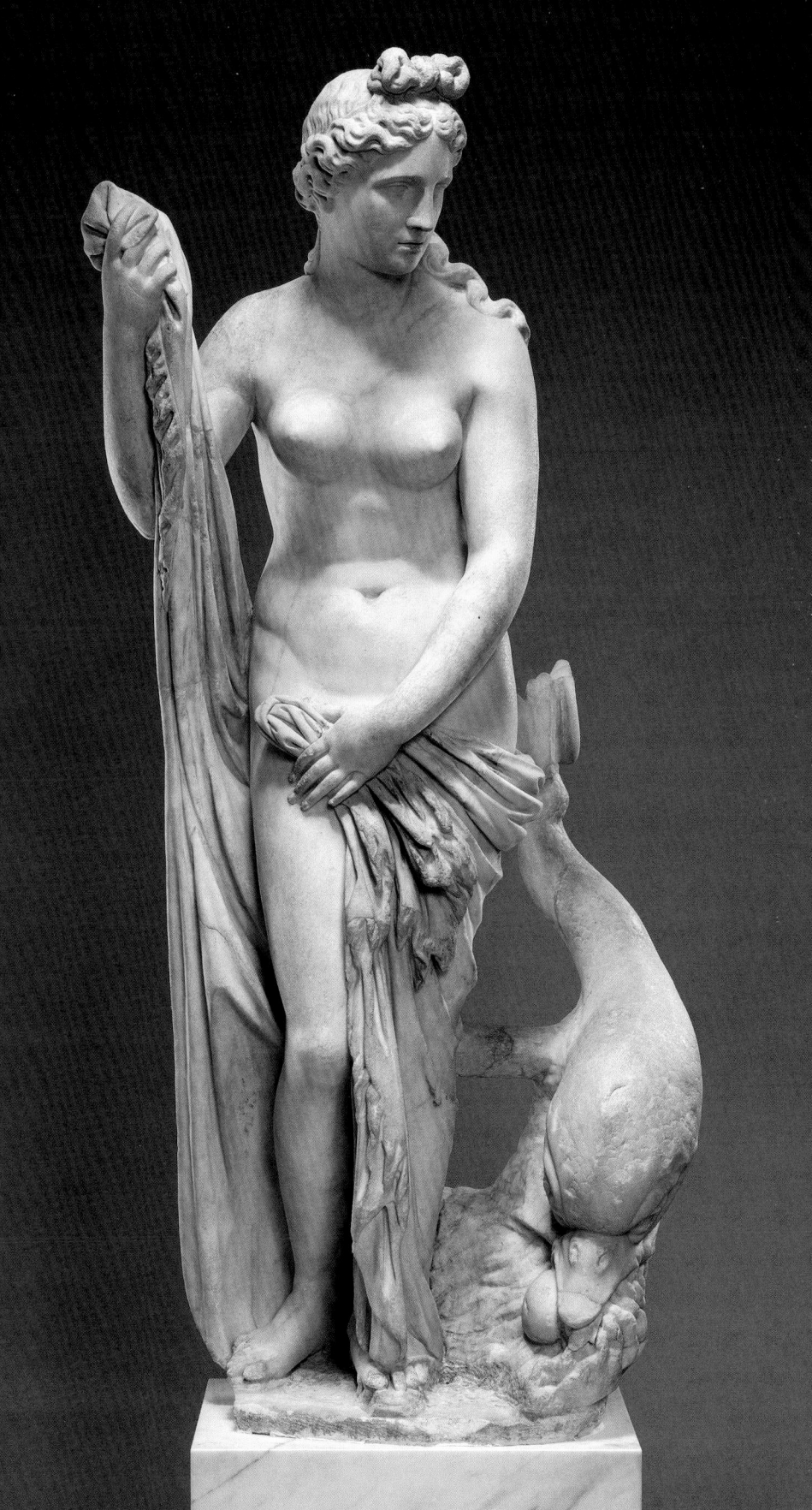

PORTRAIT BUST OF COMMODUS (THE GETTY COMMODUS)

Roman, A.D. 180–185
Marble
H (incl. socle): 92.5 cm
(36³⁄₈ in.)
H (without socle): 70 cm
(27¹⁄₂ in.)
W: 61 cm (24 in.)
D: 22.8 cm (9 in.)
92.SA.48

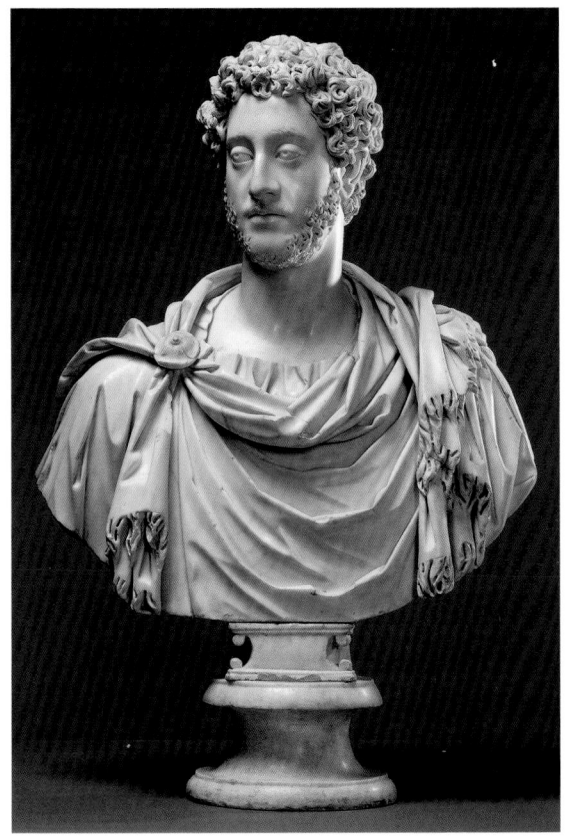

Commodus (A.D. 161–192), the last emperor of the Antonine dynasty, is represented here in a portrait type created when he became sole ruler following the death of his father, Marcus Aurelius, in A.D. 180. After several youthful portraits, this is the first to show Commodus bearded. He wears a tunic and fringed military cloak, or *paludamentum*.

When this imposing bust was first acquired for the Getty Museum, it was considered the work of a North Italian artist of the late sixteenth century. In recent years, however, there has been growing consensus among scholars that it is, in fact, an ancient sculpture from the emperor's lifetime.

The uncertainty over the bust's date is a consequence of its modern history. The piece was acquired in the 1800s, no doubt as an antiquity, for Castle Howard, Yorkshire, the resi-

dence of the earls of Carlisle. As was common practice at the time, abrasive cleaning and recarving significantly altered the surface and thus the appearance of the work. Traces of a calcium carbonate crust, however, remain in inconspicuous places in the back and the hair. Scientific analysis of these traces suggests the bust was buried for an extended period and therefore is likely ancient. The style and carving techniques such as the drilling in the hair and the rendering of the pupils of the eye further support an Antonine date for the Getty Commodus.

STATUE OF A MUSE (MELPOMENE OR POLYHYMNIA)

Roman (Asia Minor),
circa A.D. 200
Marble
H: 97 cm (38¼ in.)
W: 30.5 cm (12 in.)
D: 22.9 cm (9 in.)
94.AA.22

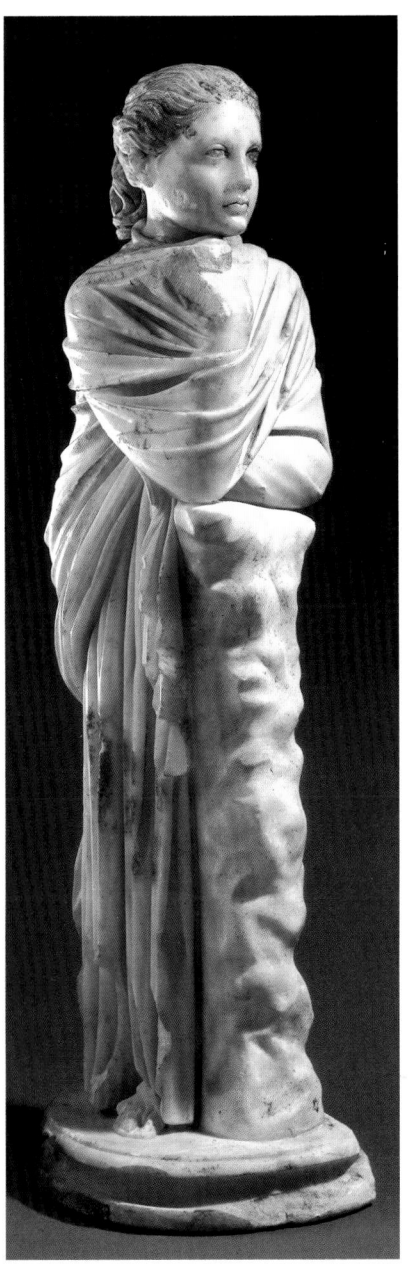

As acolytes of Apollo, the nine Muses were patron deities of music, poetry, literature, and drama. In fact, the word "museum" denotes a shrine dedicated to them. They were extremely popular in Roman art because they bestowed *kleos*, or glory, upon the humans they favored. The Muses were often found depicted on sarcophagi, where they they represented the elevated intellectual aspirations of the deceased.

Traces of paint on this figure's eyes and gilding in her hair show that color originally enlivened the surface of the sculpture. In art, the Muses are difficult to distinguish from one another, and the characteristic "Leaning Muse" posture (well known from many examples) has been associated with both Polyhymnia, the Muse of hymns and pantomime, and Melpomene, the Muse of tragedy. Ancient philosophers were often depicted in the same pose in order to associate themselves with the Muses' powers of contemplation. Here, those powers are conveyed by the figure's intense, otherworldly gaze and the way her chin rests on her fist.

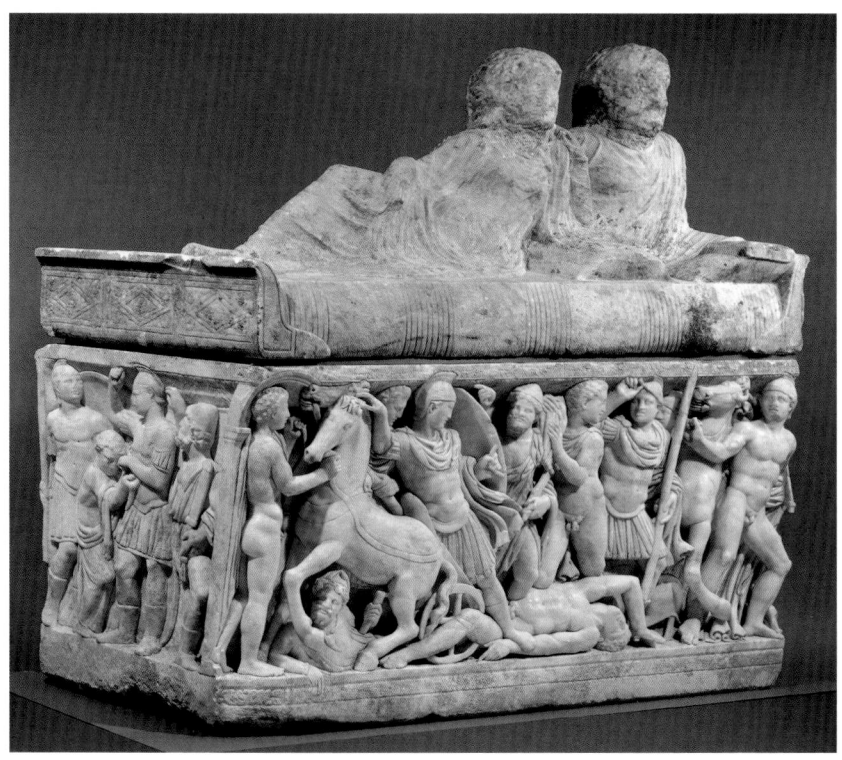

SARCOPHAGUS AND LID

Roman, made in Athens,
A.D. 180–220
Marble
H (box): 134 cm (53 in.)
W (box): 147 cm (58 in.)
L (box): 211 cm (83⅛ in.)
H (lid): 100 cm (39½ in.)
W (lid): 95 cm (37½ in.)
L (lid): 218 cm (86 in.)
95.AA.80

Tales from the Trojan War cycle inspired the three
scenes from Achilles' life that decorate this beautifully
carved sarcophagus. The right end depicts Odysseus
discovering the great Greek hero on the island of
Skyros. Thetis had sent her son to hide among the
daughters of King Lykomedes in order to avoid his
foretold fate of an early death in combat. But Odysseus
tricked Achilles into revealing himself by including a
shield among the feminine gifts he offered the king's
daughters. Achilles' subsequent decision to accept
his fate is shown on the left end, where he dons his
armor with Odysseus's help. On the front of the sarcophagus, Achilles prepares to drag the dead Trojan
hero Hektor behind his chariot around the walls of
Troy. Hektor's idealized nude body reposes in eternal
sleep, mimicking the placement of the deceased
within the sarcophagus. Achilles steps on the body
as he mounts the chariot, further defiling the corpse.
On the back, in shallower relief, Lapiths fight Centaurs. This may be a reference to Achilles' teacher, the
Centaur Cheiron, or it may represent an allegorical
image of the civilized Greeks, as Lapiths, versus the
uncivilized Trojans, as Centaurs. The lid takes the
form of a *kline*, or couch-bed, on which two figures

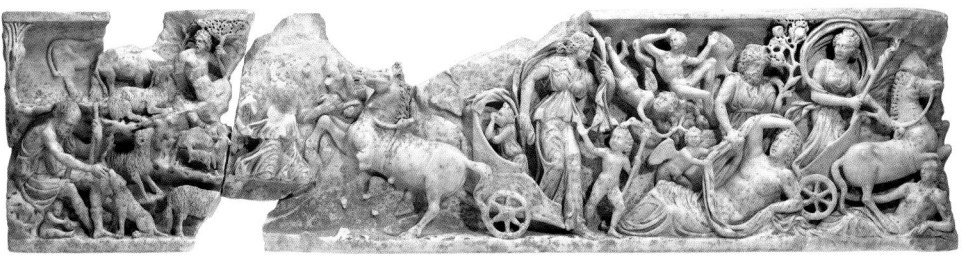

FRONT OF A SARCOPHAGUS WITH THE MYTH OF ENDYMION

Roman, circa A.D. 210
Marble
H: 54 cm (21¼ in.)
L: 214 cm (84¼ in.)
76.AA.8

This fragmentary front panel of a sarcophagus preserves two episodes from the story of Endymion and Selene. Selene, goddess of the moon, fell in love with Endymion, a beautiful young mortal. Jealous of their love, Zeus cast Endymion into an eternal sleep, but Selene visited him every night. The pastoral setting is indicated by the shepherd tending his flock on the left side of the relief. Selene is in the center, identified by her crescent-moon headdress, alighting from the chariot that she uses to draw the moon across the sky. She is accompanied by erotes, who signify love. Endymion, shown in the pose of eternal sleep with his right arm over his head, is uncovered by Eros, Aphrodite's son. Meanwhile, a standing figure, perhaps Hypnos, god of sleep, pours a potion over Endymion in order to ensure his continued slumber. Because death was equated with eternal sleep, the myth of Endymion was considered particularly appropriate for decorating sarcophagi.

To the right, in a second scene, Selene remounts her chariot to be carried back to the sky after the encounter. This method of linking a story's subsequent events, known as continuous narrative, is characteristically Roman. In this system, the same figures often appear over and over but in different scenes to show the progression of a story. Although very little of the two sides (and none of the back) of the original sarcophagus remains, a tree on the left edge and the hindquarters of an animal on the right indicate that bucolic scenes most likely continued on the other three panels.

recline. Their heads, which would normally have been carved with portraits of the deceased once the sarcophagus was sold, are unfinished.

Sarcophagi like this one were made in a few cities across the Roman Empire, including Athens. They were mass-produced, and popular mythological scenes were repeated with only slight variations.

PORTRAIT HEAD OF A BEARDED MAN

Roman, perhaps from
Greece, A.D. 200–225
Marble
H: 33.4 cm (13⅛ in.)
W: 23 cm (9 in.)
90.AA.21

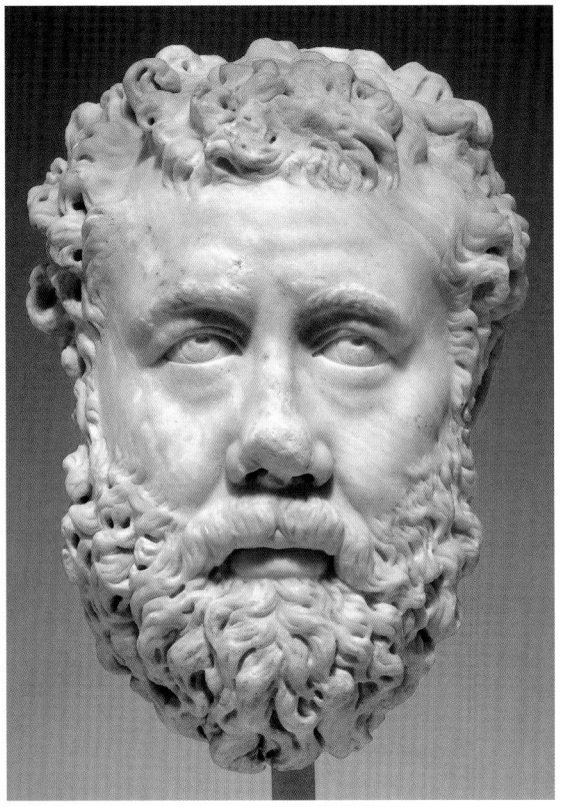

This portrait of an unknown, mature man, probably
carved during Caracalla's reign (A.D. 198–217),
exemplifies the often dynamic treatment of personal
characteristics in portraiture of the early third century. Although the deeply drilled hair and beard recall
similar features in the portraits of the emperor, the
aging face—with the upward gaze beneath the furrowed brow and the sagging flesh under the eyes and
on the cheeks—is distinctly individual. The delicately
smooth modeling of its planes, creating the appearance of real musculature and bone beneath the flesh,
stands out strongly against the rough contours and
drill work of the surrounding hair and beard. This
deliberate contrast between light and dark, smooth
and uneven is typical of the finest sculpture produced
during the Severan dynasty, which included the
reigns of Caracalla and his father, Septimius Severus
(reigned A.D. 193–211). The world-weary, sad resig-
nation of the man's overall expression suggests
the feelings of tension and uncertainty to which the
brutality of Caracalla's regime gave rise.

PORTRAIT BUST OF A BEARDED ROMAN

Roman, circa A.D. 215
Marble
H: 61 cm (24 in.)
W: 53 cm (28⅞ in.)
D: 28 cm (11 in.)
73.AA.42

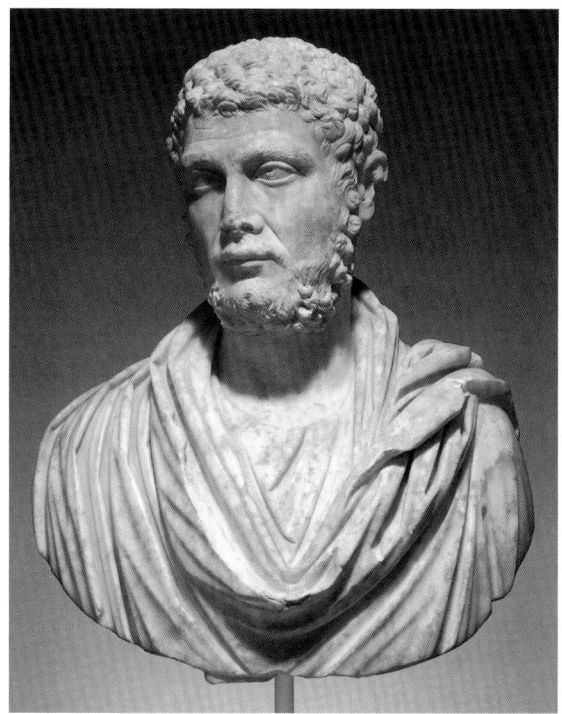

Portraits of Roman private individuals often follow the stylistic conventions of the leading contemporary public figures, such as emperors and their wives (see the Portrait Bust of a Woman on p. 163). With its subject's distinctive facial proportions and closely cropped hairstyle and beard, this bust not only emulates the physical aspects of the mature Caracalla (reigned A.D. 198–217) but also presents a somberness inspired by images of that emperor. Driven by his vision of Alexander the Great's genius, Caracalla was said to affect Alexander's intense, brooding facial expression, thus creating a look that became a part of his own iconography.

As on other portrait busts of the time, here the smooth surface of the skin contrasts with the rougher textures of hair and drapery (see also previous entry). The large eyes with deeply drilled crescent-shaped pupils placed high in the irises are also characteristic for the period. Their reflective upward glance combines with the man's pensive, firmly set lips to lend an air of psychological introspection to his appearance. The favored format for a Roman portrait bust of this date generally included the shoulders and chest of the sitter. Later the format would extend to integrate the waist as well.

PORTRAIT HEAD OF A BALDING MAN

Roman, from Asia Minor,
circa A.D. 240
Marble
H: 25.5 cm (10 in.)
W: 22.5 cm (8⅞ in.)
D: 23 cm (9 in.)
85.AA.112

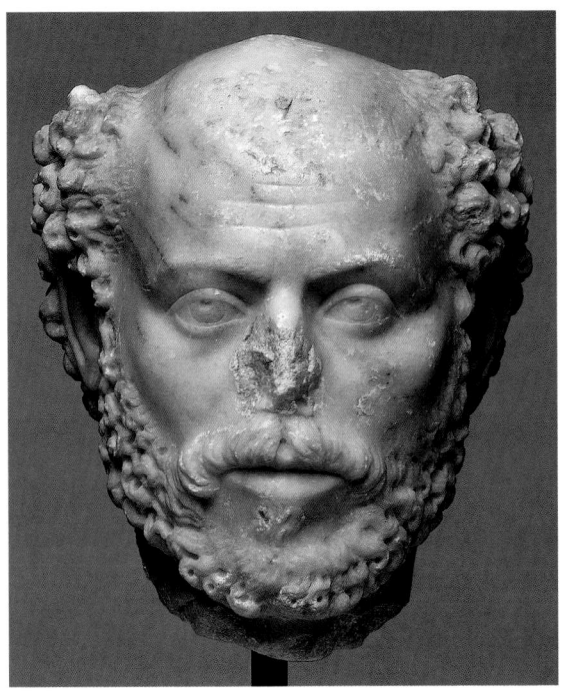

This Roman portrait depicts a mature man with an aging, lined brow and curly beard. His expression— characteristic of portraits from the third century, a time of much civil unrest in the Roman Empire— conveys a mood of concerned contemplation. The head provides a striking contrast to the idealized, clean-shaven faces familiar from Julio-Claudian portraits created some two centuries earlier (see the Portrait Head of Augustus, p. 153, and the Portrait Head of Caligula, p. 154).

This work demonstrates the tradition of Roman realism, especially through particularizing details such as the prominent cheekbones, the overall asymmetry of the features, and the inclusion of a few strands of hair atop the man's otherwise bald head. These characteristics are strikingly individual, introducing the viewer to a specific person from the past. However, although the subject of this portrait is individualized, the overall composition emphasizes certain standard components. The skillfully created contrast of texture between the highly polished, smooth skin of the man's face and the deeply drilled, undulating surface of his tightly curled hair accentuates the subject's baldness, the faint lines in his brow, and even his calm demeanor. All these elements were stock features in the portrayal of the classical Greek intellectual. This adherence to a type is further evinced by the man's sunken cheeks, which recall the ascetic look of philosopher portraits of well-known figures such as the Athenian orator Demosthenes. Altogether, this portrait reflects a careful selection of details that illustrate the inner character of the subject as much as his exterior, physical aspect.

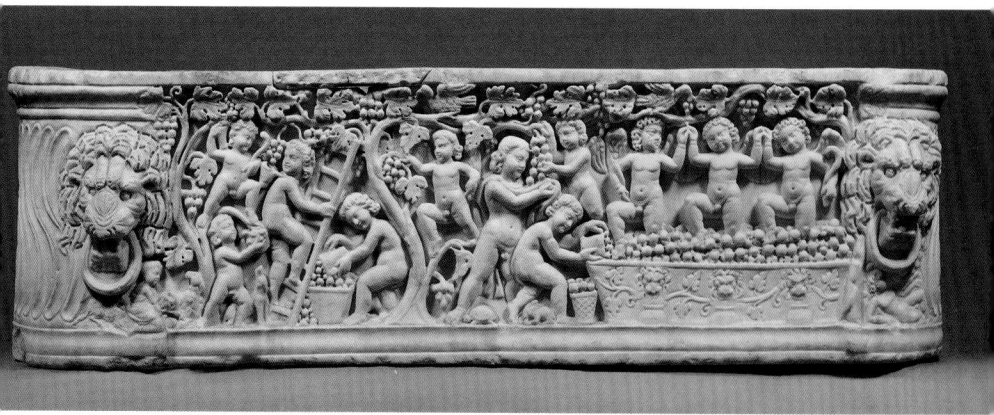

SARCOPHAGUS REPRESENTING A BACCHIC VINTAGE FESTIVAL

Roman, A.D. 290–300
Marble
H: 53.1 cm (20⅞ in.)
W: 190 cm (74¹³/₁₆ in.)
D (top): 56.9 cm (22⅜ in.)
D (bottom): 53.1 cm (20⅞ in.)
2008.14

This oval-shaped sarcophagus depicts a mythological representation of the *vindemia*, a rural Roman vintage festival. Eleven erotes harvest and stomp grapes below a leafy canopy of grapevines, while large lion's heads with fluted rings in their mouths flank the scene. Four wingless erotes on the left work together to fill a situla (bucket) with fruit. The four middle erotes also harvest grapes, and each is equipped with a *falx vinitoria* (pruning knife). At their feet sit a tortoise, a symbol of good luck, and a hare nibbling on fallen fruit. The three erotes on the right crush grapes inside a *lenos*, a wine-pressing trough. Jars, half-submerged in the earth, collect the juice from lion's-head spouts. Lion's-head spouts were a typical decoration for wine troughs, which the shape of this sarcophagus cleverly imitates. Under each of the two large lion's heads is a figure unrelated to the festival scene: on the left a girl milks a goat, while on the right a nude boy reclines.

Several visual clues date the sarcophagus stylistically to the late third century A.D. The *vindemia* scene, which was used primarily to embellish children's sarcophagi in the second century A.D., began to appear frequently on adult sarcophagi in the third century A.D. Moreover, the use of a running drill to create details on the lions' manes and the hair of the erotes is indicative of a late third-century-A.D. date.

PORTRAIT HEAD OF A MAN

Roman, from Asia Minor,
100–1 B.C.
Bronze
H: 29.5 cm (11⅝ in.)
W: 22.5 cm (8⅞ in.)
D: 24 cm (9½ in.)
73.AB.8

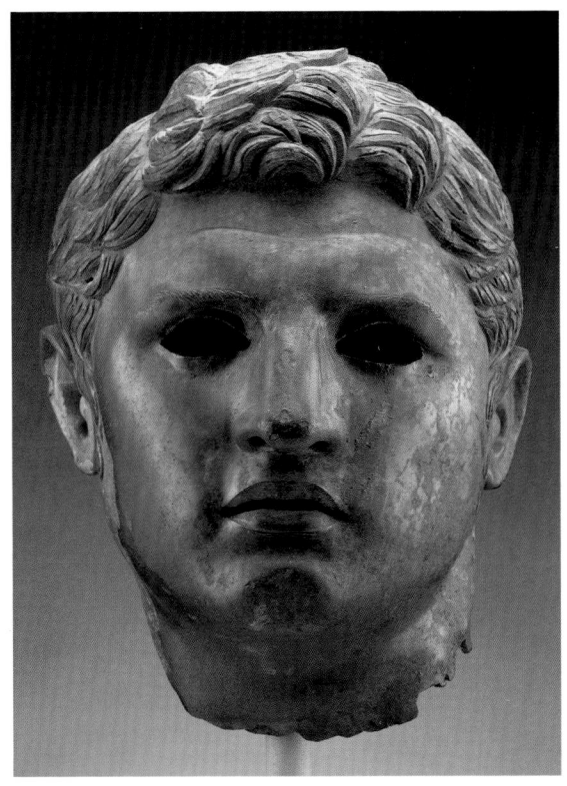

Both Greeks and Romans honored their military heroes, civic leaders, and other notables with commemorative statues. While some sculptures may have been ordered by the honorees, others were commissioned by the subjects' friends or by the local communities in which they were to be erected. Yet, no matter how lifelike the statues may have been, even in ancient times inscriptions identifying the honorees would have been requisite for most viewers.

Once part of a full-size statue, this portrait, with its bulging brow and dense mass of coarsely worked short hair, presents a strikingly forceful image of the subject. In antiquity, when its inset eyes and the copper inlay on its lips were still intact, and when its surface bore a highly polished sheen rather than its present dark green patina, the portrait would have had a powerful impact.

Although it has no extant inscription, comparison with Roman coins suggests that this portrait may represent the Roman general and dictator, Lucius Cornelius Sulla (138–78 B.C.). Sulla waged ruthless campaigns in Greece and Asia Minor, and acted equally brutally against his fellow Romans. However, close similarities to the earlier, idealized Hellenistic royal portraiture in the tradition of Alexander the Great, which stressed dynastic legitimacy and connections, also suggest that the portrait might depict a royal prince or local ruler of some eastern Mediterranean country.

STATUETTE OF A WOMAN, PERHAPS NYX

Roman, 100–1 B.C.
Bronze
H: 25.4 cm (10 in.)
96.AB.38

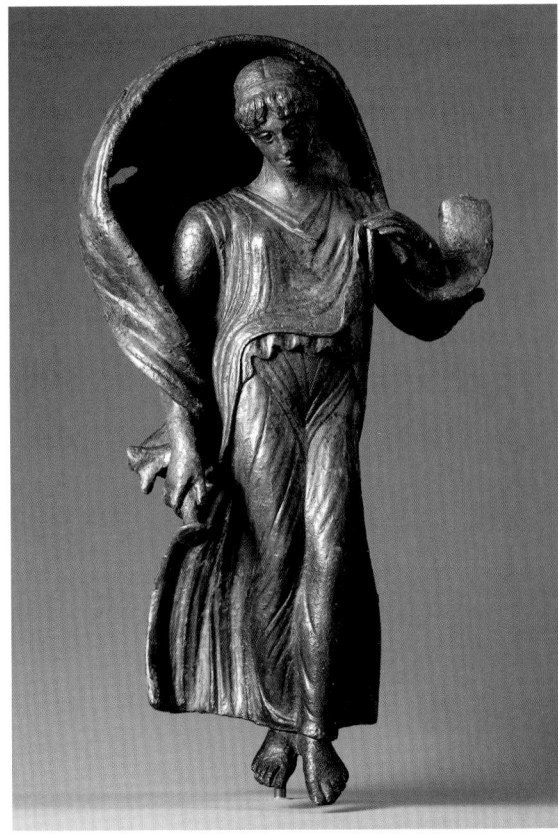

The billowing, upswept mantle that arches over the head of this figure identifies her as a celestial creature. The position of her down-turned feet, her downward gaze, and the manner in which her peplos clings to her figure and sweeps behind her suggest that she is descending from flight. She may be Nyx, the personification of night. The identity of the object she holds in her right hand is uncertain. It may be a stylized torch, an attribute normally associated with Nyx, or it may be an alabastron, a perfume vessel used here to scatter droplets of sleep on the slumbering world. An alternative identification for the figure would be the moon goddess, Selene, who is also often shown with billowing drapery. Because Selene usually wears a crown with a crescent moon, however, this identification is less likely.

The figure's details, such as the curling locks of hair on her forehead and, behind her headband, the fine lines of hair pulled back into a chignon, are carefully articulated. Her fine-boned face is delicately fashioned, as is her left hand, which gently pulls up the hem of her peplos's overfold. The drapery folds of her garment are carefully used to reveal and enhance her lithe figure. All these features help to date the piece to the first century B.C., when the Roman world was embracing the arts of Classical Greece.

The function of the statuette remains unclear, but it may have been a decorative attachment for a household item, such as the base of a candelabrum. If she is Nyx in fact , her presence on a lamp holder is more than appropriate.

STATUETTE OF ATHENA PROMACHOS

Roman, 50 B.C.–A.D. 25
Bronze and silver
H: 20.7 cm (8¹⁄₈ in.)
96.AB.176

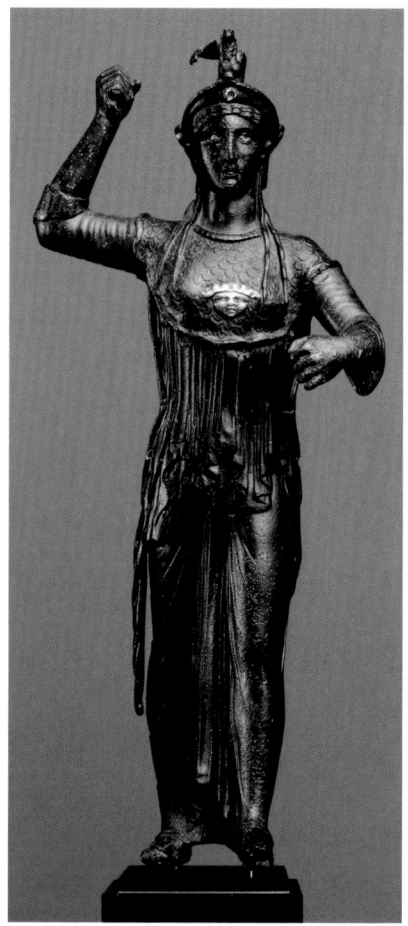

Athena Promachos forcefully strides forward in this Roman bronze statuette. The divinity, called Athena by the Greeks and Minerva by the Romans, was the virgin goddess of arts, crafts, and war. The Greek word *promachos* means "the first in battle," so here Athena is depicted as a warrior. Athena's protective aegis, bearing the head of the Gorgon Medusa, covers her chest and back to below her buttocks. Although originally identified as a goatskin, the patterning on the aegis seems closest to the scaliness of snakeskin. A griffin, a mythological creature known for its vigilance, crouches atop her helmet. The goddess holds her right arm up high to brandish a now-missing spear and has her left arm advanced to support a now-missing shield. Silver still embellishes Athena's eyes, the Gorgon's head, and the helmet's ornament, but the twenty silver snakes that originally decorated the edge of Athena's aegis are missing (with only the holes for their attachment remaining).

This representation of the goddess intentionally incorporates an archaistic, or old-fashioned, style. It depicts a statue type, known in many versions, that probably emerged in the first century B.C., with stylistic traits based on a famed colossal bronze statue of Athena Promachos created in the early 400s B.C. for the Acropolis in Athens. The Romans admired Greek sculpture and often produced works that resembled the earlier styles of the Greeks. Romans considered older images of deities, or at least images that looked older, to be more venerable. This statuette probably once occupied a place in a wealthy Roman's personal household shrine as a protective deity for his family.

MINIATURE PORTRAIT BUST OF A YOUNG WOMAN

Roman, 25 B.C.–A.D. 25
Bronze with glass paste
H: 16.5 cm (6½ in.)
DIAM (of base): 6.7 cm
(2⅝ in.)
84.AB.59

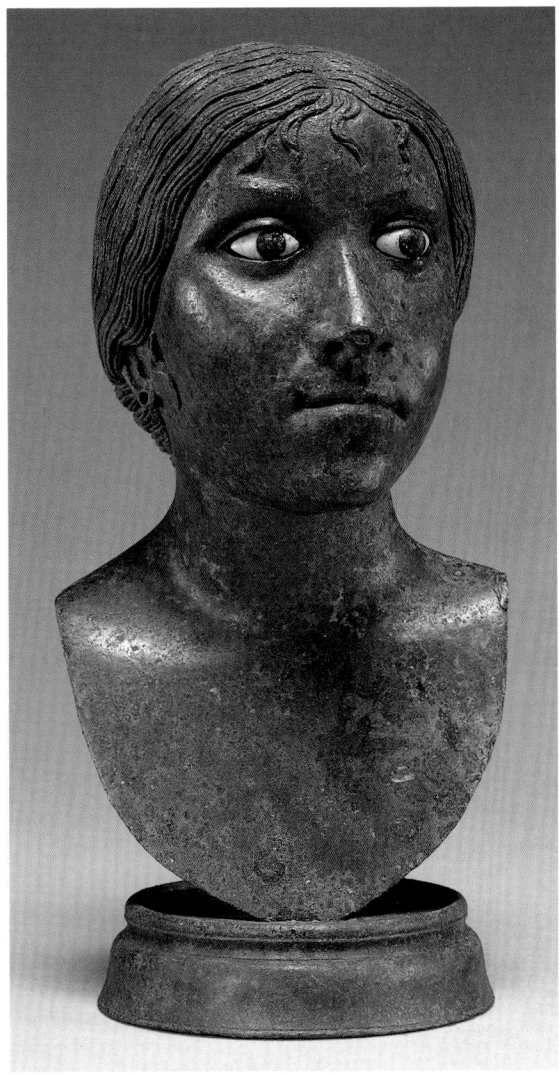

With great delicacy the sculptor has captured the portrait of a young woman. She is represented in the idealized Classical manner that was popular during the reign of the first emperor of Rome, Augustus (27 B.C.–A.D. 14). The glass-paste inlays used for her eyes are preserved here and make her expression strikingly realistic. Her complicated braided and knotted hairdo was fashionable during the Augustan period, which favored a stylistic return to Greek classicism. Her earlobes were pierced to hold earrings that are now lost.

Numerous small-scale portraits of both the imperial family and ordinary Roman citizens were produced in a wide variety of media throughout the Roman Empire. Most were intended for semiprivate, domestic settings. Pliny the Elder recounts the tradition of keeping these images in niches or shrines in order to record a family's genealogy as well as to commemorate its members' notable deeds. Therefore, they were not only a tribute to one's ancestors but also a symbol of status for the owner.

PORTRAIT BUST OF MENANDER

Roman, A.D. 1–25
Bronze
H: 17 cm (6³⁄₄ in.)
D (base): 8 cm (3¹⁄₈ in.)
72.AB.108

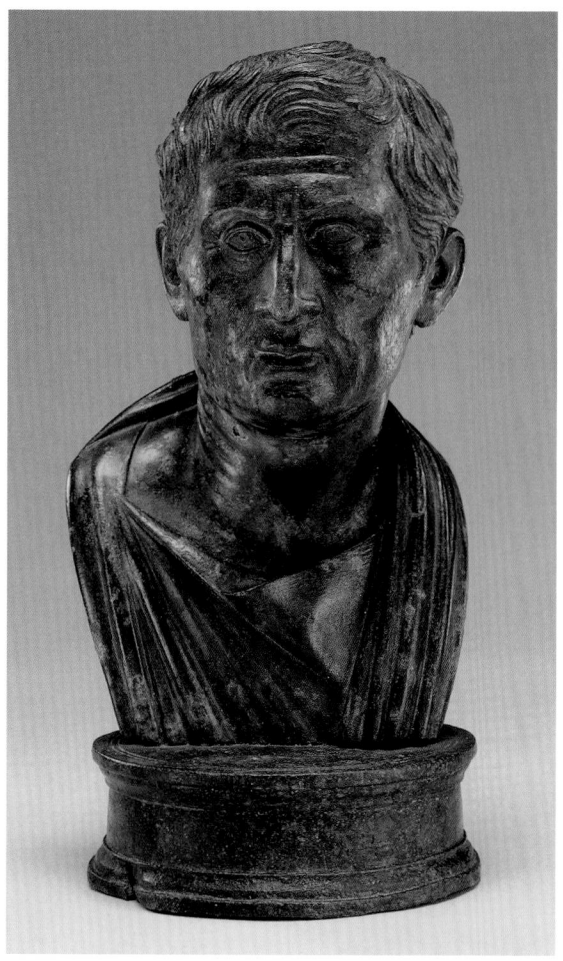

This small bust is a Roman work based upon a Greek seated statue, probably in bronze, that had been made in the third century B.C. by the sons of the famous sculptor Praxiteles (active 375–340 B.C.). An inscribed marble portrait had long ago suggested the identification of about fifty portraits of the same subject. The faint inscription of a name in Greek (MENANΔPOC) on the base of the Getty bust confirms this subject's identity as Menander (342/341–291/290 B.C.), the prize-winning Greek author of more than one hundred comedies.

Born into a wealthy family, Menander learned his craft from an uncle. The well-educated, well-connected young playwright was said to be a handsome man who dressed stylishly and enjoyed a life of ease and luxury. Yet he chose to write in a relatively simple form of Greek more readily understood by an uneducated audience. Rather than recount traditional mythological subjects, Menander developed complicated comedic plots, usually about young lovers, that reflected the dilemmas of daily life. After Menander's death, his plays continued to be staged at Athens in revivals. As a poet, he came to be regarded as second only to Homer. His works remained popular even in Roman times, when they were imitated and adapted by playwrights such as Plautus (about 254–184 B.C.) and Terence (about 190–159 B.C.).

HEAD OF THE YOUNG BACCHUS

Roman, A.D. 1–50
Bronze with silver
H: 21.6 cm (8½ in.)
96.AB.52

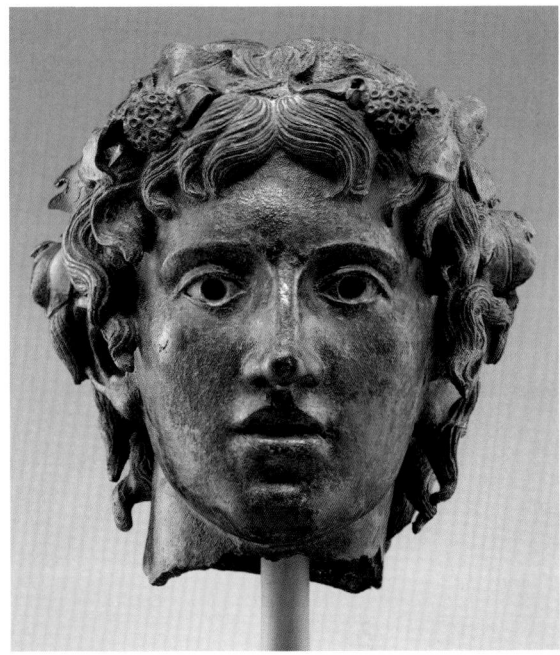

This beautifully wrought head represents the youthful god of wine and fertility, Bacchus (known to the Greeks as Dionysos). The wreath of twisted ivy entwined in his curling locks confirms his identity: ivy was associated with Bacchus because it is evergreen. The whites of his eyes are silvered, and his irises were once inlaid with colored stone or glass paste to create a startlingly realistic image. Holes preserved at the back of the eyes allowed for the attachment of the irises. The long, curling locks that hang down his neck were cast separately from the head and attached after casting.

The figure's fleshy cheeks, slightly tilted head, and wavy locks recall sculptures of the Classical period of Greek art, most notably the work of the sculptor Polykleitos, from the second half of the fifth century B.C. This style was especially popular in the Roman world during and after the reign of Augustus (27 B.C.–A.D. 14).

It is likely that this head was once attached to a full-length statue of the god. The piece may have served a purely decorative function as household ornament, or it may have been used as an elaborate lamp holder. Two statues of youths with a similar facial type that served as lamp holders were found in Pompeii; a third, which also wears an ivy wreath, was found in Morocco; and a fourth was found at Antequera (in modern Spain).

THYMIATERION WITH SEATED ACTOR

Roman, A.D. 1–50
Bronze with silver
H: 23.2 cm (9⅛ in.)
87.AC.143.1

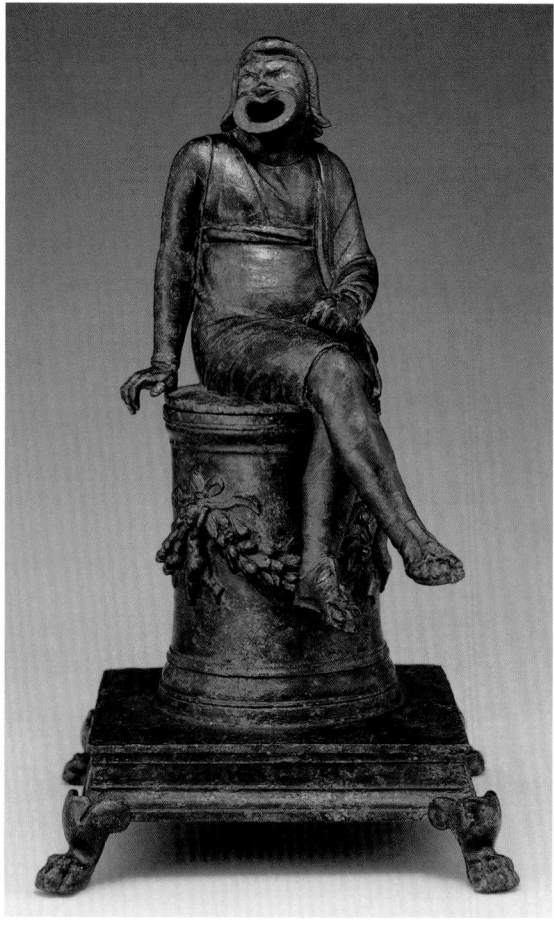

This thymiaterion, or incense burner, takes the form of an actor wearing the garb and mask associated with productions of Greek New Comedy. His costume consists of a short tunic worn over a long-sleeved garment with leggings, a mantle, and sandals. The mask, with a knit brow over the silver-inlaid eyes, broad nose, and trumpet-like mouth all framed by a rolled arrangement of hair, is designed for comic effect and would have been used for the role of a leading slave. Seated on a round altar and leaning back on his right hand, the actor keeps his left hand in his lap. That hand is pierced to hold a detachable object, probably a wig to be employed in a plot involving disguises and mistaken identities. Comic actors portraying slaves seated on altars became a familiar subject in Roman art. The motif was inspired by Greek and Roman comedies in which the characters seek sanctuary from their masters and revel in the knowledge that they can taunt them with impunity as long as they stay on the altar.

A trio of cupids holding garlands encircles the altar, which is fixed to a square, footed stand. The top of the altar is a lid that swivels aside on a single pin, and the bottom is perforated, allowing the smoke and fumes from burning incense to rise through the hollow body of the figure and emerge from the mouth. It is likely that this thymiaterion formed a pair with the incense burner in the form of a singer (see next entry).

THYMIATERION WITH SEATED SINGER

Roman, A.D. 1–50
Bronze with silver
H: 19 cm (7½ in.)
w (of base): 9.5 cm (3¾ in.)
87.AC.144

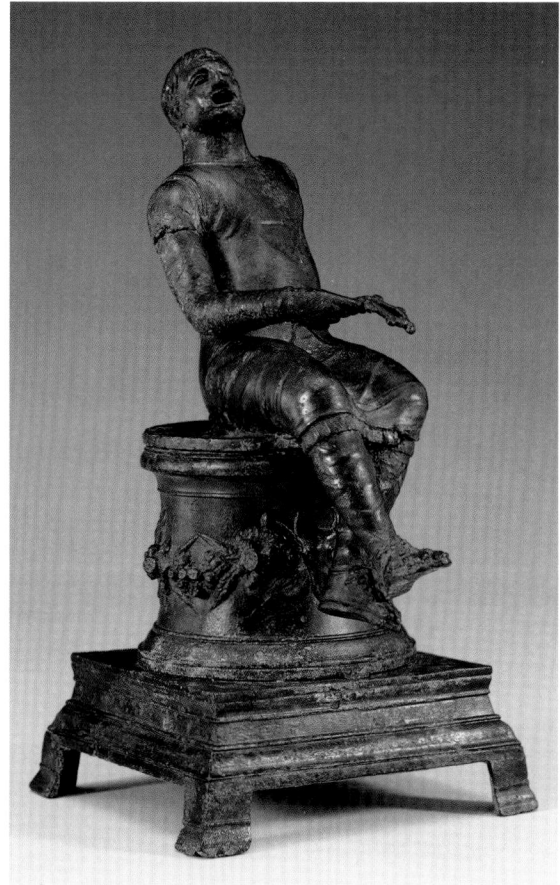

With his head thrown back and mouth opened wide, a singer performs while sitting on an altar. In a transposed, somewhat modified interpretation of the posture of the actor featured in its companion piece (see previous entry), this singer leans back on his left arm while holding in his right hand a sistrum, a rattlelike musical instrument, and crosses his legs at the ankle. Like the actor, he wears a style of dress identified with the theater—a sleeveless tunic that in this case is either fringed or worn over another long-sleeved, finely pleated tunic, leggings, and sandals. Unlike the actor, however, he has no mantle and, more significantly, no mask, suggesting that he does not play a speaking role but is a mime requiring neither mask nor special guise. Because the sistrum is associated not with the theater but with Isis, a goddess of Egyptian origin whose cult became established throughout the Greek and Roman world, he may be portraying a chanting priest of Isis.

Resting upon the squarish platform and decorated with garlands of grain, fruit, and pinecones strung on bucrania (stylized ox skulls), this altar resembles the one the actor sits on. Like that thymiaterion, this statuette serves both a practical and a decorative purpose. It also has a swiveling top to allow the insertion of incense and ventilation holes in the bottom to provide the draft for burning it. As with the actor, here the smoke and fragrance rising up through the figure's body would have curled out his mouth.

STATUE OF AN INFANT, PERHAPS CUPID

Roman, A.D. 1–50
Bronze with silver
and copper
H: 64 cm (25¼ in.)
96.AB.53

Depicted as a chubby toddler, the subject of this bronze sculpture is not immediately clear because the attributes that the figure may have worn or was once carrying are now missing. Although in the visual arts a variety of gods and heroes were depicted as children, including Hercules (known to the Greeks as Herakles) and Bacchus (Dionysos to the Greeks), few appeared as frequently as Cupid. The identification of this figure as Cupid is plausibly suggested by the remains of metal attachments, poorly preserved on the back of the infant, that most likely were for fastening wings onto the body.

Here the god stands with his weight on his left leg, leaning a bit awkwardly, as one might expect in such a young child. Empty holes now mark the place where inset pupils of stone or glass paste once were. The irises are silvered, and the figure once had silver teeth, both testaments to the high quality of workmanship. The wreath worn by the child incorporates leaves into a wrapped fillet that falls forward over his shoulders; the hanging ribbons are made of hammered sheet copper, and are reminiscent of ribbons worn by athletes or Hercules. Although resembling vine leaves, which are typically found in depictions of Bacchus, the leaves and nuts on this wreath are those of a plane tree. The shade of such trees was a popular venue for philosophers and philosophical discourse, and the presence of such a wreath may allude to a philosophical association or setting for the statue. Bronze statues such as this became popular decorative elements in the gardens and courtyards of wealthy Roman households.

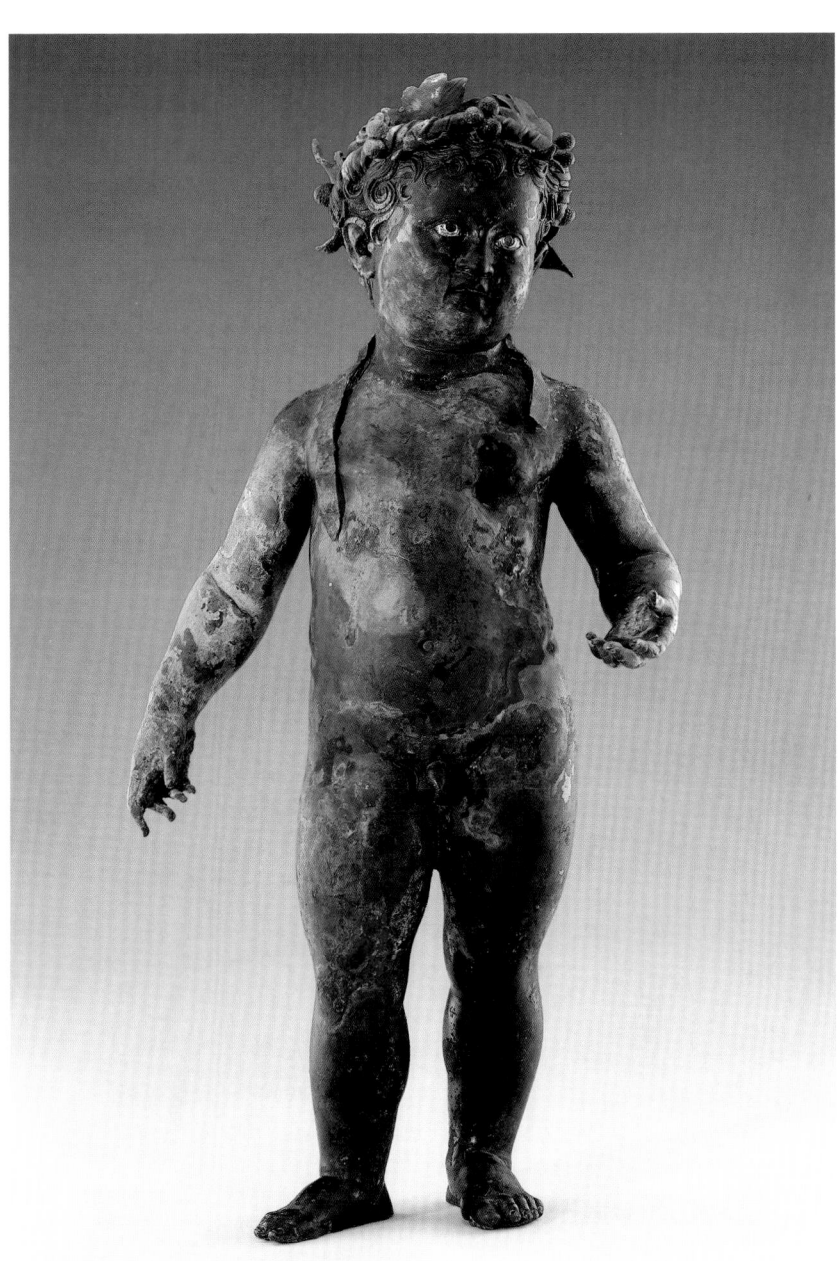

COIN BANK IN THE FORM OF A GIRL

Roman, A.D. 25–50
Bronze with copper
H: 12.2 cm (4¾ in.)
L: 13.5 cm (5¼ in.)
72.AC.99

With her right hand outstretched, a plump, curly-haired girl sits, pulling at the neck of her tunic to reveal a slot cut for the insertion of a coin. Although she appears to be begging, the girl is not portrayed as poverty-stricken. Her tunic is embellished with inlaid copper stripes and an incised zigzag pattern at the neckline, suggesting an embroidered garment too expensive for a beggar. Moreover, her elaborate hairstyle and chubby physique are indicative of prosperity. Her lively gestures may be related to figures of seated children with outstretched hands that originated in the early Hellenistic period (about 300 B.C.), when children were first depicted realistically rather than as miniature adults. The curled coiffure of the girl also is typical of Hellenistic representations of children and erotes, and likely derives from an archetype of the late third century B.C. Overall, this bank bears a strong resemblance to a statue of Hellenistic date discovered in present-day Algeria, but despite Hellenistic parallels, Greek influences have been strongly romanized. For example, here a tunic with broad, simple folds replaces the diaphanous, crinkly fabric of the Algerian statue.

Like today's piggy banks, small coin repositories were popular among the Romans. They were given as New Year's gifts, and many have been found in the graves of children and young women. Most Roman coin banks were fashioned of clay and were much simpler than this one in both form and material. Typical shapes for Roman banks were beehives, chests, and pots.

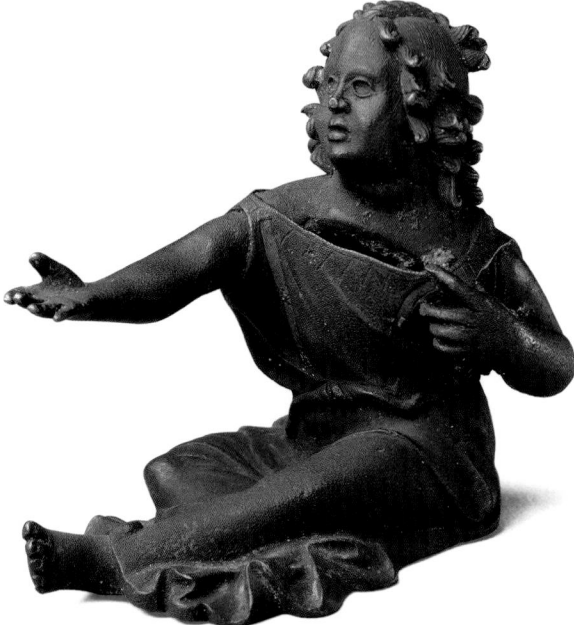

STATUETTE OF CERES OR JUNO

Roman, A.D. 50–75
Bronze
H: 32 cm (12½ in.)
84.AB.670

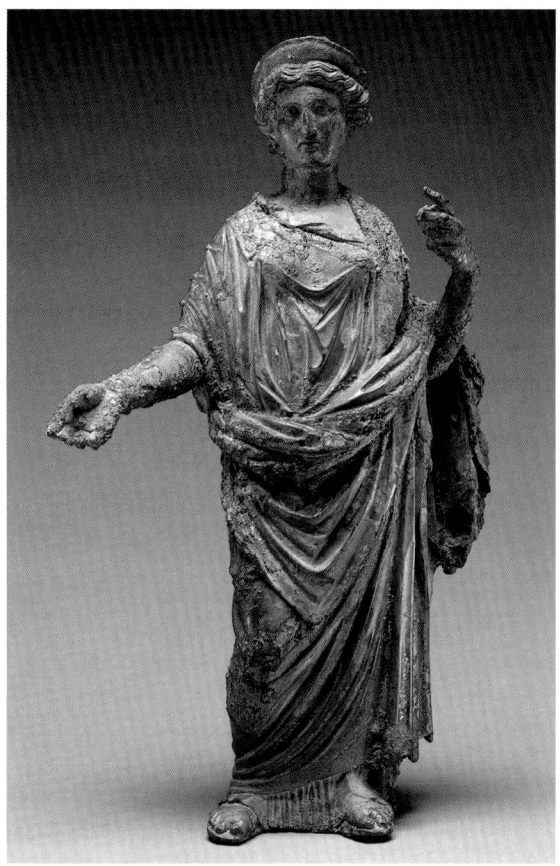

With the long tunic and heavy mantle traditionally worn by Roman matrons, this bronze statuette could at first glance be regarded as the figure of a mere mortal, but the crescent-shaped diadem marks her as a deity. She stands with her left arm upraised and her right extended. The style is classicistic, reflecting a purely Greek form of several centuries earlier. The interpretation is thoroughly Roman, however, incorporating a mannered symmetry in the hair and folds of drapery together with a stolid, somewhat heavy gravity of facial features.

It is uncertain who this deity may be. Some divinities appearing on Roman coins are similarly attired and hold objects that specifically identify them, but this figure's attributes have not survived. The position of the left hand indicates that it grasped a staff or some object with a long shaft; the open right hand held something smaller, perhaps a bowl or fruit. Comparable images on coins suggest the figure is most likely either Ceres, usually shown with a long torch or scepter in her left hand and stalks of wheat in her right, or Juno, who typically holds a staff in her left hand and a patera (offering dish) in the other.

The patina and modeling of this figure closely resemble those of the Statuette of Virtus or Roma (see next entry) and the Relief with Two Togate Magistrates (see p. 187), suggesting that all three were probably produced in the same workshop. The openings on their backs indicate that they were decorative attachments on some item, such as a large piece of furniture or a ceremonial wagon.

STATUETTE OF VIRTUS OR ROMA

Roman, A.D. 50–75
Bronze
H: 33.1 cm (13 in.)
84.AB.671

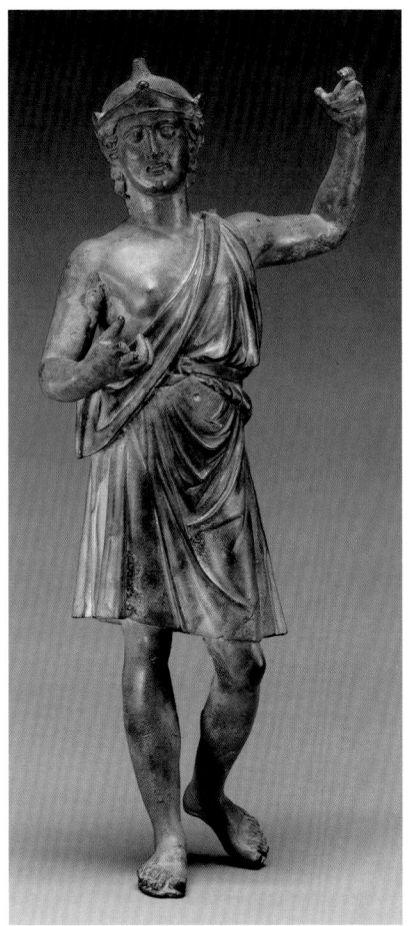

With her pose, her helmet, and the short tunic that bares one breast in the style of an Amazon, this Roman figure possesses the monumental quality of life-size works and reflects the strong inspiration on Roman artisans of Greek Classical sculpture created centuries earlier by masters such as Pheidias and Polykleitos. However, the Attic-type helmet she wears indicates that she is not an Amazon. Although the identifying attributes she once held are now missing, numismatic evidence indicates that the figure is either Virtus, the personification of valor, or Roma, the personification of Rome and her Empire.

Similar images, clearly identified by inscription, first occur on coins issued in A.D. 69 during the reign of the emperor Galba (A.D. 68–69). Like them, this figure once held a spear in her left hand. According to the parallel types on coins, if she were Roma, she would have supported in her right hand a small statue of Nike, personification of victory. Virtus would have held a sheathed short sword with the handle directed outward and the tip toward her waist. On monumental Roman historical reliefs, Roma often appears as the warrior goddess who accompanies emperors on formal occasions, such as their departure for battle and return from a successful campaign. Whether as goddess, personification, or symbol, Roma's image has persisted as one of the Western world's most long lived political-religious representations.

This figure, like the related ones of Juno or Ceres (see previous entry) and the togate magistrates (see next entry), has an opening on its back where it can be attached to another object, perhaps a vehicle or piece of furniture.

RELIEF WITH TWO TOGATE MAGISTRATES

Roman, A.D. 50–75
Bronze
H: 26 cm (10¼ in.)
W: 13.8 cm (5½ in.)
85.AB.109

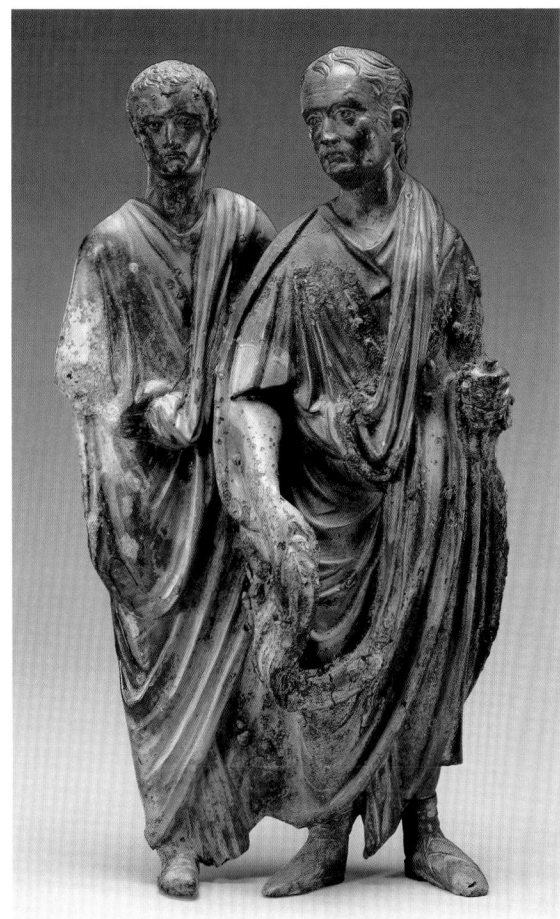

Although the detailed treatment of their faces and heads may seem to have been intended to represent specific individuals, it is more probable that the images of these two men are depictions of generic, well-known types. Based on features associated with particular roles, these two figures could represent an aging intellectual and his younger attendant. Similar figures can be seen on the Ara Pietatis, a Roman marble relief of a procession dated to the same time, the mid-first century A.D.

Whether or not the relief is meant to represent particular individuals, the men's dignified style of dress, with the togas and shoes appropriate to patricians, leaves no doubt about their status as members of the upper class.

The scroll held in his left hand implies that the older man may be a civic official or priest participating in a solemn public ceremony, perhaps an event including a sacrifice or libation, to which both he and the younger man have turned their attention.

Because of its open back, this piece, like the statuettes of Ceres or Juno (see p. 185) and of Virtus or Roma (see previous entry), must have been affixed to some object, such as a piece of furniture or a chariot. Clues to this bronze's date lie in the manner in which the togas are draped and in the hairstyles, especially that of the older man, which finds comparisons on representations from the time of Nero (reigned A.D. 54–68), in the later Julio-Claudian period.

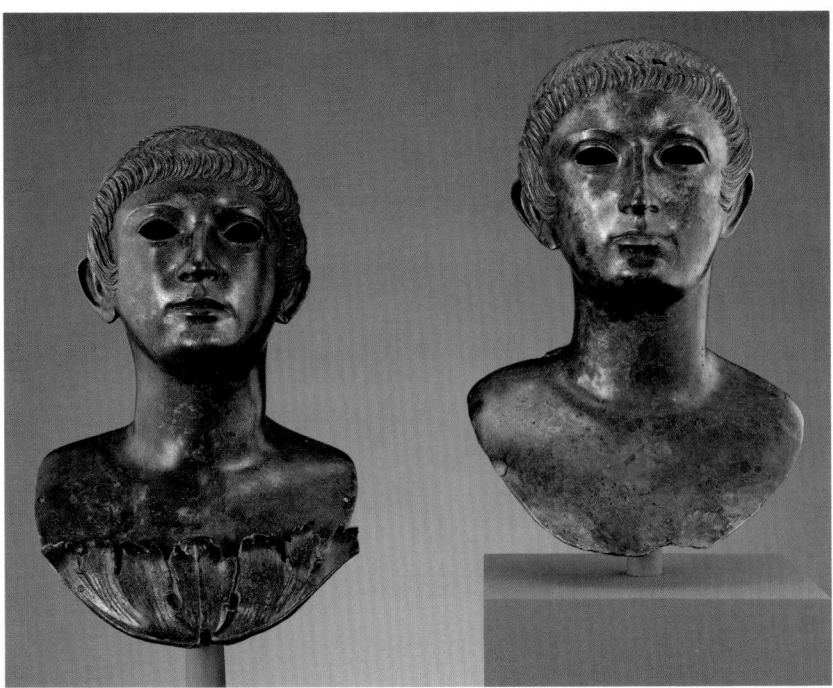

PAIR OF PORTRAIT BUSTS

Roman, from Gaul,
A.D. 60–70
Bronze
H: 40.6 cm (16 in.)
89.AB.67.1

H: 40 cm (15¾ in.)
89.AB.67.2

If these two portraits seem almost identical, it is because they were produced from the same model. One bust has a band of acanthus leaves affixed to the bottom. Originally, the other one also had an attachment, almost certainly the same kind of floral element. The now-empty eye sockets of both portraits were once inlaid with realistic eyes of colored materials such as glass paste or marble. Only subtle differences distinguish the portraits from one another. For example, the wave of the hair across the forehead, a style popular during the reign of Nero (A.D. 54–68), shows minor variations in the arrangement of the locks, helping to impart an individuality, however slight, to each portrait. The portraits originally had long, separately made strands of hair affixed to the backs of their heads in a hairstyle associated with boys who served as assistants in the ritual sacrifices for various Roman cults. The same hairstyle also characterized special attendants in a military youth organization known as the *Iuventus* (Latin for "young men"). The *Iuventus* prepared aristocratic young men of Rome and its provinces for military service and subsequent government posts. Under Nero, it also formed an imperial honor guard.

The style of the busts and the emphasis on their frontal view, together with the simplistic treatment of the backs of the heads, suggest that they were made in the Roman province of Gaul.

ARYBALLOS

Roman, from Gaul,
A.D. 70–100
Bronze with red and blue
champlevé enamel
H (without handle): 10.5 cm
(4⅛ in.)
96.AC.190

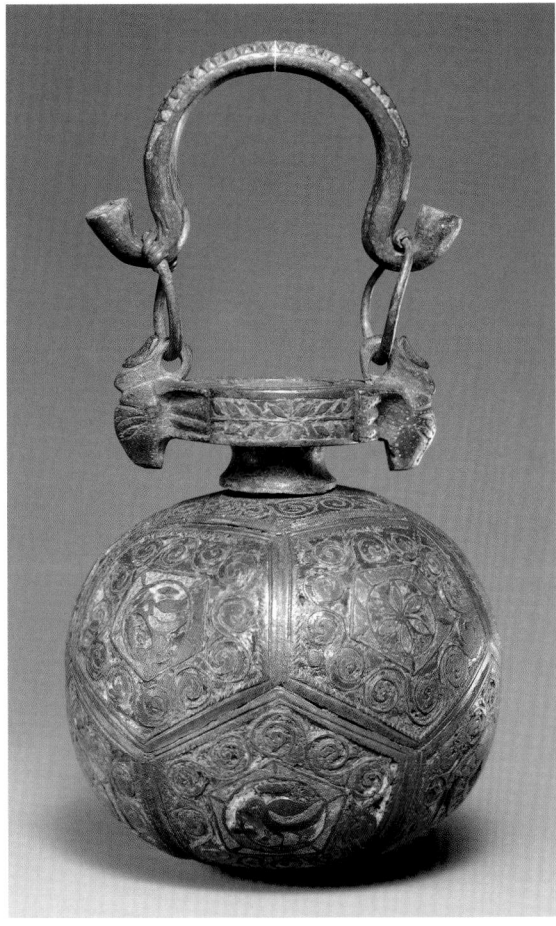

This heavy, round-bottomed *unguentarium* (a flask for holding oils or ointments) is shaped like an Archaic Greek aryballos, but the handle has a typically Roman imperial arrangement: its two elephant's-head protomes curve from the rim toward the bottom, missing their trunks (which were perhaps made and attached separately) and surmounted by a pair of rings to which the handle is attached. The handle, held in place by loops of wire, has a pattern of enameled squares flanked by triangles. The top of the flask's rim is embellished with a row of alternating red and blue triangles and its side with a stylized laurel wreath. The body, made in four separate parts soldered together, is covered with a network of twelve pentagonal panels, each of which has an inner border with a scroll on a blue enamel background, and a red central pentagon enclosing a roundel. The roundels contain either a bird, a rosette, or a radiate crown of triangles. The serrated edges of the pentagonal fields allow better adherence between enamel and bronze.

This *unguentarium* resembles a number of related bronze vessels with enameling that have been ascribed to the northern reaches of the Roman province of Gaul, in what is today Belgium and northern France. The closest parallels are a group of vessels deriving from a workshop that may have been at Anthée, near Namur in Belgium; it is possible that this aryballos was made there.

BUST OF A MAN

Roman, perhaps from Spain,
A.D. 90–110
Bronze
H: 38 cm (15 in.)
W: 17.9 cm (7 in.)
D: 22.4 cm (8⅞ in.)
85.AB.110

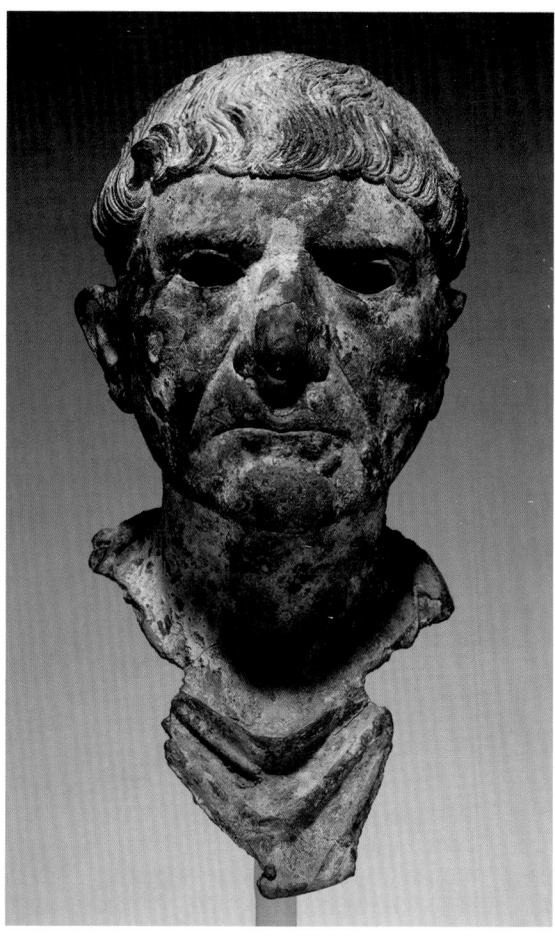

Embodied in this image and emphasized by the gaunt cheeks and thin,
down-turned lips are the qualities
of *gravitas* (seriousness) and *severitas*
(self-discipline) admired by the Roman
people. The grim face conveying the
personality and age of this man recalls
the veristic, sometimes unflattering
nature of Roman Republican portraiture that found renewed favor during
the Flavian dynasty (A.D. 69–96).
The arrangement of the hair follows a
trend set by Nero (reigned A.D. 54–68),
in which the locks are combed over
the forehead in a parallel wave pattern,
but comparable styles also appear on
portraiture from the time of Trajan
(reigned A.D. 98–117). The sitter bears
a resemblance to images on coins
and to some life-size portraits that

have been identified as Trajan's father,
a Spaniard who had distinguished
military and civil careers and died in
A.D. 100.

Rome's involvement in the Iberian
peninsula began in the third century
B.C. when the Romans fought the
first of the Punic Wars against the
Carthaginians of North Africa. In 206
B.C. the Carthaginians were driven
out of Spain, and by 19 B.C. the entire
peninsula was under Roman control.
It provided the first two non-Italian-
born Roman emperors, Trajan and his
adopted heir to the throne, Hadrian
(reigned A.D. 117–138).

STATUETTE OF JUPITER

Roman, A.D. 100–200
Bronze
H: 30.5 cm (12 in.)
96.AB.42

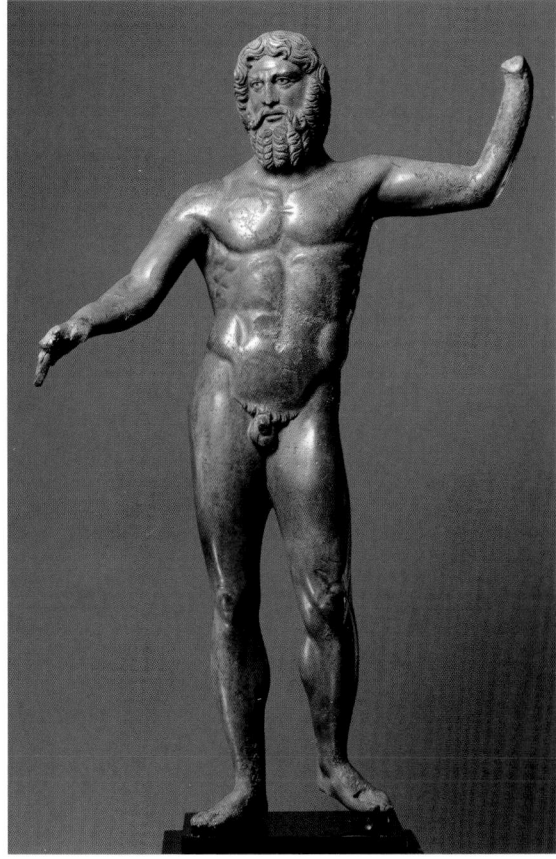

The production of this statuette in the second century A.D. demonstrates the longevity of certain figural types throughout antiquity. The original model for the image is believed to be a life-size bronze statue of Zeus (the Greek equivalent of the Roman Jupiter) from the fourth century B.C. by the Greek sculptor Leochares. In 22 B.C., three-and-a-half centuries after its creation, the sculpture was taken to Rome and installed as the cult statue in the newly inaugurated temple to Jupiter on the Capitoline hill. This statuette represents Jupiter Tonans (Jupiter the Thunderer), who once held a lightning bolt in his right hand while leaning on an upright scepter— now missing—in his left. Because of the renown of Leochares' sculpture, the image was very popular and often copied. The Getty's statuette displays a

combination of Hellenistic and Roman characteristics, including the typically Hellenistic exaggerated rendering of the musculature and the symmetrical arrangement of the beard and hair, which deliberately imitates schematic forms of Greek Archaic art.

The image of Jupiter Tonans became common in certain areas of the empire, including Gaul (modern France), where this statuette is said to have been found. The large size of the work and its derivation from a cult image in a major temple endow it with religious significance; it may have served as a devotional image in a household shrine. The sheer number of Jupiter Tonans figures that have survived from antiquity—more than one hundred are known—indicates that they may have been used as votive objects offered as dedications to the god.

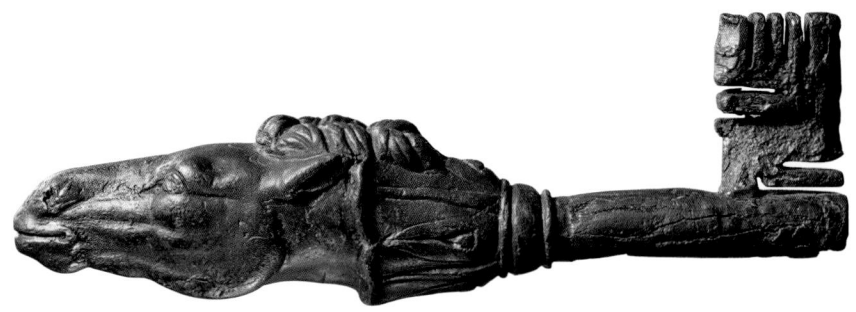

KEY WITH HORSE-HEAD HANDLE

Roman, A.D. 100–200
Bronze and iron
H: 5.5 cm (2⅛ in.)
W: 15.6 cm (6⅛ in.)
D: 2.7 cm (1 in.)
96.AC.197

The shaft of this key and its bit are forged from iron, while the decorative handle is bronze. Few locks from this period remain intact, for until the third century A.D. locks were commonly comprised of wood, but a number of the keys, often forged from iron and in some instances bronze, still exist. This particular key is remarkable for the quality of the modeling, the intricacy of the eight-slotted bit, and its state of preservation, marking it as an example of high-quality Roman metalwork.

The head of a horse extends from a four-petaled calyx that conceals the join to the hollow iron shaft. The animal is depicted with its ears flattened and mane swept back as if galloping. While horses were a popular choice for the decorative element of key handles, lions, panthers, and bears more commonly appear in this position.

The lock was invented in the Near East approximately four thousand years ago; from a simple model, artisans of the Roman period were able to devise ever more complex devices. This key would probably have operated a lever lock, in which a lever falls into a slot in the bolt and prevents it from moving until the key lifts the lever to the height necessary to release it from the slot. This type of lock has been considered the most advanced form used in the Roman period and operates on the same principle as modern lever locks.

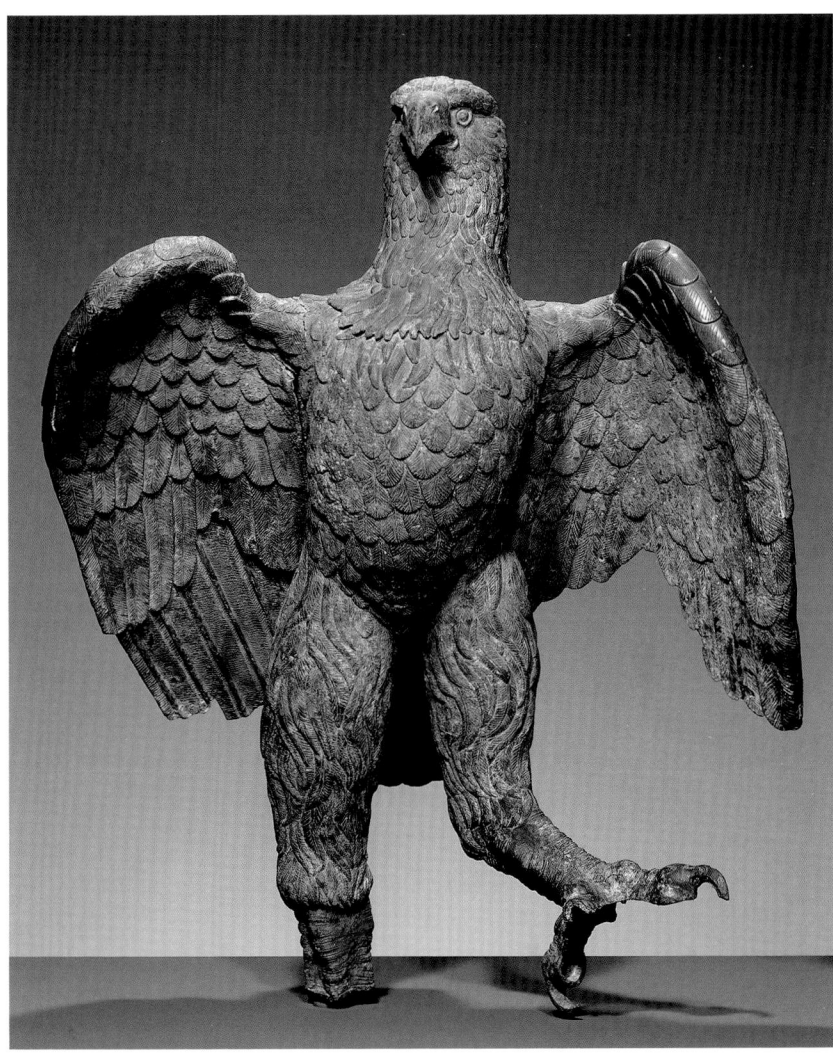

STATUE OF AN EAGLE

Roman, from Asia Minor,
A.D. 100–300
Bronze
H: 104.2 cm (41 in.)
W: 78.7 cm (31 in.)
72.AB.151

Staring ahead with a penetrating gaze, this eagle creates an imposing image. Its large hooked beak appears sharp enough to easily rip the flesh of its prey. Each feather covering the eagle's body is carefully detailed, with individual barbs incised. Its outstretched wings suggest that the raptor has just landed on its perch.

As companion and attribute of Jupiter, king of the gods, the eagle was an important symbol in Roman culture. Eagles represented victory and military might. The bird also symbolized the deification of the emperor, and an eagle was often released during an emperor's funeral to represent the ruler's spirit ascending to the gods. A large and independent sculpture of an eagle, such as this one, is rare in Roman art. Its raised left claw may have rested on a globe or lightning bolt, other emblems of Jupiter.

STATUETTE OF MARS/COBANNUS

Roman, from Gaul, A.D. 125–175
Bronze
H (with base): 76 cm (29⅞ in.)
H (figure): 65 cm (25⅝ in.)
96.AB.54

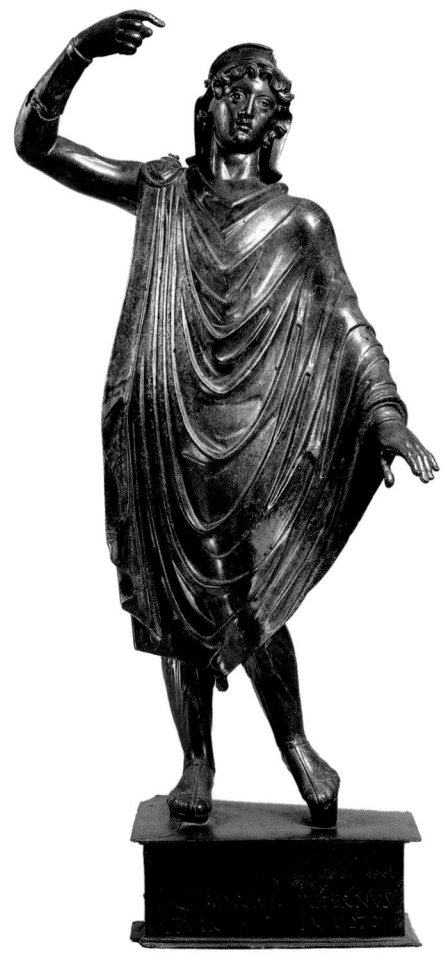

Unusual in its size, style, and the excellence of its craftsmanship, this dedication was clearly a valuable commission for an important cult shrine. The base of the statuette is inscribed in Latin: *AVG[vsto] SACR[vm] DEO COBANNO / L[vcivs] MACCIVS AETERNVS / IIVIR EX VOTO* (Sacred to the venerable god Cobannus, Lucius Maccius Aeternus, *duumvir*, [dedicated this] in accordance with a vow). Several other important bronze objects are associated with this work, including two portrait heads (see p. 188) and two additional statuettes also dedicated to Cobannus. The name of the god is rarely attested elsewhere, making this object particularly important for the study of religion in the Roman Empire. The family of Aeturnus, on the other hand, is known from other inscriptions, and Lucius Maccius himself was clearly of high standing, as indicated by his title of *duumvir*, one of the two chief magistrates of a Roman colony.

Cobannus appears to have been a deity local to Gaul (modern France) who was identified with Mars, Roman god of war. The helmet on the figure's head as well as his pose—with the right arm bent and raised, the left arm extending slightly forward—recalls Roman representations of Mars. On the basis of such images, the Getty's statuette is most likely to have held a staff or spear in his right hand while grasping the top edge of a shield with his left. In many other details, however, this figure differs from Roman works. For example, his cloak, long-sleeved tunic, and leggings reflect the local dress of the northern Roman provinces rather than typical Roman military clothing. His helmet, instead of being a typically Greek version appropriate for a god associated with Mars, conforms to a specific style worn by Roman legionaries; it helps date this piece to the mid-second century A.D. Because a number of Gallic deities were assimilated by Mars, each with its own characteristics, the unusual features of this figure may have been meant to convey specific qualities of the god rather than simply to differentiate Cobannus from his Roman counterpart.

STATUETTE OF A SNAKE-LEGGED GIANT

Roman, A.D. 180–220
Bronze
H: 14 cm (5½ in.)
W: 12.5 cm (4⅞ in.)
D: 7 cm (2¾ in.)
92.AB.11

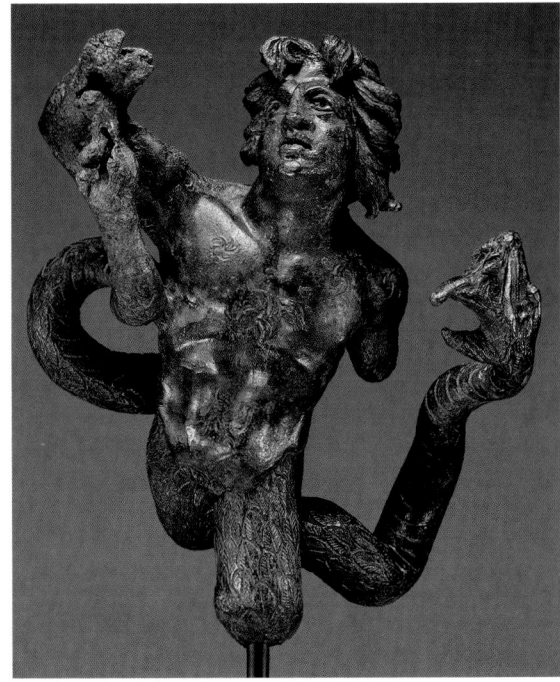

The Giants were a mythological race of monsters who were overthrown by the gods, the children of Kronos and Rhea. The battle between the gods and Giants, known as the Gigantomachy, was an artistic theme that first became popular during the sixth century B.C. It was seen as a metaphor for the contest between civilization (represented by the gods) and barbarity (represented by the Giants), and its popularity continued into the Roman period. The best-known representation of this combat is the Hellenistic relief frieze from the Great Altar of Zeus at Pergamon.

This Giant's inhuman nature is clearly evident in his legs, which are formed as writhing snakes with large, gaping, fanged mouths. If his snaky legs aren't enough, the whorls of hair on his chest and shoulders and the wild unkempt hair on his head provide other clues to his bestiality. The Giant is depicted in the midst of combat with a now-missing foe. He falls forward with his right arm held up over his head in a position of defense. Parts of his right hand and lower arm are missing, perhaps because the molten bronze did not completely fill the mold when the figure was made. His lower left arm is also missing; it may have been cast separately and attached to the figure.

This statuette was once part of a composition that depicted either a single combat between the Giant and a god, or a larger group with many figures. Such multifigured groups were often used in Hellenistic and Roman times to decorate furnishings, such as the base of candelabra; they were also mounted on ceremonial vehicles such as chariots or wagons. The Greek letter *kappa* incised on this Giant's left buttock may have been a mark to indicate the figure's original placement within a composition (that must therefore have been comprised of at least ten figures). Another small statuette of a Giant in the Museum's collection (see p. 47) was probably once similarly incorporated into a larger group arrangement.

BALSAMARIUM IN THE FORM OF A BOXER'S HEAD

Roman, from Gaul, A.D. 200
Bronze
H: 17.1 cm (6¾ in.)
2007.14

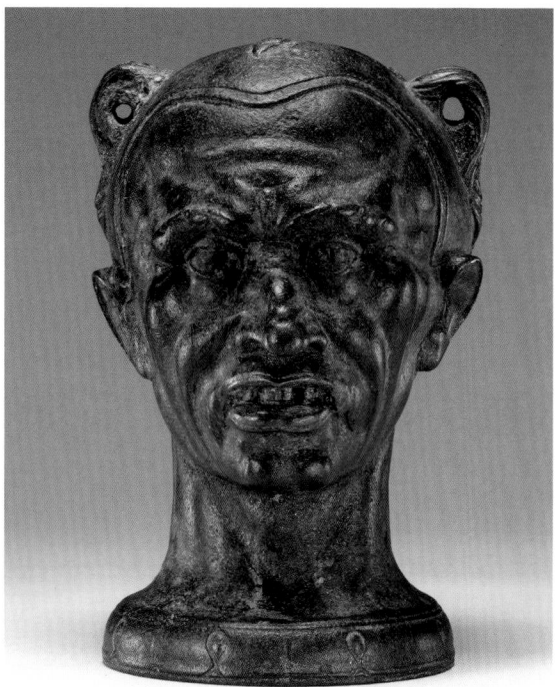

This *balsamarium*, or oil container, takes the form of the head of an athlete. The protective leather cap, the cirrus, or lock of hair at the back of the head, and the battered face all secure the identification of this figure as a boxer. Two locks of hair project from the top of the cap and create lugs for securing a swing handle (now missing). The hinge for the lid was placed at the back of the head. The man grimaces fiercely, emphasizing the flexibility of his skin and revealing gaps where he no longer has teeth. His teeth and eyes were once inlaid with a contrasting metallic foil, possibly silver. This may not be a portrait in the literal sense, yet the face is quite striking and expressive and could possibly represent either a specific individual or an artificial construction, a compilation of traits observed in a number of individuals to create a type. With great skill, the artist has captured the broken and battered face of an athlete who has survived the contest.

Athletic culture was promoted and admired throughout the Roman Empire, and successful athletes gained fame and traveled widely displaying their prowess and abilities in the games. The emphasis on honest and often brutal depictions, especially of athletes, found favor. Vessels depicting athletes seem perfectly suited to their function as oil containers, and one can easily imagine their use in the baths and the palaestra.

SITULA

Roman, A.D. 220–320
Bronze with tin
H: 33.5 cm (13¼ in.)
DIAM (rim): 27.2 cm (10¾ in.)
96.AC.55

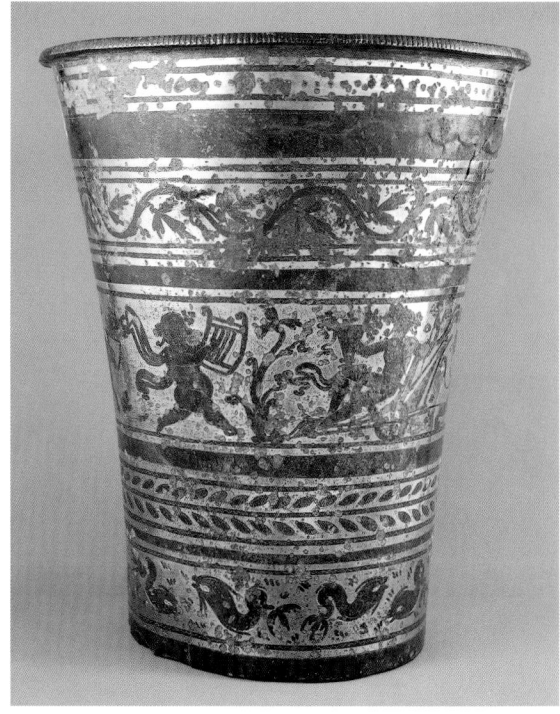

This elegant vessel, a shape known as a situla, or bucket, once had a swinging handle. The shape name derives from the Greek *kalathos*, a tall, flaring basket. In both the Greek and Roman worlds these types of baskets had many uses, but were especially associated with wool working and the harvest. The lively decoration of the vessel was achieved by the application of tin onto the surface of the bronze. The various designs were cut out of the tin plating and, set against the background, create contrasting color effects. This unusual technique is known in only a few preserved examples. The place of manufacture of the situla remains uncertain, but the closest parallels come from the area of modern Switzerland and southern Germany.

The animated figures and floral ornaments were enhanced by the detailed use of incised lines and small dots. The five decorated rows, which alternate with plain tin stripes, comprise the following (from the top):

disks; a grapevine; Bacchus (Roman god of wine) and his retinue; laurel leaves; and dolphins swimming amid stylized waves. In the main frieze, the god, holding a thyrsos (a staff wreathed in ivy and vine leaves with a pinecone at the top, a common attribute of Bacchus) and large drinking vessel, reclines on a chariot drawn by panthers (another common attribute of Bacchus), one of which is ridden by Cupid, Roman god of love. A nude young satyr with a shepherd's staff leads the group. The figures that follow the chariot include a chubby old silenos playing a lyre, goat-legged Pan playing his pipes, and a maenad. The latter holds a thyrsos, like Bacchus. The grape-filled *kalathos* that the maenad holds in her right hand is remarkably similar to the shape of this tinned bronze vessel itself.

TRIPOD

Roman, A.D. 250–300
Bronze
H: 106 cm (41¾ in.)
96.AC.203

Tripods like this one were used to hold basins in
which burnt sacrifices and libations were offered to
the gods. This tripod's collapsible, hinged legs, which
made it portable, are decorated on top with statuettes
that depict a narrative of the life cycle of a horse.
The horses stand on flat plates from which project
L-shaped hooks that supported the now-lost cauldron.
In a vignette representing infancy, a mare suckles her
foal. A bridled stallion energetically rearing beside a
small tree characterizes the prime of life. Old age is
embodied in the last depiction, where an aged stallion
with weakened legs and a bell around his neck gently
lowers his head to drink from a krater. This drinking
cup may represent a victory prize or, because it is a
vase shape often associated with Bacchus (a divinity
connected not only with wine but also with the afterlife), allude to the Bacchic paradise that followed this
life. One of the tripod's legs has a semicircular projection that is decorated with a protome of a snarling
panther (an animal also often associated with Bacchus). When the tripod legs were closed together, this
projection served as the carrying handle; when the
tripod was open, utensils could be suspended from it.

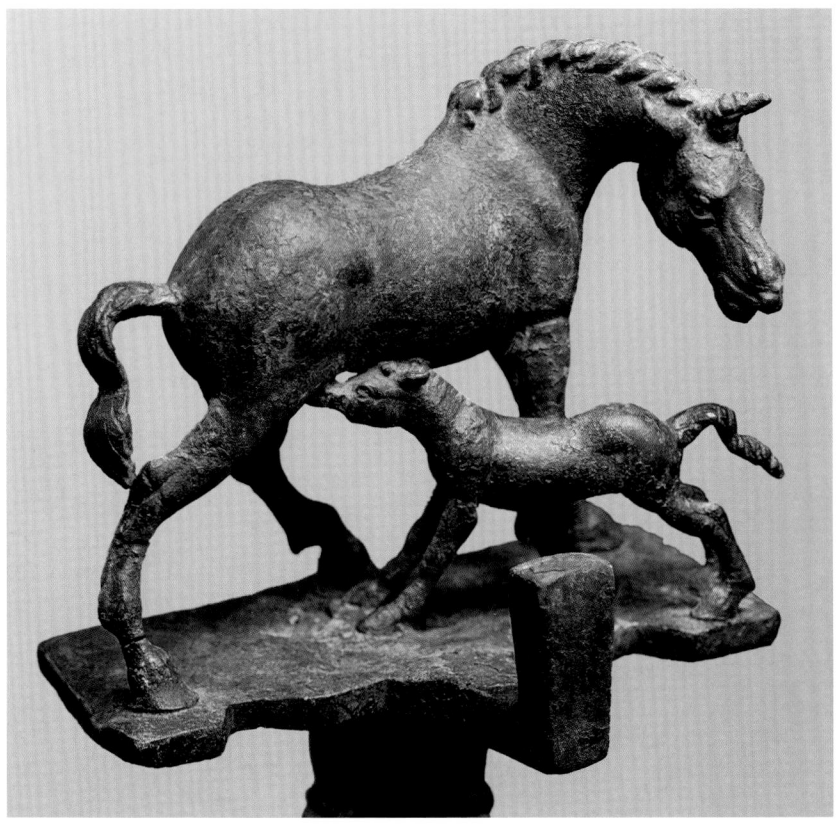

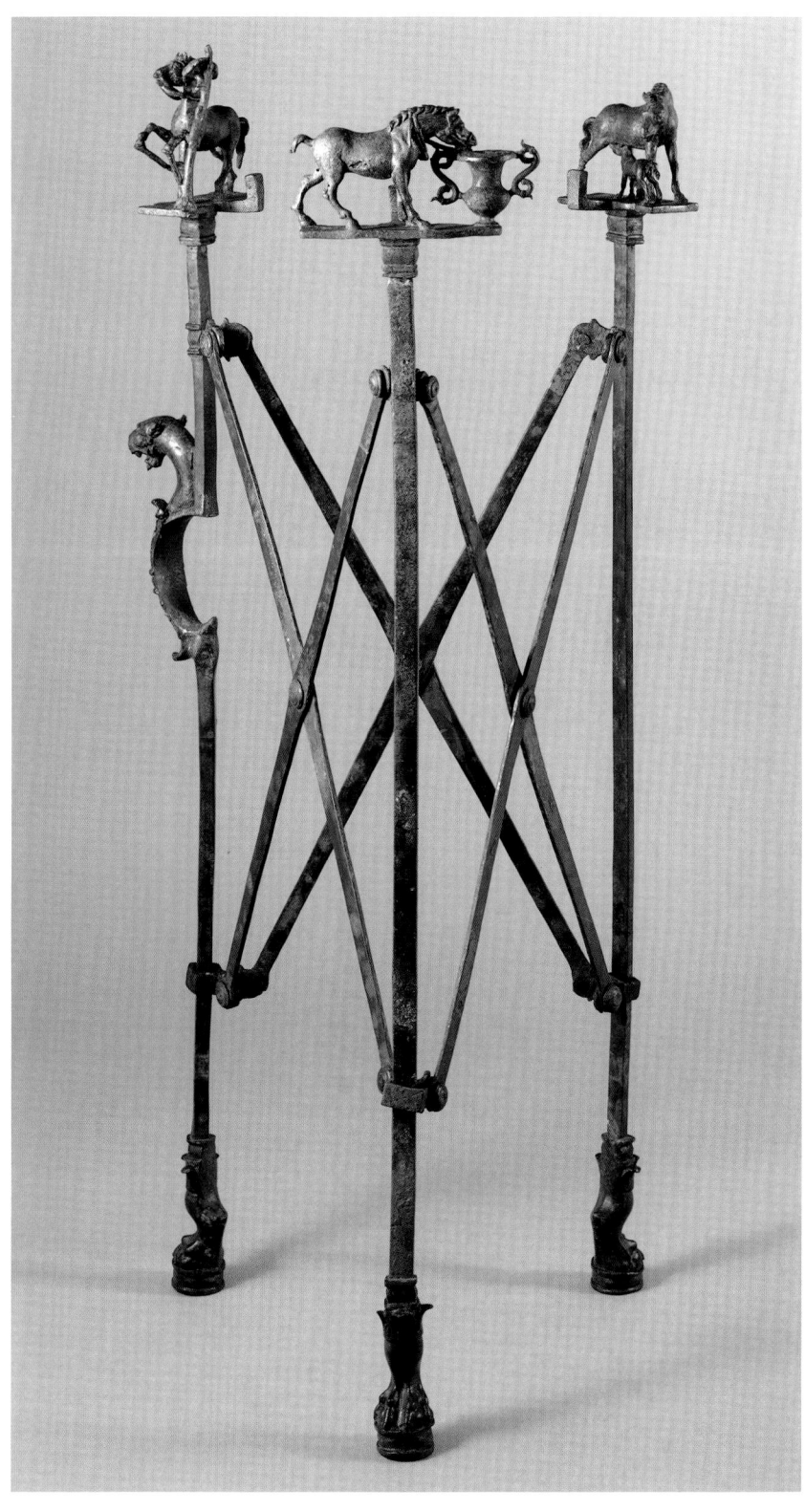

Gem Engraved with a Head of the Doryphoros Inset into a Ring

Roman, 50–40 B.C.
Dark green chalcedony and gold
H (gem): 2.24 cm (⅞ in.)
W (gem): 1.73 cm (11/16 in.)
DIAM (hoop): 2.49 cm (1 in.)
75.AM.61

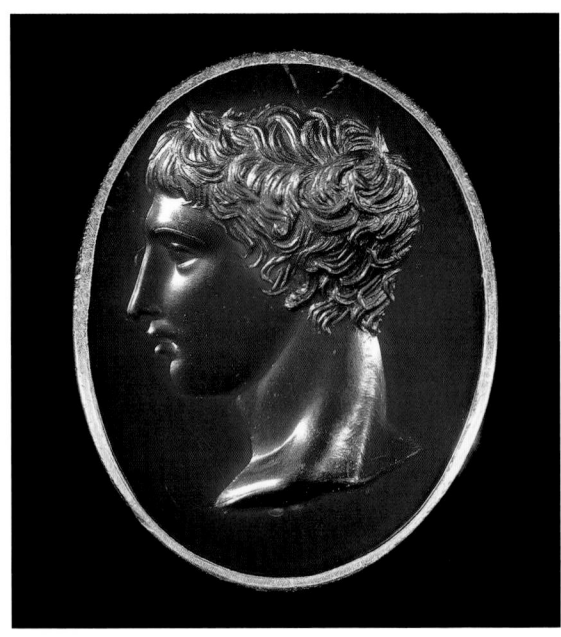

Upper-class Romans demonstrated their good taste by surrounding themselves with items that referenced Greek art, including jewelry. Carved into the stone of this ring is the head of one of the most famous Greek statues ever made, the *Doryphoros*, or Spearbearer, by the artist Polykleitos, cast in bronze about 440 B.C. Polykleitos created his statue to illustrate certain aesthetic theories that he explained in a treatise called the *Kanon*. His book has not survived, but references to it by other ancient writers imply that the Greek words *symmetria* (symmetry) and *rhythmos* (rhythm) expressed its main principles. According to Polykleitos, a statue should be composed of clearly definable parts, all related to one another through a system of ideal mathematical proportions and balance. Polykleitos's works were very popular with the Romans in the first century B.C., and first-century-A.D. Roman artists created numerous replicas and variations of his sculptures in addition to reproducing them in other media, such as engraved gemstones.

In Roman society, which emphasized display, this ring, with its carved gemstone set into heavy gold, advertised the wearer's wealth as well as his culture and learning. The ring was buried with a group of objects containing late first-century-B.C. silverware (including the silver cups on p. 208), a gold diadem, and a gold aureus of Mark Antony minted in Asia Minor in 34 B.C. The coin appears to be in mint condition, suggesting that the objects were buried shortly after 34 B.C.

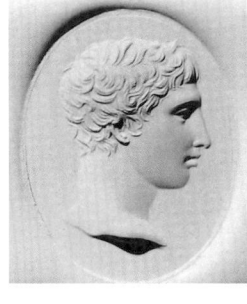

GEM ENGRAVED WITH A PORTRAIT OF DEMOSTHENES INSET INTO A RING

Signed by Apelles
Roman, 25–1 B.C.
Carnelian and gold
H (gem): 1.9 cm (¾ in.)
W (gem): 1.5 cm (⅝ in.)
DIAM (hoop): 3.36 cm
(1⁵/₁₆ in.)
90.AN.13

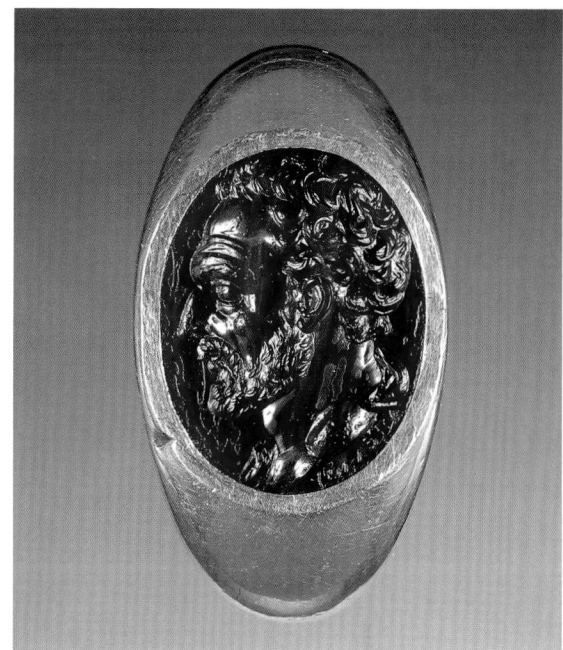

A carved portrait of the Greek orator Demosthenes decorates the gem of this large gold ring. Demosthenes, the most famous of Athenian orators, lived from about 384 to 322 B.C. He is perhaps better known today for overcoming a difficult speech impediment than for his politics. He was vehemently opposed to—and outspoken about—the gathering power in Macedonia under Philip II and his son, Alexander the Great. Although never successful in his campaign to sway political sentiment against the northern kingdom, he created many political enemies in Athens and Macedonia in the attempt. When the Macedonians occupied Athens in 323 B.C., Demosthenes was condemned to die, but he committed suicide first.

Depictions of orators on Roman gems are quite rare, but during the early Roman Empire portraits of Demosthenes in all media became popular. Many portraits in both marble and bronze have survived, but this gem portrait is one of only four that exist today.

Gem carvers did not often sign their work, except in the late first century B.C. The engraver Apelles signed his name in Greek on the face of the stone as "Apellou" indicating that it is a work "of Apelles." Apelles worked in Rome in the late first century B.C., but his name suggests that he was a Greek craftsman who had moved to Rome, the cosmopolitan imperial capital, where there would have been a larger market for his high-quality work.

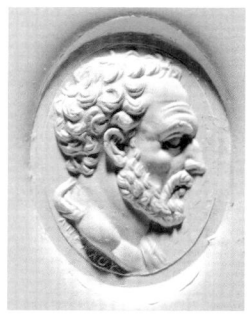

Cameo of Perseus with the Head of Medusa Inset into a Ring

Roman, 25 B.C.–A.D. 25
White on brown sardonyx
and gold
H (cameo): 1.75 cm (¹¹/₁₆ in.)
W (cameo): 1 cm (³/₈ in.)
DIAM (hoop): 2.1 cm (¹³/₁₆ in.)
87.AN.24

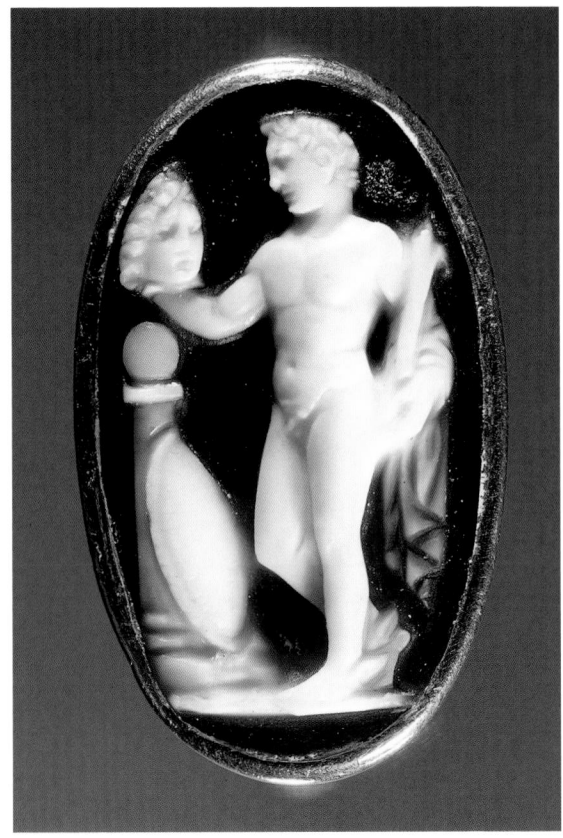

The Greek hero Perseus stands contemplating the decapitated head of the Gorgon Medusa. In his left hand, he holds the *harpe*, or curved sword, that he used for the decapitation. The naked hero has a cloak thrown over his left arm, and he wears the winged sandals given to him by the god Hermes to complete his challenging task.

The image on the cameo may be derived from a bronze statue of Perseus made in the 400s B.C. by the Athenian sculptor Myron. The depiction of the hero here is unusual and implies some confusion on the part of the artist. According to the myth, looking at the face of Medusa instantly turned the viewer to stone. This gem appears to conflate the Perseus story with a well-known motif of the period, that of an actor gazing at a theatrical mask on a column.

Popular among the Romans, cameos frequently depicted Greek statue types. Multilayered gemstones or glass were carved so that a white relief stood out against a dark background, usually blue or brown. The production of cameos originated in the Hellenistic period, after the advance of Alexander the Great's armies to India opened up the East to the Greek world. Onyx from India and Arabia was the stone most frequently used in antiquity for cameos. Like the technique of cameo carving, the ring's shape—a hoop expanding upward to form an oval bezel—was also introduced during the Hellenistic period and remained popular for centuries.

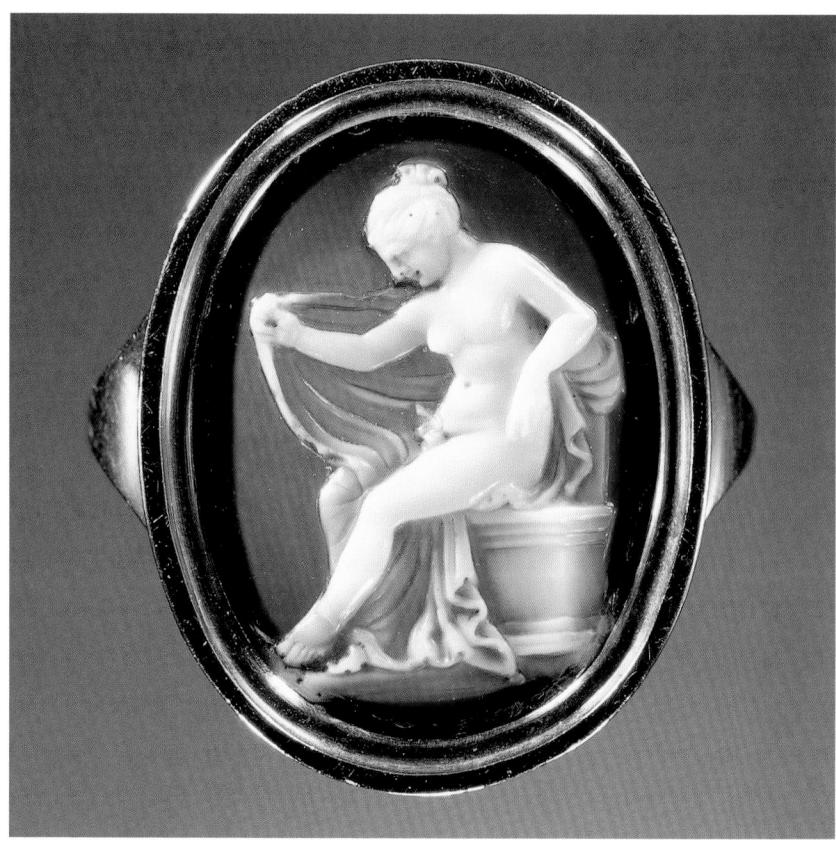

CAMEO WITH HERMAPHRODITUS

Roman, 150–100 B.C.
(cameo; modern ring)
Sardonyx, gold
H (cameo): 1.8 cm (¾ in.)
2001.28.9

Seated on an altar, Hermaphroditus pulls aside his/her drapery, revealing an erect penis as well as female breasts. The Roman poet Ovid explained in an episode of his *Metamorphoses* how the nymph Salmacis fell in love with Hermaphroditus, the son of Hermes and Aphrodite, and embraced him so tightly that the two eventually became a single bisexual being. The carver of this cameo—a single piece of banded sardonyx—has skillfully cut away the white layer to fashion the figure's body and drapery, leaving the honey-colored layer as a background. The apparent transparency of Hermaphroditus's garment and other stylistic details have led scholars to associate this cameo with the ancient carver Protarchos, who signed cameos with similar features.

ASSEMBLAGE OF GOLD JEWELRY

Roman, A.D. 250–400
Gold with various inlaid and
attached stones, including
sapphire, emerald, garnet,
and glass paste
Various dimensions
83.AM.224–.228

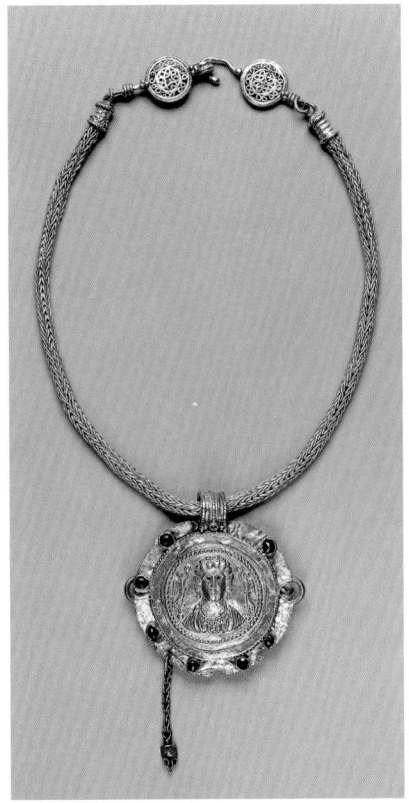

This collection of jewelry presents a
fascinating mélange of materials
and techniques. The pieces are said to
have been found together and thus
also serve as a reminder that, in times
of violent uprisings or war, treasured
valuables were sometimes buried
by an owner who did not survive to
retrieve them later on.

An elaborate gold belt is the centerpiece of the assemblage. It is composed
of twenty-two square links made from
gold coins of several fourth-century-
A.D. Roman emperors framed by green
glass, a central medallion with three
pendant attachments and inlays of
glass and semiprecious stones on the
front and a relief of opened acanthus
on the back, and an adjustable hook
fastener. Emperors in the fourth
century A.D. wore jeweled belts and
coin belts as part of their official rega-
lia, but only women of the imperial

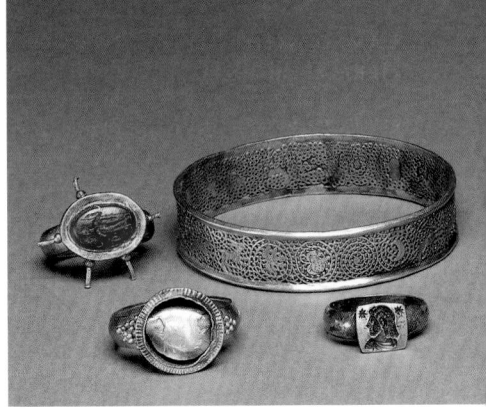

court seem to have had belts with a
central decorative ornament.

One of the necklaces has a gold
repoussé medallion depicting the
frontal bust of a woman wearing a diadem and jewelry that, together with
the flanking personifications of victory
holding wreaths, indicate she may

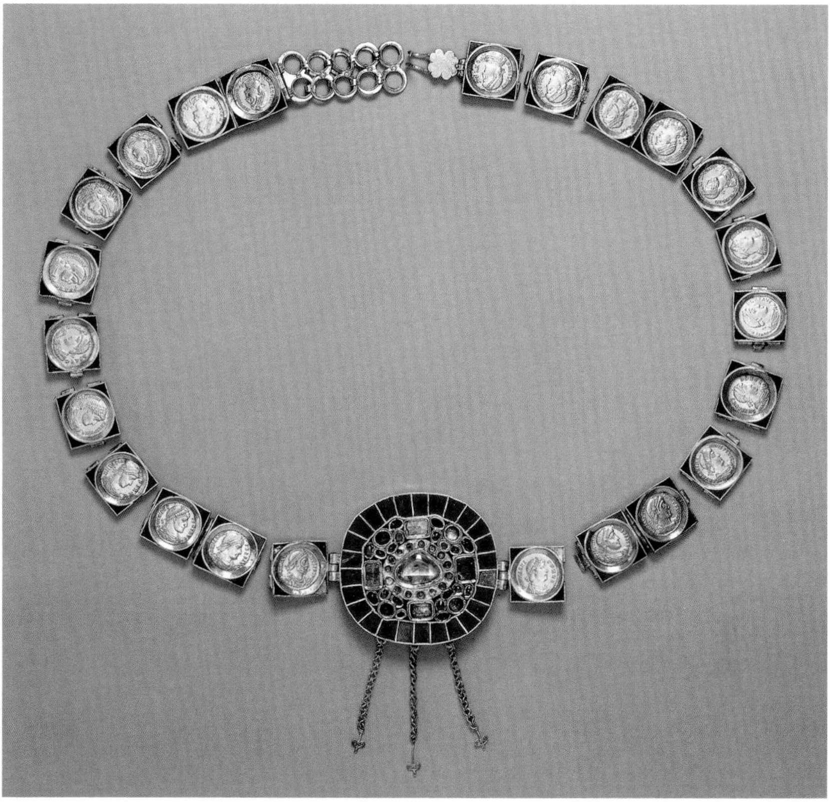

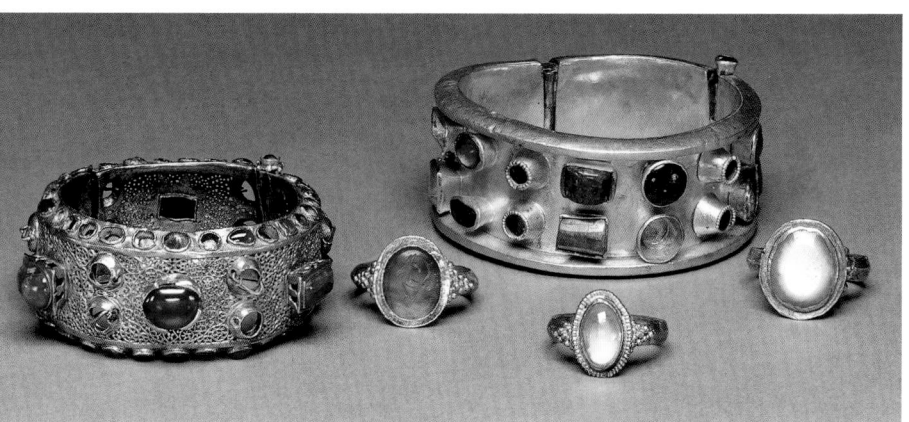

be an empty. Another necklace's pendant, a gold-mounted cameo with the facing busts of a couple, was originally a brooch; it exemplifies the tendency to reuse jewelry pieces.

Among the distinctive objects that comprise the remainder of the assemblage are two openwork gold bracelets, one decorated with animals within floral scrolls and another designed as a solid cuff inlaid with glass and precious stones. One of the rings is mounted with an engraved intaglio, four are mounted with semiprecious stones, and one has an engraved bezel.

BEAKER

Roman, A.D. 1–100
Gold
H: 13.7 cm (5⅜ in.)
2001.6

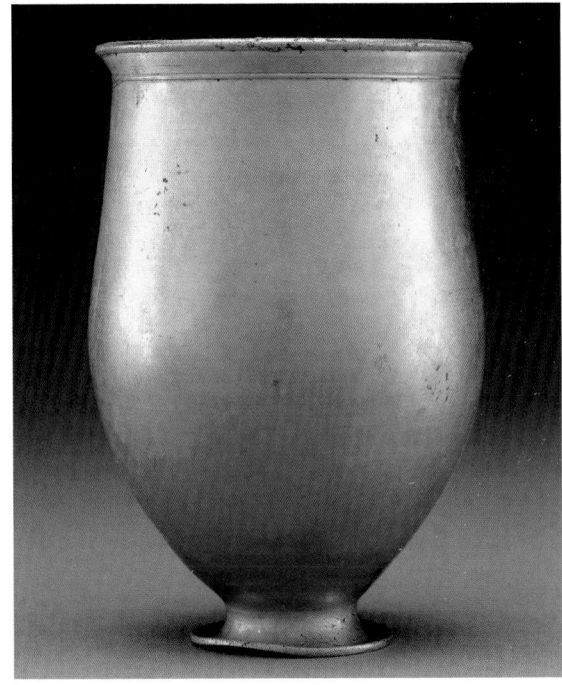

Found by sponge divers off the western coast of Turkey in the early 1900s along with another gold vessel,
now in the British Museum, this beaker is one of
only six Roman gold vessels known to have survived
from antiquity. Its deep, subtly convex body rises
from a small flanged foot and ends in a slightly flared
rim. The only decorative embellishments to the elegant profile are two incised lines below the rim. An
abbreviated dotted Latin inscription on the underside
of the flanged foot records the vessel's weight as two
libra, one *sescuncia*—the equivalent of 24.54 ounces.
The actual weight of the vessel is 23.15 ounces, and
the difference between the inscribed weight and
actual weight may indicate that the vessel once had
a lid.

STATUETTE OF A BULL

Roman, from Pompeii,
100 B.C.–A.D. 75
Gilt Silver
H: 14 cm (5½ in.)
2001.7

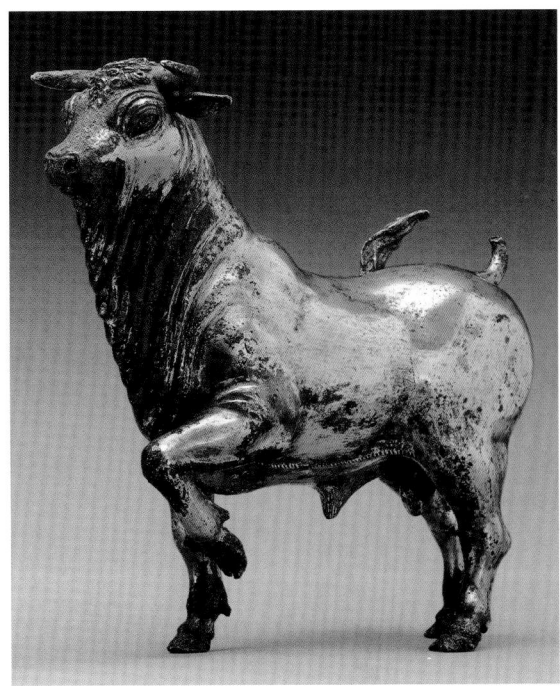

Discovered in Pompeii between 1780 and 1790, this statuette of a powerfully modeled bull became part of the collection of Maria Christina of Savoy, the queen of the kingdom of the Two Sicilies. The statuette originally belonged to a Pompeiian family who perished during the eruption of Mount Vesuvius in A.D. 79. When Pompeii was being freed in the eighteenth century from its covering of ash and volcanic debris, many precious objects, such as this bull, came to light in almost perfectly preserved condition. This figure was cast in silver and then gilt, a luxury object reflecting its original owner's social status and wealth.

The bull would have stood with other statuettes of gods, goddesses, and divinities in a domestic shrine (*lararium*), where it would have been an object of devotion and veneration by household members. The animal probably represents the king of the gods, Jupiter, who often took the guise of a bull. The bull's sculptor has modeled its anatomy after nature. For example, the loose skin under the animal's neck is depicted as a series of pliant folds. The horns curve forward above the ears and the eyes have incised pupils, irises, and lashes. The beast stands erect with one foreleg bent, tail (now partially lost) curled up onto its flank, and head raised. The bull seems to embody all the strength and power inherent in the mightiest of all the gods, Jupiter.

PAIR OF CUPS

Roman, 50–25 B.C.
Silver
H: 12.4 cm (4⅞ in.)
DIAM: 11.2 cm (4⅜ in.)
75.AM.54

H: 12.3 cm (4⅞ in.)
DIAM: 11.6 cm (4⅝ in.)
75.AM.55

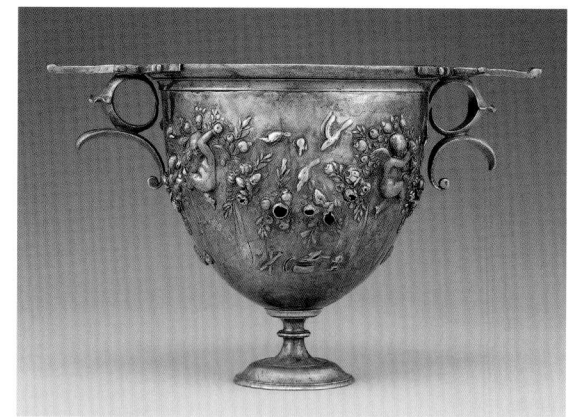

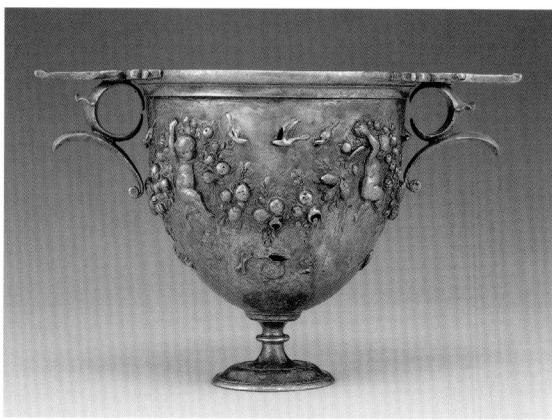

Silver drinking cups were popular throughout the Roman Empire from the first century B.C. through the middle of the first century A.D. They were often richly decorated and were used and displayed in Roman homes. These two matching cups are the most spectacular objects from an assemblage of silver vessels that were once part of a tomb group. Another silver cup, a silver pitcher, a silver ladle, and a gold ring with an engraved image of the *Doryphoros* (Spearbearer), a famous bronze statue by the Classical Greek sculptor Polykleitos (see p. 200) are other significant pieces from this group. This assemblage reflects the international flavor of metalworking in the first century B.C.; therefore, a specific location for its manufacture is difficult to ascertain. A coin in the group suggests the pieces may have been made by a silversmith employing the traditions of Asia Minor (modern Turkey) in Greece or Italy—or they may have been made in Asia Minor itself, perhaps at Pergamon, Ephesos, or Antioch.

On each of these cups, four flying cupids support a continuous garland tightly bound with *taeniae* (fillets) and intertwined with pomegranates, apples, grapes, olives, pinecones, and acorns. Birds fly above; below, various objects, including a tympanum (hand drum), a *cista* (basket), cymbals, and pipes, decorate the cups. The iconography is somewhat enigmatic, since the motif of garland-bearing cupids survives from the art of Pergamon as well as Pompeii, where Second Style wall paintings (popular in the first century B.C.) show cupids accompanied by birds and musical instruments.

Cup with Cranes

Roman, perhaps from
Alexandria, 25–1 B.C.
Silver
H: 7.3 cm (2⁷/₈ in.)
DIAM: 10.3 cm (4 in.)
72.AM.33

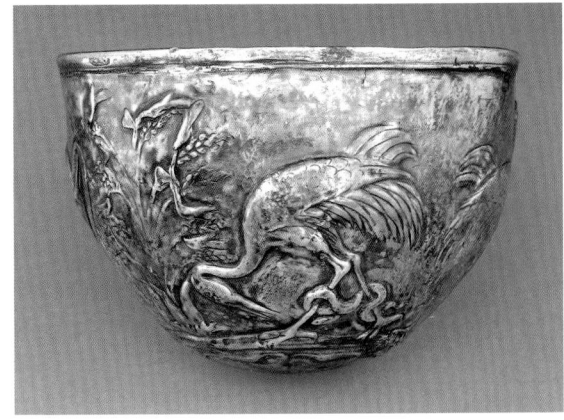

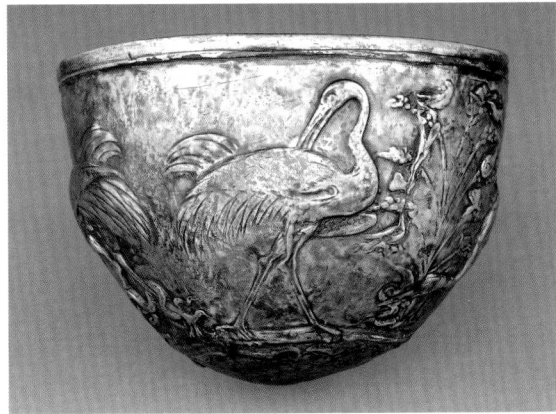

This silver bowl is decorated in relief with four cranes
in a landscape teeming with animal life and opulently
stylized vegetation. The artist has captured the cranes
in a variety of poses that convey their natural habitat
and actions. One crane battles with a snake that has
entwined itself around the bird's legs. Another preens
its feathers, turning its head to reach its back. A third
similarly preens, while the fourth grabs a snake in
its mouth.

The motif of cranes set into a landscape was a popular decoration on cups during the early Augustan
period at the end of the first century B.C. The combination of naturalism and ornamentalism on this cup
suggests that it was made by a talented silversmith
in Alexandria, Egypt. Ancient marks on the cup's surface indicate the former presence of handles and a
foot that are now missing.

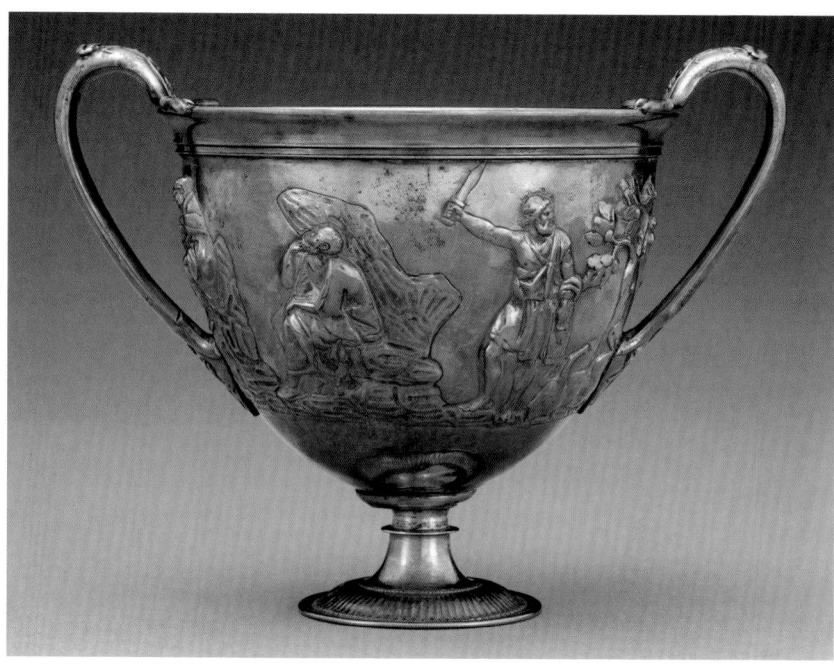

TWO-HANDLED CUP

Roman, A.D. 1–100
Silver
H: 12.5 cm (4 ⅞ in.)
DIAM: 16.3 cm (6 ⅜ in.)
96.AM.57

Complete sets of silver found throughout the Roman world attest to the fact that during the later years of the Roman Republic, tableware made of that valuable metal was no longer a luxury restricted to the very wealthy. For Romans of growing prosperity, many items in silver—trays, dishes, vessels, ladles, and spoons—replaced those of bronze and pottery.

Repoussé, the working of metal from behind with hammers and punches, was the technique used most frequently to ornament metal drinking cups such as this one. A wide range of decorative motifs are known, varying from mythological subjects to scenes of outdoor life and nature.

The primary scene on this cup comes from an episode in Homer's *Odyssey*. When Odysseus (known to the Romans as Ulysses) left Circe after a yearlong stay on her island, the sorceress directed him to sail west to the entrance to the Underworld, where he could seek out and question the blind seer Teiresias about returning home to Ithaka. To summon the ghost, Odysseus was to offer a sacrifice of sheep. Here at the right, having succeeded in his purpose and with his sword upraised, Odysseus stands beside a tree and the slain ram; its blood has brought out the shades of the dead. In the adjacent rocky setting sit Teiresias (center) and another spirit (at the left).

On the other side, additional figures engage in a discussion; they may represent philosophers or the Seven Sages rather than other shades of the dead.

AMPHORA-RHYTON

Roman, A.D. 300–500
Gilt silver
H: 38 cm (15 in.)
DIAM (body): 8.8 cm (3½ in.)
92.AM.12

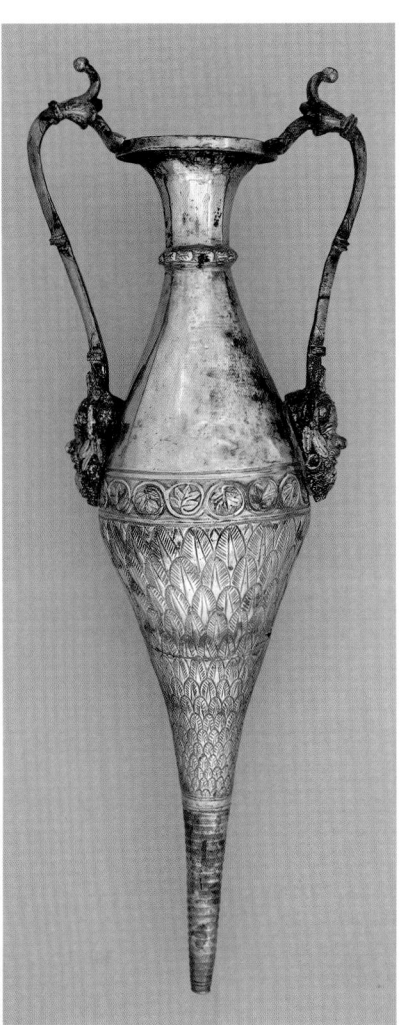

An amphora (storage vessel) and a
rhyton (drinking/pouring vessel) are
combined here in a vase type that
is unusual and survives in only a few
examples. The elegant arching handles,
decorated with foliate forms and
geese's heads at the gilt rim, are
attached to the elongated body of the
vessel with the heads of ivy-wreathed
satyrs. As members of the retinue
of Bacchus, god of wine, satyrs frequently appear as handle attachments
for vessels that most likely held wine.

This piece was probably used to
aerate wine before it was served. The
fifteen rows of overlapping vertical
feathers that adorn the bottom half
of the vessel are similar to decorative
patterns on other silver vessels (see
the bowl on p. 92). A number of
stylistic details, including the knobbed
handles and the elongated profile of
the vase—both characteristic of
fourth- and fifth-century-A.D. vessels
—help to date this piece to the end
of the Roman Empire. In addition, the
ornamental collar of overlapping
horizontal feathers is typical of later
metal and glass pieces, and the incising
on the satyrs' irises and pupils likewise points to a late Roman date. As
further confirmation, scientific analysis has revealed that the gilding, which
adds to the object's opulence, is applied
with a mercury amalgam, a mixture
that was used only in the late Roman
period.

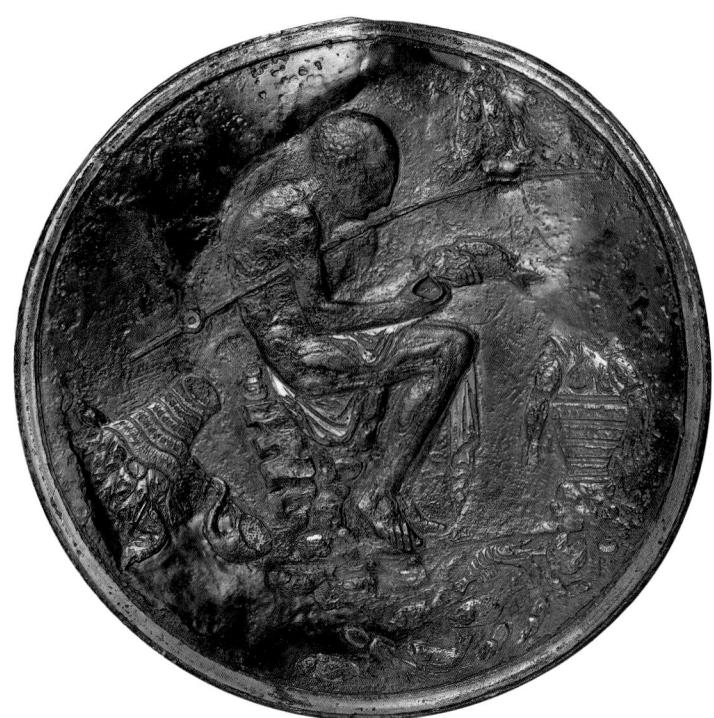

**PLATE WITH
RELIEF
DECORATION**

Late Antique, A.D. 500–600
Gilt Silver
DIAM: 60 cm (23⅝ in.)
83.AM.347

An old fisherman sits in a rocky landscape at the
edge of the sea teeming with various marine animals
and removes a fish from his hook. Two fish hang in
the background and the rest of his catch overflows
from the baskets around him. Gilding enhances the
luxurious nature of this object. The long tradition
of representing genre scenes on expensive materials
began during the Hellenistic period.

**PLATE WITH
RELIEF
DECORATION**

Late Antique, A.D. 500–600
Silver
H: 45 cm (17¾ in.)
W: 28 cm (11 in.)
83.AM.342

The allegorical scene that decorates this large plate
represents the philosophical dispute between Science
and Mythology. This is one of a number of "picture-
dishes," plates in which figural scenes fill the surface,
which first became popular in the second century A.D.
The two seated men engaged in discussion are identified by Greek inscriptions as Ptolemaios on the left
and Hermes on the right. The former was an astrono-
mer, mathematician, and geographer who represents
scientific knowledge, the latter is almost certainly
Hermes Trismegistos, an egyptianized Hermes connected with Neoplatonism and Late Antique religious
magic. Between the seated men is a globe. The
woman with her hand to her chin behind Ptolemaios
is labeled Skepsis, a personification of speculation
or doubt. The inscriptions identifying the enthroned
figure at the top of the plate and the woman behind

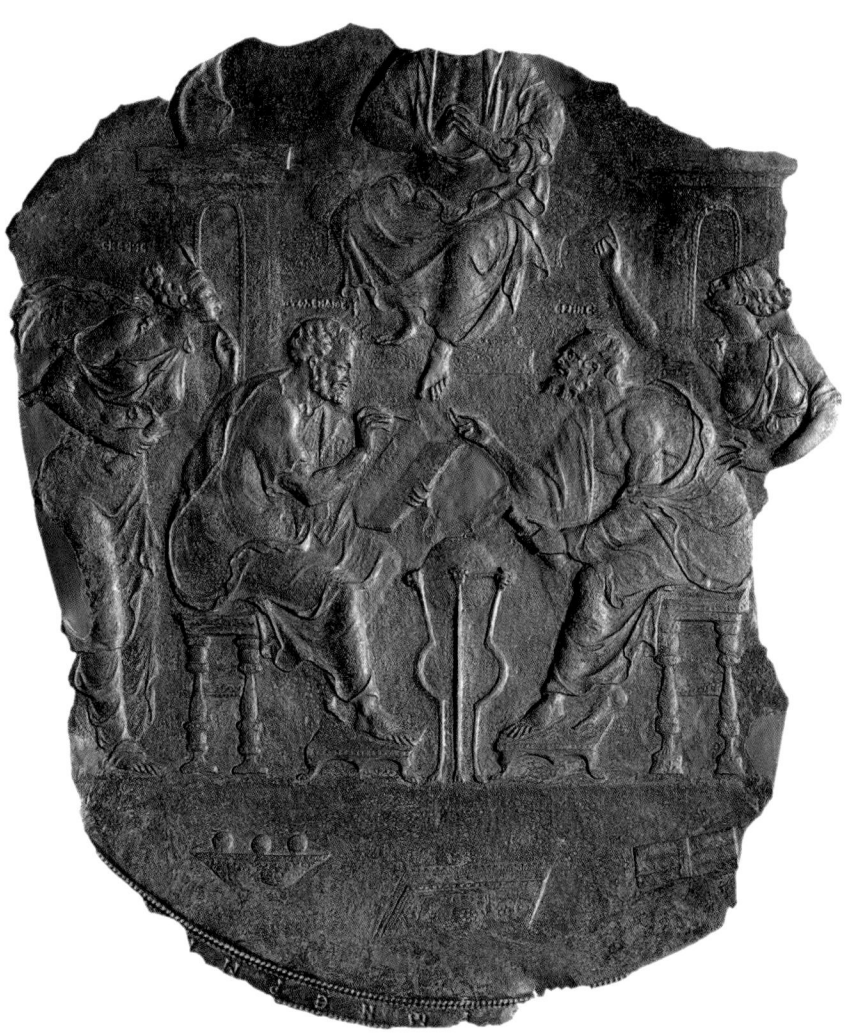

Hermes Trismegistos are missing. The subject and
style of this plate have been associated by some scholars with the European Mannerist period (1525–1600),
but its silver content and method of manufacture
point to an ancient origin. Radiographic photography
revealed a faint pattern of vines and leaves on the
underside of the plate, confirming its ancient date;
this design is characteristic of similar pieces produced
in late antiquity.

CAMEO GLASS FLASK

Roman, 25 B.C.–A.D. 25
Glass
H: 7.6 cm (3 in.)
DIAM (body): 4.2 cm (1⅝ in.)
85.AF.84

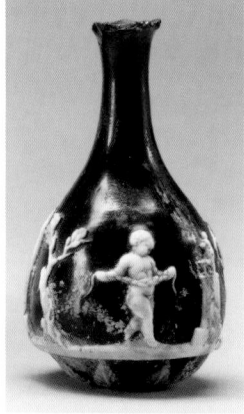

Though glassmaking had been known since the third millennium B.C., new processes and techniques for manufacturing glass continued to be developed. The method for making cameo glass was one of the highest technical achievements of the glass industry during the Roman period. Two or more layers of hot glass in different colors were overlaid and then, after cooling, carved away in cameo technique to create a low-relief scene. Cameo glass resembles precious layered stones, such as banded agate, which were carved in the same manner, and it is possible that the artisans who carved cameo glass worked primarily in stone.

The figures encircling this diminutive perfume flask are an eclectic blend of Rome and Egypt. On one side (shown here), a young boy holding a garland stands before the figure of the god Thoth, depicted as a baboon seated atop an altar. On the other side, a boy offers stalks of grain before an altar with a uraeus (sacred snake) carved on its side, a reference to the goddess Isis. Behind this altar stands the figure of a pharoah holding a crooked staff and a vessel. And finally, a tree and an obelisk carved with hieroglyphs create landscape elements. A decorative rosette is carved on the flask's underside.

Past interpretations of this scene have focused on the life of Horus, or to events in Rome, specifically to the arrival of two obelisks from Heliopolis in 10 B.C. One was erected in the Circus Maximus (an arena for chariot racing) and the other in the Campus Martius (Field of Mars). More recent study of Egyptian monuments present in Rome, such as the obelisks, has led to the theory that the flask was carved in Rome, and depicts works that would have been familiar to the artist, such as sculptures of seated baboons and striding pharoah figures in the Iseum Campense, a sanctuary dedicated to the goddess Isis in the Campus Martius.

CAMEO GLASS SKYPHOS

Roman, 25 B.C.–A.D. 25
Glass
H (preserved): 10.5 cm (4⅛ in.)
DIAM: 10.6 cm (4⅛ in.)
84.AF.85

Many surviving Roman cameo glass vessels display scenes that refer to Bacchus, god of wine, or his followers, as does this skyphos, or drinking cup. A satyr —a creature typically associated with Bacchus— stands in the center of one side of the cup (depicted here). He plays a lyre and looks back at the half-draped woman behind him, who leans against a large krater (a vessel for water or wine) and sips from a bowl. On the right, a half-draped figure holding a cup sits on a rocky outcrop. A tree and a tall stele, topped by the enthroned goddess Cybele, are situated behind him. The seated figure may be Bacchus who reaches forward to place an offering (perhaps incense) to the deity on a flaming altar.

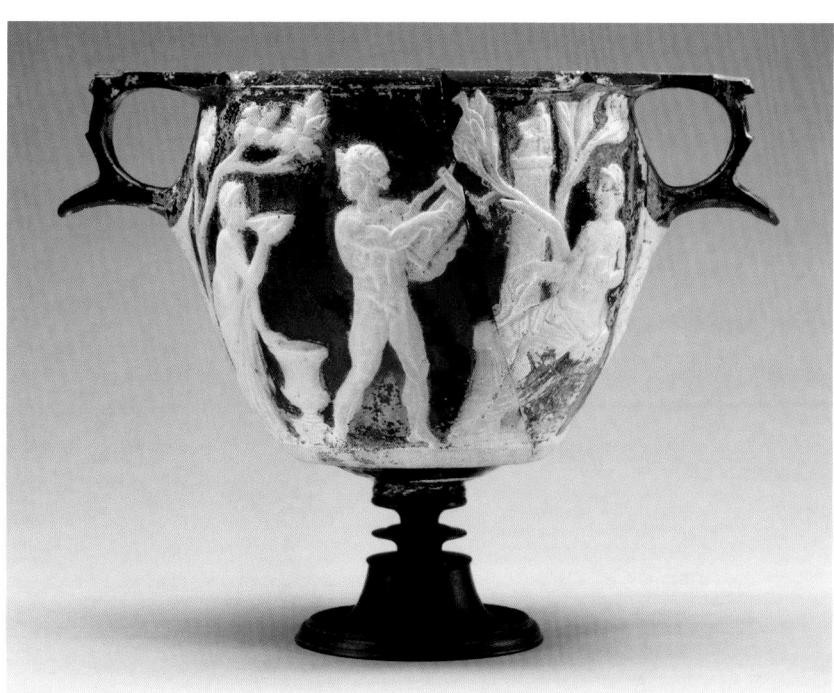

On the other side of the cup, a half-draped woman sits upon stacked rocks. With one arm resting atop her head, she looks back at the female attendant behind her, who holds out a *cista* (shallow box or basket) that is covered with a cloth. To the left, a satyr holds a set of panpipes in his right hand and cradles a *pedum* (crooked stick) in his left arm; he looks back at the two women. The trees behind the flanking figures emphasize the outdoor setting in which the scene takes place. The frontal heads of bearded Pans or satyrs are carved below the handles. Satyrs and Pan often accompanied the wine god and participated in his drunken revels. As this vessel is a drinking cup, their use as a decorative element here is quite appropriate.

The iconography of this cup's two principal scenes relates to religious rituals and votive offerings, but the identities of the figures portrayed are not completely clear. Ariadne, Bacchus's consort, may be the seated woman partaking in a scene of ritual initiation, in which the religious mystery is about to be revealed to her by the attendant holding the covered *cista*. On the vessel's other side, she may be the woman sipping from the bowl, shown as an acolyte drinking wine as a part of the religious ritual. The gaze of the lyre-playing satyr toward her emphasizes her importance in the scene.

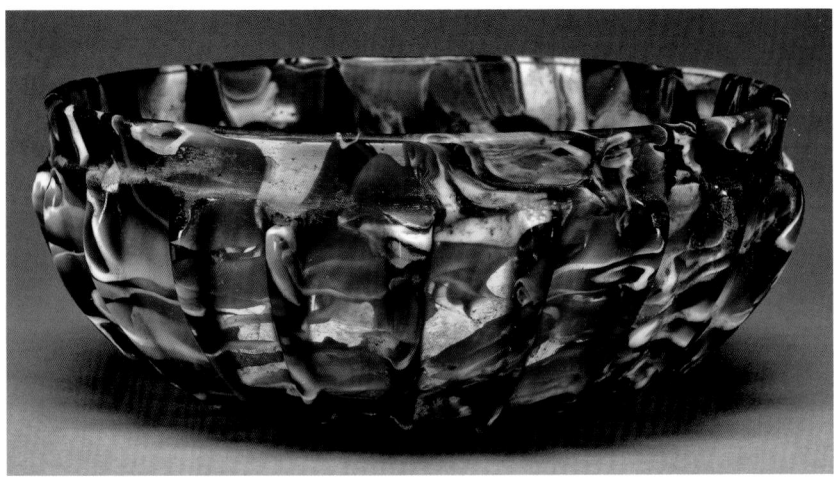

RIBBED BOWL

Roman, 100 B.C.–A.D. 100
Glass
H: 7.5 cm (3 in.)
DIAM: 18 cm (7⅛ in.)
72.AF.37

The brown and white glass used to make this bowl was deliberately blended to imitate agate, a naturally banded semiprecious stone. In antiquity, ceramic and glass vessels were often more affordable substitutes for pieces made from expensive materials such as agate.

Both multicolored and monochrome ribbed bowls were popular during the first century B.C. and first century A.D. Bowls of this shape were made by fusing and sagging the glass. First, small pieces of brown and white glass were heated together to create the appearance of agate. The fused glass was then flattened into a disk, and ribs were formed on its top. In the final step, the ribbed disk was placed over a hemispherical mold and reheated to sag and assume its final form.

This bowl was discovered in 1764 in the park of the Château of Ripaille (located on the south shore of Lake Geneva in France). The bowl was found within a round lead container and held the ashes and partially burnt bones of a cremation burial. The burial gifts found with the human remains included a fragmentary bone fibula (pin) worked in relief and formed as a rosette; an emerald cabochon; a gold ring with an engraved black stone bezel; and two glass phials, each 4 inches long. The current whereabouts of those burial gifts is unfortunately not known.

MYTHOLOGICAL BEAKER

Roman, A.D. 50–75
Glass
H: 12.6 cm (5 in.)
DIAM: 7 cm (2¾ in.)
85.AF.83

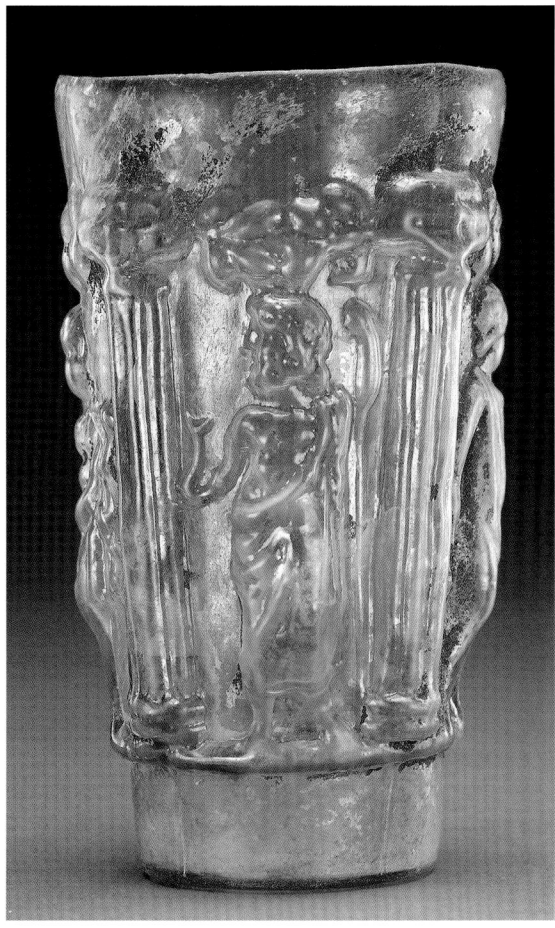

Vessels made by inflating hot glass into a mold were popular from the early first century A.D. on. Their creation was not possible until the technique of inflating glass with a blowpipe was developed in the previous century. Molds used for glass production were made of fired clay, plaster, wood, and metal. Most were simple two-part molds, but others were more complex and were made up of three or more parts. The mold used to inflate this beaker was constructed of four side panels and a base.

This vessel is decorated with a frieze of four figures standing between columns embellished with suspended floral swags. On the basis of their attributes, the figures have been identified as Neptune, god of the sea (shown here); Bonus Eventus, the personification of good fortune; Bacchus, god of wine; and Hymen, god of weddings.

The vessel is part of a larger corpus of mythological beakers that have been divided into four groups based on their figural combinations. Since there is no single figural composition from the Hellenistic or Roman period that includes all the figures found on the vessels, it seems unlikely that they were culled from a larger representation and combined together in fours on the beakers.

The function of the beakers is also unclear. The rims of the vessels were often left sharp, making them unsuitable for drinking. They may have been gifts to the deceased; at least two were found in burials.

SNAKE-THREAD FLASK

Roman, A.D. 200–300
Glass
H: 14.2 cm (5⅝ in.)
DIAM (rim): 3.6 cm (1⅜ in.)
DIAM (body): 11.6 cm
(4⅝ in.)
96.AF.56

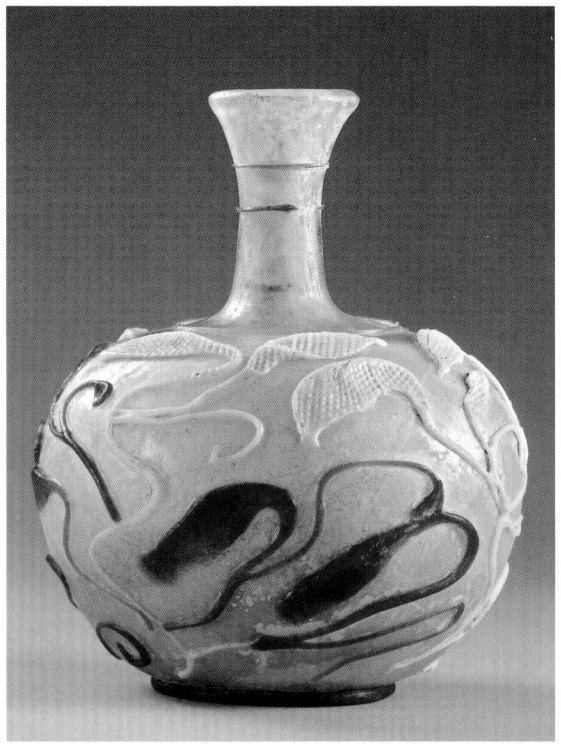

This free-blown flask of colorless glass has a globular body with a narrow neck and slightly flared rim. The neck is ornamented with an applied blue-glass trail, and a similar trail is wound on the base to provide a foot for the flask. The decoration on the body consists of blue and white trails arranged in foliate patterns. From undulating stems, flattened leaves spread over the curving surface of the flask.

So-called snake-thread glass was developed first in the glass workshops of the eastern Mediterranean. Two stylistic groups coexisted: one with freely applied trails, another, known as the flower-and-bird group, with figural representations. Shortly after its appearance in the eastern Mediter-ranean, snake-thread glass spread to the western provinces of the Roman Empire, particularly the provincial capital city of Colonia Claudia Ara Agrippinensium (modern Cologne, Germany), where many examples have been excavated. The products

of the eastern workshops are charac-terized by the use of colorless glass for both the body and trails, the cross-hatched impressions on some of the flattened trails, and the flower-and-bird patterns found on some of the vessels. The western workshops incorporated colored trails into their designs and impressed the trails with rows of single, rather than double, crosshatched lines.

This flask is an eclectic mix of shape, color, and patterning that successfully blends elements ascribed to both eastern and western manu-facture. The use of multicolored trails and the globular shape of the flask compare closely to examples exca-vated in Cologne. The decoration of the flask belongs to the flower-and-bird style, however, and its trails are crosshatched. These two elements make it more likely that the flask was produced in an eastern atelier.

HEAD FLASK

Roman, A.D. 300–500
Glass
H: 17.2 cm (6¾ in.)
W: 8 cm (3⅛ in.)
85.AF.320

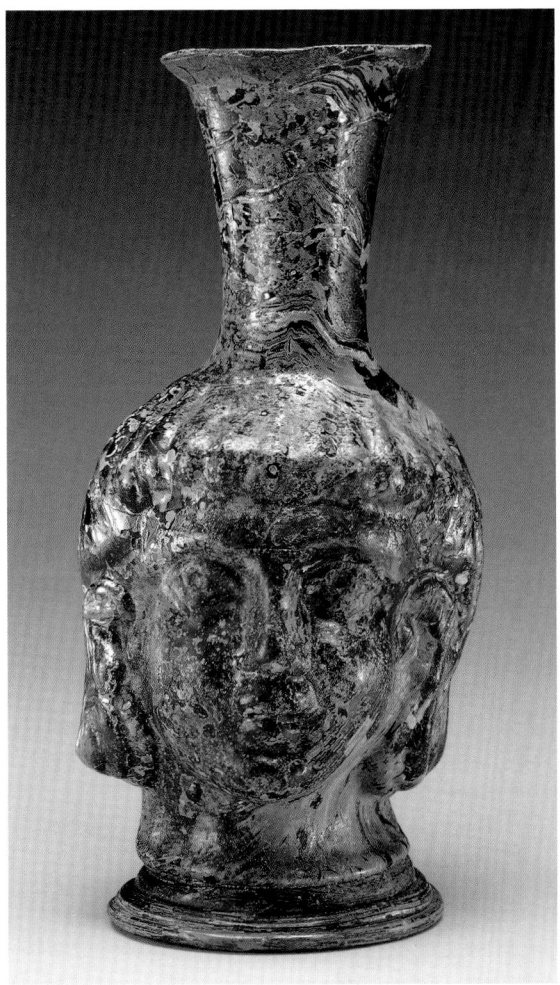

The production of ceramic, metal, and glass vessels shaped as human heads has a long history in ancient art. This flask, which dates to the fourth or fifth century A.D., shows the popularity of the type in the later Roman period, nearly a millennium after the earliest known examples. The flask is shaped as the head of a long-haired youth. His features are idealized, and he might represent a youthful god, perhaps Apollo.

The flask was made by inflating hot cobalt-blue glass into a two-part mold. Once the mold was removed from the glass, the flask's wishbone handle (attached behind the head) and circular foot were applied. In a final step, the slightly flared rim was formed

after the vessel was removed from the blowpipe; the finished flask was then placed into an annealing oven to cool. When it was manufactured, the flask was a uniform cobalt-blue color. Over time, as the glass has aged, a layer of iridescence has formed on the surface.

Five other head flasks of the same shape and size have survived from antiquity, four of which are made of the same cobalt-blue glass. The style of their handles and bases suggests that they were manufactured during the fourth or fifth century A.D. at a workshop in the eastern Mediterranean; recent archaeological finds from Israel of similar, but smaller, head flasks reinforce this conclusion.

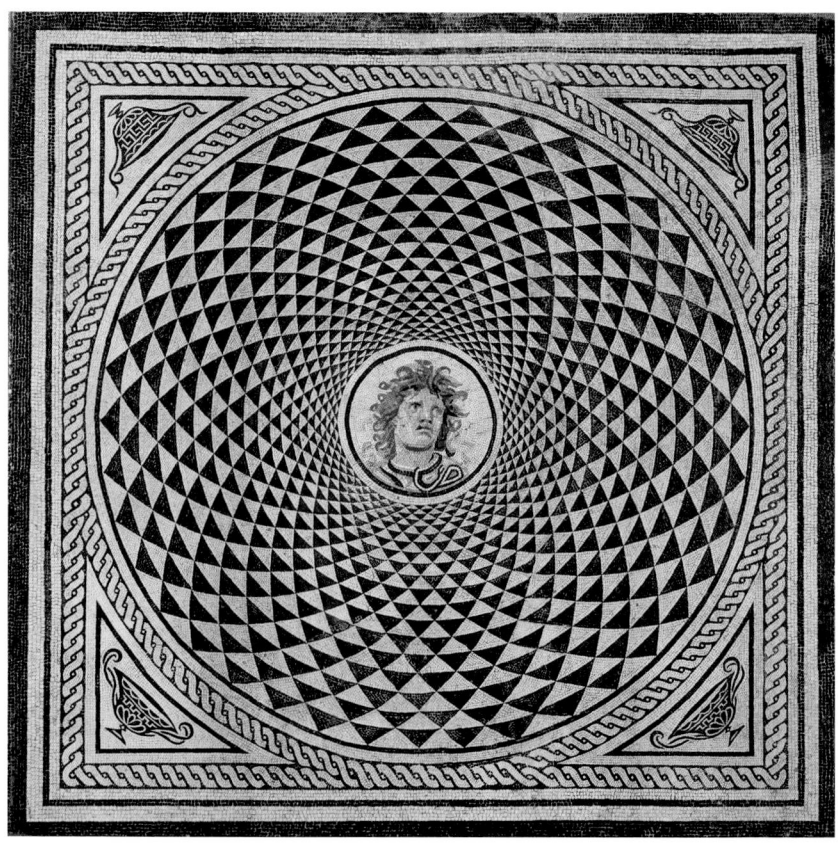

MOSAIC FLOOR WITH THE HEAD OF MEDUSA

Roman, A.D. 115–150
Stone tesserae
H: 270.5 cm (106½ in.)
W: 270.5 cm (106½ in.)
71.AH.110

The colorful bust of the Gorgon Medusa dominates the center of this otherwise completely black-and-white mosaic. Around the central medallion are circles of alternating black and white triangles that form an optical illusion of constant, almost dizzying motion. A continuous guilloche around the circle joins with another one that creates a square border around the entire composition.

According to mythology, the Gorgon Medusa with her frightening face and snakey hair could turn onlookers to stone by her gaze. She was decapitated by the hero Perseus, and her severed head was then used as a weapon. The image of the head of the Gorgon Medusa, also known as the *gorgoneion*, was one of the most popular symbols in the literature and art of ancient Greece and Rome. The *gorgoneion* is considered an apotropaic device; it was thought to protect the owner and repel any evil influences (see pp. 107, 176, and 202). The kantharos, a wine vessel sacred to the god Dionysos, is depicted in each of the four corners. Symbols of the worship of Dionysos were thought to bring good fortune and often accompanied depictions of the Gorgon Medusa.

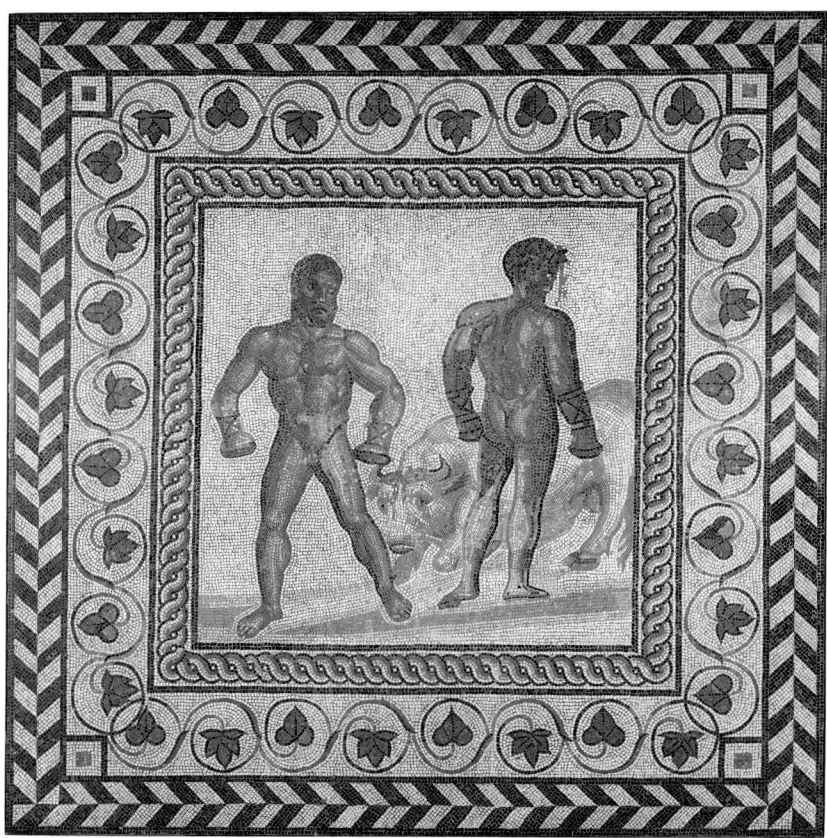

MOSAIC FLOOR WITH COMBAT BETWEEN DARES AND ENTELLUS

Gallo-Roman, from
Villalaure, southern France,
circa A.D. 175
Stone and glass tesserae
H: 208 cm (81⅞ in.)
W: 208 cm (81⅞ in.)
71.AH.106

This mosaic, which consists of small tesserae cut from different colored stones, with pale blue glass in the horns of the bull, illustrates a passage from the *Aeneid*, the epic poem written by Virgil (70–19 B.C.). According to the poem, Aeneas, Rome's heroic founder, held funerary games in order to honor the anniversary of his father's death. Included in these games was a boxing match between the Trojan Dares and a local Sicilian named Entellus. Dares, the younger and fitter of the two, was thought to be the inevitable winner, but he was beaten by the older and wiser Entellus. Entellus was then awarded a bull as his prize.

The artist has captured a quiet but tense moment at the end of the match. To the right, Dares, bleeding from his head, leaves the ring. The triumphant Entellus, meanwhile, has sacrificed the prize bull by delivering a crushing blow to its head. Illustration of this passage from the *Aeneid* is not common in Roman art, but several mosaics depicting this subject have been identified, all in the southern area of the Roman province of Gaul (modern France); this one was originally the central panel of a much larger mosaic floor in a Roman villa excavated in 1825.

FRAGMENT OF A FRESCO DEPICTING BACCHUS AND ARIADNE

Roman, A.D. 1–79
Plaster with pigment
H: 94 cm (37 in.)
W: 93 cm (36⅝ in.)
D: 6 cm (2⅜ in.)
83.AG.222.3.1

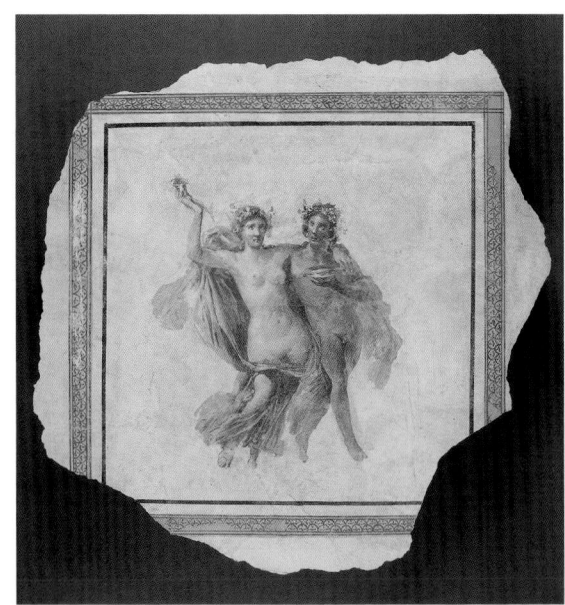

This fresco may come from the ceiling of a wealthy Roman's seaside villa in the area of the Bay of Naples. Floating through a celestial space in divine harmony are Bacchus, holding a drinking cup, and his consort Ariadne, who lifts a ceremonial drinking horn called a rhyton.

To produce the painting, artisans first stretched parcels of bundled reeds between the laths that supported the wall, a technique described by the ancient Roman architect Vitruvius as *opus craticium*. Then mortar (*arriccio*, a mixture of lime and sand) was applied atop the reed and lath arrangement. In this case only one thick layer was used, although three thinner layers were recommended in ancient handbooks. On top of the mortar a finer layer consisting of ground marble rather than lime, called the *intonaco*, was applied. Finally, the painted layer, carrying pigment mixed with water (and often lime), was applied while the *intonaco* was still wet. Because the final layers bonded together as they dried, the true fresco technique results in a very durable product. Evidence of the artisan's labor abounds: Impressions from the reeds are evident on the back of the fresco, and near the left shoulder of Bacchus numerous fingernail impressions can be seen, indicating the painter's use of the surface of the wall to support his hand as he worked. Numerous details, such as the wreaths worn by the gods, were applied *a secco* (after the fresco had dried).

FRAGMENT OF A FRESCO DEPICTING A NILOTIC LANDSCAPE

Roman, circa A.D. 70
Plaster with pigment
H: 45.7 cm (18 in.)
W: 38 cm (15 in.)
72.AG.86

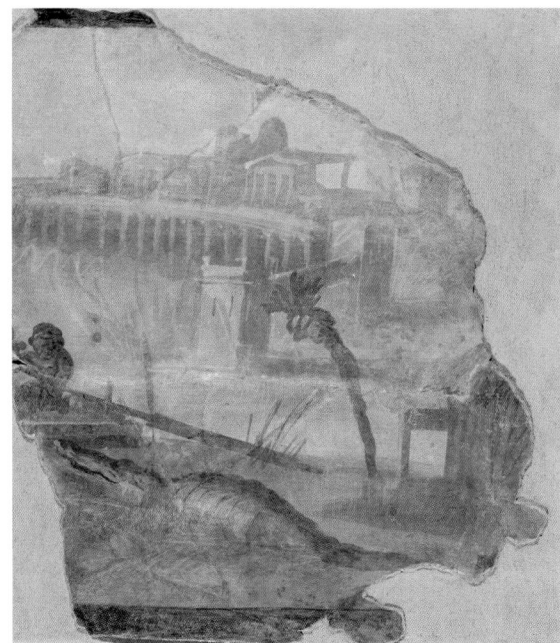

The prominent crocodile in the foreground identifies Egypt as the location of the scene preserved on this fragment of a painted wall. In a charming depiction of the annual flooding of the Nile River, the menacing reptile moves through a stand of rushes toward a boat or raft being maneuvered by a pygmy. The swaying palm tree and small thatch-roofed hut give additional geographic clues. Illusionistic architecture rises from the bluish haze of the water and atmosphere in the background, and includes a temple, a colonnaded portico, and a bridge with a tower.

Combats between pygmies and various opponents, including crocodiles, were frequently depicted as humorous subjects in Hellenistic and Roman art. Images related to Egypt became more widespread in Roman art after Egypt was annexed as a province of Rome following the defeat of Cleopatra and Mark Antony at the battle of Actium in 31 B.C., and their subsequent suicides in 30 B.C.

The remains of a red border at the top and bottom of the fragment indicate the size of the original scene. The additional, darker stripe along the bottom may belong to the painted frame of another scene below, and this fragment may have been placed high on the wall. Small landscape vignettes like this one were popular in both the Third and Fourth Styles of Roman wall painting, where they were often set within a larger field of color to give the appearance of a framed picture hung on the wall. Frescoes were painted directly onto wet plaster walls, allowing the colors to retain their vividness for centuries once bonded with the plaster.

FRAGMENT OF A FRESCO DEPICTING A PEACOCK

Roman, circa A.D. 70
Plaster with pigment
H: 40 cm (15¾ in.)
W: 24.8 cm (9¾ in.)
D: 3.2 cm (1¼ in.)
68.AG.13

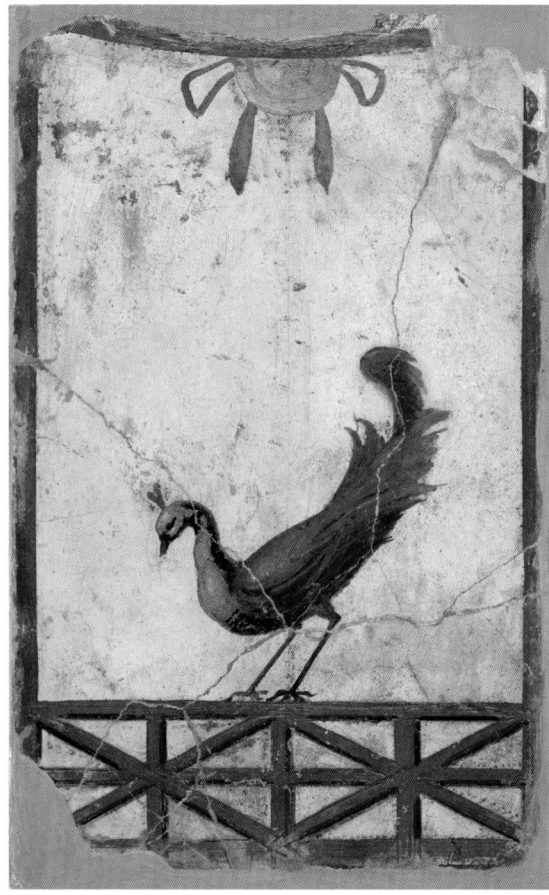

This small wall fragment depicts a peacock perched on a fence or railing. Viewed in profile, the bird is rendered in bright blues and reds against a neutral background. A pink shield decorated with red ribbons is suspended above. The fragment closely resembles a detail from the upper register of a room in the House of Siricus at Pompeii, which supports the likelihood that this too was originally from one of the cities destroyed by the eruption of Mount Vesuvius in A.D. 79.

The peacock, originally native to India, was imported and bred in Rome where it became a popular subject for painters. As well as being sacred to the goddess Juno, the extremely expensive birds were kept in gardens as an indication of wealth. Peacocks were also an extravagant delicacy

served at fashionable banquets. Inspired by the zoological gardens of Eastern and Hellenistic kings, Romans often decorated the walls of their gardens with frescoed scenes that created the illusion of greater space. Painted peacocks, fountains, and statues made gardens appear more luxurious and expensive than they really were.

This fragment came from a larger composition covering an entire wall. It is painted in a style popular in the mid-first century A.D., categorized by scholars as the Fourth Style. This is the last style of Roman wall painting, and combines the spatial vistas of the Second Style with the fantastic architecture of the Third Style. It was popular from approximately 63 B.C. until A.D. 79, when Pompeii and Herculaneum were destroyed.

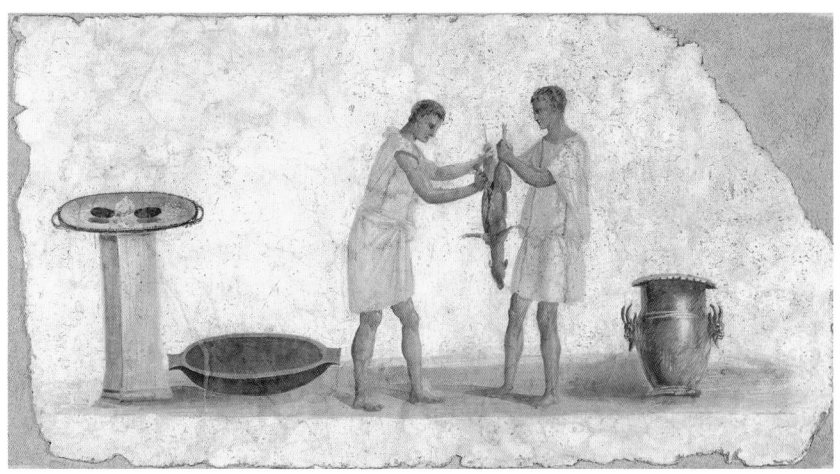

FRAGMENT OF A FRESCO DEPICTING BUTCHERS AT WORK

Roman, A.D. 100–150
Plaster with pigment
H: 69.5 cm (27⅜ in.)
W: 127 cm (50 in.)
79.AG.112

The scene painted on this fragment of a wall depicts two bare-footed men wearing short, sleeveless, striped tunics, who are cutting the carcass of a small cloven-hoofed animal, perhaps a veal calf. The figure on the right grasps the feet of the animal while the man on the left slices into the belly with a wood-handled knife with a triangular blade, a typical instrument used by Roman butchers. To the right is a large krater (mixing vessel) with a scalloped rim and handles in the shape of goat's heads. The color and sheen of the elaborate vessel suggest that it is made of silver. Details of the goat's heads are accentuated with dots and splashes of black and white paint to show their shadows and highlights. To the left, a silver tray with a beaded edge and rounded handles holds a head of garlic and what may be pieces of meat or some other foodstuff. The tray rests atop a pillar-shaped chopping block, another element typical of Roman depictions of butchers; on the floor next to the chopping block is a large basin, which here is evidently made of wood.

The shadows cast by the krater and the figures of the men suggest that this fragment came from a wall that was to the right when one entered the room. The scene seems complete, as the ground begins abruptly at the right, and appears to be fading out at the left. There are no known parallels for paintings of this type of scene, but reliefs depicting butchers carving meat appear in tombs of butchers that date from the second century A.D.

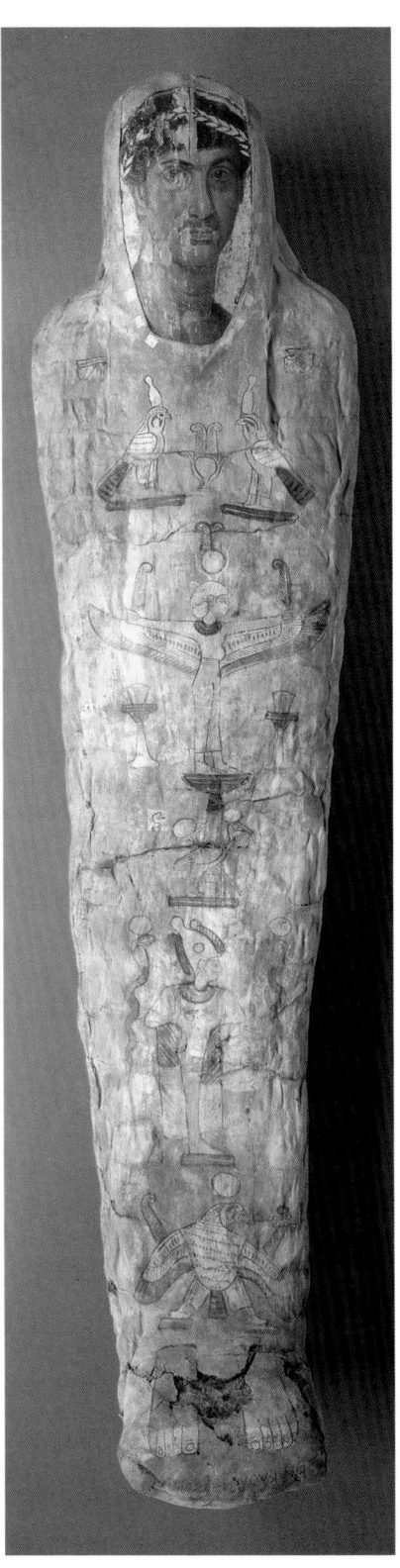

Mummy with Portrait of Herakleides

Romano-Egyptian,
probably from Er-Rubayat,
Egypt
A.D. 50–100
Wax tempera, encaustic,
gold, linen, and wood
L: 175.3 cm (69 in.)
W: 44 cm (17⁵/₁₆ in.)
D: 33 cm (13 in.)
91.AP.6

Romano-Egyptian mummies combine the Roman tradition of individualized portraiture with the ancient Egyptian practice of mummification of the dead. This example includes a painted panel portrait depicting a young man with a light mustache and loose, curly hair. His name, Herakleides, has been written on the outer edge of his feet, which are painted at the bottom of the cartonnage, or mummy wrappings. Some areas of the portrait—such as the background, the wreath, and the decorative squares surrounding the panel—have been enhanced with gilding, added after it was bound in the linen wrappings. Belonging to a small group of mummies wrapped in shrouds painted red (a color associated with life and regeneration in Egyptian religion), this one has mythological scenes connected with Egyptian funerary ritual along the length of his body. One depicts an ibis; modern CT (computed axial tomography) scans have revealed a mummified ibis inside the wrappings, suggesting that Herakleides may have been associated with the Egyptian god Thoth, possibly as a priest, scribe, or worshiper.

The portrait was painted in a technique called encaustic, in which the pigment was mixed with hot beeswax and applied to the panel. This technique dates back at least as far as the Classical period in Greece and continues in use beyond the Roman period.

MUMMY PORTRAIT OF ISADORA

Attributed to the
Isidora Master
Romano-Egyptian, from
El-Hibeh, Egypt,
A.D. 100–110
Encaustic, gold, linen,
and wood
H: 48 cm (18⅞ in.)
W: 36 cm (14⅛ in.)
D: 12.8 cm (5 in.)
81.AP.42

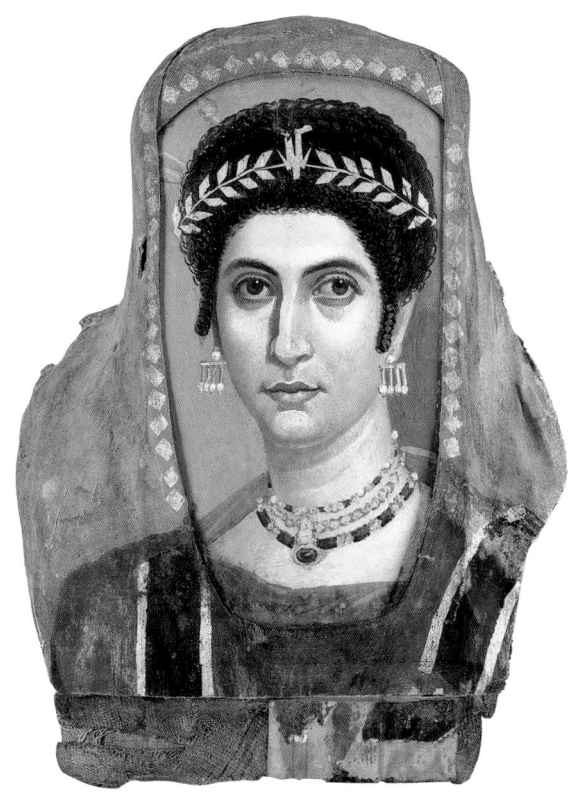

Mummy portraits from Roman Egypt fused two traditions, that of Pharonic Egypt and that of the classical world. The painting styles and techniques come from the classical world, but the inclusion of the portrait panel as part of the wrappings of the deceased belongs to very ancient Egyptian funerary practices. The mummy portrait helped the person survive death in physical form by providing a substitute body for the spirit to inhabit should the corpse be destroyed. Because this portrait is preserved with some of its linen wrappings intact, it almost certainly once belonged to a full mummy (see previous page), and it helps us understand how the panels, many of which have since been removed from their wrappings, were used.

This portrait depicts a refined and socially prominent woman. The name Isidora is painted in black ink on the left side of the wrappings and might be hers. She is shown as an elegant matron, with elaborate jewelry and hairstyle. In her hair, she wears a gold wreath and gold and silver hairpins. Pendant earrings of gold and pearls dangle from her earlobes, and three separate necklaces surround her throat. Her jewelry and coiffure probably reflect current style and help date the portrait to the early years of the second century A.D., during the rule of Trajan (A.D. 98–117).

We know that the mummy wrappings were painted after the portrait panel was inserted into the many layers of linen because some of the orange-red paint on the linen around the upper part of the panel dripped onto the panel itself. The gold for the wreath across her hair, the lozenges surrounding the panel, and the stripes edging her *clavi* (the dark stripes on her clothing that denote her social rank) were added to the cartonnage, or mummy wrappings, after the painting was completed.

MUMMY PORTRAIT
OF A BEARDED MAN

Romano-Egyptian, probably
from Er-Rubayat, Egypt,
A.D. 140–160
Encaustic on wood, linen
H: 43 cm (16⅞ in.)
W: 22.5 cm (8⅞ in.)
73.AP.94

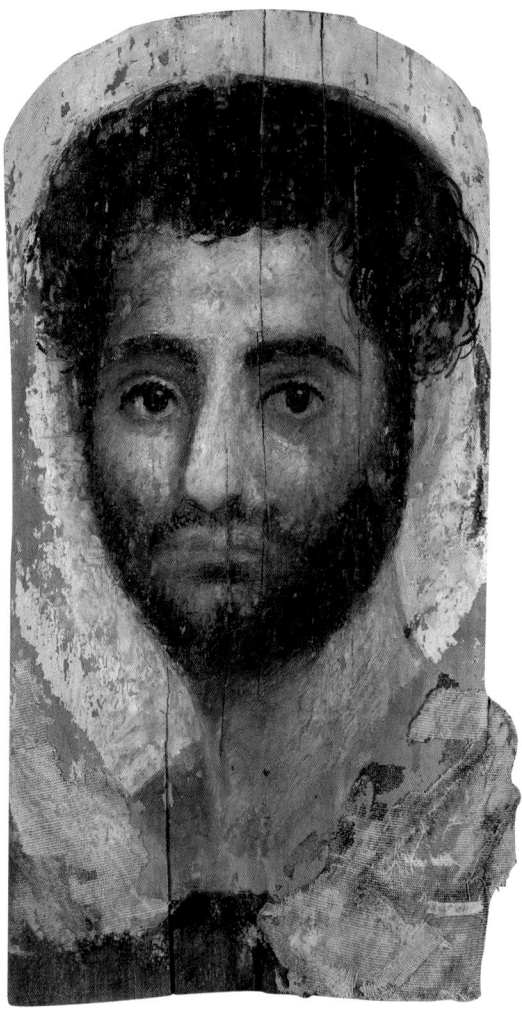

In this highly individualized portrait, the bearded man is depicted seated at an angle with his head turned to the left to gaze out at the viewer. His hair is painted in unruly curls that end at the top of his ears, while his beard appears to be closely cropped along the narrow contours of his face. The artist has used white effectively to highlight the volume of the cheeks, long nose, and high forehead. The eyes are surrounded by darker hues, with only the upper lashes clearly marked out in darker paint. The luxuriant hair and beard are characteristic of the Antonine period of the Roman Empire, dating the portrait to the mid-second century A.D.

Some of the linen mummy wrappings survive on the bottom of the panel. They are preserved at an angle on the lower corners, as the linen was wrapped diagonally around the upper part of the body to enclose the panel. Like the mummy portrait of Herakleides (see p. 226), this one is unusual in showing no traces of painted clothing on the figure of the man. In cases of younger (usually unbearded) men, such nudity could identify them as ephebes, but here it might be interpreted as a symbol of rebirth following initiation into the cult of Isis.

MUMMY PORTRAIT OF A YOUTH

Romano-Egyptian, from
Egypt, A.D. 150–200
Encaustic on wood
H: 20.3 cm (8 in.)
W: 13 cm (5⅛ in.)
78.AP.262

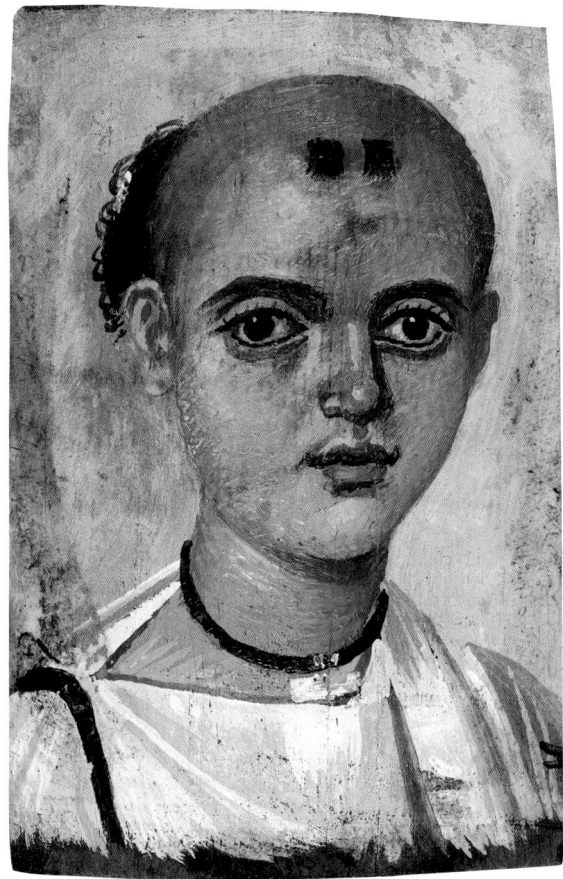

Of the portraits that have survived from Roman Egypt, the most poignant ones portray children. This young boy's head is shaved, except for two tufts of hair at the forehead and a Horus lock (a symbol of youth named after the Egyptian god of the sky) on his right side. His natural hairline is suggested by the darker hue on his scalp. An amulet hangs from a strap around his neck, and a gold pin set with miniature garnets is affixed to his Horus lock. In antiquity, children wore amulets to protect them from harm. When a child reached puberty, such charms were usually put aside as part of the rituals of reaching adulthood.

This portrait may have been done from life; the shadows beneath the boy's eyes and the pallor of his skin seem to suggest an illness. His eyes are large and expressive, with individual lashes delineated above the darker outline of the eye. After death, the panel was placed over the face of the deceased and bound into the linen wrappings of the body. The panel, which was painted using the encaustic technique, has been removed from its wrappings, but it is still possible to see their outline, both where the pigment no longer survives on the bottom edge, and along the left and right sides where there is discoloration from bitumen used to hold the linen wrappings together.

Glossary

Cross-references within this Glossary appear in **boldface**.

aegis
Divine emblem associated with the Greek gods Zeus and Athena. It consists of a scaly animal skin with a fringe of snake heads and the face of Medusa in the center (to ward off evil). In ancient art, Athena is often depicted wearing an aegis over her clothing like a breastplate.

amphora (pl. amphorae)
Medium-size pot with two vertical handles, narrower neck, and bulging body. Very common in antiquity, terra-cotta amphorae were used for storing and transporting oil, wine, grains, and other commodities. Their shape changed somewhat over time, the bodies becoming more or less rounded, the necks more or less set off from the bodies. Various modifiers of the name (for example, neck-amphora, belly-amphora) indicate a specific shape of vase.

Archaic period
The period from about 700 to 480 B.C. in the Greek world.

aryballos (pl. aryballoi)
Small vessel with a bulging body and narrow neck. It was used to hold perfumed oil.

Attika
The region of Greece around the city of Athens.

attribute
Object closely associated with or characteristic of a person, divinity, or object that serves as a symbol of identity.

black-figure technique
Style of decoration used on ancient Greek ceramics beginning in the late seventh century B.C. The figures or decoration are painted on the unfired clay and turn black during the firing process to appear as silhouettes in the finished product. Details are incised through the black paint to appear in the color of the underlying clay. See also **red-figure technique**.

cameo
Stone or glass carved with an image in relief, often banded for polychromatic effect. See also **intaglio**.

Chimaera
Mythical monster with the head and body of a lion, the fire-breathing head of a goat emerging from its back, and a snake-headed tail. The Chimaera was slain by the hero Bellerophon.

chiton
Basic Greek garment. Resembling a tunic, the chiton is made of lightweight, pleated cloth. Women's chitons were ankle length, men's were either knee length (*chitoniskos*) or ankle length.

cista (pl. *cistae*)
Small to medium-size, usually cylindrical, basket or chest made of metal or wood. Cistae were used for storing small objects such as cosmetics and jewelry.

Classical period
In Greece and the areas under Greek influence, the period ranging from approximately 480 B.C. (the sack of Athens by the Persians) to 323 B.C. (the death of Alexander the Great).

Corinthian
From Corinth. In Archaic pottery production the term denotes the phase following **Protocorinthian**, i.e., from about 625 B.C. onward. Corinthian style generally favors larger figures and often exotic hybrid creatures painted quickly.

Cycladic culture
A Bronze Age culture that flourished in the Cyclades (a group of islands in the Aegean Sea) from about 3000 B.C. to 1100 B.C. Small stone figures from this period, sometimes called Cycladic idols, are characterized by simplified, nearly abstract, renderings of the human form.

diadem
A narrow ribbon or fillet worn across the forehead, with the ends tied at the back and left hanging down the neck. In antiquity, diadems were royal insignia worn by kings and some queens.

dinos (pl. dinoi)
Medium- to large-size, almost globular vessel with no handles or foot. Dinoi were used for mixing wine and water.

erote (pl. erotes)
Companions of Eros, the god of love; a small, nude, winged baby.

Giant
Any of the large, monstrous creatures born to the gods Ge (Earth) and Uranus (Sky) to avenge Zeus's destruction of their half-brothers, the Titans. The Giants fought and lost a fierce battle with the Olympian gods called the Gigantomachy.

Gorgon
Any of three mythical Greek female monsters (Medusa, Sthenno, and Euryale) whose horrific appearance turned those who looked at them to stone.

gorgoneion
The decapitated head of Medusa, who was beheaded by the hero Perseus, often used as an apotropaic (evil-averting) device, appearing especially on the **aegis** of Athena and as a device on shields.

griffin
In Greek mythology, a hybrid creature combining characteristics of a lion's body and an eagle's beak and wings.

Hellenistic
Meaning "Greek-like." In Greece and the areas under Greek influence, the Hellenistic period ranges from about 323 B.C. (the death of Alexander the Great) to 31 B.C.

herm
Marker in the form of a square pillar surmounted by a bust or a head at the top and male genitals on the shaft. Herms were placed at crossroads or at the entry to a house, or served as garden ornaments.

himation
Large rectangular cloth of heavy material worn as an outer garment by Greek men and women. The himation was typically draped over one shoulder and wrapped around the body.

hoplite
Heavily armed Greek infantry soldier. A hoplite's equipment included helmet, corselet, and greaves; he carried shield, spear, and sword.

hydria (pl. hydriae)
Medium-size jug with one vertical and two horizontal handles. The name derives from the Greek word for water; hydriae were used in antiquity to store and transport water.

intaglio
From the Italian *intagliare* (to cut into), intaglios are seal stones with images cut beneath the surface. When pressed into wax or plaster, they create an impression in relief. See also **cameo**.

kantharos (pl. kantharoi)
Drinking cup with two vertical handles and a tall foot. The kantharos is associated with Dionysos, god of wine.

kore (pl. korai)
Meaning "young woman" or "maiden" in Greek, the term kore usually refers to a statue of a draped standing female figure.

kouros (pl. kouroi)
Meaning "young man" in Greek, the term kouros usually refers to a statue of a nude male youth. Kouroi were represented standing frontally, stepping forward on one foot.

krater
Medium- to large-size bowl with two handles and a large, open mouth. Kraters were used for mixing wine and water.

kylix (pl. kylikes)
Two-handled drinking cup with an open, shallow bowl usually set on a tall, slender foot. Variations in form are classified as Type A, Type B, or Type C.

kymation (cymatium)
Decorative border. The word *kymation* derives from the Greek word for waves.

lekythos (pl. lekythoi)
Small to medium-size vessel with a cylindrical body, narrow neck, and one vertical handle. Lekythoi were used for pouring offerings of wine or oil on graves. Lekythoi carved in marble served as grave markers.

loutrophoros (pl. loutrophoroi)
Tall, slender vessel with a high, narrow neck. Loutrophoroi were used for carrying water for ritual ablutions, particularly at weddings.

maenad
Female follower of Dionysos, god of wine. In ancient art, maenads are often shown nude or partially dressed.

Medusa
See **Gorgon**.

oinochoe (pl. oinochoai)
Medium-size, one-handled pitcher used for holding and pouring wine.

olpe (pl. olpai)
Small to medium-size pitcher with one vertical handle used to hold liquids.

Orientalizing period
In Greek art, the period from about 725 to 625 B.C., when artistic motifs were introduced from the ancient Near East. See also **Protocorinthian**.

Panathenaia
The Athenian festival held every four years in the late summer to honor the city's patron goddess, Athena. Panathenaic prize amphorae filled with olive oil were awarded to the victors of the athletic and musical contests.

pelike (pl. pelikai)
Medium-size, two-handled pot resembling an amphora, but wider toward the base.

peplos
Heavy woolen outer garment worn by Greek women. The peplos was belted at the waist and pinned at the shoulders.

phiale (pl. phialai)
Shallow, round dish used for libations in rituals.

Protocorinthian
A style of pottery decoration developed during the **Orientalizing** period in Corinth, the greatest center of pottery distribution at this time. The style is characterized by miniaturization of motifs and the use of animal friezes.

pyxis (pl. pyxides)
Small, cylindrical, lidded container for small objects such as jewelry.

red-figure technique
Technique of decoration used on ancient Greek ceramics from the late 500s B.C. through the end of the third century B.C. The figures and principal decoration are left unpainted while the background is painted so as to turn black during firing. Thus the reserved (unpainted) figures remain the reddish color of the clay. This is essentially the reverse of the **black-figure technique**.

repoussé
Technique of fashioning metal by hammering from the interior side.

rhyton (pl. rhyta)
Horn-shaped vessel that terminates in an animal or human head. Rhyta have a spout at their narrow end so that liquid, usually wine, can flow through them.

satyr
In Greek mythology, a male figure, part human, part horse or goat, with pointed ears and a tail, who was part of the entourage of Dionysos, god of wine. Often shown nude, satyrs are characterized by their bestiality and their love of sex and wine. See also **silenos**.

Severe style
Transitional style of early Classical Greek sculpture prevalent from about 480 B.C. to about 450 B.C.

silenos (pl. silenoi)

A supernatural being portrayed in art as a wild male with animal features. Silenos is associated with wildlife and with Dionysos, god of wine, and is also regarded as the father of the **satyrs**. Often represented in groups, silenoi are usually depicted as white-haired old men with horse's ears, while satyrs are generally youthful.

Sirens

Mythical bird-women who lived on the islands off western Italy. Their song led sailors to their deaths. Most famously, the Sirens were unsuccessful in shipwrecking Odysseus and his men. Orpheus famously charmed them with his own music to allow Jason and the Argonauts to pass by.

sistrum

Rattlelike musical instrument.

skyphos (pl. skyphoi)

Two-handled drinking cup.

stele (pl. stelai)

Upright commemorative stone slab, usually with painted or carved decoration and/or inscription. Stelai were often set up as grave markers.

Styles of Pompeian wall painting

First Style

Dating from about 200 to 80 B.C., the First Style is characterized by stucco panels molded in relief and painted to simulate expensive colored-marble veneers.

Second Style

Dating from about 80 to 20 B.C., the Second Style marks the beginning of figural and architectural representation in Roman wall painting; there is the illusion of perspective, often seen through a screen of columns set on a dado.

Third Style

Dating from about 20 B.C. to A.D. 50, the Third Style features images within images, enclosed by dark panels; the architecture depicted is flimsy and often fantastic.

Fourth Style

Dating from about A.D. 62 onward, this "baroque" style combines the spatial vistas of Second Style with the fantastic architecture of the Third. The style's large, narrative panels often depict subjects from Greek mythology.

symposion (pl. *symposia*)

In ancient Greece, an exclusively male drinking party where men enjoyed wine, conversation, and entertainment.

thymiaterion (pl. thymiateria)

Incense burner usually made of bronze, silver, or terracotta. The perfumed smoke of the incense would escape through decorative openings. Thymiateria were functional objects but may also have been placed in tombs as funerary offerings.

tondo

The central circle inside the bowl of a **kylix**, where an image is usually painted.

tympanum (pl. tympana)

Small hand drum, similar in size and shape to a tambourine, although often with one rounded side.

votive

Related to religious vows and devotion; any religious offering or dedication.

Index

Acknowledgments

Since the first edition of the *Handbook of the Antiquities Collection* appeared in 2002, new pieces have been added to the collection while others have left. This has resulted in the addition of new entries to this revised edition of the Handbook, as well as deletions of other entries, and, as a result, the list of contributors whose excellent work must be acknowledged has grown. I am grateful to all the members of the Museum staff, both past and present, who have been involved in the preparation of both editions of the Handbook. Most important among them are members of the Antiquities Department who wrote the more than two hundred entries in this book. In alphabetical order they are: Jens Daehner, Janet Burnett Grossman, Mary Louise Hart (coordinator of the first edition), Kenneth Lapatin (co-editor of the second edition), Claire Lyons, Marit Jentoft-Nilsen (†), Laure Marest-Caffey, John Papadopoulos, Seth Pevnick, David Saunders, Elana Towne-Markus, and Carrie Tovar. They were assisted in this process by our graduate interns and volunteers, many of whom were also authors, including Susanne Ebbinghaus, Elizabeth de Grummond, Kara Nicholas, Rachel Patt, and Lauren Rogers. Information and technical observations were contributed by our team of skilled conservators, including Maya Elston, Susan Lansing-Maish, Jeffrey Maish, Jerry Podany, Erik Risser, Eduardo Sánchez, and Marie Svoboda. Our always excellent photographs were taken by Ellen Rosenbery and Tahnee Cracchiola, supported by Lou Meluso, Anthony Peres, Jack Ross, and Stanley Smith. Additional photography of objects formerly in the Fleischman collection was provided by freelance photographer Bruce White. The search for archival photographs to accompany the introduction was achieved with the aid of David Farneth, Head, Collections Management, Getty Research Institute. In the Registrar's Department Travis Miles assisted with the compilation of images for this second edition, which was ably edited by Catherine Chambers and Benedicte Gilman. The publication of the first edition of the Handbook was supervised by former Curator of Antiquities Marion True; I am honored to be able to follow in her footsteps with the publication of this second edition.

Karol Wight
Senior Curator of Antiquities